WOMEN IN PRISON

by Kathryn Watterson Burkhart

POPULAR LIBRARY ● NEW YORK

POPULAR LIBRARY EDITION
January, 1976

Copyright © 1973 by Kathryn Watterson Burkhart

Library of Congress Catalog Card Number: 72-92195

Published by arrangement with Doubleday & Company, Inc.

For John, Mom and Alice.

And for all of us trying to build lives free from inner and outer tyrannies . . . who want to *hear*, not just listen; *see*, not just watch; *live*, not merely survive.

Contents

Acknowledgments   ix

Part I   THE CONCRETE WOMB: "Gettin' In"   1

   Money Talks   3
   A Separate Society   5
   A Personal Journey   9
   Death   23
  1. Crime: A Matter Of Power   25
     Echoes Of Rosa   39
  2. Guilty Until Proven Innocent   41
     Willie   61
     Mary   63
  3. "Ain't I A Woman Too?"   71
     Jeanette   87
  4. "Everyone Arrested Is Given A Bath"   93
     Rules and Regulations   103
     Erie   117
  5. Infancy: "We're Treated Just Like Children"   119
     Nellie   137
  6. Discipline: A Spring Wound Too Tightly   139

Part II   THE CONCRETE WOMB: "Bein' In"   169

   Pat   171
   Trinada   176
   Georgia   178
   Marta   181
   Louise   184
   Constance   191
   Proud Mary   193
   Susan   194
   Dessie   199
   Martha   201

Barbara   203
Aletha   208
Kathleen   210
Ana   213
Ana's Children   223
Martha M.   229
Anna   230
Suzanne   237
None of Us   243

Part III   THE CONCRETE WOMB: "Stayin' In"   245

  7. One Step Forward, Two Steps Back   247
       Eva   273
       Father Charles   279
  8. Industry: The Keystone of Prosperity   281
       CIW Rules   313
       Margaret M.   319
  9. Health Care: Who Plays Doctor?   321
       Lady, You Don't Know Me   359
 10. What's This About Sex?   361
       I Am A Woman   389
       Dora   391
 11. Gettin' Out: A Long Way Home   395
       It Used to Be So Beautiful Here   421
 12. Prison: An Idea Or A Place?   423
       When Will We Learn?   439

Glossary: Prison and Prison-related Terms   441
Bibliography: Consulted Works and Recommended
    Reading   453

Acknowledgments

I take this space to indulge in personal thank you's: to my dear friend, Marie Stoner, who read, criticized and discussed these pages with tireless care; to Kitty Caparella and my editor, John Ware, who encouraged and made this process feasible; to David Rudovsky, Naomi Burns, Claude Lewis, Fletcher Clarke and Donald and Carol Nathanson, who also studied and advised the development of this manuscript.

I thank James H. Neely and Julius Lester for their advice and inspiration; Terry Derry, Julie Oshana and Sue Walton for their support; Ellen McLaughlin, who shared fresh perspectives as she helped me type the final draft; Ford Burkhart, for historical research; and Rochelle Jones, for specifics on juvenile women. Last, but not least, hugs and love for my great "Hamilton Street Mafia" of Leslie, Charity, Loren, Lisa and Nini, whose laughter and play continue to cheer up my world as I write.

WOMEN
IN PRISON

Part I   THE CONCRETE WOMB: "GETTIN' IN"

Money Talks

Money talks, bullshit walks. If you're a Kennedy and you get busted for dope, you never do no time. If you're the President of the United States, you can murder millions of people in Asia, you never do no time. If you're a politician, you can cheat and conspire and steal money, you never do no time. I've watched about seventeen women go out of here after serving time for snuffing their babies, while hypes [drug addicts] still sit here. Society condones guns, but not addicts. I'm here for selling two nickel bags, yet the government is giving GIs whites to keep 'em up and reds to put 'em to sleep and getting them addicted so they can keep fighting. And the Army and the government ain't never taken to court or locked up. There's a lot of contradictions—you know, a double standard. If you're a corporation, you can fix prices and rip folks off every day, you never do no time. Me, I'm a hype. I sold two nickel bags and I'm doing life, baby, a day at a time. I already been here three years . . . and you know that's like three lifetimes of psychological warfare. They call me a criminal. I ain't no corporation; so I'm a *criminal!* I'd like to ask, just where are the real criminals?

—Mary, an inmate at California
Institution for Women

A Separate Society

The horn cuts through the quiet of the valley and echoes loudly down the halls of the state prison for women in Southern California. It sounds like a foghorn—jarring the senses, interrupting activity. It's an air raid warning, an alarm, an emergency. At California Institution for Women at Frontera it blares its demands five times a day—informing even the uninitiated to be in their rooms for "Count." The response is monotonous hysteria. Women scramble and run to their rooms. It's the usual counting of bodies taken from five to six times a day in almost every prison in the country. It's the security check against escape.

Minutes after the foghorn sounds and each prisoner is sitting on her own bed, a series of short, loud popping sounds, like staccato cannons, go off one after another, inundating the quietest mind. The doors are being locked. This particular prison is automated; there's no need for a guard to turn the key manually in every door. The matron sitting in the control room merely pulls switches that close and lock all the doors.

From behind the locked door, you see a guard walking by the narrow wicket in your door. She looks in, sees you on your bed and checks your number off her list; you haven't escaped. This procedure is somehow reminiscent of kindergarten when teacher calls your name and you say "Present." But the check here goes on the paper beside Number 8811, Number 7286, Number 7384 . . .

When her count is complete, the matron goes to the control center and calls in the number present from her unit. "Latham B—fifty-eight," she says over the public address system microphone to the guard writing down the numbers in the Control Center of the Administration Building. "Latham B—fifty-eight, okay," he repeats and confirms. When he has taken count from every living unit, the hospital, work areas, administration . . . his voice booms back over the PA into the living unit: "Count Clear!" "Count Clear," the matron echoes down the hall. The staccato cannon fire starts again. The doors are popped open.

After count, women move back into the TV room, up and down

the halls. If you have a pass, you can sit in the "rec room" between two living units and play cards for the next two or three hours. You can stay in your room to read or write letters. This particular night, on this particular hall in Latham B, the women are sitting lookout—alert and ready to stop one psychotic woman, Helen, from hurting one of her sister prisoners. The psychotic woman pulled the wires from the television last night. During the last week, she put shit in the showers and went into two or three rooms to put lipstick on the curtains. She has started several fights.

It's now on the grapevine that she's going to kill Nancy. She has stolen scissors to do the job. Early tonight she watched, sullen but with wild terror in her eyes, from the corner as Nancy fixed the television with ease—rewiring with care and skill the connections ripped out the night before. A cheer has gone up from the women who hope to see a TV special with Bill Cosby when Nancy switches the set back on and it works. Nancy bows to an appreciative audience and heads back for her room. Meanwhile, Helen looks like a cornered, ravenous wild-child. She's whispering to herself, "I'm gonna get that bitch. I'm gonna get that bitch."

"Helen's a dangerous sick woman," Marguerite tells me later as we sit in her room, aware of the tension in the hall. "But it's not something we can go to the staff with—not yet. They don't have any idea who tore apart the television—and they don't know who put the shit in the showers. The code here is *you don't go to the police—you handle the problems yourselves.* Usually we do pretty well.

"But people are petrified . . . And we're not playing with somebody you can sit down and talk to. She's the kind who will jump out and get Nancy from behind—just slash, slash, poke. Nobody is going to let Nancy get hurt. The girls want to handle it—but they aren't capable of dealing with this one. Most of the law and order around here is done woman to woman, but there just aren't enough women to handle her.

"I think on this one, I might have to break the code. It's so serious. She had wanted Nancy for a friend; now she wants to kill her. I have to think about it. It's a big thing to break the code. If I make the move, I'll be willing to accept the consequences. I have to be responsible for my decisions—but I believe that in this case, it's a matter of life and death."

Marguerite adjusted herself on her bed—the only place in her room to sit. "You know, this is a sick society," she said. "Women who should righteously be in PTU [Psychiatric Treatment Unit] are walking around on the grounds. If they actually let us run this place legally—which in reality we do anyway—things would be different."

She showed me her macrame weaving and some baby sweaters she had knit for the children of her prison friends. "In many ways this is a true communistic system, living here. You know what? We are all convicts. We don't have money. We barter for the things from the free world—barter for dope, pills, food, cigarettes. Cigarettes are the biggest bartering commodity in this community. We are just like a small community except we don't have any men. So there are women who take the place of men. And how many housewives go further than the market, the church and the school? We have fifty acres here. We don't pay any taxes—except in labor.

"There are some people who want power—and struggle for identification with the powers that be. There are also some sick women here who love chaos—house against house, woman against woman. But we deal with them, with the problems, collectively.

"This is a whole different world. It's a world I only glimpsed before. I lived in such a sheltered world. You know, I have learned so much from these women. It's something *you* learned naturally; it's something I've had to learn the hard way. People from the established society could learn so much from these women; they have so much to teach, so much to tell. I only wish people would listen.

"Usually the women treat anyone who comes in with silence; they don't trust them—so they treat them like pigs. But they know you are different; they know you are one of them. It's so apparent.

"For me, prison hasn't been the end of the world. It's been a beginning—a chance to stand aside and look. When I tell you I have grown in the seven months I have been here, I mean it. Not because of any programs—there aren't any. But because of the people I've lived with and the bed I've slept on. And I'm beginning to live with myself and accept myself. I know I am more of a woman, a valuable soul than I ever would have been if I hadn't come here. If six hundred women can each say, 'Hey, I'm a woman,' regardless of being called homosexuals or convicts or being neglected and hurt and made to live under ridiculous rules and ridiculous pressures and mental brutality and heartbreak—*they have something to teach the world*. It was a mind blower to me to see the strength, the tenderness and courage of these women and to find out, hey, I'm a woman, too. I'd just never had the chance."

A Personal Journey

Many people have asked me how I developed an interest in writing about prisons. Recently at a meeting of the Philadelphia Bar Association, the Chancellor of the Bar asked how I "got into this business" when I have written about so many other things. His question, though asked many times before, startled me. "I fell in through a trap door," I told him. "I was just walking along and then *wham*, there I was." It was a facetious answer, but there was truth in it.

Although people I knew and loved had been arrested or gone to jail, in my mind they just "went away" and "came home." It was traumatic, but being in trouble with the law was "normal"—just like alcoholism or violent, erratic behavior. I was oblivious to the quality of life inside jail, the reality of it, just as I was oblivious to the qualities and substance of my own life. I didn't examine the dimension of my own experience any more than I examined what particular experiences were doing to the lives of others. I just struggled in my own way with the enormity of life around me in isolated, non-communicative patterns and formulas for existence that gave me some sense of stability and cohesion, unaware of trying to envision that which was not visible.

It was only when realities I normally didn't see were forced in front of my eyes through someone else's perspective that I responded to what was there—whether it was classical music, racism, poverty, art, death from bombs in Indochina, prison life or the effects of my own actions. I guess you could say there was a great gap between worlds, between experience and cognition. My sensibilities had to be shattered, along with my delusions, before I could begin picking up the pieces to examine them and gain a new perspective.

Imprisonment was one of those nebulous, unexamined areas in my mind that went unquestioned until I was jolted into a new awareness through another person's experiences.

I had never been inside a jail or prison until 1969, when I came back to this country from two and a half years in Asia. I had been teaching, studying Mandarin and living in a Chinese community in Kuala Lumpur, Malaysia, where I also edited a small magazine for Peace Corps volunteers. Coming back to the U.S. was a shock. I had been so thoroughly immersed in the overseas Chinese culture that

I had trouble readjusting to the American language, the spaces, sights, smells and people. It was as though I was experiencing for the first time what I had thought familiar.

After traveling across the country from California, I returned to a newspaper in Florida, where I had worked previously, to do some special in-depth writing and research. Among my assignments was a series on rape. I worked with another reporter on the series, who took the victim's perspective. I took the "criminal" aspects as my task.

Among other things, I wanted to interview rapists and try to understand their perspective. It didn't seem fair to write about rape without getting more than one side of the story. At the time, however, I was told there was only one convicted rapist at the county jail. Others were there for rape, but they had only been accused and were awaiting trial. The man who had been found guilty agreed to the interview and so did the county sheriff.

As I sat waiting for the interview in a small, barren detective's room at the jail—I realized how absurd I was. Why did I think a convicted rapist would tell me why he had raped somebody? Here again, I was in a situation where I was totally naïve, using only nerve and ignorance as a protective cover. I was sitting there feeling ridiculous when the door opened and a heavyset young man with puffy cheeks and dry brown skin that gave him an ashen gray shadow came in the door. He wore a blue prison shirt and overalls. A jailhouse aura seemed to surround him. He sat down, seeming somewhat shocked and frightened. I felt frightened, too. We were both nervous and I became increasingly aware of the detective in the back of the room cracking his knuckles.

I was the first outsider—and certainly the first woman—this prisoner had talked with face to face in months. He was the first "known rapist" I'd met. He was twenty-one years old. He had just been found guilty of raping a seventeen-year-old high school senior, a virgin, who was black. That's all I knew. Partway through the first hour of the interview I started feeling uncomfortable about all the details I didn't know. By the end of four hours—and a shift from his helpful speculations on "why rapists do what they do" into his personal case—a lot of question marks had replaced the periods in my brain concerning this alleged rapist I'll call "Trevor Jones." The labels had slipped from their slots.

In the days to follow, Trevor Jones' story unraveled itself slowly, painfully—dislodging with small explosions whatever remaining myths of equal law and justice lay neatly hidden in my unconscious. I concluded that Trevor Jones, who turned out to be a community worker, youth recreation leader and chairman of a black grass-roots unity movement, was not a rapist. Prior to his arrest he was enrolled in a local junior college. With painstaking research and backtracking, I could substantiate none of the facts established at the trial except Trevor Jones' claim of innocence and his dedication to improving conditions in the black community. He had been arrested only once before and that was when, in response to a policeman's request for identification, he said his name was "Black, Blacker, Blackest."

Jones said he had made one mistake—the only action he was sorry for. He said he slept with someone he didn't know—a friend of a friend, the woman he was later accused of raping. That someone, who admitted she had been carrying around a newspaper clipping with his picture for several weeks before she met him, tried to withdraw the charges placed against him. But something or someone changed her mind. She testified. And Jones, who claimed innocence from the beginning, was jailed without bail, tried and sentenced to eighteen years on reduced charges of assault with intent to commit rape. The jury apparently had some doubts, because finding him guilty of rape would have meant the death penalty.

Jones had been in solitary confinement for more than nine months when I met him—most of that time awaiting trial. He was not allowed reading materials, exercise, recreation or a full diet. He was isolated from other prisoners because he was considered a "leader"—a "black militant who would put ideas into the heads of other prisoners if he had contact," according to the sheriff.

It was as though the layers of my defenses against knowing what really goes on as a matter of daily course in the criminal justice system and in jail were torn away one by one. They were shredded by the white detectives who sat around their headquarters and talked freely of the "rabbit nigger coon" Jones and graphically how they would like to "cut out his balls." They swore this was the first case of a black woman being raped in their town and that was real "equality." Black men were always convicted for raping white women; cases involving the rape of black women by white or black men had traditionally been ignored; the case wasn't considered serious. The detectives talked gleefully about circumstantial evidence they had against Jones and then went into what seemed to be euphoric reminiscing about the times they had dressed up as women in blond wigs and cruised the streets in unmarked cars—with two cops hidden in the back seat until they "got some coons followin' us around lickin' their chops to make a white woman."

"We'd idle our engine at a red light and tell the coons if they wanted to fuck to follow us . . . and then we'd lead 'em out to a dark country road," said one big-bellied white cop whose neck grew purple with laughter. "You shudda seen the shock on them coon faces when we'd get out with our rifles." The men who had been entrapped by the hoax would be charged with attempted rape and sent off "where they oughta be buried."

From one person to the next, all of whom were essential to establishing the state's case against Trevor Jones, the flimsy "evidence" continued to be revealed . . . including the situation of the medical examiner who had sworn in trial the "victim" had been a virgin—the main thrust of the prosecution. "How'd I know?" he said in a telephone interview. "You can just tell those things. Of course it's not certain, but you got a good idea. She was tight, you know." Another main point of evidence for the prosecution was the girl's claim that she had been badly bruised and beaten by Jones and several other young men who were allegedly involved but not prosecuted. The medical examiner said he had not seen any bruises on her body, but said she was "probably bruised." He said he had not personally seen the bruises because "Niggers don't bruise. If she was bruised, I couldn't a seen it anyway."

The face-to-face reality of racism and political prejudice in the criminal justice system was devastating. I realized that Trevor Jones had talked to me just to get out of confinement, just to see a face other than the one that shoved food under his door twice a day. He hadn't expected that I could change anything for him or prove his innocence. I didn't. His highly paid black lawyer didn't seem able to use any of the contradictory statements I had collected. The newspaper wasn't about to publish information they considered potentially libelous; it was only my word against the sheriff's, the detective's, the medical examiner's. Nobody I contacted seemed to have the power to right an injustice—and no one seemed to care—except Trevor Jones, his fiancée, his family, his friends and now me.

My inability to do anything about what I saw and heard was shattering. Before I left Florida, however, I decided to spend some time in the women's section of Broward County Jail. I asked to go in as an inmate but was allowed in only as a reporter for one day. ("If you want to go in as an inmate, you'll have to break a law in front of us," the sheriff said. "You'll have to go to court and be tried. The process will take you about two years.") I chose one day—and that day was enough. I was led in through five locked doors to a small inner sanctum. I became less determined about my assignment and more and more terrified as the key turned in each lock behind me. I was even more shaken by the grim, hard faces of the black and white women I saw packed together in crusting crowded cells—some sixty women in two cell blocks seemingly not big enough for twenty.

It was only after I was put inside the cell block that the receptiveness of the individual women melted my fear. They were eager to talk about the conditions they lived in—and were amazed that I had gotten in. They were like women I have known all my life. Just folks. They put me at ease and I became increasingly comfortable with familiar banter and old street talk. The heat was the only overbearing factor. There was no air circulation. We sat talking and sweating. I was aware of the confinement but became unconsciously absorbed in the deadly still aura of the environment. It was somehow enveloping and soon all-pervasive.

When I walked out of the jail that evening I was numb. I was overwhelmed with seeing the sky, touching a palm tree, breathing fresh air. I sat down in the grass outside the courthouse, awed by the earth. It was only then I realized what a totally isolated and controlled world I had just been in—how there had been no windows, no trace of outside world inside those concrete walls. I was so overwhelmed that I never wrote an article about the experience. I was too confused, too angry to make sense out of it all.

When I moved to Philadelphia later that summer and began writing for the Philadelphia *Evening Bulletin*, I still felt the urgency of needing to *do something* and get involved personally somehow in changing what I had been oblivious to for so long. After hearing the superintendent of Philadelphia prisons say "community involvement" would be welcomed in the prisons, I told him I'd like to start a writers' workshop for women or juveniles. I was told that if I wanted to conduct such a workshop it would have to be at Holmesburg Prison, a maximum-security facility for men—most of whom were awaiting trial. That was four years ago; the workshop is still active. Over the years, I got involved in the legal aspects of various individuals' cases and in attempts to change conditions both in the community and in the jail. Eventually this personal commitment carried over into my writing about the local and state systems.

That, in essence, is how I "fell through the trap door."

I never intended to write this book. I would prefer to write a children's book, a comedy or a novel. My best argument against writing it was that I hadn't done time myself; women prisoners are the only experts on women's prisons. They should write their own books about their own experiences. But friends I met in jail—and friends on the outside who had experienced jail—urged me to do it. They *would* write their own books, but I had access to more than one jail, more than one prison. As one older woman said, "Baby, you gotta be the voice for us. Cause according to society, we ain't got no voices. Numbers can't talk—everybody knows that. Besides that, we get so used to this whole thing we can't even *see* a lot of it. It's too close. You got some perspective."

"We haven't never had the chance to tell our side of the story," another jail-weary woman said. "We get processed in here and when anything's ever in the paper about our case—it only quotes the DA. They don't never ask us nothing. I always thought I'd try to write a book about all this but I never got past the title: *Jail Ain't Shit*."

After I became involved in the book, I realized one of the reasons I had resisted writing it: Like a lot of women, I didn't really like women. I didn't like myself. I didn't want to excavate the caverns of my life. I couldn't write about women in prison without looking at their reality or my reality. I didn't want to try to see past my own biases and limits at what was really happening—or struggle each day to use words that could never fully capture the pathos and actualities of our human condition. But I was already committed to the process of focusing in on that which had been oblivion. I was beginning to understand myself and, likewise, understand women.

Many of the prisoners I met said they never had the chance to evaluate the conditions they live in; and I believe it is obvious that they are the greatest overlooked source for examination and change of the system that governs their lives.

In this book, I try to give women prisoners a chance to speak for themselves—to tell about their experiences and their feelings. Whatever they say I have tried to relate without distortion or bias. Where I do make comments, my views and comments are obviously my own.

Because life in prison has been structured by reformists, theoreticians and administrators, there is often a great gap between theories and their effects on individuals. I try to examine those differences and look at realities as opposed to myths—no matter how upsetting or disconcerting they are.

I have also tried to look at what effect imprisonment has on crime; what kind of dent the system makes in alleviating crime. I am not blind to the fears people have of being hurt. I have been robbed, my apartment has been burglarized. Two dear friends of mine have been murdered by strangers. Like anyone who has been poor or lived in inner cities where crime rates are highest, I know the realities and horrors of crime on a personal day-to-day basis. It has not been uncommon for me to step outside my door and see someone bleeding from a gunshot wound or to let someone in my house who has just been robbed or stabbed. So naturally I am as concerned as anyone else in stopping crime, in curbing senseless activities. Again, people who have been convicted of crimes have untapped insights on how to stop crime. But just how often are they consulted?

My basic research has come from visits to twenty-one jails and prisons for women; sixteen county and city jails (thirteen housing both men and women and three exclusively for women), five state and one federal prison for women.[1] In addition, I visited five state prisons for men, three county jails exclusively for men and five juvenile jails. Two of the juvenile facilities included separate housing for incarcerated girls. I have received correspondence from women in several prisons I didn't personally visit and talked with women

1. The women's facilities included: Arizona State Prison; Sybil Brand Institute for Women in Los Angeles; California Institution for Women at Frontera; San Bruno County Jail; North County Holding Facility in Palo Alto; Broward County Jail in Fort Lauderdale; Cook County Jail and the House of Correction in Chicago; Iowa Reformatory for Women; Camden County Jail; New York City Correctional Institution for Women; Erie County Jail and Erie County Penitentiary in Buffalo, New York; Ohio Reformatory for Women at Marysville; State Correctional Institution for Women in Muncy, Pa.; York County Jail (Pa.); House of Correction in Philadelphia; Allegheny County Jail in Pittsburgh; Chambersburg County Jail (Pa.); Women's Detention Center in Washington, D.C.; and the Federal Reformatory for Women in Alderson, West Virginia.

The juvenile facilities that housed younger offenders were the Youth Studies Center in Philadelphia and the John F. Kennedy Youth Correctional Center in West Virginia. It should be noted that juveniles were also incarcerated with adult women in most of the county jails visited. Male prisons I visited were all in Pennsylvania. They included Graterford, Western, Dallas, Huntingdon and Eastern penitentiaries; Holmesburg Prison, the New Detention Center and the House of Correction.

who have been jailed in Massachusetts, Connecticut, Tennessee, Louisiana, Texas, Oregon, Kansas and other states.

I have interviewed some four hundred women in depth—and talked at random with perhaps five hundred more—both in and out of prison. They are as old as eighty-nine and as young as fourteen; they come from every racial and ethnic background, religious and political belief. Some were incarcerated; some were on probation or parole; and others were out on bail awaiting trial. Some have finished parole but still have many memories and opinions to relate. I talked with women in criminal courtrooms in Philadelphia and New York and met others at drug rehabilitation centers and in community organizations for ex-cons. I've also spent many hours on the telephone and in the homes of women on parole—talking with them and their families.

At first I wondered if my random sampling would be biased. The women I was instinctively drawn to tended to be labeled "aggressive" or "troublesome" by prison officials. They were for the most part fairly independent women who have "paid their dues," who are from the street and carry the humor and perspective of a woman, "S.A.P.," who wrote:

> I've played the blues and I've paid my dues
> And my race is almost run;
> I did Satan's task and I haven't asked
> If I showed—if I placed—or won.
>
> Now I'm past my prime and I've served my time
> And I've been what I could be;
> So when you get to hell and ring that bell
> That old whore on the door will be me.

She's the kind of woman I enjoyed talking to the most. Not apologetic, repenting or withdrawn. But the more I let myself talk to women I didn't normally approach out of interest, the more I felt the sample *was* representative of the human interweaving of people in prison.

"Pick your girls at random and you'll get it all together," a middle-aged woman who had done a lot of time told me. "The consensus is the same but people look at it different ways. Me, I do a lot of work up there in the administration. I keep records, type and take dictation. I make six dollars a month—and they don't bother me because I don't make trouble. But there's a lot wrong here—a lot. I've learned a lot I don't want to know. But I'm just keeping myself busy. I gotta earn my way outta here. And lord knows, I want to just maintain myself—at least ninety per cent of what I was when I came in."

The majority of women in this book are not women you've read about in newspapers. They're the women who are listed as police and court statistics. Occasionally they have been mentioned by name in a paper—"Mary Smith Charged with Homicide" or "Police Make Morals Raid on Locust Street" or "Three Suspects Rounded Up in Drug Bust." That is the last you usually hear of them, if you hear of them at all.

Because I feel what people have to say is so important, I try to quote them exactly. Many times on the street I have used a tape recorder; but inside the prisons I have taken verbatim notes. I regret that I have not been able to include information from each woman who shared her time with me, but each insight contributed to the shaping of this book immeasurably. I have been unable to use everything any one woman said. But I have tried to extract her most important messages, the most relevant of her comments. There is no composite character in this book. Each woman stands as herself, saying what she alone said, even when she is not quoted by name. Perhaps it would be less wordy to paraphrase, but I do not do this. People speak for themselves, with their own meaning, their own interpretation, their own raw, unadulterated expression. Thus the lack of conciseness, the repetition and contradiction.

Along with interviewing prisoners, I've talked with administrators of prisons, heads of bureaus of correction and more than 250 guards and prison employees, correctional counselors, deputy sheriffs, police, lawyers, judges, parole and probation officers and criminologists. These people are an essential part of any perspective on the whole system. The prison employees and administrators are most significant because they, through quirks of fate in their own lives, have ended up in posititions of power over people incarcerated in this system.

I must confess that long before I first entered prisons, I was very biased against guards and matrons. Because they wore uniforms, they seemed non-human and stereotypically brutal. My early and long-standing disdain for cops lumped police and guards into an authoritarian "enemy force." However, I have painfully discovered that guards and matrons are just people, too. It sounds simplistic and it was. I had been stereotyping them as I felt I had been stereotyped, copying a mind set I deplored. It is true that guards and matrons are in positions of control over other human beings, but they also live under stringent rules and regulations that imprison and brutalize them. They are often expected to do jobs they are untrained and poorly paid for. Some say they feel they are also being punished when they are asked to enforce rules they don't believe in and go out of their way to exercise understanding in the daily course of their work.

"All our work in the institution is so restrictive," said one young guard. "We have to follow all these rules and we're told we can't get too friendly with the inmates. All our time seems to be spent solving little problems—like keeping count or who wants to move where or who broke this or that rule. We don't ever get to the big problems or to things that will really help somebody. We never know what happens to the women when they go out unless they violate [parole] and come back."

I have tried to treat guards and administrators with the respect they deserve as human beings. This does not make the meaning of some of their actions less malignant or assume that their positions of power are not often detrimental to the best interests of human freedom or growth. But hating them or exposing them as "bad" or "evil" people is not going to change the process or the power of the criminal justice system any more than exposure of "bad" or "evil" prisoners has in the past. My purpose is not to expose personalities but to examine the tremendous power of the institutional system— and see what effect it has on people's lives.

Most of the people I interviewed asked me to use their actual names. They wanted to be credited with what they say, what they believe. Mary (Doats) Sullivan, in Montgomery County Jail, spoke for a lot of prisoners when she said: "Make sure to use my whole name. And my age—twenty-eight. I'm not ashamed of being in prison. I think they should be ashamed to put us here." I've changed a few names at the request of women who believe what they say could damage their parole status. I've also changed names of some people for their own protection at my discretion. Some guards and prison employees also asked not to be quoted by name for fear of losing their jobs or a promotion. All elected officials and public administrators are quoted by name.

Of course some prisoners and guards never had an opportunity to say anything at all. At Camden County Jail in Camden, New Jersey, for instance, Sheriff Martin Segal explained: "The ground rules here are no photographs and no interviews.

"The public has the right to know," he said, "but you can't talk to prisoners. They may not be telling the truth. I like to be accurate and exact in my remarks. People have a right to know, but they should know the truth. There will be no talking to anyone but me. We can give you all the facts and information, but we want it to be correct. Don't talk to the guards either. You can't know if what they're saying is true. I will tell you anything you want to know."

Some people may say that many of the prisoners quoted in this book are exaggerating, projecting or distorting. The same may be said of administrators and guards. They are. And they aren't. This is the way they see it—and it's adding all these pieces together that gives us a fuller picture of what's going on. No single person has a full measure of truth. There are distortions and biases in everyone—but it's sorting them out and putting them all together that gives us clearer vision to melt myths.

I've had to leave a great deal of material out of the book. As a friend of mine said, "We are all like the tips of icebergs—we show most other people only the top five per cent." Perhaps this book is like the top five per cent or less. There's a whole iceberg, or mountain of human reality underneath it.

For everything that shows, there's always more. For one person's perspective, there are a thousand more who see it another way, or experience it differently. Everyone has a separate reality—influenced by their own experiences, consciousness and limitations. Nothing is cut and dried fact, even when it appears that way. Everything is true—and at the same time, everything is false. Memories are abstractions, just as words are abstractions to communicate real feelings and emotions and smells and sounds. So this book is only a beginning, an attempt to document and draw the relevant and the authentic from the total of What Is in women's prisons and jails—as in the human experience to which we are all so inexplicably bound.

—KITSI BURKHART

December 1972
Philadelphia

Death

"When I was here the first time," Patty Velasquez says, "my husband of five years died of an overdose. The next day a friend of ours came and broke the news to me. She'd read it in the obituaries in the paper and she brought me the little article. It was only about three paragraphs long. It was just a notice of death. It didn't explain anything. I had just moved on campus and at that time they were real strict here. I asked them for a phone call to call my brother-in-law to find out what happened.

"The correctional counselor told me I couldn't call him because he had a record, but that I could call my husband's parole officer. He couldn't tell me anything but that they were still investigating the cause and circumstances of his death.

"The police [staff member] called and asked for medication because I was quite upset. She asked for medication 'cause she was trying to help me. I was standing there as she was talking on the phone and I heard her say, 'I beg your pardon?!!' She held the phone out and I heard with my own ears: 'She is a drug addict and she is going to have to learn how to cope with tragedy without the aid of narcotics.' The staff started crying. She couldn't do anything for me.

"I was up three days and three nights. My friend went to the doctor and said, 'She's just sitting there reading the article over and over. She's blowing it; she won't talk to nobody.' The second day, they came and told me I was to go to work in the kitchen. I said I wasn't going anywhere. My friend went and asked to take my place . . . but they wouldn't let her. Finally about the fourth day I went over to the doctor and told him what the nurse had said. He blew up. He gave me the tranquilizers.

"That was probably the ugliest thing that's happened to me here. It may sound like a little thing to some people but when you're locked up . . . I could have blown it. Broads have hung themselves for less.

"They used to send inmates into the room when a broad had hung herself. The inmates had to photograph her and cut her down. I was here once when the broad that took photographs was told to go into Fifty-Seven. She wasn't told what she was going to photograph. She went in and saw the broad hanging there and just blew it. She really flipped out."

Patty Velasquez's ugly experience happened several years ago—when the California Institution for Women was "rigid, strict control." Now that the prison had become more open and treatment-oriented, one might think that this sort of thing wouldn't happen. But there are still more than six hundred women inside and what happened to Francis, a fifty-year-old woman, last November gave testimony to what she called "a good example of the coldness here."

"I came in here last November. I had just been in here three days and I still didn't even know where I was. They took me out of noon count—which was an unusual thing. My counselor took me aside and just said, 'We just had a call that your husband is dead.' Just like that.

"I've never been down on my knees in my life but I was on my knees to Mr. Kehler. Wasn't there any way I could get out to make arrangements and to go to his funeral? There were only the two of us. I didn't get to go out. I didn't even know when he was buried. My husband laid in the mortuary for four days because I couldn't do anything. They did let me make a couple of phone calls and let somebody come to visit. But then to top it all, I was evaluated as 'emotionally passive' and they put me in the hospital because they thought I was suicidal. We'd been together more than twenty years. But like my counselor told me: It is awfully hard to get here.

"Even when that happened with my husband I basically understood it. I was in custody and there are rules and regulations. You can't forget you did something wrong and you're in prison.

"The only thing I resent and resent deeply is that I was promised by my lawyer and the DA that if I copped a guilty plea I'd get probation. I waived all my rights before the court—they say 'no one promised you anything . . . this or that' . . . and you swear to it. When I went to court for the sentencing, the judge sentenced me to prison, not to probation. I have cancer of the abdomen and need radium treatments. The judge stipulated I get whatever I need in here . . . but I haven't yet. The judge said he figured I had cancer when I committed the crime, so I should have considered it."

Chapter 1   CRIME: A MATTER OF POWER

I remember when I was thirteen and I was sitting on the front steps of my grandmother's house . . . My father said, "Put on your shoes, I'm going to take you downtown with me." We got into the car and we went to the police station and I kept asking him, "What are we doing here?" He told me to hush, he had business to take care of. Then one of the policemen took me and told me to wait in this little room. I was waiting in this little room for my father to finish his business and then I looked out the window and I saw my father walking towards the car.

I screamed at him, where was he going? Why was he leaving me? He never turned around . . . He just kept walking to the car and then he got into the car and drove off.

He never told me I was an "incorrigible" child . . . and lord knows, at that age I didn't know I had any problems or what they were. I just knew he left me there. From there I was sent to the Youth Studies Center and from there to Slaten Farms . . . and later on to all the rest of the joints.

I never saw my mother. I still don't know who she is. All I know about her is that she was real young when she had me, about seventeen or something, and that she left home shortly after I was born. Nobody will tell me about her or who she is. She's a big family secret in my house. They know . . . lord, with a family as big as mine, they know everything . . . they just won't talk about it.

You know, for a while I tried to deny my past. When I got out of Muncy, I wanted to be totally new and all that. But then I told myself, "Look, girl, you've done all these things, they're part of your past." I'm not wearing it all as a badge of honor, but then who should go to jail? Me at thirteen? Huh-uh, baby; not me or nobody else.

—Theresa Derry, ex-inmate, Muncy, Pa.

It's a terrible thing to grow up feeling you have no control over your own destiny. It's a feeling that is hopeless, helpless. Everything is so big and you are so small. Power seems to be something outside yourself and you just do what you can to survive.

Many people in America grow up with this feeling. Thousands of poor black, Puerto Rican, Mexican, Indian and white people have this feeling at a very young age. Women of nearly every ethnic background have this feeling. It feels like being nothing and nobody. It's hard to separate who you are from your dreams of who you would like to be. It's hard to know what you are capable of doing.

Our models—our mothers and fathers—often seem resigned or hopeless about life themselves. We may be like them, but we don't want to be, especially when we see their lack of available alternatives. The only people who seem to have options and be self-determining are middle- or upper-class white males. And of course they appear to be more immune to the overwhelming forces we feel than they really are.

Many of us have rejected our parents and ourselves in an attempt to gain control over our own lives. In a desperate search to gain power and a sense of independence, many women have copied the style of men and many blacks have copied the style of whites. We copy the people we see who seem to get the rewards for *being*. And we somehow feel we are violating our possibilities for rewards by just being *different*. We have grown up thinking we have to be other than we are to gain any real power. And we feel genuine pressures from the outside to conform, to alter our natural behavior, our differences.

It is often this sense of powerlessness and natural resentment that leads to "anti-social" actions or "crime." People who appear to have power drive nice cars, live in comfortable homes, wear fine clothes and watch color television. It is accepting these material symbols as "power" that makes us either attempt to get the same things or strike out at the people who have them. Sometimes, too, we try to escape the realities of our helplessness and outrage with drugs. In this same vein, we try to change the way things are by acting "tough" when we feel afraid. Our efforts are often molded by our fears and by our need for power over our own lives. So it is with crime.

When we talk about crime in America, about prisons, we are talking about power and powerlessness.

Several centuries before Christ, Ezekiel said: "The land is full of bloody crimes, and the city is full of violence." What Ezekiel was saying—and what we are saying today when we talk about crime—is that we don't feel safe; we want to feel protected and secure.

The machinery we have developed through law and custom to give us that protection and security is called the criminal justice system. It consists of legal standards, police, courts and prisons. The main thing we know about it is that we trust it to work for everyone to create and maintain order—but it doesn't. The land is still full of bloody crimes, the city is full of violence and we still fear for our lives.

People who live in large cities are often justifiably afraid to go out of their homes at night. They are afraid of strangers. Many people are just as afraid of police. People sent to prison are supposedly "paying for their crimes," but the plaintiff is not really "repaid" for fear, humiliation, physical damage or material loss. Society is no safer. The defendant being punished says that even if she wanted to "pay" for her crime, or learn a way to make a legal living, she couldn't do it in prison. All she learns in prison, she says, is how to commit more crime.

Because reality is so distasteful, we often compensate with myths—even though many of our resilient notions don't match the evidence. Major myths related to the criminal justice system are: "Crime doesn't pay." "Criminals are caught; therefore, prisons deter crime." "Criminals go to prison" and "Prisons reform criminals."

We believe these myths despite the very plain words of thousands of individuals and dozens of studies, including the President's Commission on Law Enforcement and the Administration of Justice, that the criminal justice system does not deter or detect crime; it does not reform and does not correct the criminal.

Detailed reports show that business and white-collar crimes cause more financial loss, more injury and death than any other crimes in America. In one year, price-fixing by twenty-nine electrical companies alone cost the public more than is reported stolen by burglars throughout the entire country. Violations of safety laws and housing codes, food and drugs sold in violation of the Pure Food and Drug Act cause thousands of deaths. Yet these crimes are rarely dealt with using the full force of criminal sanctions. Standards of right and wrong are less clear when they are committed in the course of business transactions and work.

The President's Commission also points out that organized crime is the "most sinister kind of crime in America." It says "organized racketeers, big criminals, pursue their conspiracy unmolested in open and continuous defiance of the law—stimulating corruption among police, prosecutors, judges and public officials." It supplies goods and services wanted by people but prohibited by the law: cash loans, narcotics, prostitutes, gambling.

Because the various police agencies aren't organized to halt complex business crime or organized crime, single agencies continue to deal with simpler, individual crimes that have a much less damaging effect on our total society. The focus of police, the courts and the prisons thus remains on people who commit individual street crimes —not on organized criminals or administrators, who sit in secure out-of-the-way places.

And just as it is difficult for police to focus on complicated systems of organized or corporate crime, it is difficult for us to focus our anger on a corporation or an an illegal, interwoven web of activity we don't understand or can't really *see*. But because we want to feel safe and believe that *something is being done about crime*, we stubbornly maintain that criminals are caught and go to prison.

In fact, criminals rarely go to prison.

People who do go are a minute number of the lawbreakers—*less than 2 per cent in the entire country*. Statistics compiled by the National Council on Crime and Delinquency show that Americans report more than nine million crimes to police annually. More than twice that number presumably go unreported. Yet *police make arrests on only 12 per cent of all reported crimes*. Of the number arrested, only half are found guilty. After suspended sentences, probation and other alternatives to prison are used up, slightly more than 1.5 per cent of all reported lawbreakers are sentenced to prison. One out of thirty people sentenced to prison is a woman.

The majority of women and men sentenced to prison terms are found guilty of breaking social and moral codes we have written into law. More than 50 per cent are in jail for crimes against themselves, i.e., victimless crimes. Others are petty thieves, unsuccessful burglars, bad-check writers. Murderers—the people we all fear the most—make up a minority of the prison population, usually less than 10 per cent.[1]

1. Eighty-four per cent of all known murders in this country are committed by someone known intimately to the victim, usually a family member. Twice as many people kill themselves as are killed by someone else.

Our fear of death from a stranger is an exaggerated fear. Fred P. Graham, writing for the U. S. National Commission on the Causes and Prevention of Violence in 1969, points out that rather than the FBI publicizing the fact that a person is murdered each forty-eight minutes, it could be telling the public the average person's chance of becoming a homicide victim on a given day is about *one in two million*. His chance of being a victim of violent crime is once in four hundred years.

"I asked a man in prison once how he happened to be there, and he said he had stolen a pair of shoes. I told him if he had stolen a railroad, he would be a United States Senator."

—Mother Jones, a labor organizer in the early 1900s

It would seem there are two separate systems of criminal justice in America: an "intellectual" system for crimes of basically mental process and a "physical" system for crimes of action.

As I sat in many courtrooms and watched chaotic proceedings during trials of accused shoplifters, prostitutes, burglars, purse snatchers, I was always startled at the contrast when a "professional" came to trial for embezzlement, fraud or bribery. A calm dignity would fall over the courtroom. The prosecution and defense would always be thoroughly prepared. Witnesses would be present. The judge would seem to be more focused, more thoughtful.

At first I attributed the differential approach solely to the economic status of the defendants. The process seemed like an administrative rather than a criminal proceeding for white-collar criminals or middle-class defendants. Sentences were always much lighter, even for people who had embezzled huge sums of money. A person who robbed someone of twenty dollars usually got more time than someone who had extorted more than $20,000.

What I finally realized is that discretion seems to operate according to unconscious criteria as well. When a crime is unsophisticated and "primitive," the punishment is primitive. The more primitive the crime, the more primitive the punishment. Crime in America is equated with primitive physical actions. The more intellectual synthesis, abstraction and creativity in a crime, the less it is perceived as crime and the more it interests lawyers, prosecutors and judges—who basically live by the intellect, rather than by action. The same is true of the general public, who condemn a crime of action before an intellectual crime.

Looking at these two standards of justice explains a lot of things that probably work on an unconscious, cross-cultural level.

It can be "fascinating" when a banker or an executive is arrested for having embezzled money through an intricate mental process. It is a challenge for the judge to dissect and understand the highly specialized case and its motivations. He can unravel and empathize with the pressures that drove the person of economic status to commit a crime. Likewise, a judge can understand how the arrest and the attendant publicity affects the reputation of a person like himself and how the defendant is already being punished by the shame of exposure, by loss of status or loss of employment.

On the other hand, when a person who has robbed someone, snatched a purse or offered to sell her body to a stranger comes before the bench, there is no basis for empathy from the legal profession. The judge doesn't understand the culture or realities of the economically powerless person standing before him. A physical action reflects a "lack of control." The judge can't understand the mental or emotional duress of a person of action driven to committing a crime such as this, but the action is easily comprehended and condemned. He can see that the person of little status has probably been arrested before; she hasn't seemed to *learn* that crime doesn't pay. He considers her hopeless. He doesn't understand her world and he tries to "make the punishment fit the crime."

The varying standards lead to discretion readily interpreted as discrimination: one person gets out on bail; the other is locked up before trial. One woman gets two months in jail for her part in a $750,000 hoax which was basically an intellectual game; and another woman is sentenced to ten years in prison for her part in a robbery that netted $56.43. A high society woman who is "driven" to the point of shooting her cruel and abusive husband is acquitted for justifiable homicide because of the *mental torture* she endured. The court orders private psychiatric treatment. Her less prestigious counterpart who stabbed her cruel and abusive husband to death following one of many beatings is sentenced to life imprisonment without parole.

Two crimes might be quite similar, quite brutal; the mental duress of each person involved might be equally severe—but the response differs. For illustration, look at the cases of two young women:

Heidi Fletcher, a twenty-one-year-old white woman, was accused of killing a cop in the process of robbing a savings and loan association in Washington, D.C. She pled guilty to first-degree murder, armed robbery, robbery and illegal possession of dangerous weapons.

Before her trial, Heidi was released without bail for four-and-a-half months in the custody of a high District of Columbia official with the stipulation she get a job and be in by 10 P.M. every night. The official was a friend of her father's, Thomas W. Fletcher, former deputy mayor of the District. A week before her twenty-second birthday, Heidi was sentenced to a maximum of nine years in prison—with the possibility of release any time before then. Her defense attorney said she was "starved for love." The judge ordered that she serve her sentence in California so she could be closer to her mother and father, currently city manager of San Jose, California. She was denied parole in June 1972, but will be reconsidered for release in May 1975.

On the other hand, Rose Marie Dinkins, a twenty-three-year-old black woman, was accused of killing two cops in the process of attempting to rob a grocery store in Pittsburgh, Pennsylvania. She pled guilty to two counts of first-degree murder in a Pittsburgh court. The mother of four children, Rose was held in Allegheny County Jail, without bail, awaiting trial. She had no money. No one really noticed when Rose Marie Dinkins was sentenced to two concurrent life terms in prison. She probably won't get out of prison for twenty years or more. There's a good possibility she'll never get out. Was her crime worse? Couldn't she also have been "starved for love?" Was she more of a "threat" than Heidi Fletcher?

It seems we are slower to condemn a person of economic status who lives a basically mental life—even when he or she is arrested or convicted for committing a crime of action. We are shocked when an intellectual or a bureaucrat is sentenced to prison; but very little attention is paid when a have-not person who lives basically a life of action is locked up. No one would have been so *shocked* by Angela Davis' arrest and detention, for instance, had she not been an articulate professor from the University of California at Los Angeles. Thousands of black women are arrested every day and no one winks an eye; their arrest is "normal."

Black people are generally stereotyped, however, as people who live "action" lives. People without economic power. But simply because disproportionate numbers of blacks are arrested, detained and imprisoned in urban areas does not mean there are, in fact, more black criminals than white. Nor does it mean that blacks are "worse than whites" as some people choose to believe. It only means that police focus more attention on black neighborhoods; prosecutors are not as apt to drop charges; judges are less likely to grant bail black defendants can meet; and more apt to sentence a black person convicted of a crime to prison. Once imprisoned, blacks spend longer periods of time behind bars before being granted parole.

It also means that because of social forces in ghettos everywhere, black people are more desperate to meet the basic needs of survival. They are driven to commit crimes of action more frequently than people who live in areas of greater financial security. These crimes are often essential to survival. If people want to live or eat with any satisfaction, but are not allowed to earn or gain what they need legally, they will resort to taking what they need. This has always been true. It is true of the urban poor people in Asia and Europe. When immigrants from Europe came to America in the 1800s and lived in ghettos under the same meager human conditions that still exist today, they were arrested and imprisoned in the same disproportionate numbers as black people today. The problem is that blacks have not been allowed the same assimilation; they can't just "lose the accent." Because of their indelible appearance and the persistence of societal discrimination, even blacks of high economic status are still looked upon suspiciously by white strangers, as though all blacks are still in the same desperate state of need as poverty-stricken ghetto residents. The stigma of slavery, of the ghetto, remains in the unconscious mind, and the assumption follows that because of poverty and resentment, almost *any* black person is likely to commit a crime of action at any moment.

Upper- and middle-class black people are often subject to arbitrary arrest on the basis of their race alone—because they look "suspicious" to white policemen who have been trained to look for anything "unusual." A black person with economic or social power can often clear up the case or be released on arraignment level. But it is the majority of black people living in crowded and deteriorated conditions who experience the harshest effects of prejudice on a sustained basis because they haven't the economic or political power to defend themselves effectively.

For instance, in Washington, D.C., administrators say that every class of woman is arrested—white, black, rich, poor. But after the initial hearings, it is the poor black and poor white women who are held in jail. Two women are arrested for larceny or petty theft. The bail is set at $3,000. The white woman with economic means is out of custody within hours. The black woman spends months in jail awaiting trial. One study showed that black women have a one-and-a-half times greater chance of being returned to jail after their initial hearing than white women.[2]

Another study in forty-one counties in Pennsylvania determined that bail and fines tended to be higher and sentences longer for black women than for white women on similiar charges. One exception was that the courts seemed to be more offended when white women practiced prostitution, and thus set their bail higher than that of their black counterparts.[3]

Does this mean the judge is racist? Is criminal law racist? Or is society racist? The intention of individuals involved may not be consciously racist, but the process is, the effective reality is. The fact is that our adversary system is an unequal contest, and the poor whites and blacks lose because they don't have the economic power to compete. Or the social power. Wealthy people are funneled out of the system. Poor people remain.

County Sheriff Richard Hongisto, in San Francisco, put it simply: "We can't talk about jails unless we talk about the inequitable distribution of wealth in society, the haves and the have-nots. We have to look at the emotional and cultural patterns that evolve out of the conditions of poverty.

"We have to remember that people in jail are inevitably the poor and the powerless. They don't have the power to change the system by themselves or they wouldn't be in jail. We have to change that balance of power through responsiveness and responsibility in the communities. . . .

"Jail sentences do not stop alcoholics from being alcoholics, prostitutes from being prostitutes, or heroin addicts from being heroin addicts," Hongisto said. "It never has and it never will. Jailing people as a way to solve social problems is very expensive, ineffective and inhumane. We've had rotten stinking miserable jails for years and years, and the crime rate has gone up and up. They're counterproductive.

2. Colleen Barros, Andrea Slavin, Virginia McArthur and Stuart Adams. *Movement and Characteristics of Women's Detention Center Admissions*, 1969. Research Report No. 39; District of Columbia Department of Corrections, May 1971.

3. *Report on the Survey of 41 County Court and Correctional Services for Women and Girl Offenders, Jan. 1, 1965–Dec. 31, 1966.* Reported by Margery L. Velimesis, Division Project Director, American Association of University Women in Pennsylvania, January 1969.

"Stopping crime is keeping families together, building better schools, better housing, distributing the wealth. If we encourage loving families to stay together, we discourage crime. If people feel useful and constructive, they'll be useful and constructive. Day after day, change after change, little things can be done in the jails to make the quality of life better and relieve tensions, but the real work has to be done out here."

Hongisto has made a lot of "little changes" in San Bruno's county jails, as have prison administrators in other parts of the country. But the injustices of greater proportion continue. Jails and prisons remain basically unchanged—as does the process that carries people to them. The system seems much more massive than any individual efforts to cure its apparent case of lockjaw.

The courts deal daily with people police have brought them from the streets—people alienated from mainstream economy and production, people who often are abusing themselves more than they have ever abused others. Concerned judges often feel as powerless as anyone else to change what they see as a process destructive and dehumanizing to some people who show no willingness to help themselves anyway.

"What can I do?" said Philadelphia Municipal Court Judge Paul A. Dandridge after sentencing a woman to six months in the House of Correction. "This woman is brought in the first time for a robbery and she's on heroin. I know her chief problem is drugs, so I give her probation and arrange for her to get into a drug program. She messes up that program and is brought back here before the court for violation of probation. I decide that what she needs is to go to Phoenix House in New York—something she wants to do, too. But she goes to New York and blows that program and comes back here and gets arrested again for something else—still having a fifteen-bag-a-day habit. What can I do?

"I've put her in programs and she's violated probation three times. She's out there in the street hurting herself and doesn't have any place to stay or any people to go to. So I give her six months at the House of Correction. There aren't any other alternatives. And I'm sending her there only because there's nothing for her in the community. At least in there she's safe—at least being there gives her a chance to dry out and a safe place to sleep. I know it stinks, but I don't know what else to do."

Dandridge is a rare judge to be aware of the kinds of problems and life the woman faces. But he is black; he grew up in the city and knows *the life*. Unlike the majority of judges in this country, he has visited all the jails and prisons he sentences people to. He says they are ineffective and proceeds to use constructive alternatives available. But the alternatives under criminal law are limited.

Sensitive people in the criminal justice system are aware they're dealing with people who reflect the problems and effects of social disorder, racism, poor housing, poor education.

"Society dumps all their problems in our lap," says the warden of the Women's Detention Center in Washington, D.C., Mrs. Pat Taylor. "The community wants us to do in six months what society hasn't done in the entire lives of these women. We're supposed to be undoing what they did to them for eighteen or nineteen or twenty-seven years. We didn't create these people. We didn't throw them out of the community, either. We don't have magic pills. We didn't create their attitudes and hostilities, but we become the object of them."

Pat Taylor is superintendent of a jail that books, processes and incarcerates all the women arrested in Washington, D.C. More than 75 per cent of her prisoners are awaiting trial. The rest are serving sentences, including two doing life. Eighty per cent of the women are drug addicts. She estimates 3 per cent of the population are "seriously emotionally disturbed." She says that 80 per cent of the women are kept on some kind of medication such as Thorazine or Librium—tranquilizers which make them easier to control in the overcrowded, physically deteriorating jail.

On Taylor's desk was a sign: NOTICE: DUE TO LACK OF INTEREST, TOMORROW WILL BE POSTPONED.

"Look, there's an emotional need to attain money in our society," she says. "There is nothing more important. We're all money oriented. Television, magazines, billboards—they all advertise things. We see the perfect family as having one or two cars at least, colored televisions, pretty clothes, perfume, jewelry, money and carpets on their floors.

"All of the sudden we're supposed to tell these women, 'Don't grasp for money. Money isn't as important as high moral values. Be a square.' It's a bunch of bull! Earning money as a prostitute, a booster or a hustler there are no taxes, no schedules, no time cards to punch. You expect a woman who can make up her own schedule and earn enough money to survive to take a factory job for $1.65 an hour or look forward to working over an industrial sewing machine?

"Society's taught that everyone has a right to have things—and that everyone *should* have nice things. They don't give these women any respectable way to get them, and then when they go out and get them the best way they know, we're telling them it's wrong. The community has just got to make up its mind what it wants. They're punishing these women for the very values they taught them."

When police, lawyers, judges and prison administrators—people in positions of power—feel frustrated, angry and even helpless about the criminal justice system and its effects, one can begin to imagine how defendants feel.

One day when I was sitting outside a criminal courtroom in New York City, I met a woman who was awaiting trial on a forgery charge. She was in her mid-forties and her enormous sighs as she talked about her case, one of many, reflected the powerless syndrome of her life.

"For me it was just like gettin' on an assembly line, baby," she said, patting my hand for comfort. "It all started when I was about fifteen years old. I was living on my own and they busted me for hanging around a bar. Shit, it was nice there. I could hear good music. The broads was good to me. But the officers said I'd been truant from school and I was promiscuous or something like that. They made me feel like a regular whore—a sho'-nuff down-and-out little nobody. That first time I got busted, the cop made me blow him and his partner on the way to the station. I guess they would have made me fuck 'em if there'd a been more time. That really got me, that really did me in. . . .

"I'll never forget 'em. I was so scared. I didn't know what to do. The next thing I knowed, I was in jail. And I been here mostly on and off ever since. For drinking or hustling mostly, you know.

"Shit, girl, I been to court so many times, I never could count 'em. Who knows what the fuck goes on in there? They got their own language all hooked up—it might as well be French to me. They got all their people hooked up, too, including their public defenders. I never be knowing what they're saying. All I knows is I got a subpoena and another charge. They be tellin me, 'You been bad again. What we gonna do with you?' And they preach at me some more about mendin' my ways. What ways? Shit, the only worse thing I did was come out my momma's womb. Yeah, that's where it all started, me just bein born, period. I'd like to think if she'd a known what was waiting for me, she never would a done it."

Echoes Of Rosa

One cold winter day
in New York City
Jeanette Washington
stood firm.
Black mother on welfare
refused to pay   30 cents
to ride the subway.
She got on, determined to ride,
refusing to let   bystanders
pay her fare.
"I wasn't going to be   locked
in the community
any longer.
I was going to use
public transportation
which should be   free."
Police apparently thought
          she was crazy.
They called an ambulance
and took her to see
a psychiatrist.
"He asked me why
I do what I do.
I asked him to think about   why
society does what it does to me."
Police charged Jeanette Washington
Black mother on welfare
with "criminal trespassing
on public property."
The judge set bail at $1500
and Jeanette was locked,

out of the community,
in jail.
Later she got a bill
for the ambulance.

This information was taken from a taped interview on "Radio Free People," broadcast on WBAI, New York City. I have arranged the details in poetic form to best convey the meaning of the event.

Chapter 2 GUILTY UNTIL PROVEN INNOCENT

"The way the criminal justice system is run now leaves no alternative to failure. A fundamental issue here applies as long as we use punishment to control human behavior. It's axiomatic that if you use punishment to control behavior and want to have any effect, you have to punish a person immediately following the behavior. In this system, the use of punishment just can't work. Not only do you have to wait before arrest—but by the time a person gets to court a year or two later, the behavior itself is totally forgotten. It's so long ago it doesn't even seem related and it seems you're being persecuted for something you didn't do. That's when people start feeling victimized by the system rather than being called to account for what they did.

"One other crux just as illogical is that our corrections rehabilitates people so they can adjust better to the community when they get out. Impossible! It's just impossible and illogical that you take a person away from normal society and put them in an abnormal society and expect them to adjust to the community. You just can't live inside the way we live outside."

—BENNETT COOPER, Ohio Commissioner of Corrections

The courtroom is clean, dignified. Almost pompous. Brass railings divide spectators from actors; they reflect off the shining mahogany surface of the judge's bench. Some forty people sit in folding chairs facing the judicial stage. For the most part they are a bedraggled, restless audience looking at the stage, seemingly oblivious to the decorum of the theater. Some of the women have come with rollers in their hair, dresses hanging unevenly, slips showing. Some men wear baggy pants, ill-fitting shirts untucked in the back. A few are neat, trim. Spectators include plainclothes detectives and men wearing blue police uniforms and silver badges.

A young black woman comes in, wearing a white knit dress and coat, holding hands with her sister's two small children. The children sit down beside her and then crawl up on their knees to hang over their seats, staring with curiosity at the people behind them. "Hush, sit down. Mommy's not here yet." Their mother, Beatrice, will be brought down from the jail for sentencing today. She has been in jail thirteen months. Three months ago she pled guilty to possessing narcotics and being involved in a burglary. This will be the second time her children have seen her in more than a year. They are not allowed to visit her in the county jail.

This is a tired, anxious audience before curtain time. But there is no curtain. Actors prepare in full view of the audience. The supporting cast warms up. Stenographers in designated seats check over their machines, straighten skirts, waiting to begin. Stage managers carry papers to the proper tables. District attorneys and defense attorneys officiously thumb through their thick legal files and make stylized gestures indicating readiness for performance. They rehearse lines quietly. Occasionally one actor struts over to another decorously, whispering in low tones about the first scene. Court crier and bailiffs stand at attention at the corners of the stage, surveying the audience as they seat themselves. This is participatory theater. The audience will partake, but they don't know their cues. Tension.

It is a controlled setting. Those who come to this theater regularly know the performance will be monotonously the same—yet there is always some variation, some detail or pathos, some person or outrageous crime or sentence to make it different. Rarely is there laughter in this theater. Rarer still, spontaneity. The only constant is the tense repressed anger, anxiety and curiosity emanating from actors and spectators alike.

Suddenly it is curtain time. The court crier, an old regular named Sam McGhee, steps forward and cries: "ALL RISE. OYEZ, OYEZ, OYEZ. ALL PERSONS BOUND BY RECOGNIZANCE HAVING TO DO WITH THE HONORABLE JUDGES OF THE COURT OF COMMON PLEAS IN THE FIRST JUDICIAL DISTRICT OF PENNSYLVANIA HOLDING HERE THIS DAY WILL NOW APPEAR AND THEY SHALL BE HEARD. GOD SAVE THE COMMONWEALTH AND THIS HONORABLE COURT. BE SEATED PLEAZZE." His lines have been repeated so many times, for so many years, that now they are only a loud flow, a commanding tone, the words indistinguishable except at the beginning and the end. The OYEZ repeated three times is close to music—a chant—a rhythm which could be sung to the backdrop of drums pounding while people dance to the beat. But in this theater, the chant becomes drone announcing you MUST stand, or suffer consequences: contempt of court.

Black robes swish, there is a flurry of actions that have been repeated thousands of times—and then the judge is seated. He folds his arms in front of him, clasps his hands and reads briefs and bills and psychiatric reports conscientiously, carefully, his brow wrinkled in serious effect. Like God, he sits in front of the large bronze seal of the state. Supporting cast members confer with him briefly and then the play begins—simultaneously falling apart with confusion.

"The point is, I don't have a bill of 368," the judge tells the district attorney. "No, your honor, that's the photo number, Judge. The bill is 370 and 371." "I see. Yes. I have bill 371. We can proceed."

"William Bradley, Number six," the crier demands. "ALL PARTIES AND WITNESSES IN THE BRADLEY CASE COME FORWARD." A small black man, with wrinkled brown tweed coat too large, shuffles toward the brass railing. "DO YOU SWEAR WHAT YOU TELL THIS COURT OF THE COMMONWEALTH OF PENNSYLVANIA WILL BE THE TRUTH, THE WHOLE TRUTH AND NOTHING BUT THE TRUTH SO HELP YOU GOD? KEEP YOUR VOICE UP. KEEP YOUR VOICE UP SO THE JUDGE CAN HEAR YOU!"

"Where's the police witness? Where's the police witness?" the judge asks. "Is Detective Zucker here? Is Detective Zucker here? You're taking a lot of time, Mr. District Attorney." Detective Zucker is not in the room—or if he is, he's hiding. The district attorney offers to find out where he is—why he didn't show. The case is postponed. The crier reads Bradley's name again, stating the case will be "continued" until June 6. William Bradley shuffles out with two guards.

I have come to this courtroom to see Jeanne Hardy be tried. She faces two charges of prostitution and one charge of trying to cash an American Express traveler's check at Thirtieth Street train station in Philadelphia. "ALL PARTIES CONNECTED TO JEANNE HARDY PLEASE COME FORWARD." Jeanne stands tall—in black dress, black heels and purse. She looks dignified. Calm. But she is alone and frightened. This is the fourth time she has come to court. Today will be the trial—and her life for the next six months or next six years will surely be resolved one way or another. But the case is not decided. The DA explains that he is not ready to proceed with the case; he and Jeanne's defense attorney are trying to "work something out." Jeanne's case is continued until July 8. The teller who has come to testify against Jeanne shakes his head—this is his fourth time in court, too.

Charges against another defendant are read. Andrew Moore—charged with violation of parole. Three counts: failure to report, failure to notify change of address and refusal to undergo psychiatric treatment. In a matter of minutes, the judge surveys the report and orders that Moore be returned to the state prison to complete a five-year sentence inside the walls. He has committed no new crime. But he has violated parole conditions. I realize it is exceptional that he is even coming before a judge for this decision. He could have just been returned to prison without a hearing under parole authority. I wonder if he has any children. I wonder how old he was when he first went to jail.

Finally the children in front of me have spotted their mother. She is now sitting in the front row between two matrons. Now standing in front of the bench—inside the brass railings—beside her lawyer. The two women sitting beside me—the defendant's mother and grandmother—put their arms around each other, hold their breath. The judge studies the reports in front of him, clears his throat. He tells Beatrice Connor that she has committed a very serious offense, does she realize this? Her answer is inaudible, but she nods her head up and down—like a child being scolded. A young probation officer tells the judge that he has made arrangements for Beatrice to enter a drug rehabilitation program in the Kensington section of Philadelphia. The judge listens to the details of the program. More silence. Then he tells Beatrice Conner that he is going to give her a break: ten years' probation. She will be transferred directly from the House of Correction to the drug center—where she will remain for ninety days. Following her drug treatment she will be expected to meet all the conditions of probation and have the opportunity to prove that she can be an upright citizen and a worthy mother. If at any time she violates the conditions of probation, she will be brought back before this bench and sentenced to a prison term of no less than five years. If she serves the conditions of probation satisfactorily for five years, she can appeal to him at that time to have the remainder of her sentence suspended.

The confused drama proceeds. Expected pauses, expected noise—with only some characters fumbling their lines. Some props are not available. Some actors missing. It is confused tension—an emotional circus—controlled by legal syllables and statutes. Everyone plays their part with control. Defendants stand in front of the bar stoically, yet seeming to seethe inside. I feel that if someone moved too quickly or unexpectedly, shouted, laughed or jumped up and started dancing, letting go of the dignity expected, the courtroom itself would no doubt explode or perhaps disappear in smoke. I feel like beginning to sing in a loud voice.

The bailiff is the only person who shouts when he feels like it or moves unexpectedly. He steps forward occasionally, seemingly on cue to break the tension, and hollers, "Keep it quiet back there." Earlier he has walked up to me to say I am not allowed to take notes in the courtroom. Now a man dares to wear a hat into the room. The bailiff seems outraged; his face reddens. "Take off that hat! Take off that hat!" He steps out threateningly; the man retreats, takes off his hat, sits down. I notice that "the man" is a woman.

Usually what goes on in the courtroom is unintelligible even to someone used to this scene listening carefully from the spectators' section. It is like hearing the lines from an ancient play read in a scramble without feeling; memorized lines or makeshift phrases in a language known only to the actors—words that have lost the essence, the clarity of their real meaning or original intent. The formality, the lack of warmth and awareness settles down like a fog and rocks defendants and observers alike into a maze, a daze of legal words.[1]

I walk outside the courtroom for air, an attempt to break the fog. And I realize what is intelligible is the handcuffs clicking on and off the defendants as they stand in the corridor outside the courtroom, coming from or going to jail. The overwhelming emotion and humiliation as the small dark-skinned woman in blue stretch pants and orange sweater puts her hands out together in front of her. A matron and a policewoman locking the handcuffs to each wrist. The haunting degradation on her small-boned face as the wrist shackles are secured and she walks tight-lipped and drawn down the long hall between two guards—holding her head high.

It is the memories of those handcuffs or waist chains and this courtroom scene that blur into remembrances of a woman in prison. Her anger at the time, her fear, her inability to speak for herself—the sense of not knowing what's going on when her life and the life of her children are at stake—often leave her numb, immobile when the play is almost over.

"What happened? What'd I get?"
she asks her court-appointed lawyer
or public defender.

Now the confused memory mixes with anger at the defense attorney or at the district attorney. Often the anger turns back on herself for not knowing her rights; wondering how things might have been different if she had only known the script, the rules of the game.

"I was so dumb when I went to court," Doris Jordan said as she sat in Iowa Reformatory for Women. "I got a court-appointed lawyer and I didn't know I could choose anyone. I'd never been in trouble with the law before. He told me I should cop a plea. Then when we were in the courtroom, the lawyer—MY lawyer—said, 'She's got two mixed kids by [her husband] and he's just been sent

1. Until June 12, 1972, an indigent defendant faced the prologue to this kind of circus alone—without a public defender as an interpreter at the least. Only then did the Supreme Court rule that every poor person is entitled to a free lawyer even for the most minor offense if it involves a jail sentence. Only nine years before, in the 1963 *Gideon* ruling by the court, it was held only that any needy defendant accused of a *serious crime* must be offered the services of a lawyer. Before those decisions, defendants were sentenced to months, years or life in prison without even a pretense of defense.

to the penitentiary for narcotics.' I couldn't believe it! What do my kids have to do with my case? What does it have to do with my guilt or innocence or time that my husband was black? What does his sentence have to do with my case? We'd been separated for five years! I was so stupid it's pitiful.

"We was in the judge's chambers and they told me if you plead guilty to this one charge, we'll drop the rest. So I pled guilty to one check for $44.33. I had written thirty-six of them, though, and they had me. They had my picture and my signature—so I figured I was lucky. But if I'd had any people or known anything, I probably could have gotten probation.

"I didn't have any education or vocational training and it was my first offense. They gave me *ten years*—which is a long time to get educated with a GED [high school equivalency diploma]. When I heard the judge say ten years, I couldn't believe it.

"All I could think about was my kids. It was like they was slipping out of my hands—falling away and I couldn't hold on to them or keep them safe. It was like everything I knew in the world was suddenly gone. Just gone. I couldn't even think of going to prison. And ten years? The only way I can be hurt is through the children. When I talk about them, I have to fight back the tears . . . The court took my kids when I was in jail. I was on ADC [Aid to Dependent Children], and the Welfare Department said I was an unfit mother because the light and gas bill had got to be two hundred dollars. My kids are my life; I could never be an unfit mother. When I get out I have to get myself together for me—and I only have to prove it to me. But to get my kids back I have to prove it to the court."

It is hard to imagine Doris Jordan as a "threat to the community" or someone who "belongs behind bars." No one could stereotype her visually as a "con" or a "rough, hard-talking broad in prison." Her hair is long, black and shiny. Her deep brown eyes, smooth olive-colored skin would make her a wholesome-looking candidate for the cover of *Seventeen* magazine or *Good Housekeeping*.

Doris wasn't tried by a jury of her peers. Few if any women in prison are. She was arrested, prosecuted, defended, tried and sentenced by men all with backgrounds far different from her own. Their annual incomes total more money than she'll probably see in her entire lifetime. Very few women in prison have had jury trials at all. Very few men have either, because a jury trial is a rarity. In Philadelphia alone, there were only 260 jury trials out of more than 30,000 criminal court cases in 1971.[2]

The majority of defendants sentenced to prison have big chunks of their lifetimes auctioned off in plea bargaining—a legal exchange that encourages the defendant to plead guilty to a lesser charge for a reduced sentence—getting maybe five to ten years instead of eight to twenty. Some embittered lawyers refer to it as "flesh peddling"—a gambling game between prosecutors and defense attorneys. ("You give me ten years for Green's case and I'll give you twenty instead of life for Saunders.") Off-the-record agreements are made with the judge. The process is said to speed up court efficiency and save time and energy for judges and attorneys. A defendant who refuses to plead guilty is told he will be risking the wrath of the judge—and probably wind up doing more time, not less, when found guilty.

Few people sentenced to prison have had the money to hire skilled criminal lawyers to defend their innocence or plead their case. In 1971 more than 85 per cent of the cases in Philadelphia's municipal court were referred to public defenders, who are only allowed to represent indigent clients. These same people, for the most part, were jailed awaiting trial in lieu of money bail.

The law of our land says that any person charged with a crime is innocent until proven guilty. But arrest and incarceration usually define guilt in a more pragmatic sense.

2. Even when a jury trial is conducted, it is rarely a trial by "peers" or equals of the defendant . . . "having the same legal status in society as that which he [the defendant] holds." To the present day, the Supreme Court has not ruled it unconstitutional for women to be excluded from a jury. The common rule of the law has been that juries are composed of "twelve good men." In 1879, when the Supreme Court ruled the exclusion of Blacks from state juries unconstitutional, it added: "A state may prescribe the qualifications of its jurors . . . It may confine the selection to males, to freeholders."

In "Juror Selection: The Law, A Mathematical Method of Analysis, and a Case Study," *The American Criminal Law Review*, Vol. 10, No. 4, 1972, David Kairys points out that the process or method by which jurors are selected is invalid and discriminatory. His analysis and the history of jury selection quite clearly reveal that juries are representative of the white, middle-aged, suburban and rural middle class. Black, poor and young people—the groups most often charged with crimes who most often have their lives placed in the hands of jurors, find virtually no peers on the juries. Kairys concludes that, "The one institution through which the framers of the Constitution sought to guarantee that the voice of the community would be heard in the courtroom has been undermined. The courts have done little to implement the constitutional mandate of cross-sectional juries."

The person who comes to court from jail has a feeling of jail about her. An aura. She has been treated as guilty during the days or months of incarceration. Even if she is acquitted, what is the difference between being in jail six months following a verdict and having been in jail for six months prior to the verdict?

It is also true that the longer a person stays in jail before trial, the less chance she has for acquittal. She cannot prepare an adequate defense—while, on the other hand, a person who can make bail usually is able to search for a lawyer, round up witnesses, secure a job and make a good case for herself in court. This also means, then, that women with any economic power have a better chance for acquittal or probation.

In her notes for arguments in court on the issue of self-representation, Angela Davis wrote, in part:

> I begin by directing the court's attention to the fact that as the accused in this case, I find myself at an enormous disadvantage. As a Black woman, I must view my own case in the historical framework of the fate which has usually been reserved for my people in America's halls of justice.
> . . . In a courtroom situation, the white prosecutor, white witnesses, especially white policemen, are given far more credence by the jury—usually overwhelmingly white—than the Black defendant. In the event that the Black defendant has been previously convicted of a crime, his chances of acquittal are virtually non-existent . . .
> I repeat, as a Black woman, accused of three capital crimes, I am at an enormous disadvantage. The prosecutor, representative of forces which have continually upheld this institutional racism, has enormous advantages. The history of America is on his side. There can be no doubt we are unequal adversaries.
> This inequality expresses itself not only in broad, historical terms but is also quite tangible. No one can deny that the immeasurable resources available to the prosecutor, indeed the entire state apparatus of California cannot in any sense compare to the resources available to me. His financial resources are virtually limitless—the state did not for a moment hesitate to extradite me from New York by the unprecedented means of a special military guard. I, on the other hand, must rely on the donations of concerned citizens, many of whom have had to make tremendous sacrifices in order to contribute small sums.
> On another level, the prosecutor's superior position has been buttressed by the widespread publicity in his favor. I place particular emphasis on Nixon's gratuitous and unwarranted remark when he

congratulated J. Edgar Hoover for capturing "one who engages in terrorist acts."

It would seem that the overwhelming advantages enjoyed by the prosecutor would call into question the basic presumption of the innocence of the defendant. I contend that the circumstances are *a priori* balanced in favor of the prosecutor . . .[3]

Few women awaiting trial have the publicity or excellent legal defense Angela had against the prosecution's case, no matter how flimsy. But the odds against their winning an acquittal are just as tremendous, if not more so, because they have no means of preparing a defense thoroughly challenging the prosecution's evidence.

For the most part, defendants meet their public defenders for the first time when they come into the courtroom for trial. Another public defender has interviewed them, and still another has investigated the case or talked to alibi witnesses or prepared pre-trial motions. The defendant's lawyer—often a person fresh out of law school—receives the defendant's file, along with five to fifteen other files, the night before the trial, or the day of the trial. He personally has just read over the notes taken on the case and has had no time himself to talk with witnesses, search out evidence or prepare motions which could effectively challenge the arrest procedure or prosecution evidence.

To say that public defenders are poorly paid and greatly overburdened by case loads is an understatement. Often their files are incomplete: lacking an interview, or pre-trial motions. In this case, the lawyer can ask for a continuance—and the defendant is sent back to jail, often only to meet a different lawyer and a new continuance the next time she is brought down to court. Sometimes the public defender, who may be handling as many as fifteen to twenty cases the same day, proceeds with the trial without further information.

Although the Gideon ruling provided that indigent defendants should have representation in the court, there are no standards set for the quality of representation. The young public defenders are often as overwhelmed by the courtroom scenes as defendants. Their personal commitment to winning a case is usually nullified by the frantic pace they maintain. This often results in slipshod and often meaningless representation for women and men without economic means. The interests, the lives of defendants and their families go almost unnoticed, neglected. Mothers are separated from their chil-

3. *If They Come In the Morning*, Angela Y. Davis and other Political Prisoners (New York: Signet, 1971).

dren, fathers are separated from their families. Terrible mistakes are made and remain undiscovered.

I believe that someday in history the auctioning of human life in America's twentieth-century courtrooms may be compared to the slave auctions of the eighteenth and nineteenth centuries. The powerlessness that persons who were sold as slaves felt in that moment of sudden realization that all known reality, all present time, affections, activity, warmth and routine were slipping away, fading into an unknown fearsome world—has been shared by millions of Americans in the twentieth century sentenced to enter the unknown gates of the prison world. They go into a world the public knows little about. And just as slave mothers were separated from their children, the majority of women in prison today are cut off from their children by a word, a bargain, a gentlemen's agreement.

If it weren't for the power the police and courts wield over people's lives, the courtroom scenes could be called tragic satires. The state of Pennsylvania, for instance, spent thousands of dollars to bring a woman to trial for attempting to steal her neighbor's pig to feed to her children. She didn't even get to kill or cook the pig before she was arrested. This could be funny—but the woman was sentenced to twenty years in prison. What will happen to her children without her? Rebecca Cross is in Alderson, West Virginia, for twenty years without parole on her first offense—possession of fifty-five dollars' worth of dope. Her two children in St. Louis were left without a mother when she was sent to prison. It was nine years before their first visit with her, because the trip from St. Louis to West Virginia was a trip she couldn't pay for.

It just doesn't seem real. But it happens every day. Defendants come forward—carrying with them from the streets burdens and pressures of poverty and racism not evident in this setting or in statistics on 25 million poor Americans. "Do you plead guilty or not guilty to violation of Section 174, title 21 . . . possession of narcotics?" If what you have to say fits into the slots prepared by decades of jurisprudence, you can, perhaps, say it. But there is no slot, no space, for your feelings as a person. There is just the law—you broke it or you didn't.

It didn't occur to Doris Jordan to tell the court about her life. And if it had occurred to her, what process would the court have to deal with the information? To Doris it was all a part of growing up. In an orphanage when she was seven years old. Always alone. Rejected first by her own mother, who said she was "incorrigible" because her own mother didn't know how to get along with her; because her own mother didn't know how to mother her. She was transferred to a juvenile home when she was thirteen and lived there until she was seventeen. She was never given an education, never given anything. But neglect. At seventeen she was out on her own. Yes, she did get desperate. Yes, she did break the law by writing bad checks. But should she be sentenced to ten years in prison?

"The only reason I really had such a bad time and got so much time is 'cause I didn't have no people," Doris said. "I don't get too close to people very easily."

It's amazing how many people are told they are eight-year-old "incorrigibles" or thirteen-year-old "failures." It shouldn't be surprising that they get into a process that carries them from one institution to another, a trip from one concentration camp to another. It's an A-B-C process. From being in a prison of no alternatives as a child. To Juvenile Hall. From Eighteenth and Diamond streets to jail. From the teacher yelling at you in school to getting bad grades to having your parent yelling at you to running away. Being truant. Getting arrested at age twelve or fourteen for being a truant or a runaway and being taken to juvenile court. From the Indian Reservation to the city to the Federal Reservation for women prisoners in Alderson, West Virginia. From the first taste of escaping oppression through the first taste of heroin to the first taste of jail. From a foster home or juvenile hall to jail to prison. A-B-C-D.

If you're a girl and you're a runaway, there's always the fear that you've been "promiscuous." So you're locked up for your own protection. You experience the effects of sexual and racial discrimination at a very early age—not knowing the history of this kind of discrimination. Only being told that you're *bad*.

Many women in prisons have backgrounds similar to Doris's. And while each has had experiences unique to herself, the demolition process worked on each human being seems to be a pattern repeated a thousand times over. The personal histories fit a pattern: *Gwen*, who ran away from home when her stepfather began forcing her at fourteen to submit to sexual intercourse. *India*, who ran away from home at thirteen for being locked in the house every day when she came home from school and beaten with a belt strap for "talking back." *Dorothy*, a sixteen-year-old with festering scars on the inside of her arms. She attempted suicide to get attention—to get her mother to notice her. *Susan*, locked up in Ocala, Florida, for being "promiscuous" when her only crime was being a white girl with a black boyfriend. Or *Sarah*, locked up in the same place for being black and having a white boyfriend. *Ellen*, one of six children of a family living on $200-a-month welfare. At eleven she was still sucking her thumb. At twelve she began hanging around waterfront bars in her hometown, screwing sailors for five or ten dollars as her uncle had taught her.

Some instinct to survive makes these young women run away or try to break out of a destructive environment. They are crying for help. But the "help" they get is all too often impersonal institutionalization. They are sent to reform schools and juvenile jails for truancy, running away, nebulous "incorrigibility" or "uncontrollable behavior" —actions which would never be considered crimes in an adult court. Yet they are labeled "juvenile delinquents." If their actions in the reformatory don't conform to rules, they often wind up in solitary confinement. I have seen children locked in maximum-security cells indefinitely because they are "extremely emotionally deprived." In many cases when young women have run away from a juvenile institution repeatedly, they have been sent to the state prison for women on criminal charges of "prison breach"—thus the first criminal offense on a sixteen-year-old's police record.

The President's Commission on Law Enforcement and the Administration of Justice found that more than half the girls in juvenile court are referred for general behavioral problems which do not amount to crime. Only one fifth of the boys are brought in for noncriminal behavior. And even though their offenses are not as serious as boys', girls are committed to institutions with proportionately the same frequency as boys.

Furthermore, their sentences are significantly longer. In a paper written in 1970 on "Equal Protection for Juvenile Girls in Need of Supervision in New York State," Sally Gold reported that girls average twelve months in New York training schools; boys, nine months and three weeks. Some of the people she interviewed felt parents were more threatened and less tolerant of their daughters' "acting out" than of their sons'. While girls in their teens are labeled sexually "promiscuous" if they become involved with boys, teen-age boys are thought to be "just experimenting" or "sowing wild oats."

"I was classified as promiscuous when I was fourteen because I had run away," one woman at a state prison said. "They classify you as that whether you've balled a guy or not. I was a virgin until I was twenty. But they figure you have to do something sexual to support yourself if you run away, since they think you can't make it on your own. But that's their own hang-up. They definitely play the psychological thing that you are a dependent person because you are female."

The same moral standards often follow women into adulthood, when one out of almost every five women is arrested for prostitution or commercialized vice, minor sex offenses. It's estimated that as many as 80 per cent of juvenile women are incarcerated for sexual reasons or sex-related offenses. David Ward and Gene Kassenbaum found that 68 per cent of the women at California Institution for Women had at some time in their past been officially reported for prostitution or promiscuity. Most of them got their start in the cycle of imprisonment as children.

Sheila was in Camden County Children's Shelter for being a runaway. She was fourteen years old, the daughter of a woman convicted repeatedly on charges of prostitution. She had grown up in small rooms, dark scary places. When she was five her mother went to jail and she was put into a foster home with a younger sister. An older sister and brother were in the same foster family for a while. Her oldest brother was in jail for armed robbery and for being AWOL from the Navy. Steve Cohen, working as a psychologist at the Children's Shelter, was Sheila's caseworker.

"The staff at the shelter feels that these children are criminals and have to be treated as such," says Cohen. "Mail is censored, and there is no teacher, so they get behind in school. They never get exercise except for their work cleaning and scrubbing the place and setting tables. The punishment is arbitrary. . . ."

When Sheila ran away from the shelter, they locked her in solitary confinement for two weeks, with only a thin mattress for sleeping on the concrete slab. No windows, no mirrors, visitors, mail, books or toys. Her uniform was taken away; she could only keep on her underwear.

"They wouldn't let me talk to her," Cohen said. "The assistant superintendent of the shelter told me I couldn't see her because she was on 'indefinite restriction.' The superintendent told me, 'No, she is being punished and is not allowed to have any visitors, not even therapy.'" Cohen said he tried to explain that therapy is treatment, not something that should be withdrawn for punishment any more than insulin should be taken away from a diabetic for punishment. But the final word came from the chairman of the board of trustees for the shelter [who was also chairman of the board of the Society for the Prevention of Cruelty to Children]: "No one is to see Sheila. She has to be punished. These kids are in the shelter for punishment and they are going to get it." Finally, by calling a judge and getting a court order, Cohen was able to visit Sheila. He was later reprimanded by his boss for not using proper channels of authority—and told he had overstepped his authority by calling a judge. He was placed on probation and eventually resigned from his job.

The situation described above is not unusual. The bitterness and scars on Sheila are incalculable. But like many others, she carries them with uncanny sensitivity and acceptance.

Sometimes the acceptance is frightening. Women who have been in trouble with the law for the major portions of their lives rattle off stories of physical violence and violence to the psyche that make the most hardened person shudder.

Yet it is clear to see that for many of the women in prison, going to prison was just a traumatic transition from one society that was confining and oppressive to another. The one on the outside often meant not knowing when you could get enough money together to get your baby a new pair of shoes; to figuring out how to get groceries or carfare or how to get away from the pimp you were working for when you didn't even have enough money of your own to go downtown.

For many people, the planet earth includes the liquor store, pimping, prostitution, welfare, stealing, buying any clothes you wear "hot," hiding the television when the welfare detectives come to look around for signs of a man, a television or a telephone. It's having the toilet get clogged up and not being able to flush it or get it fixed. It's having the hot water go off and not replacing the light in the bedroom that's been burned out for three years. And never being able to get the heat higher than fifty degrees in your apartment in the wintertime. Sleeping with your coat on and childhood nightmares still haunting you when you're almost thirty-four. It's never thinking of going to a dentist when you have a toothache or to the doctor when you hurt. It's trying not to believe a promise but believing it anyway and then being disappointed again.

It's knowing you're on your own. You're grown. Knowing you had to grow up fast, but you never really grew up. Because you never were a child, not really. You never had anyone love you and take care of you like it's supposed to be when you're a child. You were responsible for your own survival when you were still a baby. But now you've got children of your own.

Prisons on the outside are made of neglect and knowing no one knows. And no one cares. It's a prison of no limits. So everything's limiting. Perhaps the most horrible thing about these prisons on the outside is that you often don't realize you're imprisoned. And you don't have the motivation to change what's happening to you in any significant way, because this life is *normal*. It's the world; it's the only reality you know. It's so normal that you wouldn't begin to think about what to do to change it on a realistic level, because to you it's not unusual.

Jail and prison are a part of this reality. And although imprisonment is an intrinsic evil to middle-class people, it seems to become just another "thing"—a minor evil—to people involved in it. It often, in fact, becomes a relief after the initial fear is over.

"The first time I was in juvie, I was twelve," Pat Halloran remembers. "Mom and Pop Moriana was there. I really loved them. Like they were my parents, you know. I really dug it.

"Oh, I can remember the first night I went in, though. I was in a room by myself. And they had a window in the door. And the next morning—this is when I was twelve—they'd go walking by—the old-timers—and they'd be lookin in the window. They'd go 'Umm, nice in there. How are you, baby?' The other inmates would always do this to new girls. But see, that's how they scare you. I was so scared after being searched and everything. You don't know what the fuck's going on, but these are older people telling you what to do, so you just get right in there and take off your clothes and whatever. So you sleep it through, and then you wake up and all's you see is these faces in the door, you know, yelling at you and telling you, 'You better watch it, bitch.' I was thinking, 'They're going to kill me. What did I do? I don't know anybody—they're going to kill me.' So when I came out of my room, I was high-stepping, hanging on the wall. How funny it is we become adjusted so fast . . . because two days later, I was looking in someone else's window, 'Hey, bitch.'

"I didn't go through no court process to get there. They just pick you up and you go to juvie, period. See, what happened was that I was supposed to go to a football game, and I was in high school. I was twelve years old in freshman year and I wouldn't be thirteen until February. So I was supposed to graduate when I was sixteen. And my parents wanted me to have all the responsibilities of being a high school kid, but they didn't want me having the privileges. This one night they said I couldn't go to this football game. I was really pissed, so I took a walk. Well, my mother over-panicked. She called the pigs and says, 'My daughter ran away, go look for her.' Of course I had ran away before. But this time I was just out taking a walk. When I goes back into the house my mother goes, 'What were you doing?' And I says, 'I was out walking around.' 'Sure you were, sure you were . . . what were you doing?' I said, 'None of your business.'

"So I went up to my room and she called the pigs and she said, 'Well, she's back, but I don't know what she's been doing. I don't know where she's been.' So they came right out and they came in and my mother comes upstairs and she says, 'Get dressed.' I said, 'What for?' She says, 'The police are here.' I said, 'What for? What happened?'

" 'They've come to arrest you. You ran away.' "

Pat got dressed and was taken in a police car to juvenile hall. She said she was scared and told the police, "I haven't done anything wrong." But like many other young women, under the law she was a runaway; she was taken to jail.

"I was so scared at first," she said. "But within a week or two, by the time it took to take me to court, I liked it there so much I didn't want to go nowhere." When she met with the probation officer she was recommended for a foster home. Her mother didn't protest, nor did her father.

"I wanted to stay at juvenile hall, I didn't want to be in a foster home," Pat said. "They put me in a foster home, and I didn't like it. I had a little problem with the foster father, most foster kids do. And even later, when I didn't, it's a good excuse. I told 'em and they put me in another foster home, and I ran away from it. I really fucked up bad. But after I ran away from the foster homes, they'd put me back in juvenile hall. I was in and out of there. I think I held the record for a long time. It was something like forty-six arrests and times in juvenile hall in six years. For runaway.

"It's good when you sit back and reminisce. 'Cause like we brought out a good point. I didn't know . . . it's funny, I was always afraid to admit that I really liked coming back. You know, when you get there you always say, 'Oh fuck, I don't want to stay here . . . let me out of here.' And all the time, you know, you're staying there. It's that security. It's that instant gratification . . . coming back and having everybody holler and say, 'Look, Pat's back,' all happy to see you."

Pat didn't stop going back into juvenile hall or into other jails until she was charged with a crime she didn't commit when she was nearly twenty-four years old. She said she was sitting in jail waiting trial on an arson charge and was talking with another inmate about seeing her at the state prison. "All of a sudden I had this flash—I realized—hey, I didn't do anything. Why should I go to prison? I must be crazy—just accepting going like this. It really blew my mind. I was sitting there and I knew for once that I *wasn't* guilty—but I was talking about going to prison and just accepting it. Like, well, that's the next step."

Pat managed to get out, raise money for a lawyer and beat the charge. Now she is living in San Francisco, working with an organization called Connections, which serves as a link to people inside prison, assisting in their problems and working with their families.

If it hadn't been for her "flash" of questioning *why* she should be in prison for something she didn't do, Pat might still be in prison. The "normalcy" of going to prison and the security of the concrete womb after a lifetime of oppressive circumstances lulls many people into never asking *why?* The idea of changing *the life* is as alien as going to Mars in a steamed-up spaceship. "Treatment" or "rehabilitation" are just words; a matter of lip service. Jail has just become a bigger part of the world—an extension of *the life* and the "family"; a reinforcement of *natural* self-destruction learned during formative childhood years from models who never asked *why?* either. Abuse for many people is a way of life. It's the world.

Willie

Willie King got busted on an 11721,
being under the influence of   narcotics.
The judge told her 180 days,
but when she got to jail,
the papers said nine months.

(Another nine month scar
in Willie's mangled 39 years on earth.)

"I couldn't even count all the times
I been here."

Willie's been going to jail since she was 17
and busted for prostitution.
Next she got three years for forgery,
then petty theft with a prior conviction—
which means prison time.
Next time, for parole violation . . .
"In '52 I got me a public defender
to send me to the penitentiary.
P.D., yeah, prison deliverer."

"All this time . . . Now I could see it for robbery
or killing, but not for misdemeanors.
I'm always incarcerated."

Willie's a trustee in the jailhouse laundry.
"Whatever officer is on tells you what you
have to do. Today the officer she asked me
to help on the mangle and folding gowns.

"I don't do no officer's blouses.
If I did they wouldn't wear them."

Between trips to jail, Willie lives near
her mother in Los Angeles.

"*The police out in the street dislike me.*
They try to proposition me and I go off on them.
I just get out and they start coming around.
They tell me when I get out, they'll send me back.
They keep harassing me.
They know me real well.
My mother lives in the district
and I like to be close to her. But at this rate,
I might as well move away.
I'm always incarcerated.

"*You know, I'm not going to let them rehabilitate*
me. I'm the only one who can rehabilitate me.

"*If the police wouldn't harass me,*
I'd straighten up. I'd get off dope
and try to get my children back and not commit
no crimes.

"*But as long as they try to keep me away from it*
and demand I don't do it
I'm gonna do it!"

Mary

My legal name is Mary Lynne Wilkins* aka Mary Johnson, I was born and raised in Detroit Michigan, May 20, 1931. The origin of my crime career started in 1949, when I started using dope. I was doing ninty days for prostitution, at the termination of the ninty-day sentence the Federal agents put a "Hold" on me for three counts, Mail theft; Breaking and Entering; and Forgery. I was sentenced by Judge Thormton for three counts, the sentence was 18 months, 18 months, 1 year [respectively] running concurrently into 18 months, at Alderson West Virginia. I was denied parole, and maxed out in April, 1951.

In 1952, I had a son, he lives with my mother. In 1953, I was arrested and sentenced by the Federal agents for Interstate Commerce, transporting stolen money orders, across the state line. I received 2 years in Alderson, or two counts running concurrently into 2 Years. I was denied parole and maxed out in June 1955.

In 1956, I was arrested by the Feds. and pleaded guilty to Interstate Commerce and sentenced to 5 years in Lexington, Kentucky. In April 1960, I was released from Lexington, and around October violated my CR and was sent to Alderson, to max it out. I was released in November 1961.

In 1963, I was arrested for Grand Larceny and pleaded guilty to a lesser charge, attempted Grand Larceny, which is a 2-year maximum. I received a one-to-two-year sentence. I was granted a parole in 9 months and the Michigan Parole Board made it clear to me that the only reason they was granting me a parole, was that in all my convictions, I had never had a parole. In 1964, I received my discharge from parole.

In 1965, December 26, I was arrested in Ohio for Grand Larceny, and Narcotic Implements. I pleaded guilty to Arrangments on Information, and received 1–5 and 1–7 running concurrently into 1–7. The State appointed me an Attorney, by the name of Samuel Jones III, (if memory serves me correctly). On January 1966, I was admitted to Ohio Reformatory for Women. While in Isolation, I got some matches [contraband in isolation], was caught with them and spent 8 days in punishment.

* This account was written by Mary Wilkins (not her real name) and is reproduced with her permission exactly as she wrote it. She asked that her name be changed for her family's sake.

After being released from Isolation, I was in School, Gospelettes [a gospel group that practices unsupervised], Choir, Drug Therapy, and had honor status. *But when I met the parole board in December, eleven months after entry, they gave me two additional years!* This place and its petty rules just made me sick, you cannot touch another inmate, can't comb each other's hair, the personnel talks hostile to you, you can't get medical attention over the weekends, because there is no nurse. If a relative expires, and you're from another state, you cannot attend the funeral services.

A couple of weeks later I tried to run away, in fact I did get as far as town. I was returned and placed in a cell with a steel bunk, three dirty blankets, and not fed for 24 hours. I went to Displinary Court January, 21, 1967, and was told that when I met the Parole Board in 1968, I would automatically be given two additional years for running away. This would have meant I had four more years to do.

Immediately, I started planning to run away. Successfully I went on a diet, and on July 1967 I squeezed through the window and made a successful escape. I went to Los Angeles, California where I got a job at the Sunset Uniform Company. I worked under "Mary Ann Richmond" (I think). I left California and went to Detroit, Michigan and got a job under another alias. In 1968, I went to New York City, and worked under Betty Sue Prophet, at the Bevolry Dress Company; I am an experienced power machine operator, working for $1.65 per hour. This did not even pay my expenses, so I started cashing checks. I was caught at the Hanover Bank and Trust Company and while in the House of Detention in New York City, then Ohio dropped a fugitive warrent on me. I did not fight extradition and was brought back and placed in a cell, for thirty days of punishment with another group of runaways (4 others), 3 in Maximum Security and another in Upper Isolation.

Finally all 5 of us were released in November, we was put in an Isolated area, called P.Q. [punishment quarters]. On November 28, 1968 a balmy Thanksgiving evening, we five got together and tied up the guard and matron, taking the keys off the matron, and escaped. Four of us were captured 3½ hours later, the 5th was captured about 12 hours later. We was held incommunicado for 28 days in Maximum Security, and for two months or more we went without a shower (once a week they would bring a face basin with warm water in it and set it outside the cells we were in). The cells are approximately 6 by 8 feet, with iron bars. We would have to sit down on the floor and stick our arms through the bars to touch the basin, in order to wash up. No one had told us (5) what was going to happen to us or anything.

I had a meeting with the Parole Board in December, 1968, they came

ck to Max to speak to me, 5 days later the Superintendent told me the
ole Board would see me in 5 years, December 1973. Meanwhile back to
x. The 5 of us started banging and shouting we was tired of staying back
re, not knowing when we was going to court. Miss Wheeler came back
Max and told us we was going to court January 9, 1969 (this was Decem-
1968). On Monday, January 9, 1969, the snow was very deep and driv-
was hazardous, so we didn't go, in fact noone told us we was not
ng, other than one of the matrons insinuated that the snow was so bad
t the Grand Jury probably couldn't get into Union County. In February
started making noise again, asking for a shower, three meals a day, and
arettes. We got a shower once a week, and to smoke once a week too.
e also got three meals a day.

Febuary, about the second week we all went on a hungry strike, we re-
ed to eat because we said we wanted to know when we were going to
to court. We fasted about seven days, and on or about the 17th of
uary, Miss Wheeler came and addressed us saying, "You wanted to
w when you were going to come out, well you are getting out today,
u're going to Lima."

Febuary 17, 1969 two Penal Transportation guards came into Max with
g chains. They put the chain around my waist, the chain was so long
t it hung between my legs when I walked. Then they put hand-cuffs on my
ists, escorted me to a truck and drove us 4 to Lima State Hospital.
ss Wheeler had already sent one of us, named Wilma, to Lima, in Decem-
1968.

Discription of Lima: An isolated dirt road, leads to a paved road where
re is a high tower about 100 ft. tall. A guard with what looks like a
chine gun, but the nurse said that it was only a high powered rifle.
ese women that work at Lima claim the title of nurse, although some are
even nurse-aids).

The high towers also consist of hugh flood lights. There is, about a ten
ot fence, that is also bob-wired. This fence is also alleged to be
arged. We were unshackled and lead to a dining room where you eat
h only a spoon, and you are not allowed seconds on any food. You
y receive two slices of bread. The food is placed on a sectional tray
de of steel.

After dinner we were assigned to wards. Two went to ward 22, and
self, and Norma, went to ward 23. Boy were we lucky to get ward 23,
t's supposed to be the honor ward.

They fingerprint me and photograph me, now I'm sitting in a chair waiting

to see the Doctor. The Dr. breezes through, and one of the officials t
him he has to see us. He says he haven't got time, he'll see us later.

When he sent for me, he asked me how many times I had been arreste
I told him about 25 times. [He] blew, in a whistle, then he asked w
the date and the year. I explained that I have not seen a calendar an abc
three months, but I think it's Feb. 17, 1969. [He] then asked me why
was sent to Lima. I told him I did not know, that it must have been f
displinary reasons, because I sure wasn't crazy for wanting to get out
Marysville. He said, 'Well!' thats all. I then asked him how long would I ha
to be there? He said he did not know, that I was sent there for an indefin
period. I asked him how long was that, and he said *that depended on m
I could stay there five years, ten years, or maybe life.* This is verbatim an
get nervous every time I think about it. Can you imagine how I felt, knowi
what I do about law, I know the first thing it takes some MONEY. I'm fr
an indigent family, I do not have any money saved, and I'm from out
State. I'm not asking for sympathy, I'm just telling it like it is.

Mrs. . . .: From the moment she saw me she seemed to take an attitu
towards me. (Hostile) She was the Head Nurse, passing medication c
really her status was a citizen. However, I swallowed a many lump t
cause, I knew that she wanted to put me on medication. I would f
worms, bugs, and paper in the food, and never say anything, at least not
the officer.

If the nurse gets angry at you, she'll say, "You better be quiet, or I'll p
you on medicine. And she had this authority, because if she told the
that a patient needed medication, the Dr. did not question the nur
And once you're on medication the patient must be off medication
to 6 months before he can meet Staff, which is like a parole. Sometin
the nurse would give the patients a stronger dosage so the patient wo
be dormant, and sleepy and not ask the nurse for different things, like to
paper etc. All the nurse had to tell a patient was, you're too worrysome, c
the patient knew what that meant. That if he or she kept doing what th
were the nurse would either put them on medication, or have their dosc
increased. Some of the nurses had a bad habit of kicking the patie
Mrs. [   ] was one. She wouldn't kick them hard, but its the idea, of putt
your feet on another human being.

At shower time approximately 2:30 they have a room where its someth
like a supply room, about 8 feet by 10 feet. As many as can goes into
room and undress, for your shower. Then you walk across the hall NU
and there is another room about the same size. The only difference is it
three small shower fawcets. With very little water dripping from them. Th

are as many women as can squeeze in this area. About 15 women crowd into this space, because the nurse wants them to hurry up and get through with their showers so that the nurse can sit back down. The nurse *all* of them do the same thing. They sit on a stool in the hall in front of the shower room and yells, to different patients that are staying under the water too long, "Alright Sally, Mary, etc. get away from that shower so someone else can use some water." "Move over so Mary, can get wet." When you get soaped up, you are then allowed to get under the shower and rinse off. The nurse sitting on the stool holds a can of Right Guard, and you hold your arms up and she sprays them for you. Then the nurse puts some lotion in your hand, to lotion with.

There was an old Chezslovia woman named Frances with catteracts on her eyes who almost never said anything to anybody. She just sat, and stare. Now when Lima calls SHOWERS that means everybody. So one day this poor old lady didn't feel like taking a shower, because she had just told me how bad she was feeling. But the nurse insisted. And poor old Frances was trying to get to the Head Nurse, and ask permission to not take a shower. On her way to the office, she fell, and some 9 hrs. later the lady was Dead. Now I agree that some patients needed to be reminded to take showers. But they never even stop to ask "WHY."

Another patient named Carrie Hayes, complained that she was sick and bleeding. Nobody paid her any attention, they just said that she was lazy. She was 56. They transfered her to the punishment ward, where they have no compassion at all for human lives. They put Carrie Hayes in a punishment cell, with a pissy smelly mattress on the floor and one blanket to serve as anything you want to share it for. Something like a sheet, a pillow, or just to cover yourself. They even take your shoes, and you have no toilet, no water, and Nothing else, unless they have changed it since I have been there. Carrie stayed down there and caught something and DIED, TOO. The day before we left, about the middle of March, [another woman] hung herself, because she was threatened to lose her cigarette smoking privilege for 6 months, and she just couldn't take it.

I feel these deaths might have been prevented, if someone had done something. That is why Lima was such a mental strain on me. I never was on medication the whole time I was at Lima. Lima really did something to me. I can never forget.

March, 1970, we five were released from Lima State Hospital, and turned over to the custody of Union county sherriff, Ameron. The shirrif drove us to Union County Jail, where he served us with one indictment: Assault on a prison guard. We five women said we would fight the assault charge because we did not assault Mr. Redder, the guard, we only tied him up along with the matron, Mrs. Mary Mitchell. My court appointed attorney, Mrs Jeanne Dailey told me if we fought the assault, the proscutor would serve us with another indictment, "Escape." I asked Mrs Dailey to show me the other indictment. She went to the court building and returned with the indictment. The proposition was that we plead guilty to assault, and the escape charge would be Nole Prosque. Although I have a carbon copy of the escape being Nole, the Parole Board Members have no knowledge of such a decision whereas the charge was nole.

April 1970 we five were sentenced to six months in the Dayton Workhouse, sentenced to run consecutively with our prior sentence.

P.S. (I met the parole Board in December, 1968, and was deferred for five years, only for escapes (3) Double Jeopardy.)

May, 1970. The Sheriff, Mr. Ameron told us he was transfering us back to O.R.W. but that only four of us were going back to O.R.W. The fifth Wilma, was to be returned back to Lima State Hospital, because she had not been "cleared" through staff. About 5 weeks later she was transfered to Ohio Reformatory for Women.

Now that I'm back here again, I have tried to comply with these petty rules, for instance now, if an inmate is disagreeing with the matron, the matron might tell the inmate, "To shut up," or the matron will just cut the inmate off and say, "You have three nights early bed." This place now ha approximately 12 guards here, and two guard houses. The guards now harass the women, especially if the woman is not too popular at the "Front" where Miss Wheeler presides.

If you're at the clinic, and are caught asking a sick inmate, is she feeling better, even though you are whispering, you get 3 nights early bed, plus your hospital privileges are taken. The matrons have found pills on some inmates, so now to prevent the inmate from swinging with her medication the medicine is crushed and put into a cup. Now, common sense tells any one, that if an inmate wants to swing with her medication, she will. And the nurse makes you stick out your tongue. But let me add, where there's a will you'll find the way.

The "only" reason I'm complaining about the crushed pills, and opened capsules is that the different medicines irritate your tongue, makes the insid of your mouth sore.

If a matron has a personal grievance with an inmate, she is in a position to send the inmate to punishment, any time she chooses, all the matron ha to say is the inmate was insubordinate. After you have been in Max you go to displinary Court, to tell your side of the story. You can't talk to anothe inmate twice or you are branded as a homosexual. They think everyone is homosexual.

However, I managed "not" to get a punishment slip from December, 1968 to August, 1971.

May, 1971. The Grapevine said that the Governor was no longer assessing time, it would be a "continuance" since all assess time was either for hitting a personnel or running away.

There were 17 of us runaways, and matron hitters. So in June 1971 Mr. Worley, the Review Parole Man, called me and told me since I had not been in any trouble since 1968, I was eligible to meet the Review Board in one half of my five years assessed time.

My name was added to meet the Regular Parole Board in August. They acknowledged my very good work, I reminded them I am a power machine operator with 23 years experience. I am going out of state, I was discharged on the last parole I had. My old parole excepted me. I have a home placement, and a job waiting, as a housekeeper, and I intended to go to I.B.M. key-punch school at night.

But, you know, when the answer came back—I was continued for another year. I meet them in June, 1972. How much longer will the Ohio State Parole Board punish me? Why would they even put my name on the board if they were not going to let me go home?

Chapter 3 "AIN'T I A WOMAN TOO?"

The existing criminal code makes it a crime to commit adultery and fornication. It's been the law since Colonial times. We know a lot of people commit adultery and fornication, but we don't condone it. It's the function of the state to protect the family unit.

But in this bill [proposed new state criminal code], they've deleted adultery and fornication, and I want to put them back. I can't visualize anyone in his right mind that would oppose this amendment.

. . . The whole purpose of the Legislature is to set up standards which everyone is to follow in the morals field. We should make it clear it's wrong to commit adultery, and it's wrong to commit fornication, too."

—*Representative* MARTIN P. MULLEN, *Democrat from Philadelphia, during debate over exclusion of adultery and fornication from criminal penalties in Pennsylvania. The House voted eleven to seventy-three to reject Mullen's amendment to impose criminal penalties for premarital and extramarital sex.**

What *kind* of women commit crimes? What kind of crimes? What are women "criminals" *really* like?

Although these questions have been asked often, no one knows for certain whether women are involved in a lot of crime, a little crime or even what kind of crime. The overwhelming majority of all crimes go undetected, and we can only assume that women are included in the vast majority of lawbreakers who live lives uninterrupted by criminal detection.

The only women in crime we know anything about are the women who are arrested, tried, convicted and sentenced to probation or prison. And we know very little about them. In fact, there is a dearth of information on them. Even in the President's Commission on Law Enforcement and the Administration of Justice's ten-volume report on crime and corrections published in 1967, not one chapter or paragraph is devoted to women.

From varied and limited state and private sources, however, a few

* "Mullen Loses Bid to Put Adultery in Crime Code," by Forrest L. Black, Philadelphia *Evening Bulletin*, Nov. 11, 1972.

basic facts appear to shape the picture of women in the criminal justice system:

—There are more than 7,730 women in local and county jails throughout the country on a given day, and more than 15,000 in state and federal prisons.

—Approximately seven men are arrested to every one woman on a national level.

—The ratio of men to women widens to eighteen to one in county jails and thirty to one in state and federal prisons.

—Women are arrested and convicted for the same crimes as men, for everything from vagrancy to homicide and rape. The concentration of types of crimes for which women are arrested and prosecuted in significant numbers, however, is theft, prostitution, violation of narcotics laws, drunkenness and disorderly conduct.[1] The chief area of criminal law grossly discriminatory to women is prostitution.

Although most other written laws express formal equality between the sexes accused of crimes, in practice men are arrested, tried and convicted indiscriminately more on all charges—and disproportionately more for sodomy, public exposure, statutory rape and nonsupport. It is apparent that discrimination by sex occurs at each stage of the criminal justice procedure, and that men are grossly overrepresented as a group.

In Philadelphia, for instance, a study of the cases of 1,034 persons indicted in 1971 for one of four major crimes of violence (rape, aggravated robbery, murder and aggravated assault and battery) showed that men are more likely to be sentenced to jail than women and for a longer term. Men pleading guilty or convicted of a serious crime are sentenced to jail in 64 per cent of the cases, while women pleading guilty or convicted are sentenced in 21 per cent for the cases. Men receive jail sentences of seven months or more in 68 per cent of the cases as compared to 12 per cent for women.[2]

Ironically, minor offenses which could be considered social rather than criminal problems are the areas of behavior for which women are sentenced to jail more often than for crimes of violence. It would appear that more than 50 per cent of the women in county jails are charged with disorderly conduct, vagrancy, drunkenness and drug

1. U. S. Federal Bureau of Investigation. *Uniform Crime Reports.* Washington, D.C., U. S. Government Printing Office. Annual.

2. Donald L. Bartlett and James B. Steele. "Crime and Injustice." The Philadelphia *Inquirer.* February 18, 1973.

addiction. In major urban centers statistics show that more than 80 per cent of the women confined are there for drugs or drug-related crimes, usually minor property offenses. Only a small percentage of women in prison are there for violent crimes. The same is true of men.

In Pennsylvania between 1967 and 1968, 2,300 women were confined for various terms in 41 county jails. Their most frequent offense was disorderly conduct. The second most frequent offense was prostitution. The average age of the woman offender was 29.[3]

In this survey, the most valuable to date in the United States, the Pennsylvania Division of the American Association of University Women found that 80 per cent of the women arrested were unemployed, also that 80 per cent of women on whom records were available had dependent children. Their studies indicated that judges saw only 35 to 50 per cent of the women sentenced; the rest were adjudicated by justices of the peace who have great discretionary power, few guidelines and little training in law.[4]

A lot of people were shocked when the Uniform Crime statistics in June 1971 reported a "drastic rise" in the female crime rate. Front-page headlines broadcast the news that women were committing more violent crimes. Federal Bureau of Investigation figures showed that from 1960 to 1969, male arrest for major crimes rose 61.3 per cent and, for females, 156.2 per cent.[5] The increase is startling, but it seems upon closer examination those figures can be questioned with good reason. Are women committing more violent crimes or just being arrested more often? How are both the male and female percentages affected by the different crime reporting processes, which varied from city to city during those years? Haven't the Uniform Crime reports made a vast difference in the frequency of reported crimes and in the way statistics have been manipulated and tabulated? And what about the population increase in the age group of people traditionally arrested for major crimes?

Certainly, some women do perpetrate horrible and harmful actions against others, but it is not at all conclusive that women are committing more violent crimes than they used to. In fact, it is not even certain that there has been an actual increase in crime—and if

3. Velimesis, Margery L. "Criminal Justice for the Female Offender." *Journal of the American Association of University Women.* October 1969.

4. Ibid.

5. U. S. Federal Bureau of Investigation. *Uniform Crime Reports.* Washington, D.C., U. S. Government Printing Office. Annual.

there has, whether it is at all significant, proportionate to the increase in population or in the variation of crime statistics historically. Despite the headlines, despite the data, no one really knows for sure. It is still a matter of speculation.

As I interviewed prison administrators, I asked them why fewer women than men are arrested and sentenced to prison and whether they believed women were becoming more violent and committing more crimes. Their answers, for the most part, were as divergent as their biases:

—"There's a general breakdown of inhibitions among women. They are committing more crimes because they aren't tied to the home like they used to be. They want to do everything a man does, even crime."

—"Women aren't committing more crimes, they're just being arrested more. Women have always gotten away with murder before now."

—"Women are getting younger. When I first came here, in April 1949, the average age of the inmates was between thirty-one and thirty-four . . . and it's been slipping down since then. One factor is the increasing mobility of youth. They're coming out from the home at a much earlier age."

—"Women are becoming more violent, but so is the whole society. It's observable in all parts of society—not just in the criminal element."

—"They talk about women's liberation—Ha! Women already have it. In our society, men are the ones who decide on who goes to prison. The legal profession really decides—between the prosecuting attorney, the defense attorney and the judge. It's a matter of copping a plea and all goes on. The result of the attitude that women are the weaker sex winds up with giving them every opportunity to adjust short of having to confine them."

—"It's true the women we get today are much more hostile, aggressive and more dangerous than they used to be. It always amazes me that people think incarcerated women are like Sunday School teachers. They're not! Every woman here is capable of aggressive, assaultive behavior. Any time a tour goes through, we have to think who's on the floor—and what danger they represent."

Many people stated flatly that there is no increase in women's crimes. Many stated there was. One of the most uninformed and humorous bits of speculation was given by the Attorney General of Ohio, William J. Brown, known to his colleagues as Billy Joe. I asked the young Attorney General (elected to office at the age of thirty-one) about his perspective on women's involvement with crime. He said that in his opinion "very few women commit crimes.

"Some of the biggest things they do is pass bad checks—not crimes against nature or persons. They commit crimes against the pocketbook. They're not violent. Girls just aren't brought up to fistfight and shoot guns. That's just a woman's psychological and physiological makeup.

"I did a lot of defense work before I came in office. And I never represented a woman. I was going to represent one for a bad check but the case was dismissed or never came up or something, so I never met her. So it doesn't seem that women are very involved in crime.

"It's the way people are brought up. Women have a different makeup than men. They don't have as many opportunities. Women can't be cat burglars, for instance. ["Cat burglars" climb up sides of buildings or scale walls to rob safes or break into second- and third-story apartments and offices.] There might be a couple that are that agile, but the average girl can't do it. *The usual American woman doesn't want to get dirty* [my emphasis].

"Most women don't have criminal type minds. When you talk to a girl, she doesn't think about making a quick buck. There might be a few, but not frequently."

I had to laugh at the Attorney General's stereotypes when I remembered women I met convicted of armed robbery, "fraud of a garage keeper," kidnaping, hijacking and cat burglaries. Also when I thought of one woman I talked to the day before, who had said, "I loves to steal. I *loves* to steal." What *isn't* so hilarious is that women who get arrested are subjected to hostile or lenient treatment based on such varying and fragile myths, which often have little or no relationship to their lives.

Many of the headlines reporting the Uniform Crime statistics in June 1971 concluded the "increase of violent crime" among women was linked directly to the growing emancipation of women. The New

York *Times* quoted Sheriff Peter Pitchess of Los Angeles to that effect: "As women emerge from their traditional roles as housewife and mother, entering the political and business fields previously dominated by. males, there is no reason to believe that women will also not approach equality with men in the criminal field."[6] Law enforcement personnel, sociologists, criminologists and other students of crime at the time attributed the "rise of crime among women" to three broad causes: the changing attitudes of society, the women themselves and the police.

Certainly many attitudes are changing about women in general, and specifically as examined here, about women in crime. One strong indication of this is the fact that in 1968, the FBI for the first time listed a woman on its "Ten Most Wanted Fugitives" list. This list, which originated in 1950, to date has included six women considered by the FBI to be among the "most dangerous and vicious criminals" in the country.

It is significant to note that four of the six women listed were *accused* of being involved with political crimes. The six "fugitives" were: Marie Dean Arrington, for interstate flight, murder and manslaughter; Ruth Eisemann Schier, for kidnapping, extortion and interstate transportation in aid of racketeering; Angela Davis, for murder, kidnapping and interstate flight; Bernadine Dohrn, for interstate flight, mob action, riot and conspiracy; and Susan Saxe and Katherine Ann Power, for interstate flight, murder, theft of government property and bank robbery.

When a reporter from *Off Our Backs*, a women's news journal published in Washington, D.C., queried an FBI Special Agent as to the criteria used for the list, however, he said it was a "difficult question"—a lot like his asking her "what made her decide to wear a green dress or a pink dress in the morning."

Until Otto Pollack's study on *The Criminality of Women* (University of Pennsylvania Press, 1950), there had been no thorough examination of the concept that women could be involved in criminal activity on any large scale. Pollack emphasized the "masked character" of female crime—showing that shoplifting, prostitution, thefts, abortion, perjury and disturbance were infrequently reported

---

6. In contrast to this theory, Italian writer Gino Faustini reports that the gradual emancipation of women in Italy has resulted in a steady *decline* of female crime—particularly the more serious offenses. (From "La delinquenza fra le adolescenti in Italia," *Esperienze di Rieducazione*, 1969.)

crimes. He also concluded that homosexual contact and exhibition-
ism in women were rarely reported, and that the roles of women as
mothers inclined them to use different methods in homicide. His
theory was that women's "devious methods" were misleading to law
enforcement personnel. He noted that, "At least in our culture,
women are particularly protected against the detection of criminal
behavior on the one hand and exposed to a wealth of irritations,
temptations and opportunities which may lead them to criminal behavior on the other." Pollack was basically saying women can get away
with murder.

In an unpublished paper for the President's Commission on Law
Enforcement and the Administration of Justice in 1967, Walter C.
Reckless and Barbara Ann Kay also groped for the reason behind
differential selection of women for prosecution and imprisonment
and came up with the "chivalry factor":

"A large part of the infrequent officially acted upon involvement
of women in crime can be traced to the masking effect of women's
roles, effective practice on the part of women of deceit and indirec-
tion, their instigation of men to commit their crimes (the Lady Mac-
beth factor), the willingness of men to 'cover up' for them and the
unwillingness of the public and the law enforcement personnel to
hold women accountable for their deeds (the chivalry factor)."

My conclusion about women and crimes—which is not based on
empirical evidence—is a simple one. I think it is obvious that many
women are involved in behavior which is technically illegal, whether
it's victimless behavior that violates the social norm or harm to
people or property. And just as the majority of men who break laws
aren't arrested, the majority of women aren't either. I think the dif-
ferentiation of treatment for women being arrested, tried, convicted
and sentenced, though, is simple. For one, I think that men are discriminated against with proportionately higher arrests and convictions because they are *considered* more dangerous, not because they
are more dangerous. People are more afraid of being hurt by a man
than of hurting him. This is not so true with women.

I think that people in general, including law enforcement personnel, judges and prosecutors, are more reticent about hurting
women, especially women who could be their mothers.[7] No matter

7. This could explain some of the favoritism shown white women by white
judges—discussed in Chapter 2. It could also explain their added outrage at white
women being prostitutes.

how sophisticated we become, or how hardened, there is still something sacred about mothers. (Remember when the Egyptian soldiers threw down their guns and ran when they first saw Israeli women in the front lines approaching them? And how, as a result, so many were shot in the back—running away? Or how many fights start on the street when one child insults another child's mother?) Women who appear to be moral by conventional standards or who seem "proper," warm and soft can and probably do get away with behavior men serve time for.

On the other hand, women who appear to have different moral codes or who have stepped far enough out of line to be arrested are no longer protected by stereotypes. When they appear to be living disintegrated lives or violating their roles as "ladies" or mothers in a way considered socially harmful, they are often subject to a great deal of additional disdain and abuse based on subjective definitions and moral judgments. Stereotypes work both ways.

In Washington, D.C., for instance, the D.C. Citizens Council for Criminal Justice found that bail agency personnel and officials believe women "pose a higher risk of flight." A far greater percentage of women than men, they said, are required to post money bonds, and many women are unable to meet those money requirements. The standards of the Bail Reform Act appear to allow an unsuspected bias toward women offenders. The act empowers a judge to substitute less tangible ties to the community—employment, family associations and residence patterns—for money as indicators of the suspect's reliability in showing up for court. The D.C. Citizens Council said that because so many women offenders are jobless and don't usually live in one residence for a long period of time, they are considered poorer risks for conditional release.[8]

In addition, women sentenced under discriminatory statutes in some states are given longer sentences than men (see Chapter 7). Women who are caught and sentenced are often scorned as "tramps" or "cheap women"—basically as "anti-mothers." Women report incidents where they have been the objects of hostility and ambivalence because their open defiance of the law offends the revered or idealized notions of motherhood. This applies to women who sell their bodies for a living as often as it does to political activists or bank robbers. Men and women of the dominant culture have often reacted

8. *The Treatment of Women Offenders in the District of Columbia*, a report of the D.C. Citizens Council for Criminal Justice, March 1972.

vindictively to women who step "out of place" and threaten the status seemingly integral to their purpose on earth.

But legislation of morality is not unique to the Judeo-Christian ethic of twentieth-century America.

Throughout history women have gone to trial and heard lectures on their demeanor, the violation of their roles and what they have done that is unbefitting their sex and their station in the church. In 1429 Joan of Arc stood before the court to hear twelve indictments of heresy against the supreme authority of the church and state read against her. In her day, Joan was considered immoral and seditious: She would not give up the clothes that fit her purpose as a soldier. She was vilified for maintaining her virginity—an obvious blasphemy in not following the edict to bear fruit and multiply. Anne Hutchinson was banished to the wilderness from Newtown, Massachusetts Bay Colony, for holding meetings in her home and speaking against the church in 1637. The infamous witch trials of Salem Township in Massachusetts in the 1600s resulted in the hangings, drownings or banishment of dozens of women for "consorting with the devil" and being "possessed." Guilt was confirmed if they actually drowned or died at the end of a hangman's noose. If they had been "one with God," they supposedly would not have died. People justified their fears in those days by retaliation through "divine command."

In recent years, however, the government has in many ways replaced religion as the ultimate source of authority over human behavior. And most of us trust the state's authority to punish violation of its laws as if divine command were still the rule of the law. A crime is considered an act that is "socially harmful" or that "is believed to be socially harmful by a group that has the power to enforce its beliefs and that places such act under the ban of positive penalties."[9] The definition of crime thus depends on the interpretation of the group which has sufficient power to make its beliefs an effective and functioning part of the social order. Thus the thin line between what is considered sexually normal or harmful sexual misconduct or deviance is so vague that it blurs our conceptions of what is "crime" and the severity of punishment in relation to the concerns of the time.

Since each state jurisdiction in the United States has its own penal code, what is criminal in one state may not be outlawed in another.

9. John L. Gillan, *Criminology and Penology*, New York, London: Appleton-Century Co., Inc., 1945.

n Oregon, for example, fornication can be punished with up to five ears' imprisonment; but in New York, California and twelve other tates, it is not a crime. In Colorado, Georgia and Nevada, sodomy an bring life imprisonment, while in New Hampshire and Vermont t is not a crime. Similarly inconsistent is the division of offenses into nisdemeanors and felonies. What is a misdemeanor or a petty offense in one state may be a felony, or presumably a serious crime, in nother.[10] In Ohio and several other states, for instance, a second onviction on prostitution becomes a felony offense for which women are sent to the state prison for one or more years.

Certainly as we experience variations in the power structure and moral climate over time and place, we see differences in what is considered "criminal." The national experiment in the prohibition of lcohol dramatized this lesson of change, as does the recently revised iew of abortion as illegal. It has been estimated that as many as one hird of the acts today declared criminal were not defined as crimes at he turn of the century.[11]

Yet in reading literature about women in conflict with the law during their time—whether they were abolitionists, suffragettes, prostitutes or pro-union women speaking in public places—there seems to be a firm dogma, still retained, that condemns them as "wild," "loose," "immoral" or "fallen." The general public has consistently eemed upset and more distracted by a "general breakdown of inhibitions" than the issues involved. In 1840 the *Public Ledger* in Philadelphia published an editorial about wives of poor workingmen in he Kensington section of the city who had stopped a railroad rom being built through the heart of their community. From newspaper accounts of the confrontations, the women apparently towed way wagonfuls of rails and tore up foundations where the rails were o be laid. The *Ledger* entitled its editorial "The Mob." They wrote:

> A singular and most disgraceful feature of the disturbances was the active participation of women. The most efficacious leaders of the rioters were females. Unsexing themselves for the occasion, these Amazons led on their forces, and both by precept and example incited them to mischief. They prompted the destruction of property, they assailed with blows the officers who attempted to restrain them, they gave life and impulse and energy to the whole proceedings.

10. Marvin E. Wolfgang and Bernard Cohen. *Crime and Race: Conceptions and Misconceptions.* New York: Institute of Human Relations Press, 1970.
11. Ibid.

It is a sign of evil times when they [women] thus forget what i
due to their sex and station, and rush into the turmoil and conflict of
lawless strife. It is a sign of evil times, also, when their husbands and
fathers tolerate such misconduct.

Another editorial on the same event warned:

Once cut loose from the gentle restraints of sex, and taught by
experience that when united they are not only formidable but ir
resistible, what shall hinder them hereafter from renewing and re
peating upon every provocation, real or imagined, the turbulence
which, once tasted, to ferocious natures never loses its relish.

Women in prison today feel they still bear the brunt of stereotypi
cal 1840 standards for "immoral" women. As only a minute number
of female lawbreakers they are considered the "sample" population
for most projections about "criminal women." They say they are be
ing punished for breaking not only social laws, but also unwritten
moral laws. Oversimplified conceptions still portray women in prison
as "Amazons," "weak, ignorant and immoral women," women in
violation of innate codes of motherhood. Movies with exotic titles
such as *Women in Chains* and *Women Behind Bars* portray in
carcerated women as "bull dikes," nymphomaniacs, "toughies" and
mentally deranged human beings.

"Women in prison are less than a criminal in society's mind," said
one woman with a laugh. "They think of us as summertime whores
who don't have phone numbers."

"Most people have exaggerated ideas about people in prison," said
another. "Most of us are judged as a whole—not as individuals. We're
as different from each other as anyone anywhere is. I know I had ex
aggerated fears myself before coming here—but I've met a lot of really
beautiful sisters. Of course we do have some people here for Grand
Stupidity, but that's the way things go. People just forget that every
body in here is somebody's daughter, or somebody's wife, or some
body's sister. We're not no more bad or dangerous than anybody
else. We just carry the stigma, that's all."

Martha Wheeler, superintendent of Ohio Reformatory for
Women, plays down the concept that women in prison are even really
criminal. "There are a relatively small percentage here who are in
volved in criminal behavior. Most of the women who are involved in
criminal behavior we never see. Every now and then we get some

people who have been involved with shoplifting or narcotics rings on a big scale, but it's rare.

"The other women, the women who end up here, are acting out of their inadequacies as individuals—not with criminal rings or real criminal intentions. They have two or three kids and nobody to help them, so they write checks. Most of our homicides come out of long-standing volatile situations—a person who had meaning to the woman and the situation blew up. It's a personal interaction kind of thing—very often a drunk and abusive man, a husband, boyfriend, next door neighbor who's been picking on the kids . . .

"A woman who gets into trouble with a supportive family who has money will get sent to a shrink or to live with Aunt Suzi and the court approves. She can be diverted from incarceration. *Incarceration is for women without resources—financial and human.* If she has economic support, she doesn't end up in an institution. This is not always true, but it's true for the majority. In this state, some nine thousand women are arrested in a year, but only three hundred are incarcerated here. There are all kinds of diversionary things going on for women.

"For the most part, courts are good at sorting out crimes where a woman is actually stealing bread for her children. But I have seen a lot of cases where it's directly the reason for the crime . . ."

Dr. Seymour L. Halleck, professor of psychiatry at the University of Wisconsin and chief psychiatric consultant for the Wisconsin Division of Corrections, argues that what the public normally calls criminal behavior is more likely than not an individual's desperate effort to try to alter an internal state of helplessness, a lack of autonomy, and hopelessness.

"I think all crimes are really either efforts to change oppression that is real or to change perceived oppression," he said at a psychiatric conference on crime and violence last year. "Of course in some crimes it is perfectly clear that the effort to do something about a social system such as family or community is obvious. In other crimes people are reacting to more oppression in a situation than actually exists; they are acting from their internalized sense of oppression. But certainly much of this internalized pressure is related to real external oppression they have experienced previously.

"For the most part those people—not criminals—who get sent to prison are people who have been sorely oppressed by the society, who lack skills, who are inadequate in almost every conceivable way.

They generally lack the capacity to make it as criminals. I would argue that perhaps over 90 per cent of those people you'd find in our institutions are not violent, they're not greedy, not enemies of society, they are just very, very unfortunate losers."

Halleck said that one of the things he likes to do when he goes into the prisons is periodically sit down and pull a hundred prisoners' charts at random.

"It is extremely rare to find anybody," Halleck said, "who has ever earned as much as a thousand dollars in a criminal career. And these are people who have committed many, many crimes and may have spent years and years in prison. It is extremely rare to find anybody who has any kind of decent hourly wage for his criminal activities when you gauge it against the risks entailed."

Halleck said that in his experience it's most common to run into people who do "life on the installment plan" for cashing checks for twenty, thirty, forty and fifty dollars, who commit small burglaries.

"If you look at the behavior of offenders during a criminal act it becomes even more disturbing to see how few precautions most of these people take to avoid being apprehended. You know the stories about robbing places next door to a police station and things like that. But I think one of the more startling statistics has got to do with the use of alcohol. Various studies indicate that *up to 72 per cent of felons at the time of arrest are in a state of inebriation* [my emphasis].

"Now, I would hold that if one wants to commit a crime and get away with it, he should not try to commit a crime when he's drunk. It would be as ridiculous as trying to be a successful surgeon while operating while inebriated.

"What this suggests is that what we call criminal behavior is more likely than not a desperate effort to try to alter an internal state of helplessness, lack of autonomy, and hopelessness. The criminal act is a way of trying to adapt and change that circumstance."

"I was drunk to start with—and I was even drinking during the robbery—right there in the laundry . . ." said Jeanette Spenser, who is now out of prison and off parole in New York City. "But I don't know why I wore that purple coat. I should have known. All they said was, 'She was wearing a bright purple coat.' Now, how many people wear a bright purple coat to pull off a robbery? They had me picked up in five minutes. . . .

"I guess I was screaming to get caught. I guess I was screaming for help. And that purple coat helped me scream. Lord knows, I needed help. I was drinking so bad . . . I had lost my husband. I had lost my baby. I had really hit the bottom of the barrel."

Jeanette

"My only point of reference when I'm talking about prisons is what I've heard about men's prisons plus my personal experience in one county jail and one state prison. There is no real information on women in prison."

Jeanette Spenser, a strong-looking woman with deep brown skin and a subtle twinkle in her eye, grew up in Harlem. When she was twelve she moved to the Bronx with her mother, who worked as a domestic, and her new stepfather, a factory worker. "I was a scholarly kid and even though my mother didn't make much money, she always dressed me nice. I always had a good coat to wear to school and I looked neat and clean. This made me unpopular to start with, besides being scholarly. I had to fight to defend myself. Most every fight I had was for being called a bastard. I'd seen my father, but I didn't know him. I was insecure. And I didn't like my stepfather. I didn't know how to tell my mother anything, either. It had been our own little world till he came in. I got married at nineteen to escape. The only way I saw to get out of my house was to get married. So I got married for all the wrong reasons.

"My husband loved to drink. I loved the taste—but not what it did to me. It got to be a necessity for me. The doctor told me when I was twenty-one I was a potential alcoholic. I was drinking too much and it was interfering with my life, which on the whole was pretty ordinary except for my extra problem.

"I had the home and the daughter and the husband with a decent job. But as years passed, I was less able to function as a housewife or a mother —and, eventually, I was unemployable. I lost my husband and my home and eventually my daughter was taken away. Then I had nothing. I was on the fringes with drug addicts, alcoholics and people considered sick.

Society has made a lot of people outcasts—and they have their own little bars they hang out in. I had become an outcast and I hung out in those bars. I cared about my child, but I knew I couldn't do anything about it. The people I was with didn't have the answers. It was like being in a rat race and wanting to get out but not knowing how to get out. My people had turned their backs and I couldn't blame them. I was terrible.

"Then one time in this 'Bucket of Blood' bar, I met a guy who had just come out of jail. He took a liking to me and I liked him, I guess . . . but I don't know, I was so numb at the time. Anyway, we started hanging out together. All I was interested in was, did I have enough money to get my bottle? It didn't bother me, nothing else did.

We committed a robbery of a laundry in the Bronx. I was in the back, drinking out of my bottle while he was taking the money. And I was wearing a purple coat . . . When we got the money we ran out, but somebody had called the police. Police cars came from every direction and they caught us and handcuffed us. They couldn't miss me running in that coat. . . .

"In the beginning it was like it was happening to someone else. It wasn't happening to me. I didn't feel I had done anything wrong. I'm very glad I didn't get away with it the first time. I'm glad I was caught—or I might have been dead today. I was taken into the precinct and charged with armed robbery. Then to the old House of Detention.

"An old friend of mine came to visit me in the jail. He said, 'What's happened to you? You've gone crazy since your mother died. She's not even cold and look at all the trouble you're in.' I had been deteriorating and destroying myself for fifteen years—and this was like the end of the line. I had sought help, but not in the right places. I didn't want to be a drunk. I didn't want to be the kind of person who doesn't care about someone else, but I was. I only cared about my kid . . . and I knew the best thing I could do for her was stay away from her. I don't think I knew what love meant, 'cause I didn't love me. You have to love yourself before you can love anybody else.

"I had laid aside my own sense of right and wrong a long time before to meet my own needs. I had to get rid of all the garbage and re-evaluate my old set of standards. It's hard—and that's why most people don't want to go through the changes.

"Anyway, I never did understand what happened to me legally. Emotionally, I was given a sense of degradation from the time of arrest. On the one level, women aren't supposed to do anything wrong. If a man is arrested for drunk, he's still treated like a man. But the attitude of the arresting officer was one of disgust that he had to be bothered with me. His feeling was, 'If you don't respect yourself as a woman, we won't respect you either.' The pattern goes all the way through. Even the probation officer checking me out at the House of Detention assumed I was a prostitute since I hadn't been working—in spite of the fact I was arrested for another crime. It's like you're automatically loose if you've been arrested. The laws are unfair

—for a girl it's promiscuity; for boys it's natural experimenting. Like with prostitution, a man goes home and the girl gets sixty days.

"Anyway, I laid in the House of Detention for six months. When I went to court and they read four indictments, I was scared to death. I was thirty-three years old and this was my first real brush with the law under these circumstances. I had a Legal Aid lawyer. He recommended that I take a guilty plea to robbery in the third degree. I was sentenced and served my time and I still don't know what robbery in the third degree is—except that it's better than armed robbery time wise. I was sentenced to one to ten years and they told me I was lucky. . . . I didn't expect anything else. I had committed a crime and punishment for committing a crime against society is prison. But the officers at the House of Detention were shocked at the time I got. And I couldn't even picture ten years. But one CO said I really was lucky—that yesterday the judge was giving out three to ten years. I did six months in the House of Detention before I was sentenced to Bedford Hills. I did fourteen months in Bedford Hills and did five and a half years of parole before they released me.

"When I was arrested, I felt I was some kind of moral leper, some kind of bad seed. I didn't know alcohol was a sickness. I actually had thought I was keeping myself alive drinking—'cause if I stopped, I got so sick. But I came to the realization at the House of Detention that alcohol was the problem, and I began to deal with me.

"I was scared when I went to Bedford Hills. But I knew a few things by then. Like if you act quiet and hostile, people will consider you dangerous and won't bother you. So when I got out of isolation and women came up and talked to me, I said, 'I left my feelings outside the gate, and I'll pick 'em up on my way out.' I meant I wasn't going to take no junk from anyone. I made a promise if anybody hit me, I was gonna send 'em to the hospital.

"When you go in, if you have certain characteristics, you're classified a certain way. First of all, if you are aggressive, if you're not a dependent kind of woman, you're placed in a position where people think you have homosexual tendencies. If you're in that society long, you play the game if it makes it easier to survive. And it makes it easier if people think you're a stud broad. I played the game to make it easier so they would leave me alone. I didn't have money to use makeup and I couldn't see going through any changes. You're in there and the women are looking for new faces. Since I was quiet and not too feminine-looking, I was placed in a certain box in other people's mind. I let them think that's what box I was in—'cause it was a good way to survive. My good friends knew better. But I had three good friends and they were considered "my women"—so they in turn were safe, too. You have to find ways to survive. You cultivate ways to survive. It's an alien world and it has nothing to do with functioning in society better. What I learned there was to survive there."

Jeanette says that what she saw happen in prison—to herself and others —is what pushed her into her present work with other ex-cons in the Fortune Society* in New York City. She talked about a sixteen-year-old, who came to the prison before she had ever had a date or knew what sex was. "I watched that kid when I was there and the changes she went through about herself and about sex and who she was. One day some of the women put makeup on her and she ran. She was frightened by what she saw. Her sex drives had been misdirected by women older than her. A lot of women are caught up in that process who come out thinking they are lesbians just because they've been institutionalized. I got angry one day and said, 'I don't think there are five true lesbians here!'

"I did hard labor at Bedford Hills. I unloaded trucks at the storehouse first and then sat down and did records work. I had to figure out mathematically how much coffee each kitchen needed and proper distribution of supplies. I was a bookkeeper, too. I was paid five cents a day and got a bonus each month of one pound of sugar, one pound of coffee and one can of evaporated milk.

"When you're in prison, time stops. You come out with the same problems you go in with—and start all over again with their twelve extra rules of parole in addition. While you're there, you just learn to survive and manipulate any extra pleasure you can. A comparatively honest person who just committed a crime of passion would end up becoming a manipulator in prison. A girl who works in the kitchen takes extra slices of meat and gets cigarettes for them. Cigarettes are money in prison. There's nothing there to foster the qualities society wants. You become dishonest just to make it. All the qualities you're being sent there to get, they forget you won't have when you get back. You wind up doing all those little things just to make life more comfortable for yourself. Sixty per cent of what you do is against some rule. If you have more than four slices of bread in your room, it's against the rules. An egg or rice—you get three days in punishment. I know a woman who got nineteen days in punishment for refusing two slices of burnt toast. They'd have raids on your room. But they'd only look where you hide things. So I'd leave whatever I had that was contraband out in open view. I never got busted.

"When I think back, the only reason my time wasn't wasted was because

* Fortune Society is a self-help organization headquartered in New York City and composed of ex-prisoners working for changes in the criminal justice system.

I had come to the end of the road before I went there and was looking for answers. When a weekly alcoholic program came in from the outside, I found a beginning. When I got out on parole, that's when people in the program really helped me out. The day I got home, people from the program picked me up. A woman who had spoken at the prison became a friend. I don't think she knew how much she helped me. I was on parole and I was living with a sick aunt. This lady gave me keys to her apartment so I could go there after work or whenever I needed to get away from my aunt. She trusted me. I couldn't believe it. My references were all to jail, then. She said, 'Listen, that's behind you.' And she told me to stop thinking about my past life and start living in my present life.

"My parole officer said, 'You aren't considered a criminal.' And I said, 'If I'm not, then why was I locked up? I wasn't violent. I might as well have been.' Anyway, I got a one-room apartment of my own finally. I told the landlady I was a parolee and she was very nice. I stayed there almost two years, using the phone in the greeting card shop down the block. The man in the shop said I had a nice smile. But I'd use his phone and go out and look for work.

"When I was honest, I couldn't get a job. I'd been out about nine months then and the man in the greeting card shop told me to go to the hardware store—that they needed a bookkeeper. I went and the man hired me. He told me not to worry about not being a bookkeeper, that I would learn through the work. My starting salary was $85.00 a week. Can you imagine how good that was after a nickel a day? I felt so good making a decent salary.

"I worked five years for this man and his wife and finished my parole on that job. I worked a year before I told them I was a parolee. I was turning gray worrying about it. By that time I had hooked up with Fortune Society and was using a different name on speaking engagements because of the job. When I finally told him, he gave me a raise. He was very honest, though, and told me he didn't know if he would have hired me or not if he had known I was an ex-con. My daughter and I eased back into our relationship again. At first we went to the movies every Saturday or Sunday. Eventually she came back to live with me out of her own choice. It took about six months.

"I was tired. I was very tired. What I had for a life wasn't anything like I had pictured in my teens—where I wanted to be a schoolteacher, get married and be a wife and mother. So it was like starting all over again.

"I was scared to death of decisions. All decisions had been taken away from me in prison . . . and coming home is so hard. The only thing you've been responsible for is being on the job when you're supposed to work. How can you come out and make a good decision? I was scared to make any at all. I finally had to say, I'll just make the decision and live with it—good, bad or indifferent.

"After I'd been home a while, I wondered if ex-cons were doing anything for ex-cons. I couldn't forget what I'd experienced—the sixteen-year-old kid, the inmate who was put into punishment behind two doors and wound up in a catatonic state because she couldn't stand it . . . she couldn't stand being in a steel cell with only a Bible and a book of rules, a toilet and a bed, with a matron coming by three times a day with a cigarette . . . I couldn't forget the claustrophobia I'd experienced and what it was like to go to the library to look for a book and find that anything pertinent or relevant must have been printed in the 1800s.

"I had come to believe that people destroy themselves by committing crimes and going to jail. It's a way of self-destruction. And I didn't see anything in there to help. Prisons don't serve any purpose but removing women from society. Even though the physical facilities and surroundings where I was at are better than men's prisons, and there is less physical brutality unless a woman fights . . . all the demands made at Attica could fit very well into any women's prison.

"Well, I was struck by the honesty of the people at Fortune. And I found out that I cared, I cared a lot. I became committed then. Both to dealing with myself and to maybe help other people avoid my mistakes and to expose what prisons really are.

"I have a new way of life now. I don't take ordinary things for granted anymore. Ordinary things are gifts to me. I enjoy food. I enjoy going to a good show. I enjoy people. I've had a lot of luck, a lot of good breaks."

Chapter 4   "EVERYONE ARRESTED IS GIVEN A BATH"

Being in jail is harder on a woman than a man. Men are always together. They grow up taking showers together, sleeping together . . . they've been in the Army with other men and are used to being around each other naked or dressed. Women are taught to undress in private and be modest. They don't like to undress in front of other people. Women have stall showers, men have one big shower room . . . so think how much harder that would be on a woman. She comes in here and we undress her and tell her to "bend over, lady," to look for contraband. We make her bathe in front of everyone. Right off that gives them mental problems that are hard to handle. The initial shock is the toughest thing. That sort of thing can break your spirit.

—MALE WARDEN

The word "reception" is usually associated with a friendly, hospitable event. Wedding receptions, welcome-home receptions and "warm" receptions call to mind an entirely different image from the "receptions" women receive after arrest when they are processed into jail. When they are stripped and searched, when they *become* the name on whatever identification they carried at the time of arrest and are given a prison number. When they hear the sounds of doors closing and the turn of the key for the first time.

The popular euphemism for a woman's initial orientation to jail or prison is "reception," but it doesn't usually ease the initial shock of confinement. In state prisons, women are confined to a cell block for two to six weeks for "reception and orientation" while they are examined medically, given tests, interviewed and assigned jobs before they are taken out of isolation and put in with the general prison population. Prisoners in county jails are given a shorter "reception" before entering their new homes.

Deputy Sheriff Georgia Walton at Los Angeles County's jail for women explained the reception process in straightforward terms from her own perspective as a guard who helped process more than 30,000 area women into that jail in 1970. We began at the point where women are escorted in handcuffs or waist chains into the jail from police districts.

"For a new booking," Deputy Walton explained, "the officer types up a booking slip while another officer has the inmate in custody. She gives her a number and then goes through her purse to search for contraband. After everything is complete, the inmate is sent through number three gate and delivered to a female deputy, still in full view of the control center and hall leading to the administrative offices. At that time the deputy gives her a pat search. She removes her wig, rings, shoes and socks. Anything such as a leather belt, drugs or medication is taken. She can keep up to ten dollars—but no more than two dollars in change. More than two dollars in change is not allowed because it could be put into a sock and used as a weapon.

"This is where I am generally assigned. The pat search means I also look in your ears, your nose and mouth. I search your bra and around your waist and look up your pants legs. If they have dentures I ask them to remove the denture and look at this for contraband possibly being concealed under it. Then we put them into one of the two holding tanks."

The three walls of the two holding tanks are bare except for names and messages and telephone numbers scratched into the concrete. The wall facing the hallway is half glass, which allows the deputies to keep constant observation on the women inside. One of the tanks has two pay telephones and no toilet. The other has one pay telephone and an open toilet bowl and sink exposed to full view from inside and outside. Thin aluminum benches line two of the walls. Officer Walton notes that they are too narrow and "women fall off of them all the time."

"They're kept out here approximately two hours," she says. "They can make telephone calls because this is run just like a police station. If they don't have any money, I give them a dime and tell them to call collect. Before I put them in, I tell them what they're charged with and how much their bail is—whether it's a misdemeanor or not. We take new bookings right off the street and women are sent here from other jails. If someone is intoxicated and can't stand up, we put her in a reception observation room."

The "reception observation" rooms were two tiny padded square holes seemingly dug out of concrete blocks. "You see the walls are padded but not spongy. The floor is the same—and it's softer than the cement in the holding room. It's for their safe being we put them in here. Before they're placed in this room they are seen by a nurse to make sure she is drunk, and not having a seizure. Then the officer checks on them through this little glass window every fifteen minutes to get some form of response. They're kept in here a maximum of four hours . . . and then if they're sobered up they can come out and make their calls or whatever before they continue the processing.

"We also put inmates in here who are combative—someone who doesn't want to be here. If in the process of searching her she is swinging, kicking or biting, she is put in the observation room until she settles down. She is also checked on by the officer. When she's ready to behave she can come out and make her calls in the holding tank.

"Some say they don't want to call anybody, they don't want anybody to know they're here. Then we make a notation of call declined or incompleted. After I have that response, they are taken out of the holding tank and into the reception room.

"Everybody that is arrested is given a bath. They are instructed to remove all of their clothing, including their underwear. Then we give a narco search. Do you know what that is? Well, I'll explain. I would have a flashlight—and I would feel through her hair, and use the flashlight to look inside her ears, behind her ears, in her nose, in her nostrils and her mouth. I would look between her fingers, both sides of her hands, under her arms, and around her breast area. If her breasts are so heavy, I would have her lift them up—sometimes they tape things under them. I'd have her spread her toes apart. Then I'd have her turn around and do the same thing down her back—hair, arms and all. Then I would have her spread her legs and bend over and I would look up into her vagina area to search for weapons, contraband or narcotics. The only area I touch is her hair. I can see into her vagina because her legs and buttocks are spread and I use the flashlight. I don't touch her. I couldn't say I look into her rectum—I look into her buttocks area. I have her lift her feet and check the bottom of her feet. That's a complete narcotics search.

"Then she is instructed to get into the bathtub. Then I take the tray and search her clothing—the seams, the shoes themselves and the soles. She may have her underwear returned along with her comb and lipstick. If the shoes are similar to tennis shoes, I would return them to her—as long as they have no metal buckles, along with the money she had. Everyone that comes through has a clothing bag—along with a clothes tag that lists her name and everything she has. Jewelry, money and license go to the cashier for safekeeping.

"After she has completed her bath, she's instructed to get out and clean the bathtub. Then she is sprayed with Kwell Lotion." She points out a large tank of Kwell Lotion with a spray nozzle on the end of the hose. "She is sprayed under her arms, under her breasts and in her pubic area to get rid of any body bugs she may have.

"Some people come in and appear to be very clean and I don't suppose they have body bugs, but everyone has to be sprayed. It would be terrible to have bugs spread around the institution. If an inmate has lice in her hair she is given Kwell Shampoo and instructed to shampoo her hair. It works the same way as Kwell Lotion—it kills the bugs. If somebody comes in with a cast on, we make an exception about the bath, but she'll still be sprayed. After they have been sprayed, they are taken back and given their underwear, a jail dress, thongs and a sweater. If an inmate comes in with a dress that needs laundering, we do it. If they come in in a nightgown or a bathing suit, we wouldn't send them to court in it. We would provide a dress.

"After they are fingerprinted and photographed, they go up to see the nurse. The nurse asks questions—ranging from "Are you pregnant?" to "Have you ever had seizures, heart problems, diabetes?" and a number of questions. If it's confirmed, we would give her medication. If an inmate is booked with medication on her, we cannot use her medication . . . even if we confirm that she needs it. We must use our own medicine prescribed by our medical department. If she's an epileptic, the nurse at her own discretion would give medication or have the doctor check it. We just can't take the word of an inmate. If you were coming in, and say you're an epileptic, you might just want your medicine—but we don't know what's in that medicine you have." (Women who have been at Sybil Brand complain of getting no medical attention for the first week or two weeks after arrest— and some have said that although they put in requests, they never saw the doctor. Others who have had needed medication confiscated said that if and when it was replaced, it often was the wrong dosage or the wrong prescription.)

After leaving the photo-fingerprinting room, we walked down a long hall, passing another holding tank, where women wait to go to court. Across from the holding tank is the dressing room where women are given a search and change of clothes when they return from court. Beyond the "court holding tank" we walked out into an open area where some twenty-five mops were lined up parallel on an iron rack.

"The jail is divided into two halves," Officer Walton said. "The left side is the minimum side—that's the sentenced inmates. The right side is maximum security—that's for unsentenced inmates. This is the mop area. Trustees are assigned to ring out the mops and deliver them to the housing areas. They are required to work seven to three each day in the laundry, or on the freight and trash crew—going around and picking up trash and dumping it. The laundry does all the washing and ironing for the whole institution—dresses, sheets, towels, officers' white blouses. Tank trustees wash the personal underwear of all the inmates in their block, sweep and mop the area. Others work in the kitchen or in the sewing industry."

We walked down two long halls and through three electrically monitored gates, past the dorms for sentenced inmates—sixty women to one dorm. Attached to the front of each dormitory was the officer's watch station—separated from the room by a glass cubicle. From the watch station you could see all areas of the dormitory, the bathroom and a connected dayroom, which is open to the women from 12 noon to 2:30 P.M. daily and for two to three hours during the evening. The dayrooms contained one television set, one table and several benches secured to the floor. Women said later that each dorm is allowed to watch one television station only. They are not allowed to turn the dial to a different station. According to prison staff, this reduces the possibility for friction over what program to watch and reduces the chances of the women breaking the television sets.

It was about 11:30 A.M. when we were walking through one of the maximum-security dormitories on our way to the dining hall, but no one else was in the area. Officer Walton said this was because everyone was at lunch. "Everybody goes out for lunch, because the officer doesn't want to leave them unsupervised," she said. "The officer goes with them to eat. She doesn't eat with them. She watches them. They're moved by ramps—not by stairs—because we're moving large numbers. They walk two by two. There's no talking after they leave the cellblock. There's no talking in the maximum-side dining room. Yes, these are all unsentenced or untried inmates. There's no talking returning to their housing area. They come through the dining room door single file and they get a tray and a spoon. They slide the tray along the line and food is placed on the tray. There are no forks or knives and no pepper. They could throw pepper in an officer's eye. If someone was talking in the dining room, I'd say, 'Stop talking.' If they did it habitually or didn't stop when I told them, then an incident card is written on her and it's up to the lieutenant what to do with her. If somebody burps, we set her at the diet table. ["Oh, you wrote that down—make it belches, not burps," she said.] We have her sit up here so she won't be offensive to the other inmates who are trying to eat."

I asked why no talking was allowed in the dining room. "For security reasons," she said. "You have approximately two hundred and fifty-one people in here at one time for approximately twenty minutes. We feed approximately four hundred and fifty people during one hour. It's basically because of the number of people in the dining room. You cannot talk quietly. You cannot talk at all. You have people who have just been booked—and here she is sitting worried about her case. If someone even said, 'You touched my toe,' she might get belligerent. Or if two people were booked on the same case and the arresting agency wanted them separated before court we would try to comply. If they could talk, they might holler back and forth and it would be disrupting. The same would be true of old friends or people from the same neighborhood.

"On the minimum side, the sentenced inmates are permitted to talk when they leave the housing areas or while they are eating as long as it is quiet. They can also talk quietly when returning to the cellblock. Sentenced inmates are assigned to jobs they are physically capable of doing. They get knives, forks, spoons and pepper. They know they have got a certain amount of time—and they are stable; they're adjusted to being here."

As Officer Walton talked, in an absolutely secure reality, I remembered what Connie Powers said she felt about her reception into prison life:

"What really happens is that when you come in they search you and poke you. They give you fourteen needles, pull what teeth they think need pulling, dump you in the shower with your mouth full of blood, shave all your pubic hair and dump a lye disinfectant over your head."

"They try to strip you from the very first minute," another woman said. "They try to strip you of any dignity or self-respect you have as a woman. When they brought me in county jail the first thing they did was take my wedding ring and my earrings. Then they stripped me stark naked and made me jump up and down on the floor in a squat position—while they all stood around watching. They have to forget we're human beings to treat us that way."

Georgia Walton kept walking—she pointed out the dining rooms, the kitchen, the garment shop. A sign held onto a desk with masking tape in the large industrial sewing room read: "IN THE DUNGEON OF YOUR MIND, WHO IS CHAINED TO THE WALL?" The letters of each word were penciled carefully in large block letters.

Finally we stopped for a cigarette in one empty officer's control room. From the room we could see through glass and screen into every nook of a large dormitory. The women's beds were divided only by foot lockers—small chests. Each bed had an army blanket covering it, tucked in smoothly in military style. Bunk beds lined the back wall of the dormitory. ("We would not assign an epileptic or a pregnant woman to a top bunk bed," my guide noted.) Only two women were in the large dormitory; the others were at lunch or on job assignments. The two remaining were "day workers" who scrubbed the toilets and floors and did laundry for the other women. There was no music, no sound in the area. "An officer is not permitted in that dormitory unless there is another officer in the officer's station," Officer Walton said. "That's for the officer's security.

"If two inmates are fighting, I cannot just go in there," she said. "I have to call for help. I can give orders from here to break up the fight—but I am not allowed to go in by myself." I asked Georgia Walton, who seemed unruffled by this whole tour, what her feelings were about punishment for rule infractions.

"If I instructed an inmate to do something and for absolutely no reason she used profanity on me—I would have to report it to the lieutenant and a disciplinary would be written up. Say I instruct an inmate to get out of bed and report for duty. If she said, 'Oh shoot,' I wouldn't report it. But if she was more profane towards me personally, I would have to report it. I'd have no choice.

"Another reason someone can go to discipline [solitary confinement cells] is if she refused to work. If she asks to go to the cell, in essence, she's refusing to work. If she refuses to work, she's asking to go to the cell. If she's in disciplinary, she's not allowed to smoke and can have no reading material, no writing material, no candy and no cigarettes. She is given exactly the same food as other inmates with the exception she does not get dessert. Before each meal her bed must be made and she must be dressed—in her jail dress, not her nightgown. She's required to clean her cell three times a day—sweep and mop it and clean the toilet and sink or washbasin, after each meal. In a regular cell for exclusions and in disciplinary, I would pass the broom and the dust pan through the bars and she would use it. If she needed cleanser, I would pass it through. I would pass the mop through the door and she would use it and return it, the same. She does not leave the cell with the exception of going to court or seeing an attorney. They are not allowed to receive or write mail. But quite a few of them are quite ingenious. They might go to court and get a pencil and make playing cards on toilet paper. They also try to write letters on toilet paper if they can get a pencil.

"They do not necessarily stay down there long. Lieutenant Hess goes down with a sergeant and does board. She talks to the inmate—and depending on the case, they get more or less time. Each circumstance is different. But we do have rules and regulations they must abide by."

Rules and Regulations
General Rules for Inmates at Cook County Jail[1]
Chicago, Illinois

1. Address all correctional officers as "OFFICER."
2. DO NOT use slang in addressing an officer.
3. NEVER argue with an officer.
4. Obey all orders given to you by an officer or civilian personnel immediately. If you feel you have a legitimate complaint, you may put in a request to the person's superior only after you have done what you were ordered.
5. You cannot give anything to other inmates without permission.
6. Report all threats, acts of violence or pressures to an officer immediately.
7. Clothing, like everything else is county property. Take care of it. Destruction of ANY County property may get you more time.
8. You will not have cash in your possession at any time.
9. You cannot transfer money to another inmate at any time.
10. No gambling of any kind is permitted.
11. No food, tobacco, stamps, stamped envelopes, or medication can be brought in or sent to you.
12. Turn in all out going letters to officer in housing unit. Letters being written to Attorney, Judges, Court of legal nature may be given to the officer sealed by you.
13. Only books which have been approved are permitted.
14. When moving from one place to another, you will go straight to destination always with an officer or a runner.
15. When in a line, always move quietly, in an orderly manner.
16. Your family or friends may bring clothing 3 days before your out date.

1. I have included two sets of rules to illustrate typical regulations for prisoners in county jails throughout the country. Although inmates do not always receive written copies of these rules, they are expected to obey them. One section from regulations for guards is indicative of restrictions on personnel.

BEHAVIOR:

1. Do not shout or yell at any time.
2. Do not change cells or bunks in dormitories.
3. Do not visit in other cells, dormitories, or housing units.
4. DO NOT FIGHT. No reason or excuse will be accepted.
5. Unnatural sex acts will not be tolerated. Anyone involved in such acts is subject to charges and prosecution.

CLEANLINESS:

1. You must keep yourself personally clean at all times.
2. You must keep your living area clean at all times.
3. You may obtain a razor to shave from an officer. When you have shaved you must return the razor to the officer.

CLOTHING:

1. You can have only 1 set of regular issue clothing at any time. No other clothing is permitted.
2. Do not wash clothing in housing unit. All clothing is washed in the Institution Laundry. Unless permitted by Superintendent Directive.

SMOKING:

1. No smoking in bed or in sleeping area.
2. No smoking in any dining area.
3. No smoking in the hospital. Except by directive.

MEDICATIONS:

1. You are not allowed to have any kind of medication without written permission.
2. All medication must be taken in the presence of a doctor, a nurse, or an officer.

CONTRABAND:

1. You must turn in any contraband you find to an officer. No excuse will be accepted for having any contraband in your possession.

REMEMBER:

ANYTHING NOT ISSUED BY THE INSTITUTION OR SOLD IN COMMISSARY IS CONSIDERED *CONTRABAND!*

In addition to the above, your housing unit may have some additional rules. If so, you will be told about them or they will be posted. Obey them. Violation of rules will subject you to a conduct report and the possible loss of privileges and/or Good Time.

OBEY THE RULES! STAY OUT OF TROUBLE! DO YOUR TIME! LET US HELP YOU HELP YOURSELF!"

MAXIMUM

(for untried and unsentenced inmates)

THIS INSTITUTE IS A BRANCH OF THE LOS ANGELES COUNTY JAIL. IT IS KNOWN AS THE SYBIL BRAND INSTITUTE FOR WOMEN.

Time Schedules

Maximum—4:40 A.M.—Rising Time
5:00 A.M.—Breakfast
10:00 A.M.—Lunch
3:30 P.M.—Dinner
8:45 P.M.—Everyone in own bed area
9:00 P.M.—Lights out

Conduct Rules

Bed Areas—Bed assignments are made ONLY by an officer. Do not change your bed without permission from the officer. There are to be NO more than three inmates in a bed area or cell at the same time. Only two inmates are permitted on one bed at a time, and both are to be sitting up, with feet on the floor. When lying down on your bed, your shoes must be off. Do not hang towels, clothing or laundry in such a way that officers cannot see. Do not hang anything on the bars in cellblocks.

Bathroom Areas—Except for toilet facilities, not to be used prior to lights on. Personal underclothing is not to be washed in the wash basins. Dorm or cellblock trusties ONLY to wash and dry all personals including tennis shoes for entire area in Day Room. Showers are to be used only as scheduled. You must shower every day.

Smoking—In Dorms smoking is permitted in bed area ONLY. In cell-blocks smoking is permitted inside a cell ONLY. You must not smoke in the cellblock corridors. Ashtrays must be kept empty and clean, and remain on the shelf of the locker or writing table. Never place on beds. Never smoke while lying down.

Talking—There is NO talking after lights out, during count, or when going from housing area to meals, work areas, visitation or Infirmary. There is no loitering outside of housing area. Inmates must walk by twos and close together in meal lines and when going to or from work areas. No talking is permitted in lines.

Red Lines—In Dorms a red line is painted on the floor at the grilled gate. In cellblocks it is painted on the floor between the showers and the first cell. Anytime a line is formed to leave the housing area, the formation is to begin behind this red line. If you are called from your housing area by an officer wait behind the red line until the door has been opened and the officer has instructed you to step out.

Count—Count is regularly taken after lights out. However, it may be called at any time. When count is called over the public address system, inmates in Dorms are to go to their own bed areas, inmates in Cellblocks are to go inside their own cells. When the officer enters the officer's station inmates are to line up at the foot of their beds in Dorms and in front of their cell in cellblocks. Do not lean against the walls, beds, or bars. There is absolutely no talking while count is being taken. Remain standing until excused by the officer. Inmates in work areas will line up as designated by the officer, according to housing area. No movement out of dorms, cellblocks, or work areas until count is verified.

Meal Lines—Meal Lines are called over the public address system. You must go to meals. There is no talking in meal lines or in the Dining Room.

Personal Contact—No personal contact is permitted. This includes playing, wrestling, massaging, plucking eyebrows, etc.

Borrowing, Lending, and Exchanging—You are not permitted to give, exchange, borrow or loan ANY personal items such as clothing, shoes, commissary, money, etc.

Disciplinary Actions—The BEST way to avoid disciplinary actions is to follow the Jail Rules and do as instructed by the officer. If you feel an order is unfair, the best policy is to do as told at the time and then write a request to see the Classification Board.

Identification Bands—Identification bands are not to be removed and if showing signs of wear or if cannot be read, report to your officer at once.

Property Slips—Property slips are to be kept on your person at all times.

Clothing and Linens

Undergarments—Each inmate may have a maximum of five (5) sets of underclothing (bra, panties, slip). All personal items must be marked with your initials. Pettipants and girdles are counted as panties.

Street Clothing—You are permitted to receive one exchange of street clothing during your incarceration. If you receive a clothing exchange, the original clothing must be returned with visitor. No exchanges will be accepted on Saturdays, Sundays, or Holidays and may be made only between 8:00 A.M. and 4:00 P.M. and between 6:00 P.M. and 9:00 P.M. during the week. No socks are to be brought in.

Needlework—Permitted in reasonable quantities in Dorms only. You may work on one (1) needlework project at a time—knitting, crocheting, or embroidery. Visitors may bring you five (5) skeins of yarn at a time or enough thread to complete one embroidery or crocheting project.

You may knit or crochet the following items: sweaters, stoles, afghans, baby clothes, socks or hats. You may *not* knit or crochet pants, skirts, long coat sweaters, dresses or shorts. Visitors may bring you only those pattern books, plastic needles or crochet hooks to complete one project.

Completed articles must be turned in to the Officer (along with your authorization or sales slip) to be placed in your property.

If you wish to release articles to a visitor, you must inform the officer when you turn in your completed article. Excess yarn, thread, needles, and pattern books should be turned in at the time the article is completed.

You must retain your authorization or sales slip with your needlework at all times, or articles will be confiscated. You may not knit for another, nor may another inmate knit for you.

Appearance—Cleanliness—Neatness

Cells and Dormitories—Each inmate is required to keep her own cell or bed area and surrounding area neat and clean at all times. This includes your assigned share of showers and general cleaning of Dorm or Cellblock.

Lockers—Only cup and ashtray on outside locker shelf in Dorms. There are to be no liners on the inside locker shelves. Locker contents must be orderly and not excessive. Any amount over Five (5) of each cosmetic item is considered excessive and will NOT be returned to you. Dresses, etc. to be hung on rack inside locker. Do NOT hang anything on doors of locker.

Beds—Must be made prior to breakfast and kept neat during the day.

Floors and Walls—Nothing is to be left on the floor during the night except one (1) pair of shoes or thongs per person. Do NOT deface or paste pictures on walls or lockers. No blankets or pillows on floor.

Trash—All trash which will burn is to be placed in the trash can. There are to be NO individual trash receptacles (boxes, paper bags, etc.) in bed areas or lockers. Soiled napkins must be wrapped securely in newspaper and placed in trash cans. Glass and metal are to be turned in to the officer.

Personal Appearance—Each inmate is required to keep herself neat and clean at all times. You must be fully dressed and presentable when leaving your housing area for any reason; do NOT walk around in stocking feet or barefooted.

Showers—Shower is to be taken daily. You are allowed ten (10) minutes to shower. No showers one-half hour prior to any meal line or after lights out.

Hair—Beauty Shop schedules are posted in individual housing areas.

Hair Preparation Orders—Inmates may order permanents and/or have hair dye (only to maintain present color or return to natural color). Write a request to Special Services Sergeant for permission. Only one (1) request filled during month. The orders will be taken on the first Wednesday of the month. You must have sufficient money at time of order. No refunds will be made if you are released before dye is received.

Headscarves or Pin Curls—Headscarves or pin curls are not permitted from 7:00 A.M. to 5:30 P.M. unless special permission is granted.

Nightcaps—May be worn after 5:30 P.M. only if hair is in curlers. May be worn from bedtime to 7:00 A.M. whether or not hair is in curlers. Are to be worn above eyebrows.

Money

Ways you may receive Money—Visitors may leave any amount at time of visit, to be deposited to your account. Visitors may leave up to $5.00 at time of visit, with the officer in the visiting room—to be given directly to you.

Mail—Cash received in the mail will be deposited to your account. A notation on the front of the envelope will show the amount. Checks and Money Orders will be placed in your property.

Checks and Money Orders—Cashier's checks and bank or postal money orders for amounts under fifty dollars ($50) are automatically cashed when received and the money deposited to your account. If it is over fifty dollars ($50) it is placed in your property. Personal checks are NOT accepted. If anyone has mailed these in, they will be placed in your property.

Money Receipts—You will receive a money receipt for any cash deposited to your account by visitors, deposited to account through mail, or after checks and money orders have been cashed.

Withdrawal of Money from Account—Money withdrawal slips will be issued in the housing area on Tuesday evenings. You may not draw more than eight dollars ($8.00) from your account per week. Slips will be processed and money issued to you the following Saturday morning. Special request for money withdrawal should be sent to Inmate Personnel Sergeant. You are not allowed to have more than $12.00 in your possession at any time. Bills of larger denomination than $5.00 will be confiscated.

Commissary—County Line

Commissary Rules—You may not buy commissary for another inmate, nor can another inmate buy commissary for you. If you are going out to court, you should give your commissary order (sealed in an envelope with money) to your officer in the morning.

Regular Commissary—Regular Commissary shopping daily except Saturdays, Sundays and holidays. Commissary Wagon will be in your housing area each weekday morning. A list is posted in the areas showing what can be purchased and the cost. If you wish to shop you must have a list written on a piece of paper including what you want to buy, how many, and the cost of each item. All inmates wishing to shop are to line up when the Commissary Wagon arrives. There is no talking while in the line. You must have a ditty bag.

Cosmetic Commissary—Cosmetic Commissary shopping on Wednesdays only. No shopping on holidays. Commissary envelopes are available for cosmetic shopping and must be filled out prior to breakfast and deposited in the Commissary Box enroute to the Dining Room. The purchase is bagged and stapled closed. Any money to be returned will be placed in bag for return to inmate. Purchases will be distributed by the Sales Clerk and should be opened in the presence of the officer.

County Line (Fridays)—If you have no money on deposit and are not receiving any from visitors, you may write a County Line Request for necessary supplies. Make this request each week that supplies are needed. Note MUST be in the mail box by Wednesday and County Line is delivered on Friday.

Visiting—Mail

Visiting—Visiting hours are daily from 10:00 A.M. to 2:30 P.M. Monday through Saturday and holidays, and from 12:30 P.M. to 2:00 P.M. on Sunday. You are allowed two (2) visits per week. Each visit is limited to twenty (20) minutes. No children under eighteen (18) years of age will be permitted to visit. Ex-inmates are not allowed to visit. Visitors cannot visit more than one (1) inmate.

General Information about Mail—All mail is inspected. Letters may not contain institutional gossip or information about other inmates. Inmates without privileges may not send or receive personal mail. Mail pertaining to case is permitted. Incoming mail will be delivered when privileges are restored. There is no written communication permitted between inmates. No packages will be permitted.

Special Permission—must be obtained by writing a Request Slip for permission to: Correspond in a foreign language; send enclosures (except Sunday Church Bulletin); or send letters without inspection stamp or return address.

Outgoing Mail—Each letter is limited to four (4) pages written on one side only. Do NOT write in margins. Top first page must have your NAME, BOOKING NUMBER and HOUSING AREA. The envelope must have the following return address:

> NAME (as booked), BOOKING NUMBER
> BOX 54320 Sybil Brand Institute for Women
> Los Angeles, CA 90054

Leave envelope unsealed and drop in mail box on way to Dining Room. Letters will be returned to inmates if they are not prepared in accordance with those rules.

Photographs—You may receive small photographs through the mail, but may have no more than five (5) in your possession. Excess will be confiscated. You may not trade photographs and your name and booking number must be written on the back.

Other Information

Catholic Services—Confession at 8:00 A.M. on Fridays. Mass is held at 8:00 A.M. each Sunday in the Auditorium.

Protestant Services—Held at 9:00 A.M. every Sunday in the Auditorium.

AA Meetings—Held at 7:30 P.M. every Wednesday in the Minimum Dining Room. All persons booked on any drunk charge are automatically okayed to attend. Others wishing to attend must have special permission obtained from the Inmate Personnel Sergeant.

Sick Call—Nurses' Line will be called at 6:20 A.M. Monday through Friday for those who have illness complaints. No Nurses' Line on holidays.

Court—Items which may be taken to court are only the following: lipstick, compact, cake mascara, brush, cigarettes, matches, property slip, deposit slips, court papers, money, unpeeled fruit or eggs.

RULES AND REGULATIONS FOR THE DIRECTION OF THE OFFICERS AND EMPLOYEES OF THE MASSACHUSETTS CORRECTIONAL INSTITUTION FRAMINGHAM

"Deportment and conduct between employee and inmate"

12. Your relations with the inmates may be of necessity dual in character. You may be both counselor and disciplinarian at one and the same time. This will enjoin your utmost tact and diplomacy. You should aim to be friendly not familiar, sympathetic not maudlin, firm not harsh, constant, not obstinate, vigilant not unduly suspicious, strict not unjust. Let the inmate feel the impact of your leadership. Do not discuss the discipline or management of this or other penal institutions, or the affairs of your fellow employees while in the presence or hearing of an inmate, nor inform her as to the nature of comments, entries, or reports regarding her made by another employee. Do not show or otherwise allow these rules to be made available to an inmate. Do not intercede personally for an inmate relative to release or outside employment, nor endorse a petititon for granting parole, pardon or commutation without the permission of the Superintendent. You must not associate, accompany or consort with an inmate on parole or others permitted to be at liberty without specific written approval of the Superintendent and the Parole Board. Do not grant any inmate special privileges but treat all inmates impartially. Let your relations with inmates, or with their relatives or friends, at all times be such that you would have them known to any superior officer.[2]

2. Rules and Regulations for the Direction of the Officers and Employees of the Massachusetts Correctional Institution, Framingham. Reprinted from hearings before Subcomittee No. 3 of the Committee on the Judiciary, House of Representatives, 92d Congress/first session on Corrections, Part V, Prisons, Prison Reform and Prisoners Rights, Massachusetts, December 18, 1971, serial no. 15 (Washington: United States Government Printing Office, 1972).

Erie

It is a late winter afternoon and the tiny "waiting room" in Erie County Jail in Buffalo, New York, looks like an old disaster area left over from a World War II movie scene. Yellow paint peeling from the wall. Exposed pipes. Stuffy heat and smoke-filled air. Three black men sit on a thin wooden bench, waiting for visits with their women. Two white guards in uniforms of motley gray stand by.

I'm here for a "knitting class" in the women's section with Mara Seigel, a student who works with the Buffalo Women's Prison Project. The project runs knitting and art classes at the jail, and helps women with bail, court and family problems. I carry only my purse, a notebook and a paper bag with a sandwich in it.

We sign our names, addresses and occupations on the visitors' sheet. "Any medications?" the guard asks. He takes a small bottle of Bufferin I have in my purse and puts it in an envelope. He also takes a small bottle of eye drops and tells me I can pick up both items on my way out. Then he looks in the paper bag. "A sandwich?!!" he nearly shouts. "A sandwich?! You're not going to share that with anyone, are you? You can't take it in if any woman is getting any!" As we go through the door, he reminds me again not to share the sandwich or he will confiscate it.

Inside the barren room used for the knitting class, a hefty black matron walks up and stands over me as I take a bite from half the dry roast beef sandwich. She scowls at me for a couple of minutes in silence and then says, "I won't let any women in until you have eaten your sandwich. Because if you're eating—you can't give them any food, and if they saw you, they would probably ask." I put the sandwich away in my purse and assure her I will eat it after the class and not offer so much as one bite to any hungry woman.

Satisfied, she opens the door to let the prisoners in. As they slowly meander into the room and begin to gather up their yarn and needles from the week before, the matron sits down beside me again. "Remember, there is to be no smoking while you knit or crochet, either," she said. "We don't want ashes on the floor."

Chapter 5   INFANCY: "WE'RE TREATED JUST LIKE CHILDREN"

You can tell the difference between the staff and the prisoners by the fact the matrons wear blue uniforms, the prisoners wear yellow.

—COUNTY JAIL ADMINISTRATOR

—"I think I have a mental problem. I've started talking to myself and answering myself. I sit in the rec room and hear people saying such dumb shit I just want to get up and choke them or scream at them. I like to have fun and when I can't I feel like I'm going crazy."

—"You start losing your identity when you get locked up. You stop seeking things, you stop doing things for yourself, you stop looking for things. You feel nothing's gonna be all right again . . .

"You can dress only one way, you can adjust your uniform only so far, you can wear shoes only so high and so much makeup. When you start doing jobs that are a man's jobs, you start having female problems and that breaks down your feeling about yourself. The attire does a lot . . . I still feel like a woman but I can't have what I want and I want these things."

—"It's not that a person is so mean or violent. It's just that you have to let the emotion out. I have to relieve myself of that feeling. I do it by going off at a matron every now and then. It might be a little thing that she says, but all that bottled-up emotion comes out."

—"You do the same things day in and day out. You lose a sense of what day it is, what date. I find myself losing the days. The most difficult thing to adjust to is not being able to be who I want to be at certain times . . . not being able to do certain little things I want to do when I want to do them . . . not being able to do anything without pressure. It's a continual choice between what I want to do and what I can do.

"The pressure starts in the morning. You get in line the first thing in the morning for breakfast. If you're one minute early, they say, 'Wait a minute, wait a minute.' You want to knock 'em down, but you know you can't. The hardest thing for me is not being able to say what I want to say. Like why should she be called *Miss* or *Mrs*. and me be called Betty? Why should she be over me? Why can't I say the things to her she can say to me as far as defending herself and saying what she thinks?

"They only have to go by what they hear about you, rather than find out who you are or what you're all about. I will not speak to certain matrons. I will speak only to a few. I can count them on my fingers. We're just called by our first names. You have to call them by their last name or be sent to punishment or apologize."

—"You just can't let out emotion. If you laugh or halfway try to enjoy yourself, you're called silly. The other night we were laughing and the matron called us fools. She told us to be quiet or we'd be sent to bed—just like children. A lot of times it's only because we're getting on their nerves or they can't cope with the situation, so we get three days' lock-up. The officers bring their family problems in here and go off at us for them. A lot of them talk about inmates, not only with each other, but with other inmates.

"It's just like people out in a community, though. There are all types. We can't just blame it on the staff. The women are a lot of the problem, too. They have a tendency to be jealous. If you have a knitted sweater they don't have, or maybe you get more mail or more visitors or wear better shoes . . . they start talking to each other and signifying on you because they feel left out or jealous. But there are enough pressures without the staff making it worse."

"It's like Miss Arn the other day. I had to see her and when I sat down, she asked me, 'Why do you have on one earring?' I said, 'I lost the other one.' It was in my room, but I like wearing one earring and I didn't want to have to explain that to her. She said, 'You know what that means. It means you're going with someone and she's wearing the other one!' "

—from rap session with Mary Jo, Tiki and Betty
at Ohio Reformatory for Women

I know it is not logical to treat anyone who is grown as an infant. But as a way of examining reality from a different perspective, I will in this chapter use the logic of rehabilitation in a custodial prison system, and look at administrators as parents and prisoners as infants.

If you can, try for a minute to imagine that you are a female infant.

First of all, as an infant, you are taken away from your real home and led into a big scary place with concrete walls and locks on all the doors. You are told you have been taken here because you are bad, and this place will help you learn how to be good. You are immediately probed and examined to make sure you are not carrying any toys or food on you. Children about your own age have been put in charge of you. Your new parents have apparently ordered that these strange children in neat, clean uniforms and shiny shoes look into your vagina and rectum and make you stand naked and humiliated in front of them. They handle you roughly and tell each other jokes. They take everything you brought with you away from you. They whisper to each other about you.

Then they make you take a bath in front of them, spray you for lice and give you a set of ugly clothes. The clothes they give you are hand-me-downs; they're not made for you. They're either too big or too small.

Then you are given a paper bracelet to wear with a number written on the paper to identify you. The paper is enclosed under plastic. You are told this is your new name, and you are never to take off the bracelet or destroy it. "We have to have a way of identifying you," the strange children say. "There are a lot of other girls here, so there's no other way we can keep track of who you are. Only this number will identify you, so don't forget it—because anytime we want to talk to you we will call out your number."

Then you are led into a cage or large dormitory, where you see other children wearing ugly old clothes exactly like yours. They are your new siblings. They also wear paper bracelets and some even have numbers stamped on their clothes to identify them. This is your new home. You have to go to the bathroom in front of all of the other girls and you never can find a place to hide when you want to be alone.

After a few days, you find out that the strange children who poked you and ordered you around are actually members of a military gang. You find out that you might never get to meet your new parents—you are not even sure of who they are. The gang members are your parents' favorite children, so you have to follow their orders or you will be punished. They say they take orders from the parents and even though they aren't any older than you, they're in charge. You're not supposed to say anything disrespectful to them. You're supposed to act like they're adults, but you know they're just the same as you, and it doesn't seem fair.

Nevertheless, you have to follow their rules—and every different one of them plays by different rules. They tell you the rules are inflexible and equally enforced for all number-children, but you see other number-children getting away with behavior you are punished for, so you resent them. You learn that if you want to do something fun or something you enjoy, you have to sneak. If you want extra food, you have to steal it. You also know that if your surrogate parent-child asks you to "tell the truth: did you do it?" and you say, "Yes," that you will be severely punished anyway. So you learn to lie, because maybe lying will help you get away with it and honesty doesn't help.

You are awakened every morning, fed and put to bed each night if you are good. You are given a job scrubbing the floor and you have to make it shine. If you never laugh too loud or cry or throw anything, the gang members will usually leave you alone. For being good, you are left alone and nobody bothers you too much. But if you are caught doing anything they decide is *naughty*, you are put to bed early three nights in a row or locked in a dark closet for two or three weeks or more and somebody pushes a bowl of food under a six-inch crack in the door a couple of times a day.

While you're locked in the closet, you can't ever come out to play and you can't have any toys or crayons. If you ask why, they tell you it's because they don't want you to hurt yourself. They say you're being punished, so you can't talk to anyone either. And you don't get dessert or anything sweet. Being locked in the closet is terrible. Sometimes you see rats and roaches staring at you. If you scream or cry to get out of the closet, you will be locked in the closet for at least an extra week. If you bang your head against the wall, they might leave you there forever.

Pretty soon you've forgotten even what you're being punished for.

A lot of times you're cold and you want an extra blanket or you're hot and want to make the air cool—but there's nothing you can do about it. If you get sick and want to be taken care of, a gang member just tells you to be quiet and says, "If you hadn't been a bad girl, you wouldn't be here in the first place." Sometimes you have been locked in the closet because you felt sick and didn't go to work.

In this new home you cannot play with boys. And if they are ever around, you are not allowed to look at them or laugh with them or talk to them. If you ever do, you will be locked in the closet again. You are not allowed ever to play with boys or make boy friends— you can only stay by yourself. The gang members can have friends— girl friends and boy friends, but you can't.

So you are left to play with the sisters who look like you in their ugly clothes. You play with them, and you learn to love them. They have to scrub the floor, just like you. But you also hate them and fight with them. They're the only ones you're allowed to holler at when you feel like you have to holler at somebody. You smell them and understand them and live with them. Since you don't get to hug a parent and you can't trust those other children who always order you around, you can reach out only to your sisters for warmth and comfort and love.

But then you are told by the gang members that your parents said this is against the rules, too. You are not allowed to love your favorite sister-friends. You can't touch them or hug them or anything. If you are caught on your little sister's bed combing her hair or bandaging her knee, you will be punished very severely. If she is sick and you want to take care of her, you are told to go to your room and be quiet. If you are *ever* caught playing doctor or playing make-believe and kissing, you will be locked in the closet again. So you are very careful not to let anyone see that you like your sister or want to hold hands with her—because then you might be separated from her forever or locked into the bad girl's closet indefinitely. Some bad girls never get out of the closet.

You can see that the parents don't stop gang members from being friends or holding hands, but they stop you. The parents don't want their favorite children to be friends with you. They tell the military gang members that it is against the rules for them to do you any favors and that *they* will be punished if they ever are friends with you or treat you differently from anyone else.

You can tell your parents don't like you. If they did, they

would understand. They would let you be friends with people. They would also protect you from other number-children who are bigger than you who force you to play naughty or bully you. But your parents don't care what happens to you. They just want you to work and keep their house clean. They must not care, because they never talk to you and they don't give you comfort or understanding or protection. They won't even let you play or have fun. They don't know how it feels, and they don't even care enough to find out. They make you and their favorite children do everything, and they don't even know what happens to you during the weeks.

Since you're all left alone so much, you start playing a game with the gang members—sort of like cops and robbers. You use a lot of your energy seeing what you can get away with. The gang members play the cops and you play the robbers. They sneak around trying to catch you, so you always have to be on guard. The object of the game is not to get caught. Sometimes when you figure out ways to get extra food and they don't catch you, it's great fun. Especially when you know they know, but they weren't as fast as you were. They get mad when they know you've fooled them, but the parents told them they can't be mean to you unless they catch you, so you learn how to outsmart them. You and your sisters form sort of a gang to fight them and when you stick together, you can almost always outsmart them. It's a problem sometimes, though, because they will often take some members of your gang aside and give them extra food or toys to tell on you, so you can't really even tell your own gang everything.

Some of your sisters even try to act tough and order you around because they want to be like the military gang. And if they don't like what you're doing, they'll hit you. You always gotta watch out for people who are going to hit you.

Pretty soon you start to realize that your parents never want you to grow up. They won't let you make any decisions of your own. They won't let you find any new playmates or see any boys or encourage you to grow or to take responsibility. They make you feel silly and dumb and retarded—and even if you *know* you're *not* the names they call you, you begin to wonder if they're right.

After you've gotten really used to your new home, your parents open the door one day and say, "Okay, you can leave now." They tell you to leave, even though you don't know if you want to. They tell you to go out and take care of yourself. "You're grown up now.

Now you're an adult, so you can leave. You said you wanted to leave, what are you waiting for?" They don't give you any money to take with you, or any food or any toys. The gang members stand around and whisper and joke with each other. They laugh and declare: "You'll be back. That's a big world out there—you probably won't be able to take care of yourself. You'll be back to see us 'cause you need us. We'll still be here when you get back." You get to turn in your number now and to take off your paper bracelet. They tell you to use your real name again when you're out in the world, not your number. They tell you you can't play cops and robbers anymore because now you don't have anybody to play with. They tell you to be friends with boys again, but you've almost forgotten what boys look like, and you don't think you will know how to act with them. You don't know what to expect. You don't know what it will be like out there and you're afraid.

Strange as it may seem, this analogy touches at the core of much of what is going on in prisons today. I had often heard the myth that women prisoners were especially "babied" compared to men. And while it was obvious to me that women prisoners were not babied or "coddled," I kept hearing statements that baffled me.

—Lieutenant Archibald at Riker's Island, New York City: "They're grown up, but they act like they're in kindergarten." Pointing out one forty-year-old woman who was quarreling with another inmate over a seat in the auditorium, the lieutenant said, "She's my problem child."

—The superintendent of Riker's Island, Mrs. Essie Murph: "We're a lot like a family here . . . this is home for most of them. I was captain for ten years before becoming a deputy, so we've sort of grown up together, you could say. Most of these women I've known off and on for years . . . I even know some mother and daughter and grandmother sets . . ."

—Marjorie T. Ward, director of the women's division at Arizona State Prison: "They don't have that much time to lollygag around. They're generally busy . . . we keep them busy . . . plus we're constantly watching them."

—Another guard: "When they act like children, we treat them like children. When they want attention, they break out the windows or throw temper tantrums just like two-year-olds."

Inmates had repeatedly told me, "They treat us just like children," and, "They think we're four years old. They think we can't think for ourselves." "They call us girls, but we're *women*."

In a letter to Ericka Huggins, Angela Davis wrote of her experiences in the Women's House of Detention in New York and said: "I have often heard the rumor that as compared to men's prisons, women's institutions are humanely benign, the gravest problems being the tendency to "baby" the women captives. This is a myth which must be immediately smashed . . ." She said the "notion of mildness in the midst of coercion is a blatant misrepresentation."

It is obvious that babies are not locked up in cells, put in isolation, forced to work, disciplined for laughing out loud or neglected when they are sick. But the myth bothered and baffled me every time I heard administrators talk about "feedings" and "controlling the girls" and the women "acting just like babies." I knew there was some piece of reality in the misperception but I couldn't put my finger on it.

Then one day I was talking to Missouri Beckton—an older woman who had spent time in Muncy, Pennsylvania's State Correctional Institution for Women. Missouri had gone up for parole one year and been denied. The next year she was supposed to go before the board but they didn't see her. They had given her a one-year setback for having had a bad record. She said the setback came from an incident where she had been punished for "talking impudent to a matron."

"*The main thing I think kept me in Muncy so long was they was trying to rehabilitate me down to be a two-year-old. I refused to be retarded*," she said. "*I'm grown. I'm forty-nine years old. They can't make me be a two-year-old.*"

The same day I talked to Missouri, I got a letter from Bernard Orr at Graterford Prison, outside Philadelphia. Bernard was writing me about a newspaper he and some other men had started at that institution:

"At present, subscriptions for 'outsiders' are out—so say the omnipotent administrators. Because we are only in the infant stage, I think it's a question of watching the baby's feeding. But as soon as they find out how silly the games they play are and do what should have been done in the first place, I'll send you a copy of our first edition."

I remembered the other conversations: "You can dress only one way, you can adjust your uniform only so far . . ." "You have to eat everything on your plate. You can't even decide for yourself what you want to eat."

The simple truth to the "mystery of the myth" I was probing is that total institutionalization is synonymous with forced dependency. The controls of prison which attempt to regulate lives, attitudes and behavior are synonymous with those used during infancy.

The only other time we know of in life where nearly every moment is dictated for us by outer tyranny is infancy. Children are told when to get up, what to eat, where to go, how to spend their time—what to do and, moreover, what not to do. Parents or adults literally tell you what to wear. They set feeding times, make decisions, reward and punish behavior. If they are wise they are delighted when you begin to make decisions for yourself that don't hurt you. They are delighted to see you grow, change, take new steps and use initiative. Good parents are not arbitrary or irrational but observe your response to the world, encourage you to explore it and watch your development with love and care.

They know you will make mistakes, because they know mistakes are part of learning. But if you played with matches, and burned yourself, they wouldn't punish you further or hurt you for hurting yourself. If you were sick, they wouldn't punish you for being sick.

Institutions which control the *total* lives of people confined in them have accepted the role of parents. People confined in these institutions are forced into childlike status by the fact of their incarceration and isolation. Thus the role of the prison system to the prisoner becomes parent to child. Authorities have total power over the lives of the people they govern, just as parents have power to control and direct their children's lives. The more isolated the institution from public view, the more helpless inmates are to defend themselves—just as private tryanny over the life of so many children continues when not exposed.

We would call parents who really treated their children in the manner described cruel and abusive and we would refer to their children as neglected and battered. We would not wonder why their children might have problems adjusting to the world.

Prisons have this same kind of power over prisoners. And what we have in our prisons today is mass infancy treatment. The treatment is abusive and battering in its very nature. Mass infancy treatment of adult human beings seems illogical—especially when we say we want those human beings to be independent and responsible citizens.

I believe that it is irrelevant whether the system was an evil design to strip people of responsibility, independence, human contact and dignity—or whether it just evolved that way. What is important is that we see what it is now. Because at this point in time, it has trapped many people into roles they're often not even aware of. Even progressive and humane administrators who want to encourage growth and responsibility are pressured or coerced themselves by a structure that negates almost any positive actions they take. There is no way of dealing with large numbers of people in a constructive manner when your chief responsibility is to regulate and control their actions. What good does it do to offer counseling or education to help a woman become self-sufficient when she still has to get up by a bell, eat at a prescribed time, walk a certain way and be locked into a cell at night? What good does it do to encourage people to be responsible and independent when the majority of all their decisions are made for them and they are punished for initiative?

In jails and prisons which adhere to the old methods of strict custody, orders are given as to what prisoners wear, what they eat, how much they eat, how they work, where they work, what they read, whom they see, whom they write, when they can write, when they can talk, and what they can say. Prisoners are made to do everything at the same time, the same way, every day.

In more progressive institutions where administrators believe in an emphasis on treatment rather than strict custody, and on reintegration into the community rather than retribution, there is still a basic conflict: summed up in the *Manual of Correctional Standards*, issued by the American Correctional Association:

"The fundamental responsibility of prison management is the secure custody and control of prisoners. This is universally prescribed by custom and public opinion. Although at times such a concept may seem at variance with attempts to introduce rehabilitative services, it is doubtful that any correctional program which ignores this reality will long endure . . ."

In a progressive institution which has made a humane effort to individualize treatment of the inmates, women may be allowed to choose what to wear each day, wear their own street clothes and choose how to fix their hair. They may be able to hang pictures on the walls of their rooms and even be allowed the choice of whether to eat certain meals or participate in certain education or self-improvement classes. But even with these possibilities for self-expression, authorities and the controls of prison life still dictate a prisoner's lack of contact with the outside world. A woman's choice of friends and her expression of beliefs are still monitored and censored. Her life is still regulated and dictated by the limits of the institution and the majority of her choices are determined *for* her, not by her.

MORAL FORCES, ORGANIZED PERSUASION AND SCIENTIFIC TREATMENT SHOULD BE RELIED UPON IN THE CONTROL AND MANAGEMENT OF OFFENDERS, WITH AS LITTLE DEPENDENCE UPON PHYSICAL FORCE AS POSSIBLE.

> —Principle XX, Declaration of Principles
> of the American Correctional Association

What she *should be*—in the opinion of the institutional staff—as opposed to what she *is* is still dictated by someone else's standards. If she is being *treated*, the parent models are expecting her to accept their moral values and standards of proper behavior, according to their cultural expectations. They are often totally unaware or disdainful of the different culture she came from or the different set of moral values she has. She is expected to mold herself in their image.

Prisoners are placed in a double bind. If they accept custody and allow other people to make their decisions and set up all the rules, they will try to play the game properly. They will repress their anger, never talk back to an officer, obey all the rules and follow all instructions without complaint. They will then be rewarded with positive staff reports and be released on parole before the expiration of their sentence. But with the acceptance of custody comes the natural erosion of self-determination, independency and a sense of responsibility in making decisions.

On the other hand, prisoners who fight custody and control, who refuse to be dependent or to agree with the authority's determinations about their values and actions, maintain a sense of autonomy and control over their own lives. If they express themselves, they may continue to let out their anger or laugh when they feel like it or behave in a manner much the same as if they were in general society. Even if they don't fight the system, but ignore the regulations and maxims laid down to govern their behavior, they cause conflict. It makes them "problem prisoners" and they are apt to spend a lot of time in "close custody" or segregation and be labeled "incorrigible." At the least they are viewed as unco-operative by staff and maintain a poor institutional record. They are often denied parole for the *unorthodox* prison behavior that would allow them to adjust more quickly to society than their less independent counterparts. They often stay in prison until expiration of sentence.

Seymour L. Halleck, psychiatric consultant for the Wisconsin Division of Corrections, suggests one way of looking at the whole issue of incarceration is that "if one had systematically and diabolically tried to create mental illness and tried to create situations in which there were no alternatives, he could probably have constructed no better system than the American prison system.

"If you think about what qualities one could define as being conducive to mental health and then take a look at what actually exists in prisons," Halleck said, "the argument that the prison is there to create mental illness is well put.

"We all agree to be mentally healthy we have to be able to feel intimate towards others and others towards us. As you know, any kind of intimate expressions in prison are repressed. Certainly contact with the opposite sex is not available. Contacts with the same sex are looked upon as homosexual, and are punished. Contacts with the officers—real camaraderie and all sense of sharing—are absent.

"Also to be healthy one has to express a certain amount of aggression. Now, I'm not talking about violence. I'm talking about being able to use one's aggressive impulse to argue verbally, to gain mastery over the situation. Any kind of aggression in a prison situation is punished. Not thwarted, *punished*.

"Also to be mentally healthy one must have a certain sense of autonomy. One must have a sense of dignity. One must have a sense that there is hope. That he is not totally helpless and dependent. Obviously these things are gradually stripped away from prisoners.

"Also to be mentally healthy, one must have a sense of responsibility. One must feel that he is accountable for what he does. That he is not totally dependent. And that he is master of his own destiny. Again, the prison system systematically strips inmates of these kinds of very, very basic needs essential for mental health."

Halleck said there are very, very few things a prisoner can do to change this situation. But there are several kinds of *adjustments* to it. One is saying to herself: "Well, I will change something about my own physiology or my own attitudes so I can live with this situation." And indeed, some inmates do. They blame themselves. They work hard. Religion helps enormously if they believe in an afterlife or in a time when things will be better.

The most useful kind of adjustment, according to Halleck, would be "organized, legitimate-within-the-system grievance, i.e., legitimate efforts to change the society, the prison society in this case. These efforts are what have been used in reforming other institutions. *But these outlets are simply not available to the prisoner.* There are very few inside prison organizations or inmate councils which have much influence on the authorities. There is very little power that prisoners have, ultimately.

"What's left for prisoners are some other kinds of adjustments," he said. "When other legitimate outlets are closed off, another type of adjustment is simply to attack the prevailing community. So far this has not been used excessively, but I think now there is greater awareness of the possibility of using it," Halleck said. "Now that there are more riots in more prisons, we are probably going to face more of this direct attack upon the institutional system."

NO LAW, PROCEDURE OR SYSTEM OF CORRECTION SHOULD DEPRIVE ANY OFFENDER OF THE HOPE AND THE POSSIBILITY OF HIS ULTIMATE RETURN TO FULL, RESPONSIBLE MEMBERSHIP IN SOCIETY.

—Principle XIX, Declaration of Principles
of the American Correctional Association

It is true that some people need or want to be controlled by others. It is true that some people put themselves in prison-like bondage and need to be cared for. Both inside and outside prison. They are people who want to have most major and minor decisions made for them. They are the people who literally need infancy as a way of life— maybe because they are emotionally or mentally unable to grow up. Or maybe it is because they have been so warped and stretched out of shape by life that they have gone beyond the elastic point of return to a natural, healthy shape. They are dependent on care—whether it's adequate or inadequate, they need outside direction and support. But these people are few in number and are easily indentifiable. As a minority of the prison population, they are mainly neglected or locked up in solitary for being "emotionally disturbed."

What is tragic is that the regimentation molded for protection against these very few dangerous, violent or psychotic women prisoners estimated by administrators to be 3 per cent or less of the total prison population—dictates the controls on all the women in an institution. It is not even the kind of treatment those sick few need—it is only ineffective control mechanisms that force dependency on everyone.

Mary Vangi, imprisoned at California Institution for Women at Frontera—known as a relatively progressive institution with an emphasis on *therapy*—wrote about this problem in *The Clarion*, CIW's convict newspaper:

"The fact is that *some* convicts are violent and dangerous. The fact is that no or little provision is made once they are in prison to get them adequate psychiatric care. There is not enough money in the budget, we are told, and the State Mental Hospitals refuse most convicts treatment while they are doing time. None the less, patients deemed unmanageable by the Mental Institutions of this state are sent, without being convicted of a felony, to the state prison for control. None of this is publicized. The fact that most convicts just want to do their own time and get the hell out of prison is not often made public."

Mary was responding directly to an eleven-part series on CIW that was being run on local television. The series was called "Ladies in Waiting." It depicted the surface realities of the prison in a manner Mary believed was akin to creating a fairy tale leading people to believe it was "comfortable, constructive and cozy here." Since the green prison yards of Frontera look much like a college campus, prisoners felt the public would mistakenly believe that curtains on windows and rugs on floors indicated a relaxed freedom and a setting for constructive growth and dignity in contradiction to what they felt was a degrading, confining infantile reality.

Mary wrote: "It begins to seem that the public is more interested in sensationalism than in reality. The society out there is not interested in how their tax dollars that go to support prisons and pay salaries of people who work in prisons and related fields are spent. They are not interested in whether or not there is anything worth salvaging from the warehouse called prison. They are more interested in getting the thrill of seeing what the inside of the prison looks like —room, curtains, rugs, food—not the need for or the lack of reality within the gates to prepare the convict for returning to the community.

"This, though, is a typical sociological phenomena of the Amerikan society. *We have been programmed to reject reality.* Perhaps because the realities that make this country a great world power are so very ugly. I recently read an article by a man on death row that suggested that all executions be televised, so that the public that screams for convictions, for blood, may see their work realized. I think it's a good idea. If we cannot face the truth then we should change it so that it is acceptable to us, instead of trying to build fairy tales around it.

"I would like to suggest that the woman who is doing this eleven part television series [commentator Terry Mayo], voluntarily commit herself to the prison for one week. In the booking-in process, instead of staff who might try to treat her like a human being for the public opinion that will come of it, convicts should book her in, search her just like they were searched on their arrival. All of the very real things that happen to us should be allowed to happen to her: lost mail, disciplinary measures for things like 'silent disrespect,' visits with male friends denied until she chooses just one of them . . . all of it. Perhaps then she would be well versed enough in loneliness, indignation, hunger, alienation and desolation to tell the truth.

"We are not physically abused, we are demoralized drop by drop, that's all. We are not physically uncomfortable, we are involved in a psychological war about ten out of every twenty-four hours, that's all. We are not starving to death from self-inflicted and other kinds of pain we live with; we are not cold from lack of proper clothing or heating. We are freezing from the cold, icy reality that even though we've done time for a crime, we will pay for it for the rest of our lives."

From infancy.

Nellie

When Nellie Parker was thirteen years old, a man killed her mother. "It was a sex murder," she said. "He split her head open with an ax. I didn't find out who did it until about a year later, when I heard the man had bragged to my aunt that he was the one who did it.

"I went and got a gun and shot him," she says matter-of-factly. "When police arrested me, they asked me to tell who I got the gun from and they would let me go. They also told me to tell them where the gun was. I told them I'd dropped it in the river. They told me they'd let me go, but I knew what was what. I never told them who I got the gun from . . . and twelve years later, when I got out, I went right to the place I had hid the gun and took it back to the man who had loaned it to me. He had forgotten about it by then."

Nellie Parker is seventy-one years old now. She lives in a project in South Philadelphia with her husband, William, but she carries her years in prison with her as indelible scars. She is small, with a soft old wizened brown face. She moves slowly, painfully with arthritis. I met her at a prisoners' workshop preceding a production of *The Cage*—a play produced by members of the Barbwire Theatre from San Quentin Prison in California. Mrs. Parker and her husband had taken a subway and two buses to get to the performance in northeast Philadelphia, a white section remote from the heart of the city.

"I knew why I was in prison," she recalls. "A man killed my mother and I killed him. I still have no regrets. I never did have. Not even when I was in Clinton [the state prison for women in New Jersey]. When I was in Clinton, I worked in the laundry and milked cows two times a day.

"We used to get up at four A.M. to milk the cows. That was fun to us. I was always on punishment, so I was only fed bread and water. So on those cold mornings, I would wash off the cow's titty and put it in my mouth and drink warm milk directly from the udder.

"The first seven years, I just didn't care. I was always in punishment. Punishment was terrible. They would beat you and give you cold water showers with fire hoses. Afterwards they'd give you the needle to keep you from getting pneumonia and throw you in the hole. Sometimes they'd strap you on a rotating table and raise it up and you'd go around. Five or six matrons would whip your naked body as you went past them until you fainted. Then they'd rub you down with salt and vinegar. They'd punish you like that for fighting or cussing or something like that. You don't have to do much to get punished. But I got used to it.

"I guess the worst thing is to be locked up on Saturday and Sunday. Those are the days you're locked in all day, and if you don't go to church on Sunday, you won't get out. I'd go to every church service they had on Sunday. I'd go to every faith just to get out of my cell."

Nellie Parker talked on—in present tense, occasionally slipping into past tense, about her adolescence in prison during the 1920s. She talked about her mother and her sixteen older brothers and sisters. She talked about her own son—who was born six months before she went to prison. She also has a daughter—and twenty-three grandchildren. "My son has seventeen children, just like my mother had," she says proudly. "My daughter, she ain't worth a cent."

After twelve years in prison, Nellie Parker served twelve years on parole, completing the remainder of her sentence on the street working first as a live-in maid, later as a day maid. But in 1958, nearly thirty years later, Nellie Parker went to prison again—this time to jail to wait trial, and then the Federal Reformatory for Women in Alderson, West Virginia, for nine months. The mistress of the house where she was working as a maid had accused her of taking a check, and pressed charges. With her prior record, Mrs. Parker said she didn't have "a chance in hell" to beat the charges. She pled guilty.

"It wasn't so bad at Alderson," she said. "They knew I had a heart condition, so they let me work in the garment factory. It was a pretty good job. In the House of Correction, you only got slop to eat. But in Alderson, there was good food—all you can eat."

When Nellie Parker got out of Alderson, she put in another eleven years on parole—which she successfuly terminated in 1969.

"You know, for years I been walking around with all this inside me. I never been able to talk about it to nobody before. Nobody would listen. But I know it's still the same. I just know if you're in there and your parents or your people don't come to see you, they just bury you like a dog."

Chapter 6 DISCIPLINE: A SPRING WOUND TOO TIGHTLY

At this moment the King, who had been for some time busily writing in his note-book, called out, "Silence!" and read out from his book, "Rule Forty-two. All persons more than a mile high to leave the court."

Everybody looked at Alice.

"I'm not a mile high," said Alice.

"You are," said the King.

"Nearly two miles high," added the Queen.

"Well, I shan't go, at any rate," said Alice; "besides, that's not a regular rule, you invented it just now."

"It's the oldest rule in the book," said the King.

"Then it ought to be Number One," said Alice.

The King turned pale, and shut his note-book hastily. "Consider your verdict," he said to the jury, in a low, trembling voice.

"There's more evidence to come yet, please your Majesty," said the White Rabbit, jumping up in a great hurry: "this paper has just been picked up."

"What's in it?" said the Queen.

"I haven't opened it yet," said the White Rabbit, "but it seems to be a letter written by the prisoner to—to somebody."

"It must have been that," said the King, "unless it was written to nobody, which isn't usual, you know."

"Who is it directed to?" said one of the jurymen.

"It isn't directed at all," said the White Rabbit; "in fact, there's nothing written on the outside." He unfolded the paper as he spoke, and added, "It isn't a letter, after all: it's a set of verses."

"Are they in the prisoner's handwriting?" asked another of the jurymen.

"No, they're not," said the White Rabbit, "and that's the queerest thing about it." . . .

. . . "He must have imitated somebody else's hand," said the King. (The jury all brightened up again.)

"Please your Majesty," said the Knave, "I didn't write it, and they can't prove I did: there's no name signed at the end."

"If you didn't sign it," said the King, "that only makes the matter worse. You must have meant some mischief, or else you'd have signed your name like an honest man." . . .

"That proves *his guilt," said the Queen.*

—*from "Alice's Evidence,"*
Alice's Adventures in Wonderland *by Lewis Carroll*

Women Riot, Attack Guards At Jail Here

A band of women inmates stormed the Philadelphia House of Correction dispensary, apparently in search of drugs, touching off the second of two disturbances here Sunday.

No one was injured in the first melee, which erupted about 9 A.M. in the G-2 cellblock and took about 30 minutes to quell.

But four male guards, a matron, and an inmate were injured in the second disturbance, which broke out shortly after 11 A.M. It involved 50 women—half of the 92 held in the prison—who wielded broomsticks, kitchen utensils, and legs pulled from chairs. . . .

—from the Philadelphia *Inquirer*
Page 1-A, February 19, 1973

Whenever you have exaggerated repression, you have exaggerated response. A spring wound too tightly will recoil with extra force. A child who has no natural, direct outlet for his anger will throw a temper tantrum. A people who have been held down too long and denied alternatives will explode in anger—over a police brutality incident in the ghetto, over a prison guard insulting an inmate in a crowded cafeteria. We call the response "riot."

A woman abused by her man continually over a long period of time will "riot" just as "unexpectedly," and the relationship often ends in violence or death. Parents "lose" their children to drugs or hatred over a seemingly small incident, sometimes only casually related to the process of oppression the child has experienced for years. The overwhelming nature of disasters can often cause delayed reactions which the individual may not even associate with the accident or disaster. After a death, a hurricane, a horrible train crash, a tornado or flood, people often protect themselves unconsciously from the terrifying experience by mentally putting it away and not thinking about it. When the response finally does come forth, it can be devastating.

It seems that going to prison, in and of itself, is an emotional and mental disaster. Further, the judgments and punishment that continue once imprisoned create terrible repression. The response, the outlet, is manifested in broken windows, senseless fights. Sometimes a "riot." Although the occasional news we hear about prison rebellions would give the impression that only male prisoners stage uprisings, women also rebel. They strike, they negotiate, they boycott. At California Institution for Women alone, one fifth of the population successfully escaped in 1971, one or two at a time. The same pressures that lead women to escape often result in riots. And sometimes the incident that sparks response seems minuscule. But the reaction is one that has been pent up from day-in-and-day-out pressures, coercion and anxiety.

It may be sparked by the fact that a woman's father died and the administrative staff delayed its decision on her pleas to go home to his funeral—despite the fact that her prison friends were willing to pool their funds to pay her expenses of a guard-escort and transportation and she was collapsing with grief. This ignited a "riot" in the administrative building at Muncy, Pennsylvania, when women who went to protest were confronted by locked doors, male guards and maintenance men.

It may be the fact that two womem were very ill but were unable to get medical attention from prison authorities. This sparked the so-called "riot" and break into the dispensary at the House of Correction in Philadelphia, after legitimate avenues for help were exhausted.

A minor riot can happen because a woman with hepatitis is not getting medical attention. This happened at Bedford Hills in New York. "Full investigations" can be launched, but they rarely focus on the pent-up frustration of no change after agonizing conditions have been ignored by "proper channels" even when women have gone about expressing their grievances in a reasonable way.

"What people fail to realize is that being locked up at all is punishment enough," said Barbara Collins, now out on parole after four years in a state prison. "They think you come to prison to be punished—and so you're punished in all kinds of ways while you're there.

"But there are times you can get pushed too far—and you just can't keep your mouth shut. You can't lose your pride one more time without giving up some part of yourself, and that's the only thing you have. . . ."

Like our society at large, prisons seem crisis prone. The response to disruptions is a microcosm of the American Way, where we condone or ignore the violence of racism, poverty and imprisonment—but condemn the violence of resistance or reaction to it.

We denounce violence and riots, but we fail to equate daily violence perpetrated in more subtle ways. Women at the House of Correction "hurt" four male guards and a matron. But how closely do we consider that seventy-seven out of the ninety-two women there were *awaiting* trial? Further, how adequate are the social welfare services in providing for the children of these women? And what are their feelings and experiences as confined people, helpless mothers?

When we witness any violent outburst, we seem to forget that this kind of predicament doesn't happen in a vacuum, that it is a response. To examine the crisis alone is myopic and sensational. We must probe more deeply for the real causes—otherwise we continue blindly and blandly to place Band-Aids on cancerous sores.

The origin of every outburst in prison is woven into the day-to-day fabric of prison life. First of all, women being punished for violating society's standards by being incarcerated enter a new social order with its own regulations and status quo. The order dictates a picayune system of discipline, where crime and punishment revolve around behavior issues which could never be "taken to court" in the larger society. Central to the system is the fact that prisoners have privileges, not rights. A sign in the dining room of the women's House of Correction in Chicago, Illinois, expresses the core focus of prisoner "rights":

> Words were made to be spoken
> Voices were made to be used
> If you speak lightly, and also politely,
> This privilege will not be abused.

In prison speaking can become a privilege, not a right. Visitors are a privilege. The smallest things we take for granted on the outside become a matter of rewards to be allowed or withheld: showers, mail, laughing out loud, touching, walking slowly, running, dancing, smoking, eating. Even the quantity of sugar or milk in coffee is of consequence.

"I went to get sugar for my oatmeal," Marlene Riffert says. "I took a spoonful and then the matron came up and took my bowl away and threw the cereal in the garbage. I was so shocked, I didn't say anything, I just looked at her. She said, 'You know you already used sugar in your coffee.' I was given three nights' early bed." Marlene had violated a sacrosanct rule at the House of Correction in

Philadelphia: she attempted to use sugar in her coffee *and* on her cereal at breakfast. Her option was one or the other, not both.

Marlene told this story when she was testifying about conditions at the House of Correction for a Philadelphia court. Inmates from three male institutions and the women's section of the House had filed a class action suing the city for violation of the Fourteenth Amendment—cruel and unusual punishment.[1]

She sat dwarfed in the witness box and explained her history: she ran away from home at age sixteen, was declared "incorrigible" by the state and locked up at the House of Correction. That was 1962. She was there again in 1963, 1970 and 1971. She is in detention this time for possession of narcotics. Her voice is small and shaky as she talks about her unresolved drug problem, her husband at Graterford prison and their two-year-old son. She says she is testifying because she thinks "things should change" for the women who will follow her into the jail.

She tells the judge that when she finishes her testimony and goes back to the jail, she is scheduled to go into solitary confinement for another infraction of rules at breakfast. "Men work back in the kitchen," she says. "They're from over on the men's side. . . . I was on the line getting my food. Well, the men were bringing the food in from the outside and the door opened and I looked at one of the men. I didn't wave or call him or nothing. I just looked at him. When I got to the end of the line the matron said, 'Marlene, you're going to get lockup when you get back from court. I said, 'What for? For looking at the men?' She said, 'Yes.' "

Bizarre as it may seem, this kind of infraction is not uncommon in institutions that hold both men and women in separate sections of the same jail. At Cook County Jail in Chicago, which warden Winston E. Moore describes as "one of the best-run jails in the country," women are put in lockup for talking through the window in sign language to men in other sections of the massive jail complex. Passing "kites" [notes] is an automatic lockup.

More rarely prisoners are disciplined for "talking on the wall" to the men on the floors below them. By getting down on the floor and putting your ear to the wall, you can hear voices from the other floors through the air vents. Men and women signal each other with

1. *Bryant vs. Hendrick*, 444 Pa. 83, 1971. The court found conditions at the three jails to constitute cruel and unusual punishment. The city is appealing the decision.

specified numbers of knocks on the wall and sometimes carry on long, intimate conversations throughout the day and night. Since it's almost impossible to stop the conversations, inmates and guards have established a truce; matrons usually tolerate such an exchange as long as they don't personally witness it. Women shout, "Respect" when a matron's coming, and conversations cease as the women stand at attention for the matron passing their cells. ("The time goes fast when you're down on that cold floor talking on the wall," Toni says. "You get tired of talking to women all the time. Man, on Saturday nights those walls be steamin'.")

The only opportunity male and female prisoners have to see one another close up at Cook County Jail is when they go to co-ed concerts Winston Moore has instituted since he became warden. Lou Rawls, Joan Baez, Dick Gregory and several other artists have performed at Cook County in the last three years. On these oc-casions, the women are ushered to the front of the prison yard and seated. Then the male inmates file in and sit down. Women inmates are not allowed to turn their heads, wave, nod or look at the men. After the performance, the women walk out single file. "Heads for-wards, girls." Any woman who looks to the right or left, acknowl-edges someone with her eyes or turns around is banned from future concerts and subject to lockup. ("They seem to think we're going to take our clothes off and lay right down," one inmate said. "They treat us like we're a bunch of nymphomaniacs—not just normal women who like to look at a man every now and then. The whole thing is in their heads. It doesn't have shit to do with what's really going on. . . .")

"Women here are locked in for 'silent insolence' if they raise their eyebrows at an officer or refuse to answer a stupid question," said a caseworker at one prison. "They are never allowed to let go except when they're watching television or having a dance. Even then they're told to keep it down. Sometimes I feel as if I were living in the middle of a nightmare; I don't know how long I'll be able to take it. I've been here one year—and it's the incredible intelligence and sensitivity of the women that's made me stay this long. They need someone to talk to. But I'm just overwhelmed by the needs they have—and my inability to meet them.

"There's no way the unexpected can be incorporated into the living situation here. Custody depends on a known and strict schedule so that the unexpected cannot happen and harm 'security.' No matter what rhetoric they have here about treatment and rehabilitation, any disruption of the schedule or the routine is a security risk. And any woman who does anything she is not supposed to do—even like talk while she's eating—means that she's a 'security risk' and must be locked up or disciplined."

In many county jails, there is no pretense of a disciplinary hearing for women sentenced to solitary jail within a jail. The women are just locked up, period. If there is a disciplinary hearing, it comes sometimes four or five days after the punishment. When women at the Detroit House of Correction refused to work in protest to humiliating search procedures and abhorrent prison conditions, in June 1971, participating strikers were locked in their rooms for several days, some up to two weeks. Before they had been locked up, they sent letters out to the mayor, city council and prison board listing their grievances. In answer to a city investigation of the incidents that followed, then the superintendent, W. H. Bannon, said that "each girl was interviewed to get the facts on how this started." He admitted they were locked in their rooms before they were interviewed, but maintained that "after a period of six or seven days we released each of them without any punishment whatsoever."

In state prisons, disciplinary hearings are more common—but if I were to describe how they seem to a stranger, I would call them "pretend trials"—with the concept of "proving" guilt only make-believe. Although the disciplinary hearings are often called "tribunals, behavior clinics or adjustment hearings," the process is not impartial, nor is guilt or innocence the issue. Guilt is an *a priori* assumption. As one administrator bluntly put it: *"The process used for determining punishment* [my emphasis] includes a hearing with a senior correctional officer, a senior counselor, the warden and a psychologist when he can attend.

"Theoretically a woman can have an attorney present if she wishes, but think of it logically. With court processes so slow and lawyers with so many clients, how many would even consider taking time to come here for a disciplinary hearing? And even if a woman could get a lawyer—how would she pay him?

"A woman can speak on her own behalf and try to convince us she's telling the truth, but *we know what really happened"* [my emphasis].

Inmates say the process is one-sided from the get-go. A matron or guard does a "write-up" or a "blue-slip" which is a summons to come to court. Sometimes offenders are put into solitary before court. If not they usually receive no prior written notice until they are called to behavior clinic or the hearing. The woman is not allowed to call witnesses in her behalf. And the board is not required to give a decision based on evidence.

"It's your word against hers," said one woman who had been in solitary confinement for a week when I met her. "She's always going to win because they're her people, they're going to listen to her. You're just a number or a blank space in their minds. You go in and sit in front of that board and you know you don't have a chance in heaven to get out of going to solitary.

"I got nine days here because Miss Brown in Central Food Service said I refused to drop a pan and clean the grill. She was just upset about her husband being sick and she was taking it out on me. She told me to quit what I was doing and I said 'Just let me finish this pan first.' She just went off on me—started hollering about my 'insolence' and then she wrote me up. Of course she blew it up in front of the Behavior Clinic. They asked me to step into the hall, and about two minutes later I came back in and heard my sentence. Then the guards brought me up here."

Getting "locked up" is a common occurrence for women prisoners, as it is with men. They are all familiar with the "bing," "hole," or "strip cell." These cells are drearily the same in every jail I've visited—windowless and bare. Some have one thin, dirty and bloodstained mattress on the floor. Some have no mattress. Some jails provide blankets for the women confined, some do not. In some quarters, women locked in solitary are allowed to wear prison shifts—in others they are allowed to wear only their underwear or are stripped naked. Toilets are most often flushed from the outside, and women complain that on occasion sadistic matrons play games with flushing the toilets —either flushing them repeatedly until they overflow or not flushing them at all for a day or more at a time. ("If the toilet backs up, there's nothing you can do about it but live with the stench.") Food is passed into the room two or three times a day between the bottom of the dusty door and the unwashed floor, as are sanitary napkins if the woman is menstruating.

"You can't even take a shower or comb your hair. Sometimes they'll remember to pass a comb into you, or toilet paper, but sometimes they forget. And you can imagine what it feels like to use a dirty

Kotex. Last winter I was in solitary for six weeks and they'd leave the windows open and I'd just freeze on that floor. . . ."

A joke among women is the names used for solitary confinement. What was originally called "the hole" changes to "solitary"/"max" "administrative segregation"/"punitive segregation"/"isolation"/ "the quiet room"/"security cell"/"control center"/"reflection"/"behavior center" or, currently, among the satirists, "loss of privilege module." At Cook County Jail, Lieutenant Dorothy Zeno explained, "We don't call this the hole or confinement, we call it the Blue Room." [It was painted blue.]

Although the euphemisms may be more tolerable titles for outsiders or administrators, the reality for prisoners in max is unchanging. Often women say they are afraid they will lose their minds or whatever sense they might have of who they are, where they are. Women sent to solitary who are experiencing severe emotional difficulties are sometimes driven to hurting themselves by trying to slash their wrists with any sharp object they can find (such as a piece of metal from the window) or burning the mattress if they can get matches. Often they are kept even longer in solitary for having tried to hurt themselves. Some administrators say they have no other means of coping with such problems.

"You lose track of time, you start feeling crazy, even though you know you're not there for anything," one woman said. "It's hard enough if you're strong or you can direct your anger on the people who deserve it for putting you there. But some women are sick to start with and just plain need help. When you put them in there, they're going to go crazy. I'll never forget one night listening to an eighteen-year-old girl just crying and screaming. She kept saying, 'Please somebody talk to me. Please just talk to me. I think I'm losing my mind. Oh, God, help me.' Any one of us would have gladly gone down and talked to her, but we was locked up, too. It just made me cry to hear her. And you know the matrons weren't going to talk to her. Those two be sitting down there saying to each other, 'She'll get used to it. She gotta learn sometime.' "

Becky Careway, at Ohio Reformatory, said, "I guess it used to be a whole lot worse in here. Miss Riley, the warden before Miss Wheeler, would shave your head bald for walking on the grass and put you in maximum security for no less than six months."

Becky said she had been in max several times for short periods of time. Once for refusing an order from the matron while working in the kitchen and another time for stealing supplies from the storeroom. "They didn't have no evidence on me. My room was clean. But I went to max anyway. I usually go peacefully. But one night the matron, who's a drunk, told me I hadn't swept the floor good enough, and it was swept good enough. Besides, she had just been drinking and she was all loud and sloppy. I told her, 'Bitch, call the guards, 'cause you ain't taking me nowhere.' The motherfucker . . . if I didn't have two more years before parole, I would have liked to slam into her. She called the guards, though, and I went with them."

A constant source of tension for women is discretion in enforcing rules and handing out punishment. "You never get away from it— it's always different strokes for different folks." When two women behave in the same way and only one is punished, others naturally are incensed at the injustice. Often women involved in the same incident are dealt with in different ways, even when the basic infractions are just plain silly.

Sharon Wiggins, sentenced to life at the State Correctional Institution for Women at Muncy, Pennsylvania, for instance, was charged with possession of fifty cents—which is "contraband" on "campus." All official monetary exchanges are transacted on paper.

"I was sitting on the steps in front of Sproul Cottage, and Mrs. Spaulding and three guards and three maintenance men drove up and told us to come into the building. They didn't say what they wanted. She stripped us and searched us. She made me pull down my Kotex to look. She found fifty cents on me, so she wrote me up. The male guards and maintenance men were there in case we refused to be searched. But we didn't.

"I was charged with possession of fifty cents, but on the behavior sheet, she wrote that she had searched us for narcotics and implied she knew we had it on us, but she didn't find it. At the time we asked her to take us down for urinalysis after she looked at our arms. We didn't have any narcotics and hadn't used any—so we wanted a urinalysis. She said she didn't have the authority. We asked if she had the authority to search us, she could give us the urinalysis instead and that would be less humiliating—plus it would prove whether we were taking drugs or not.

"But we didn't have a chance to prove ourselves. When they searched me, they said they would have to have a hearing on the fifty cents, but they didn't say nothing about searching for dope. They just wrote it on the behavior sheet and read it out loud at the hearing.

"I spoke in my own defense at the hearing. I was guilty of fifty cents but I said it was not right to write stuff about drugs on my record when she flatly refused to give us a urinalysis which I thought was my right. After the hearing I waited five minutes in the hall and when I went back in they told me what I had. I was locked in my room for three nights from 6 P.M. to 6:30 A.M. for the fifty cents. There's no way to appeal. None of the other three who were stripped and searched were charged with anything because they didn't have nothing on them."

Many prisoners have told me that addicts are discriminated against; at other times I have been told that Chicano women, black women or white women are the ones who are more apt to be "written up" or "called on the carpet" for rule infractions.

Occasionally I heard racial antagonisms from both black and white women. "They're always complaining about how they get the raw end of everything," one white woman said, referring to black women. "But I'm a living testimony to the fact that whites get fucked over just as bad. You can't tell me any different. If you ask me, they got more privileges than I ever had. I get tired of all their bellyaching. I got some black friends, but they're not into that bag all the time. If you lived here, you'd know what I mean. I just get tired of hearing black this and black that and black, black, black. . . ."

"We don't get shit around here," a black woman said. "Don't tell me no white girl has to do time like I have to do time. They get the best and they still be carrying that white thing around on their shoulders, signifying and strutting—like ain't I somethin. . . . You'll see it, they get away with all kinds of shit we get locked for."

Although some racial hostilities give vent to "disciplinary problems," most of the women in the prisons I visited maintain that tensions are created by the staff and staff policies, not by the women themselves. They say staff tactics are used to "divide and rule."

"There is a lot of racial tension because there's the feeling that whites get treated better," Sharon Wiggins said. "They get the better job assignments and they don't get sentenced to Clinton (maximum-security "cottage") as much. So they get parole sooner, too. If a white girl breaks a rule, she's more likely to get a warning than get written up. Inmates are ready to fight then because they say, 'Hey, I did the same thing but I got written up for it.' Then they take it out

on the other women instead of the matron. There are fights, but nobody's been hospitalized.

"The guards and the officials are the problem. Some of them do it
on purpose because they're very prejudiced. Others have just never
been around blacks so it's a natural thing. The problems don't come
from the white inmates, but from the officials. The administration has
started a group for the staff to talk about things like that—and it has
made a small difference." [Out of the staff at Muncy, there's one
black guard and seven whites; one black matron and sixty-three
whites. All the administrators are white except the head of the school.
The religious leaders, medical staff and counseling staff are white.
Up to three years ago, there had never been a black person on the
staff.]

"The general policies favor whites," Sharon said. "Fifty-three per
cent of the population is black and 47 per cent is white. But there's
only two black girls on the farm who have higher paying jobs and
I'm one of them. I make $1.00 a day. All the other office positions
—nine of them—are held by white girls."

At Cook County Jail in Chicago, where 85 per cent of the staff is
black, women say the policies and jobs and discipline favor blacks—
who are 80 per cent of the prison population.

"A girl from a southern state came in here and three of the women
were gonna beat her up," said Maria Fisher, an inmate in Cook
County. "She was from Alabama or Mississippi or one of those states.
It was three against one and I told them, 'If you wanna fight one by
one, that's okay. But three against one ain't fair.' I had just been sick
and didn't feel too good, but I told them they were forcing me into
it. 'She's a whitey, you gonna fight for a whitey?' I said, 'I don't care if
she's a greenie, three to one ain't fair.' The officer was there but she
wasn't doing anything. She was just sitting at her desk pretending
nothing was happening 'cause she wanted to see the white girl get
licked, too. Anyway, it was really wild in here; I got hit in the chest
with a wastebasket and hurt pretty bad.

"But I'm not gonna beat her just because she came from a southern state. She can't help where she comes from any more than anybody else can. The officer locked her up after the fight and spit on her
and threw water in her cell. I used to think it was whites against
blacks in America, but in this jail it's blacks suppressing whites and
blacks."

Maria, thirty-four, had been in Chicago's House of Correction waiting trial on a homicide charge for more than a year. She said she was maligned at the jail for having been previously associated with the Black Panther party: "They're just so afraid of revolution in here. I'm not with the Panthers, any more, but I'm a revolutionary. I been a revolutionary since I was born.

"One of the officers she says to me 'Look what they've been doing to us for four hundred years—it's about time they got theirs.' I told her, 'Hey, look, I'm not four hundred years old, but I know I'm black. You're just finding out. I was born in Jamaica and when I first came to this country, black was the worse thing I could have called you. You're not black just because your skin is black. The way you use your power is just as bad as the way white people use it. It looks to me you're trying to be just the same."

In general it seemed to me that the imprisoned women I met had broken through prejudices and racial barriers in positive, if not remarkable, ways. "We all come out of the same bag, baby," a thirty-year-old black woman told me. "They can't put that old divide and conquer thing on us. We know where it's at. It's the same in the free world, really, but people don't dig it yet."

Although women work through most of the problems themselves in individual friendships and group sessions when they're needed, the effects of class and race prejudice are still an institutionalized and personal strain. Latin and Chicano women, for instance, are not allowed to speak Spanish in many institutions. In spite of changes at some prisons, they are generally not allowed to read or write letters in Spanish (because the censors can't translate), subscribe to Spanish-language newspapers or magazines or converse with visitors or friends in Spanish.

Lydia Amada, a Puerto Rican woman from New York, said that even though there was one Cuban, one South American and two other Puerto Rican prisoners who didn't speak English "except for 'Yes, yes,'" they were not allowed to speak Spanish at Muncy. "One day another girl and I were talking and an officer snuck up and yelled, 'No foreign languages can be spoken here on the farm,'" Lydia said. "I told him 'It's not a foreign language to me.' They make you feel you're a foreigner because you can't speak English. I tell them, 'As far as I'm concerned, *you're* all foreigners.'

"It's not so bad for me since I speak some English, but I speak Spanish anyway when the matrons aren't around. My attitude here is, since you have to do time, why be miserable and get locked up in solitary . . . so I get along pretty good."

Although it may seem ludicrous that a woman is punished for speaking her native tongue, harboring fifty cents in change or "insubordination" because she didn't clean the grill in a kitchen, what is put into a woman's file is serious business. The behavior record could be said to be a matter of life and death to prisoners who want to get out. Although the individuals are never allowed to hold or see their own files, staff members, parole board members, law enforcement officers and commutation board members can see and use them. On the basis of what is in the file, institutional personnel write progress evaluations or recommendations for parole. On the basis of staff evaluation, and their own brief contact with prisoners, parole board members determine when a woman can be released under supervision to the community. When "threat to an officer," "contraband," "fighting" or "assaultive behavior" is written on her record, it doesn't appear that a woman is working in her own interest, obeying rules or "prepared to respect law and order in the community."

Because of "indeterminate sentences" for women in so many states (see Chapter 7), parole depends totally on a prisoner's institutional record and ability to convince the parole board within fifteen minutes or less usually that she is "rehabilitated." A poor behavior record almost guarantees an extra year or more in prison—and sometimes determines as much as five or ten more years. Of course most women count on getting paroled before their maximum possible sentence is served (up to twenty-five or even sixty years for robbery alone), but the pressure of possibly "maxing out" still provides the feeling of trying to balance on a tightrope. Every woman is aware that her immediate behavior affects her future.

Some women give up caring about when they will get out. "I could have did a year," said a parolee from Clinton, the New Jersey state prison for women. "But I did three 'cause I was a sho' nuff bitch. I had that attitude, 'You can throw me in here, but I'm gonna do my time my way.' Once I spent thirty-six days in the hole. It was the same day Kennedy was killed and everybody was watching TV. Some of us wanted to put records on instead but the matron said, 'This is your history in the making.' We said, 'Whose history? Ain't our history!' Anyway, somebody set fire in the cottage. I knew who set it. It wasn't me, but I wouldn't tell who did it and they knew I knew.

"This guard took me to the cell and he told me to take my clothes off. I told him I wasn't gonna take shit off in front of him, the honky white motherfucker. He snatched me and tore my clothes off. I kicked him and jumped him. I knew I wasn't gonna win 'cause he was too big, but I wasn't gonna strip in front of him. He beat the hell out of me and handcuffed me spread-eagle to the bed. The matron was out there in the corridor and she didn't do nothing. My bra and dress had been ripped off but my panties were intact. I lay spread-eagle like that for about six hours. Then another dude, he was pretty nice, he came in. He took me out of shackles and gave me salve for my face and a slip to wear. He told me he was sorry. Yeah, I was sorry, too. That motherfucker had closed my eye. Believe me, I called his mother every name in the book. . . ."

"Lois" said she figured she couldn't handle worrying about when she would get out; and saw no alternatives to serving three years rather than one. Other times women say they just "go off"; they "can't take it any more." They say their write-ups are "worth it"—like the time Theresa Derry got nine months in solitary for taking a bath in a female officer's bathtub: "It was hot and I was tired of taking a shower standing on the bare concrete floor. So I went up to Miss Taylor's room in the administration building, filled the tub with water and bubble bath and crawled in. The girl who was my lookout fell asleep and the next thing I knew, Miss Taylor came up, opened the door and asked me, 'What do you think you're doing??!!' 'What the fuck does it look like I'm doing? I'm taking a bath.'"

There are also peer rewards in being a rebel. ". . . You live in a whole fantasized world of Miss Bad Girl," said Fran Chrisman, who did time in both New York and California. "And the badder you are the more strength you have because you're looked up to by the inmate population. Also, once you've established yourself, they don't mess with you so much. The guard who says she's not scared of the women is lying. . . . She says 'move' and you say 'make me.' That's why they have male guards put women in the hole. Some male guards can't believe what they see out there. . . ."

For the number of women who play "Miss Bad Girl" there is an equal number who are pushed to the opposite extreme of becoming passive nonentities in response to the pressure. But the majority seem to concede to the power structure and adjust to doing "easy time"—getting prison wise to stealing extra food, trading favors, sneaking to see friends. Superficially, the threat of confinement and a poor behavior record contribute greatly to management and control of the institution for administrative purposes. But in the long run, ironically, the repressive security considerations add to the development of all the qualities prison is supposed to erase, not promote: dishonesty, cheating, stealing, hustling, evasiveness. These attributes are usually necessary for prison survival. They are necessary for co-opting the system, staying out of the hole, getting parole. Honest or direct responses to the conditions—like openly asking for extra food, striking for better work conditions, sticking up for someone else, asserting your rights openly—mean punishment and a poor record. Another irony is that it is just as often the little or insignificant things—not the big issues—that give a woman the "bad" record that denies her parole or commutation.

When Evelyn Newman applied for commutation of her life sentence, she had had a "good record" at Muncy for ten years. She had been convicted of conspiring to murder her husband in 1959 following a three-day trial and a jury verdict that took less than three minutes to determine. Although Evelyn maintained her innocence, she said she pled guilty under an intense threat from the district attorney: Don't plead and you'll get the electric chair. Do plead and you'll get life.

Under Pennsylvania law, someone doing a life sentence can apply for commutation when she has served nine years of the sentence. After ten long years in the mountains on the isolated Muncy farm, Evelyn was sure she would get commutation. During her time in prison, she had worked every day and conducted herself "well." In the ten years, she was separated from her children, who had been five, four and sixteen months when she went to prison. They were put into foster homes and shuffled from one shelter to another. She gave her youngest son up for adoption. "I didn't want to do it," she said. "It broke my heart. I couldn't bring myself to sign the papers, but they kept pressuring me. I felt I just couldn't sign my baby away—but I finally realized I was being selfish. I realized I couldn't be mother and father to him with the time I had. So I signed the papers and adopted Charles out."

Despite the heartbreak, Evelyn hung onto the dream of getting out and being mother again to her two oldest children. She lived with a sure faith of getting commutation. When the time came to apply, even her mother-in-law wrote a recommendation for her release to the state commutation board. "She knew how her son treated me, and she wrote a beautiful letter on my behalf. Everybody was for me, except the state." Evelyn was denied release on lifelong parole. She was never given a reason. Her bitterness made her tremble as she sat in her cell telling me about it. "I mean, I thought ten years with a good record should mean something.

"Sure, I got a lot of demerits—there's no angels in jail, but mine were always for contraband—perfume, makeup, eyebrow pencils, earrings. I had my connections and always got busted for it. I couldn't never understand why . . . something that a woman wants and needs. But they wanted to strip you of your femininity. . . ."

Evelyn was not the only person looking forward to her commutation. "When my daughter found out I didn't get commutation, she got rebellious and ran away from home," Evelyn said. "I got bitter, too, and decided I'd leave this joint of my own accord. That's when I got the additional time [five years] for attempted prison breach . . . and we didn't even get out. I just had the screen off my window. But the whole thing had taken me out. My mother said my daughter asked her, 'What does it feel like to have a mother?'"

Just as Evelyn Newman eventually decided to make her own freedom by escaping after having no explanation, no legitimate outlet for her despair, people otherwise seemingly oblivious to their inner hysteria in a pressure-cooker environment will either recoil or explode eventually if they're not already thoroughly shattered. It's bound to happen.

Sometimes it's an individual response to an affront; sometimes it's a delayed reaction. Because of the numbing effect of everyday humiliations, tension among prisoners sits like dry kindling ready to burst into flame spontaneously.

Whether or not outsiders hear about it, there's some kind of eruption in a jail or prison every week, every month. But as Sydney Shaw, at California Institution for Women said, "When they go too far with the women, there's bound to be an explosion. . . . But if there's a riot and I'm killed, I don't want it to be over a sandwich."

In fact, a "taco search" at CIW was one such event that disrupted the delicate balance of emotions at the institution. Windows on buildings and a vehicle were smashed one day in February 1972 after all the women in the dining room had been "searched" for tacos as they left the cafeteria. Later the women referred to the incident as "The Great Taco Shake."

"It's a no-no to take food out of the dining room, but usually we can manage surreptitiously to stock up for midnight snacks," said Joanne (Friday) Fry. This particular day women looked forward to Mexican food and the expectation of a snack before bed. ("Eat one, stash one.") But officers were waiting at each door, patting each woman down, checking pockets as women started to leave the dining room. ("Check that out! That police is chasing that woman half-way across the lawn to try to take her tacos. What a trip." "Hey, haven't they got anything better to do?")

"It was a very tense situation," Friday wrote later in *The Clarion*. "A small thing like this can be the spark that starts the holo-caust . . ." she wrote. "As we said, it is against the rules to take food from the dining room. Perhaps this is one of the many small rules that needs looking into, changing. Obviously we can't have grocery stores or restaurants in our cells. Aside from the stench of spoiled food, the mass invasion of ants and other insects is discouraging. But why not a reasonable quantity of food for eating later?

"It is this kind of added frustrations and tensions that make tem-pers short. Short tempers lead to unnecessary violence. But these things can be avoided. Communication is important. So far we can't find anyone who will admit to ordering the 'taco shake.' We can't even ask why; we have no one to ask. When the line of communica-tion is broken, all that is left is frustration. In a caged society like this, frustration can be a dangerous, deadly thing—when there is no where to go with it, no way to alleviate it."[1]

With no way to alleviate the anger or agony of different policies, sometimes the entire population at a prison will respond to vic-timization or alienation as a body—in collective resistance to the af-front to personal dignity individuals are experiencing. A parolee from California Institution for Women wrote to me in detail about a re-bellion at that progressive prison while she was still incarcerated. I say "progressive" because relatively CIW is very progressive. Women wear their own clothes, have pre-parole furloughs, keep birds and fish in their rooms and have an Inmate Advisory Council. I quote her in lengthy detail because these details tell us a great deal about what

1. "Friday's Child," *The Clarion*, California Institution for Women, Frontera, California, Jan.–Feb. 1972.

often happens with "good" intentions designed to protect the women, about inmate-staff communication, about administrative steps used to alleviate or agitate an impending crisis and about the process involved in what is later often termed a "riot" or "militant resistance":

In early March 1971, a woman was hospitalized for an overdose of narcotics, taken while in her cell at CIW. She was a Mexican woman. On the 11th of March 1971, at approximately 1 P.M., a frozen count was called at the institution. A frozen count is a count taken when there is either evidence of an escape or when an inmate is missing from a designated area. Everyone, without exception, returns to her cell, locks in and gets counted. Frozen counts sometime last as long as three hours . . . On this particular day, though, the frozen count was for another reason. We were told as we went to our cells to turn on our telexes for a special bulletin from the superintendent.

Over the telex we were told that we had ten minutes to get rid of any contraband we might have, that at the end of ten minutes a room to room, person and room search would be made. The reason given was that there was an abundance of narcotics on the reservation, and that some people were in danger. Reference was made to the Mexican woman who had taken more than she could handle. There were no incidents, everyone—both inmates and staff—got over the search with as little discomfort as necessary.

Rooms were searched systematically and nothing was destroyed. But in their eagerness to gather contraband, personal, legally issued articles of clothing, jewelry, pottery, shoes and so on were taken in error. The search of the entire prison, every woman in it, took a little over three hours.

Women who had had things of theirs taken as contraband, which were not in fact contraband, and could prove it, petitioned verbally to have these things returned. They were given excuse after excuse and very little was returned to them. After two weeks had passed, tensions were building due to the lack of positive response from administration in regard to the return of personal property, also due to the clumsy, uneducated efforts of staff to bust people using drugs. Even medication that was issued by the nurses became suspect. Because the woman who had almost overdosed was Mexican, the Mexican American Research Organization in the prison was told that they could not have outside guests until an investigation was made. Nor could any of the other groups, but the only group under suspicion was MARA.

Visitors were frequently, during this two weeks, searched, and turned away in some cases because some eager guard decided that some one's mother was a hype, and children were also asked to be searched. Women returning from visits were searched as well. They told us staff were also being searched, but this writer has well founded reason to believe this was a statement made to pacify the tense convicts. In fact, the main source of drugs, a staff member, continued all during this time to supply those women who had cash money with drugs.

A chart, circa 1959, was placed in each control area, describing the symptoms of various drugs and their effects. This was a guideline, supposedly for staff to use in case of suspicion.

On about the 26th of March, thirty-five state employees were called together and told to go to one of the living units and search it thoroughly for drugs. These thirty-five people held various jobs in the prison. Some were cooks, nurses, typists, clerks and some were off-duty custodial staff. But the fact that most of them were not taught how to search, nor were they given any instructions as to what to look for added to the outcome in a disastrous way. Nurses, cooks, clerks and typists are not paid by the state to search convicts or their cells. They are not, in fact, supposed to participate in this kind of thing because of their ignorance of the ways to do it.

At about 1:00 P.M. on the 26th, everyone living in the unit to be searched were locked *out* of their rooms. If they were in the cottage, they were locked in the recreation room that separates the two sides of the unit. The search ended about 4:00 P.M. Behind them these thirty-five people left torn up photographs of children and loved ones, disheveled linens and in some cases footprints on sheets, plants un-potted, gravel in fish tanks torn up, fish dead, parakeets hysterical from being searched, coffee spilled out of jars, makeup dug out of jars, creams probed—and in general a total disrespect for the personal propriety of the convicts that lived there. They were unnecessarily destructive of things that in many cases hold the sentimental value such as children's photos. Things were taken in the guise of being contraband—again that were not in fact contraband. Jewelry, wigs, dentures, toilet paper, bibles and even a bowl or two of guppies were taken as "contraband."

Dinner that night was tense, uptight, angry and ready to explode. I thought that night was awful, but the next day I was to learn what it feels like to be in the midst of a human explosion, with enough input into it to either help it explode or help to detonate the bomb the pigs had created . . .

The next day, at 1:00 P.M., thirty-five employees at the prison descended en masse on the unit in which I was housed. I was at work. The women in the unit across the path came and got me. They were angry, upset and demanding that we do something to stop this madness. I went illegally—out of bounds—to the superintendent's office. She had the associate superintendent and the chief of institutional police (a WCS IV) with her . . . I demanded that they go at once to the unit I lived in and stop the destruction taking place there. They said they couldn't do that, that it was a necessary precaution against drug use in the prison. I then told them in blunt, hostile words that unless they stopped the pigs in the unit, I was going to incite a riot that was already well on its way to becoming. They told me I was too smart to do that . . . They then proceeded at a very slow pace to go to the unit and survey the holocaust that their subordinates had created under the title of searching. The administrators did not stop the search, they did not request that the staff be more careful not to destroy, they in fact merely looked on for over an hour.

At four that day, the yard was a bubbling boiling sea of indignation. It was decided by some of the women who are usually looked to for leadership by the rest of the population, that the next day no one would go to work nor would we lock in. We would lay out on the grass and refuse to move until our requests were met, our property returned or paid for by the state, and a guarantee given that this kind of thing would never happen again.

The cooperation of some six hundred women did not come until they were pushed so far up the wall by the staff they had no choice. Women with parole dates were ready to forfeit their freedom for this cause, others who intimated they would not cooperate were told in vague terms what their station within the prison would be if they didn't. It is not easy to be told by the forty women you live with that none will ever speak to you again if you do not join with them.

By that night the feelings in the units were that we shouldn't wait until tomorrow, we should sit down in the TV rooms, refuse to be counted at ten or to go to our cells until our things were returned. Since tear gas had been used on three women not too many weeks prior, this idea had its dangers and most of the constructive women in the prison wanted to avoid any physical violence that the pigs might incite by their attitudes and/or actions.

At this point, this writer and several other women were called to a special meeting with the associate superintendent as representatives from each living unit . . . His offer (broadcast at ten over the telex): by eight the next morning every article of contraband would be returned, and a meeting would be held with every counselor present and representatives from the convict body as well as the Inmate Advisory Council. Everyone locked in by ten thirty that night, with the agreement that if at 8 the next morning things were not returned, they would not go to work but would proceed to the original protest plan. The only ones exempt from this were hospital workers . . .

At the meeting the next day, the only agreement we could reach was that the superintendent should have a face to face confrontation with the entire campus as soon as possible. At eight that morning, almost everything was returned, but the women had not been given any assurance that this would not happen again . . . So as we ended the meeting, we were told that the lawn was covered with convicts, that they refused to eat, work or move. We were asked to go out and tell them that the superintendent would meet with them and hear them out at 2 P.M. in the auditorium. We were also asked to keep things under control, which we refused to do. We felt that we were all together on this, and none of us could make a commitment or decision for all of us.

I told the women in my unit that I was with them, if they decided not to listen, or if they felt they were not being given honest commitments from the prison, we would all go to the rack together. That if one of them got into it, all of us were in it. This same thing was said in every unit that day.

At 2:00 P.M., the auditorium was packed. There were four men, in suits, whom we had never seen before, escorted by staff and seated at the back of the room. Earlier that day, myself and another convict had heard the WCS IV [guard] telephone one of the men's prisons nearby and request support, extra guards, etc. Thus, the four men were in fact armed with guns of some kind, and were not merely observing. We'd been told they were reporters, but when I asked one where he was from he said CIM [California Institution for Men].

The confrontation went on and on, not only the searches, but many grievances were aired. Nothing much was accomplished, unless you consider a promise made by a cornered prison administrator an accomplishment. We were told: we would not be abused in this way again; the clothing and property cards would be brought up to date; staff would continue to search but would be required to leave things as she found them and to have the women called to the unit before the search. Staff would also have a form to fill out with room number and convict's name and a complete list of anything staff removed from the room on it.

Two things that came out of the confrontation that had more of an effect than the searches did: One, a woman who had spoken out in the auditorium was give a 115 [a write-up] later that day for a minor thing, and the Parole Board prolonged her release date for thirty days. The other thing was that certain convicts were labeled leaders, inciters, agitators, militants and several other words that the staff evidently didn't know the meaning of. And these labels are still stuck on us. Our mail was read thoroughly, we were watched, baited, and verbally attacked by several staff. The fact that we could have blown the prison apart with not only a loss of staff lives, but our own, was never recognized. It still is not recognized. When one of those "leaders" or "militants" asks for anything that is usually granted to other convicts, they are denied—but in such a way that there is no recourse for them. I recently received a relatively short time by the Parole Board for parole consideration. This was because they know that to keep me here can only bring my boiling point down lower, that they have not been successful by any of their tactics in trying to force change upon me, and that there is no real reason to keep me here that could be justified in a courtroom.

There are two especially significant points to be made about this crisis at CIW, though there are many more that could be examined at length. First—although the collective resistance and work stoppage could be called *political* because the action aimed to change the use of power more in favor of the prison population's interest, the effect of the resistance was only to change degrading procedures. The most obvious result was the promise of a sophistication or "humanization" of search procedures—not abolition of them. The reaction to the search was no doubt part of a larger perspective and real feeling about the whole institutional structure. But the response came directly from the specific abuses. The resistance thus did not depend on overall political perspective or the collective interest of its victims in subverting the exploitive structure. The outburst subsided pretty quickly after it began—as most prison "riots" do. (No matter how mild the incidents above sounded, they would be termed a *riot*.) And the prison structure remained intact. So, for staff to label a woman involved as a *militant* or *revolutionary* is, as the writer said, an exaggeration or a misnomer. Effective, organized resistance would work underground to subvert the entire institutional structure—to gain real power—not just affect procedure.

It could be said that prisoners as a whole—like citizens at large—respond to exploitation on an individual and collective basis—not because of political theories, but because of their sense of themselves as human beings and their quality of life. Acts of non-co-operation and violence are subject to many interpretations—and a defensive interpretation is to label the actions "sabotage" or "militant activity." The defensiveness stems from people afraid of losing their power or control.

The other significant point is that the writer said, "The cooperation of some six hundred women did not come until they were pushed so far up the wall by the staff they had no choice. . . ." For prisoners to rebel or to take collective action at extreme jeopardy to themselves is the exception, not the rule. Every day in prison, there's non-co-operation, "malingering" and disdain for the structure, resentment of authority. But this differs from conscious political attempts to overthrow the criminal justice system or the prison structure itself. A lot of people in this country theorize that if we were ever threatened with totalitarian government, people would fight back relentlessly, would take up arms and lay their lives on the line. In theory this sounds fine, but in actuality a totalitarian society co-opts the majority of people it controls. It has its system of rewards, incentives, punishments and coercion—just like the society of prison.

Prisoners develop independent standards of personal satisfaction and fair treatment within the prison system that controls their lives. Only those willing to risk death, the future or indefinite solitary confinement will consistently revolt in an open manner. No one in the "Free World" should doubt that they would behave much differently under the same totalitarian system. Many analogies could be made to our everyday lives, but I will leave that for others.

The writer also noted that women who "intimated they would not cooperate were told in vague terms what their station within the prison would be if they didn't [co-operate in the strike]. . . ." Inmate loyalty is part of the expectation of the prison code. But as we have seen before, staff policies, administrative prejudices and an individual system of rewards and punishments, from "extra privileges" to "honor status" to parole considerations, serve to break down solidarity and unity on a day-to-day level. The result is the individual woman's need to create personal strategies for accommodation and survival that will still meet the basic requirements of the code. And in such rule-clad, total surroundings, survival becomes the most important thing to every woman.

It is also true that at times peer pressure can be stifling, adding to the status quo of tensions within the prison. James Ward, a young black correctional counselor at CIW, for instance, said he had been "ineffective" in one cottage, despite his belief that the prison was desperately in need of change.

"I felt my approach was pretty much rejected," he said. "I assumed the women would appreciate a new concept and as a result I made a lot of mistakes in dealing with this population at its own level.

"One thing that hurt me more than anything else was I felt that some of the women would like to do what I'd suggest. . . . But the culture is so strong that if they're accepting the staff, the person is automatically interpreted as rejecting her peers and culture.

"It's hard to work with a group that's rejecting you outright or sitting silently while others do—or to have women come into the office afterwards and tell you what they really feel but not say it in front of the group. Some of the women would be one person in the group and another in my office. This was hard for me to accept."

Whatever the consequences, the "code" remains intact. And in the prison structure, it seems a necessity for survival.

It is amazing there are as many petitions, grievances and revolts as there are—considering pressures on individuals to stay in line. It is indicative of the conditions prisoners live in that they rebel in spite of the personal consequences they face.

But inmates are becoming increasingly aware of their rights. Administrators say they're getting "more militant." Women and men in prisons all over the country are beginning to question more and more *why* they are in prison.

As a result of massive civil rights and anti-war actions in the last sixteen years, prisoners otherwise isolated have been exposed to the politics of college-educated people and intellectuals sentenced to prison, as well as white, brown and black militants. These middle-class newcomers, including those sentenced for narcotics offenses, are shocked by the blatant violations of their rights inside prisons. Their families and supporters have been outraged by the physical conditions and mental anguish. These people have shed new light on many conditions that long-time prisoners previously saw as a way of life, "normal" for prison.

Increasing numbers of prisoners are beginning to look at the entire system from a new perspective. They are seeing it from the outrage of the liberal middle class. The pieces begin to fit together and they are beginning to see themselves as the victims of class and race oppression. They are also looking beyond the immediate conditions to the system in broader terms—realizing that anyone, for instance,

who expressed their intentions to be politically involved upon release, would probably be denied a parole. And that a person who
is to be considered *rehabilitated* must present an attitude of repentance and conformity to prison norms.

A demonstration at the Federal Reformatory for Women in Alderson, West Virginia, beginning September 14, 1971, reflected the increasing awareness and sophistication of demands affecting the entire
system. Following the deaths of prisoners and guards at Attica, the
women held a memorial service for their slain brothers. Following the
service and a march around prison grounds, which was approved by
the administration, some of the women gathered to sleep in the
prison yard. Earlier in the summer 300 women had signed a petition
urging clarification and reform of parole procedures. It was part of a
petition campaign in many federal prisons. Nothing had been done
about it and there had been a growing dissatisfaction with the lack of
results.

About 130 black, white and Latin women then occupied the old
garment factory on the prison grounds and drew up forty-two demands to present to the administration. Representatives from various
"cottages" sat in on the sessions and after the first day, some 500
women out of the 600 inmate population stopped work and school
for four days to support the demands. Prison officials, along with a
lawyer from the Federal Bureau of Prisons, agreed to a number of the
demands but said that many of the others were "out of their jurisdiction." They told the grievance committee the demands agreed to
would need to be rewritten in "legal language" and then would be
implemented. The women said they would wait to see how the agreements were written up.

On Saturday, September 18, male guards wearing gas masks and
carrying sticks were called into the prison. The women left the building to avoid a violent confrontation. Prison officials announced the
incident was over and that agreements about grievances had been
negotiated successfully.

But women in various cottages were still talking about continuing
the work stoppage until the demands were implemented. On Monday, September 20, about forty guards from neighboring correctional
institutions again came on "campus" with gas masks and sticks. A
Greyhound bus was parked nearby. One of the men called out names
of prisoners through a bullhorn and sixty-six women were ordered

without warning to board the bus. When some resisted they were maced and dragged aboard. The women were transferred to the Federal Youth Center at Ashland, Kentucky. About ten days later, fifty-nine were flown to the federal penitentiary at Seagoville, Texas, and the others were returned to Alderson. Their families and lawyers were not informed of the move.

Some of the women from Alderson said they'd like to know what programs could have been set up at Alderson with the money the Federal Bureau of Prisons used to finance the flight to Texas alone.

The women's demands related directly to the prison itself, including the establishment of a work-release program; an open mail policy, more caseworkers, sufficient diet planning (pork-free, bland, salt, etc.), more complete commissary stock and lower prices. They asked for a complete law library, as well as medical examinations as prerequisite for job assignments, and sufficient reasons for severe disciplinary punishment. Also related to institutional life were demands for the freedom to choose cottages, and washers and dryers in all the cottages.

The chief focus of the demands, however, was on the larger, total system. They asked for contracts for halfway houses and that Congress appropriate enough funds to enable educational rehabilitation programs to function properly. They noted that the budget for educational facilities had been cut from $18,000 to $11,000. They also demanded that funds be appropriated for emergency furloughs— such as critical illnesses, family deaths, childbirth, etc.

Much of their concern was directed at the parole system. They, along with federal prisoners in Danbury, Connecticut, and Springfield, Missouri, demanded changes in the operation and effect of the U. S. Parole Board:

1. The Parole Board should recognize that prison is destructive of our personalities, our humanity, and our ability to cope well with society. Since this effect is contrary to the Bureau of Prisons' expressed aim of "rehabilitation," the board should adopt the policy of speedy release for all prisoners.

2. The Parole Board should be required to give reasons for its decisions.

3. Parole Answers for both hearings and write-ins should be given within two weeks. [Alderson inmates said it takes six to eight weeks or longer to hear from President Nixon's board. Under the Johnson administration, women said it took two to three weeks.]

4. A person should have access to all the material in the file that the Parole Board uses to judge her case.

5. There should be no parole restrictions that interfere with a person's freedom of association, freedom of travel, and freedom to participate in legal, political and social activities. Parole should not be revoked without a positive conviction on a new charge.

6. People released on mandatory release rather than parole should not be under restrictions.

7. There should be a party beyond the Parole Board to whom parole or mandatory release revocations and Parole Board decisions can be appealed.

8. The Bureau of Prisons should insure that there is institutional cooperation for prisoners who want help with their release plans (jobs, furloughs, contacting potential employers and community resources, etc.)

9. Lawyers should be made available to represent or advise people before and during their parole hearings, when this service is requested.

There has still been no real response from the U. S. Parole Board. Women are still kept waiting in the isolated hills of West Virginia from eight to twelve weeks following their interviews before they hear whether they'll be granted or denied parole.

Ninety-eight per cent of them will eventually get out—whether it's on parole or at the termination of their maximum sentence. Ninety-eight per cent of all prisoners are eventually released. Will their voices be heard before they hit the street? And will anyone listen then?

Part II THE CONCRETE WOMB: "BEIN' IN"

When you starts measuring somebody, measure him right, child, measure him right. Make sure you done taken into account what hills and valleys he come through before he got to wherever he is.

—Mama Younger's advice to her daughter,
from Lorraine Hansberry's A Raisin in the Sun

I felt that my world was gone. That I was dead. Just dead. I was totally numb to everything that was happening—completely numb. I had no feelings, no emotion at that time. I felt very cold and very cut off. I felt like my life had ended. You must realize, Kitsi, that I had committed the act of murder . . .

—SUE MOSS, after the stabbing death of her husband

Pat

"Coming here to prison wasn't too much of an adjustment for me. It's a lot like Indian boarding school was. I was raised on a reservation and then they took me to boarding school on the same reservation when I was five and a half years old. I never left until I was thirteen. So for eight years I was confined to just that one area. The school was very confining, very strict."

The woman talking was "Pat Red Cloud,"* a member of the Blackfoot Indian tribe in Canada. Pat, a tall, elegant woman with smooth umber skin, strong facial bones and long, straight black hair, guided me around the grounds of California's state prison for women. She spoke in low tones; her words deliberate and sometimes spoken after long pauses of thought. We stopped repeatedly, comfortable with the silences to watch birds, to study two fat goldfish in a small pond by the greenhouse, to appreciate the sky.

"We can have birds and fish in our rooms," she told me after pointing out where the lawn crew works and telling me of the job details women prisoners have as auto mechanics, electricians, plumbers, tractor drivers and maintenance "men." "A man drives the dump truck, but women haul the trash and do all the work. They repair lamps and TVs and radios and do all the painting. The place is pretty well run by inmates themselves."

Pat had been at the prison at Frontera for eight months on a forgery conviction. It was her first offense. "I was lucky, though," she said. "They could have gotten me for a lot more checks than they did. I wrote more than I can even count now."

While pointing out blatant contradictions such as the green recreation yard which was closed for the Southern California "winter" and opened for three "summer months" in marvelous understatement, Pat said that in spite of the pressures, "I've learned a lot about myself here. In some ways it's been good . . . and now I just want to learn more about myself and how to better communicate with people because that's my number one problem. It always has been.

* Not her real name.

"They say problems here develop because of lack of communication between staff and inmates. But it's not lack of communication between staff and inmates. It's lack of communication between staff and staff. That's what creates problems. We really run our own lives. For me the problem has always been lack of communication between me and other people, period.

"When I was thirteen, they closed down the boarding school I attended, and sent me to a city about a hundred miles away from my home to junior high school. The adjustment was tremendous. There were three Indian students there. By the next year I was the only Indian there. I stayed there through the twelfth grade—as the only Indian. A lot of the students there used to make cracks at me for being a 'savage.' The only Indian they had seen was the Hollywood Indian. They thought I was non-verbal and illiterate—only making little grunts and 'ughs' here and there. That's how Hollywood had portrayed Indians.

"I lived with five different foster parents, who were paid to house me from the ninth grade to the twelfth grade. All they were keeping me for was the money. They didn't take me in as their own. Some of them tried, but they didn't know how to communicate with me. I was backward and shy.

"A lot of times I was tempted to go back to the reservation and just live there. If it wasn't for the encouragement of my parents I probably would have gone back and still be there. I was just going through all sorts of turmoil. The only place I ever felt at home was in the Indian organization they had for Indian people that lived in the city. I felt they were the only people who understood what I was going through. No one seemed to have the interest or understanding about what I was going through except my fellow Indians. Somehow I managed to go through high school—but I wasn't a very good student. If I didn't have all those adjustments I probably could have been a better student. But it was lonely.

"Like many other Indians just coming from the reservation, I had that problem communicating with people. So many times I wanted to communicate my thoughts and feelings—but it didn't seem important enough. I was afraid no one would listen, because they never had; they never had gotten down to the core. I guess I just more or less withdrew into myself and I felt that no one really gave that much care, really.

"Then I wanted to keep on in school but I wasn't happy with that sort of life. I thought changing my environment might be better and people would be more understanding. So I enrolled in a church-oriented school in Provo, Utah—where I thought I might be able to help myself with the help of others. I felt I wouldn't be too far away from my people because I knew there were other Indian people there. And so I journeyed down there not knowing anyone or anything except the fact that I was getting away from this previous environment where I felt like a stranger . . . and knowing I did not want to return to the reservation, knowing I would never be happy staying the rest of my life on the reservation and knowing I couldn't leave if I didn't get an education.

"So when I went to school in Utah, I got involved in Indian activities they had there at the time. It was a very beautiful experience. I was more at ease there. The Indian students were able to communicate with each other and we could express our feelings to each other. The students were more open and accepted me so much better. There were about six or seven of us from Canada and all of us tremendously enjoyed that environment . . . free from the red tape we had to go through in Canada just because we were Indians from the reservation.

"I think those were two of the most beautiful years I had in my life. I felt so happy. I was starting to open up. Before I'd been so afraid to talk to any stranger.

"I wanted to stay and finish school, but I didn't have the funds to finish my education. We had had a grant from Canada, but after two years they dropped it. They thought we could get educated in Canada as well as we could in the United States.

"I was quite indecisive in what I wanted to do. I was debating whether to go back to Canada—but the experiences there . . . there were too many bad memories. I wanted to investigate and kind of look around to see where I could find a place—so I came to California. I had heard about California and so many opportunities and I thought I could come to L.A. and possibly get into the modeling field. I guess I made a big mistake—coming unprepared, not knowing anyone.

"I was scared. I was lonely. The first people I met that made me feel accepted and at home were some black people who were into another way of life. I hung on to them as my friends. I guess they knew I was an easy person—I didn't know much about city life. They made their game sound very easy and very exciting. Their game was forgery.

"One thing I had in my mind was to get some money saved for going back to school to finish my education. So their game sounded very inviting. It sounded like easy money and I thought this is one way I could get money to return to school.

"Before I knew it I seemed to get further and further into the mess. To tell you the truth—it was exciting. It was sorta fun to just walk into a bank and come out with all that money. It was a different way of life for me. I had never had a lot of money and so many pretty clothes and money in my pocket all the time. I'd never lived in a luxurious apartment and had a luxurious car. We had a 1970 Mark III . . . and I guess I was very adept and so I just kept on cashing those checks until I got busted."

The inevitability of Pat's getting busted made me laugh. Seeing her face—her regal Blackfoot appearance—is really an inerasable experience. To think that she walked in and out of banks, oblivious to being identified, getting caught or being remembered in black and white Los Angeles made us both laugh.

"After I got busted, I got out on bail. My old man even convinced me that money could buy my freedom. So after my first bust I even tried harder to get the money, but I knew then I would end up in some prison or jail. But it seemed the further I got into it, the worse it was to get out of it. I was into forgery for a year. But the deeper I got, I really didn't enjoy getting the money. It was a hassle. But the people I was working with counted on me. Plus by then I was paying lawyers and bail bondsmen. I felt it was my job. At the end I wasn't doing it for good times—I was doing it for necessity to set me free. But it didn't set me free. It just sent me to prison.

"The last time I got busted, the fourth and final time, all the holds popped up from all over. There were so many holds there was no way to get out of it. There were detainers from all over the place. It seemed like an endless thing—it seemed like I'd never get through all those court proceedings. I thought, 'Well, this is it.' I guess that was the moment I had been waiting for all the time. I knew this would happen, I might as well accept it. It was kind of a relief for me.

"I had fourteen counts of forgery. I had so many different names I can't even remember them. I went to the first county—the one I got popped in—and they sent me to prison for observation. I dreaded go-

ing to all the other fourteen counties. I went crazy in county jail.
Every time they would take me out to court I would just look at
everything I could see. A tree. The sky. It meant so much to me. It
makes it much easier for me to do time when I can see life around
me. Inside a jail with those bars and everything, you start to forget
there's a world. You miss the earth.

"So anyway, the second county I went to, I said, 'Well, I give up.
I don't want to go to all these other counties. Send me to prison, I
may as well get started doing time in prison.' By some miracle they
dropped all the other charges on me—so I'm here on one commitment. So here I am on another reservation, feeling lucky I didn't get
more time.

"My old man's on the lam—so I can't see him or write him. One
of the stipulations of my parole is that I can't see him. That's going
to be hard . . . but maybe its best, because I don't want to get back
into that life. I love him though . . . and I'm going to keep our
baby. He's a beautiful child." [Their son was almost a year old—and
was in a foster home while Pat was in prison.]

"While I was in L.A. before, I wanted to go down to the Indian
Center but I never got a chance to. I was too busy running in and
out of banks. . . .

"My greatest desire now is to possibly work in a city and help my
fellow Indians that are coming from the reservations, to help them
in their problems in adjusting to city life. One thing my brother Indians need is a helping hand and a listening ear from someone who
understands. . . .

"It's hard for me even now. I guess I never really knew what I
wanted and I really didn't know what was being offered to me. I
was just confused, I guess. This experience sort of stopped my world
and gave me time to think. But now just knowing what I do now and
experiencing what I've experienced . . . I think the biggest thing is
to know me better and communicate with the world better. I still
have my whole life ahead of me."

Trinada

Trinada has been on heroin since the early 1950s. She has been in jail off and on for short stays frequently in the last twenty years—"so many times I can't even count 'em no more." I met her in county jail in California shortly after I had turned thirty and she had turned thirty-eight on the same birthday—February 4. I was feeling young, like my life was just beginning—and she was feeling old and like her life was almost over—"It *is* old, if you think about it in terms of running around in the life," she said.

Trinada had been found guilty of violating 11500.5 Health and Safety Code: possession of narcotics with intent of sales. She got a one-year sentence with a five-year parole. The six months she had spent in jail awaiting trial was "dead time"—it didn't count toward her sentence. When we met, she had three more weeks before release. If she violates parole anytime within the next five years, she will have an automatic two-to-twenty-year sentence to serve in the state penitentiary.

"When I got this sentence here, the court put me on methadone . . . so when I get out with that help, and my own, I should stay drug free. I also have Naline parole and probation for the next five years. Naline is a shot they give you to test your eyes to tell if you have any trace of narcotics in your system, period. They also give you a urinalysis test whenever they want; it's up to your parole officer. That's why so many people are being returned to jail."

The jail Trinada was in was strictly regimented. There were no educational or vocational programs or drug therapy. The women just worked manual jobs and slept. They were not allowed to dance, or to laugh out loud in the dining hall. It was run by deputy sheriffs—the same as other county jails in California.

"A place like this there's less chance of any type of drugs or alcohol getting in to the institution. Here, it's discipline. You learn to control yourself. Your wants and your needs are inside yourself. And you can't do anything about it. Plus, you're doing short time so

you can't sneak anything in. It's telling me, 'You can do without'—
'You don't have to have'—so I guess it's good for me.

"But locking up addicts or alcoholics is not the answer. It's only good on a thirty-to-sixty-day basis to dry you out—'cause your body can only take so much. But it really doesn't make sense. But then, neither does California Rehabilitation Center. I was there, and in my personal opinion, it's a farce. What can one dope fiend do for another? They're the same people you've shot drugs with all your life. What good's it do? Maybe it would be good for youngsters, fourteen- and fifteen-year-olds—but not for us. Besides, the staff are all these people who've learned from books and don't know shit.

"People who get jobs there should have knowledge of life, not books. Then maybe it could mean something. You have these fresh-face, naïve little things trying to find out what it's all about and they can't begin to get to your problems. They're hung up with all the details on the way.

"I don't know why the state feel they're God Almighty and can tell you how to live your life. There's too many strikes against you. Society on the one side, the man on the other, parents on the other, and you jump right off in it.

"The first thing I'm gonna do after I get my first drink is go and see my new grandbaby and see my kids. I might have to go see the parole and probation officer before I get home, though. They say I must maintain employment. But at my age, I'm not thinking about it. I'll probably sit home and knit and crochet—there's good money in it to sell the stuff. At this stage of the game I don't want to spend the rest of my time behind somebody else's bars and gates and things.

"My man needs me, and my kids. I still got three at home. They're six, twelve and eighteen years old and staying with their dad's family. I'm still with him. There's too many years and memories wrapped up in that—can't cut that loose. We can stay together and we will stay together, even though he's still a junkie. We always been together. They tried to keep us apart, but we went to court about that years ago. We fought it and won. They don't give us no trouble now.

"No . . . my main fear now is, will I be able to maintain myself without getting involved in any things that are unnecessary? I have a real fear of getting busted and returned. And I don't wanna face no twenty years in the penitentiary. I don't wanna die in no penitentiary. So I'm gonna try. Just try and maintain myself. I know I can make it."

Georgia

Georgia Walton is the kind of all-American beauty you see in Geritol advertisements in *Better Homes and Gardens*. At twenty-seven with her teased blond hair, slightly lightened and bouffant, she still carries the self-assurance of a high school cheerleader going with the captain of the football team. She tells me she has been at Sybil Brand Institute for Women for three years, four months and four days, and there is no question in her posture: she is a deputy sheriff, a guard, not an inmate. She loves her work. She's made for it and it's made for her. She walks tall and proud in her deputy sheriff's military green skirt and regulation jacket. Her white blouse is spotless, neat, ironed with starch. Her flat regulation oxford shoes—polished to a spit shine—are the only police feature that make her look more like a deputy sheriff than an airline stewardess.

At twenty-seven, she is wife, mother and model of military discipline in the long sanitized corridors of Sybil Brand Institute for Women. She turns keys and recites rules meticulously, almost automatically, with no need to pause for breath or curiosity.

As we walk from the "heartbeat of the jail," the name she calls the control center, Georgia Walton begins to explain the booking process, the "pat search" and the "narco search" in great detail. Her recitation seems automatic, chronicling each step of inmate-guard process, but she is constantly alert, vigilant to inmate movement. On guard, in control. She has to be, she says. That's the way it is.

"After the inmate has been booked, given the pat search, the narco search, bathed, sprayed and dressed, she is brought over here," she says, pointing out all the equipment in a small room. "Everyone is required to have fingerprints and photograph. If her hand is burned, we put her on Identification Room Hold. If it heals while she is here, then the fingerprints are taken. If she's ready for release, and her hand's not healed or is still in a cast or something, she is allowed to leave without having been fingerprinted. And then we are left with no fingerprints. That happens rarely, but it has happened."

This is one of the few exceptions to rules Georgia Walton pointed out. Generally, there are no exceptions. Security reasons don't allow them. She points out the security telephones. "These are all security phones, just like the one I showed you in the fingerprinting room. You can just pick up the phone. I don't even need to say where I am. The light on the main control board shows the exact location. The moment you take it off the hook, the light goes on in the control room and they send in reinforcements within seconds. It's a very effective system."

Georgia Walton understands her job and respects it. She is upset when she hears criticism of the training she got or the job she does. "Some people think that law enforcement officers are inhumane or uninteresting," she says. "Personally, if I became personally involved with every person sitting there crying, I couldn't function in my job. I'm not inhumane—I'm just removed from the emotion.

"If I became upset and showed it, I would lose my self-control and my control over the inmates. If someone has a bloody nose, I say, 'You got a bloody nose. Sit down. I'll call the nurse.' I cannot lose my self-control. I cannot become emotionally involved. Even though I'm concerned sometimes, I cannot show it.

"I really love my work. This is the kind of work I always wanted to do. My father was a policeman. My husband is a policeman. Ever since I was a little girl I said I wanted to be a policewoman. Now I am one. Even though I'm called a deputy, it's the same thing really. It's just a different name."

Mrs. Walton attributes her self-control and ability in her work to her training for the job at the Sheriff's Academy, where she had a stringent sixteen-week training course. "Other people criticized it in an article in the L.A. *Times*," she said, "but I really enjoyed it.

"It was wonderful training for me. I think the stress training was especially valuable. Every word out of your mouth began with 'Sir' or 'Ma'am.' We had tests every Monday—sometimes after no time off. We had to shoot with the men, run long distance with them, work out with them, everything just the same. If we were allowed to smoke, we could go get our cigarettes and smoke. But we had to go to our lockers or wherever we kept them. That's because we carried utility bags, not purses. All we could have in them was our handcuffs, revolver and keys. Women weren't allowed to put lipstick or anything else in there. We couldn't carry cigarettes in our utility bags. If you were caught with cigarettes in your utility bag, you would be up for discipline and punishment. I never carried cigarettes in my utility bag.

"It really is a form of stress training. You have somebody screaming orders at you for sixteen weeks. It's just like the military training. And you get used to the screaming without getting upset. It really developed my self-control. I was yelled at and I had to follow instructions. Now if an inmate yells at me, I don't get upset.

"Classes were also stress. Although there were a couple non-stress. One time we were sitting there and there was a loud noise—like a boom—from behind. You can't turn around in class. Those who turned around had to write a paper on why they turned around. It was like a test to see how much self-control we had, but we didn't know it then. Oh, no, I didn't turn around—I really wondered what it was. But I wouldn't dare turn around."

Marta

The petite Chicano deputy sheriff said good night at the control center and walked with small, precise steps up to the entrance building to the county jail for women. She went to a small safe-deposit box, opened it with one of her ten keys, pulled out a small automatic revolver and put it into a brown leather holster inside her small brown leather purse along with her badge. She punched her time card, told the two officers in the room good night and walked out to her small gray '90 Porsche. She was wearing her sheriff's uniform —a tight green skirt, white blouse and military green jacket.

Marta Fernandez* was giving me a ride back to my hotel from the jail. She hadn't spoken to me from the time we had met until we started to drive down the winding road from the jail back toward the city. Still somewhat shaken at the sight of the gun and the knowledge that she always carries it with her, I commented on what a nice car it was.

"I keep a small car because I don't like to haul people around— and this gives me a good excuse," she said. "I can never fit more than one person in—so it's sort of a built-in safety valve."

She told me that she was single—which put her in a minority of the personnel at the jail. She said that more than half the deputies are married, and half of those are married to other sheriffs. It was 10:30 P.M. and the car was loud on the curving roads into the lights and shadows of the metropolis.

"This work is more liberating than most jobs for women," she said. "We get equal pay all the way and equal opportunities. Less than 1 per cent of the people in the department are women—but we get the same jobs and promotions the men do. We're very lucky. There are not that many jobs for women where you can get this kind of pay.

"But one thing about this job is that it makes social life difficult. The requirements here are more stringent for women than they are for men. They expect us to be more than the average woman. I have

* Not her real name.

to be very careful. The public expects us to be super human—or not be human at all. Therefore the requirements are quite strict on our behavior. People will quickly fink on a policewoman. Personally, I don't like to tell people what my job is. If they really push me, I tell them I work for the county. People don't trust you if they know. They have so many attitudes.

"Most police officers associate with people in the same field. I personally don't. I find it too stifling. But unless they're very sensitive, it's hard to retain a friendship with people in other areas when they know what kind of work you do, because they don't approve or they don't trust you.

"The work is a real strain—it takes a lot out of you. It's heartbreaking sometimes . . . I really couldn't take it after work. I need a totally different environment. Even when I get together with girl friends who are policewomen—and that's rare—we avoid talking about work. You gotta maintain your sanity."

We had arrived in front of the hotel, but Miss Fernandez kept talking about her struggles with her work in controlled, carefully chosen words. "I don't expect to stay in this work for all my career. It takes too much out of me, it's just too draining. I'd like to go into an administrative position—maybe in corrections or in the adult authority—where I could have some effect on the decision-making process. You see, I have a little different background than many of the officers —so I have a little different attitude. I see the women and their problems and I think there but for the grace of God go I. That's why I'd like to do work that's more involved with them—and that's why I'd like an administrative job where I could really effect some change.

"At the jail it's not our duty to become personally involved or to try to rehabilitate or counsel. We're not supposed to. And actually we're so busy booking, fingerprinting and all, there isn't time anyway. The women come in so upset. Some are crying. They think we're so callous and have no human emotion. But we're just so busy processing we don't even have time to get a drink of water half the time. The correctional officers for the state have more freedom. They're not chastised for becoming involved with the girls' problems and personal matters. We are chastised; we are not supposed to become involved in any way. Our duty is custody and security, and that's it. We're there to keep them safe.

"The girls don't think of us as human beings—or as people. Just the little questions they ask—like 'Do you dance?' or 'Would you wear that kind of dress?'—show it. They only see us as robots in green. They must think when we leave here we crawl into a little box. They don't think of us as people.

"And I guess I can understand why—but that doesn't make it any easier. A lot of it is because the deputies are in fact only working for the money. The money really attracts people. When I got my B.A. in fine arts, I had a hard time deciding where to go to work. I didn't want to teach in our schools—they're terrible—and this was one of the only good paying jobs. I had worked as a student in the sheriff's office one summer and I had a very negative attitude towards policemen. They really turned me off. When I was going to graduate, they said I should try it from the other side—and learn what it's like. So I went into it as sort of an experiment. And I've been here three and a half years.

"The problem is that many officers go into the field just for the income . . . to help their husbands or pay for the mortgage. I think they can be more detached because they're only in it for the money. If they were screened more for interests in the work itself, they could have people be more sensitive. There has to be some kind of balance."

I was still trying to deal with the fact that Deputy Fernandez was an artist, a painter, working as a deputy sheriff, when it was time, finally, for me to get out of her car. I was thinking about my own early attitudes toward cops and her statement, "They must think when we leave here we crawl into a little box," when I got out. The pain in her face was clear.

Louise

Louise Bezie's face is round and beautiful. Her hair is white. Her eyes sparkle—with interest, with anger. She is seventy-one years old and she's been imprisoned at California Institution for Women for nearly twenty years. She's been totally deaf for forty-five years.

Early in 1953, she was arrested and charged with second-degree murder. "I was accused of not being deaf from the time I was arrested," she said. "The women deputies at Los Angeles County Jail refused to call out for me. They said they would let me use the phone but they would not use it for me to call two witnesses I had. They told me, 'You can hear as good as I can.' But if my life had depended on it I could not have called to save my *own life*.

"I wrote three letters to three doctors that I had gone to back in 1925, when I first lost my hearing after I had scarlet fever. They had given me tests and treatments but the one doctor finally said I'd never hear again barring a miracle and not to pay out any more money to other doctors. He told me I'd never hear again because the auditory nerves were completely dead. Well, my letters were picked up but the next A.M. I found them sticking right back between the bars. When breakfast came, I asked the woman deputy about it and she said, 'They could not go out.' When I asked why, she gave no answer, only her back."

Mrs. Bezie talks loudly, drawing deep breaths between statements. She pauses often to make sure I have written down exactly what she is saying. We are sitting on the bed in her room—which is in a CIW cottage for older and handicapped women. When I have a question, I write it down for her—she nods her head and thinks a minute, then answers in precise, loud words. There is an aura of the fifties about her—as though somehow her world has changed only into a series of details in the last twenty years, leaving the essence of her prior development life untouched.

She tells me she had to go to court without any witnesses because she had never been able to call them or get letters out to them. When she went to court she had an attorney, secured by her half sister who

was out of state—but she had never met him before the trial: "I did
not see him until I went to court and he came up to me with a piece
of paper on which was written, 'My name is Kenneth Lynch. Your
sister sent me to defend you.' That was *all*. Then he walked over and
sat on the other side of the courtroom with some court attachés. I
was not allowed to have an interpreter."

Louise said "no one wrote" her anything concerning the trial. In
other words, no one told her anything about what was going on. "It
was my first felony, so I regret to state I was too ignorant to know
about court procedures. After I'd been tried and found guilty, some
inmate at county jail asked about my transcript and when I told her
I had none she became furious and said, "You cannot hear that trial,
you have been denied the stand, you've been denied a Polygraph
test, you've been denied a witness, you've been denied an interpreter.
You make that crook give you your transcript when you go back for
sentence."

Louise said that she did get transcripts after she was sentenced, but
only after she got back to the jail and read the transcripts did she find
out what had happened during the trial. "I had been lied on right
there in front of me without me having any way of knowing what
they were saying." She said she turned in the copies of her transcripts
when she was admitted to CIW, but that they were never returned to
her.

"I just lost all hope. No one told me anything about appeal and I
was not well versed in the law, not enough to know it was my privilege, and I am not denying that after reading my transcripts and
having been denied every request . . . I tried my best to wreck this
jail when I got here. I was so shocked to find justice a thing of the
past in this country of my birth—which now I'm ashamed to admit. I
was put in the padded cell in just a jail shift and it was very cold in
December, with only the stone floor and no cover.

"After the initial outrage of feeling I'd been lied to and deceived
—as well as everyone thinking I was a fake—I began to do my work
and go along the best I could. I have worked here until '65 at housework—mopping, scrubbing and cleaning windows—until in '65 I
was forced into idleness and been idle these past seven years! From
this inactivity I contracted kidney trouble and arthritis from nothing
but idleness and inactivity. I came to this place strong and healthy.
The first year I was kept inactive I contracted both diseases."

"Have you asked to work again?" I wrote.

"I raved about it for several years and they refused to give me anything to occupy my mind. It was the doctor—who left here in January, thank God—who wouldn't let me work."

In November of 1970, Louise Bezie was given parole to a nursing home called the Beverly Manor, in Riverside, California. She was checked out of the institution after seventeen years with an official listing of all her worldly goods. She had saved the receipt. She carefully unfolded it from a collection of papers, to show it to me.

Property Receipt Release

I, Louise Bezie, No. 2004, hereby acknowledge receipt of:

Jewelry: 1 pr. of tweezers, 1 gold filling, 1 silver filling.

Personal Effects: check $1,931.00
                     check   88.20
                     check   20.40

The above property constitutes all jewelry and personal effects held for me by the officials of this institution.

Date *November 12, 1970*   Signed *L. Bezie*
Witnessed *N. Weaver*   Institution *C.I.W.*
                property clerk

"I left here with over two thousand dollars. It was the money from my husband's Social Security. I don't spend much. I had saved it. The home took it from me—and my sister will verify this. You can see the amount of money listed on the form," Louise said. "My parole officer kept my receipt. I asked to be transferred to another home. Instead, they brought me back here. My sister wrote her Congressman about the home taking my money and the whole thing. He advised her to get the receipt from the parole officer. It's been fourteen months since then.

"When I left here for the home in Riverside, I was told by my correctional counselor and parole officer due to my deafness that I was going to a place where I would pay a hundred and forty-five dollars a month. When they got me in and the door locked on me, I was informed that I was paying five hundred dollars a month. And when I tried to contact the parole officer, the management at the home told me she had no name or telephone number. I had to smuggle a letter out to my sister giving her all this information what was being done to me. She wrote this adminstration with threats of having an attorney go to the home and tell my story. Then the superintendent contacted the parole officer to come for me. I lacked four days of being there two months and paid nine hundred and seventy dollars and the parole officer still had my receipts for the money paid out.

"I had been told they had Medicare there. But you can't believe anything they say here. When I got there I had no Medicare. They were even more strict with their rules there than they are here. I couldn't have a radio in my room. I couldn't go out. They mainly kept me locked in my room. I could hardly breathe in that place. They sprayed almost continually, like we were a bunch of insects.

"The very first night there I had my shower and then went and pulled back the cover to retire. The bed was soaked—a big brown circle reached from one side of the bed to the other—with urine, and the stench almost knocked me down. I went out and said to the aide— 'Look at this bed, we do not have to live like varmints even in jail.' Right then I wanted out of that place, my very first night. So we changed the bed.

"They did not even have a throw rug on the floor, which was shower tile. I have a parakeet and there was not even a table to set his cage on and no library, no handwork in the rooms, no knitting needles or crochet hooks; not even my mother's picture, no face lotions, or shampoo bottles, or cold creams were allowed. They allowed nothing but a few clothes brought from storage. I said, 'Why, I'm shocked. I had small work scissors, knitting needles, hooks, etc., for seventeen years even in jail! I had jars, bottles and in fact my own Gillette safety razor with removable blade all the time at CIW.' I said, 'This place is worse than jail!' All the mail had to be left open and if it did not please them it was destroyed, all incoming mail was opened and checks and money removed. My sis called long distance and wrote me about it later. The manager never let me know one thing about that call.

"Finally, when her letters kept asking me, 'Why don't you write?' I cultivated a maid and made her a promise to pay her and then she smuggled letters in and out for me from general delivery at the post office. My sister and I wrote to the superintendent here asking her to transfer me to another home. Instead, the parole officer brought me back here January 1971 on a parole violation for 'refusing to co-operate with parole officer.'

"At CIW at least I can shop every week at the canteen—soft drinks,

candy, cookies, nuts, canned meats . . . and our former superintendent [Miss Carter] let me go to town with a friendly staff member I'd
known for fifteen years who was very good here.

"Believe it or not, last year when I went to the parole board about
my return from Beverly Manor, I wrote all the details out for them—
over nine pages. I told them how I had no parole officer for six weeks
when I wanted to appeal for a move. I told them how *before* I had
checked in that all my money had to be left at the office to 'protect
it for me' so that I could draw on it when I shopped once a week
with a staff member. I also told them how that Christmas 1970
when I wanted twenty-five cents to get my sis a Christmas card,
they refused to give it to me. The parole officer had not left any
name or phone number so I was helpless and wrote to another state
to my sister to get help out of there. Well, I handed the nine pages
to the board member and he tossed it back to me without reading.
Then they showed me what the PO had charged me with—'refusing
to sign checks.'

"My letter and testimony was ignored completely. They called it
"Refusing to Co-operate with Parole Officer," and my God in heaven
knows *I had no parole officer* to co-operate with . . . How they do lie
on people in these places.

"Anyway, I was given two more years here by the parole board.
This is paradise compared to that place. I have seen my parole officer
only once since I came back from the Beverly Manor and I ran up
to her and asked, 'Where are my receipts? My sister and my Congressman want them.' She did not even grunt, she just tossed her
head and looked down her nose and brushed past me as if she were
defiled. Miss Carlson would not even give me a chance to take it up
with her—it's easier to get an interview with the U. S. Supreme
Court. Miss Carter was trying to recover those receipts when she retired one year ago this month, but after she left everything stopped.

"But they do not treat inmates who have families nearby, or who
are going back to the outside world like they do the ones they know
will never go back, and if the truth as it is has been lived and
breathed, as I have—you are sure in for the *hard way*. I tell them,
'You can do no more than kill me, you can't eat me.' I have kept
right on talking.

"The problems here are with the staff, not the inmates. There was
a television show and Dr. Drieser, a psychologist, said *on the television,* 'The inmates do not make the trouble here, it's the staff that

makes trouble for us.' She speaks the truth. The whole campus was happy when she said that. She is in charge of the Psychiatric Treatment Unit and knows what she speaks of. She is a very brilliant woman and since her truthful statement on TV she is (like me) not so popular with administration and staff at large.

*　　*　　*

"I think it should be against the law where any totally deaf person is concerned for a psychiatrist to refuse to write out questions. That is not giving us a break. Reading a stranger's lips is very very difficult. But before I was given my parole in 1970, I had to have an interview with the psychiatrist. I do not know one question he asked me, I just groped and floundered in an attempt to guess what he was asking me—I wanted to hurry and get away from that man, for I knew he thought he was talking to a hearing person—so I just answered at random, 'Yes, No, I don't know, etc.' How can one answer a question correctly if they do not know what the question is?

"I do not know his name, because he came from the outside. I do not even hear my own voice so I do not even have the pleasure of talking to myself—I cannot hear what I have to say. [smile]

"It is very hard being handicapped in a place like this. Here in CIW I was once put in solitary with not even a shift, not even panties, just like I came into the world, no water in the cell, no toilet, just a hole in the floor with a pipe. No towel, no mattress, just a stone floor and my bare skin. I was sixty-five years old at the time, seventy-one now. I was in there for three weeks' lockup over crackers. Just because I had a few illegal crackers that were given to me by a kitchen girl in my room. I was sent to PTU from Walker after three weeks' lockup.

"I'm in the same kind of spot that the Jackson boy was in San Quentin. He had given out the rotten truth and also told his attorney, friends and parents that he would never leave there alive. *I do not believe* that boy was killed trying to escape. They—the guards—just knew it was the best opportunity they would ever have to get him. I have talked to any number of inmates here who have brothers, husbands, etc. in that same prison and write all the lowdown direct from there. That boy was doomed and he knew it, for he kept right on putting out the truth regardless of the punishment, just as I have done and will continue to do until death stills my tongue and hand.

"I do not believe anyone is out to kill me. They have other plans for me and that's to keep me where I can never talk. . . . You are the first outsider I've had a chance to talk with in private in eighteen years and I think the Good Lord must have sent you to me."

In August of '72, I got a letter from Louise that began

DEAR BUDDY

. . . I will not put your name here until I'm out of this isolation for it might be lifted. An old wore out whore and bootlegger from Little Rock, Ark., told a lie on me and got me in deep trouble. Been locked for three days now and have had not one person stop from CC, adm, or committee even stop to ask me if I'm guilty or not. Been taking dope from clinic to knock myself out so I will not go crazy. No sound in the world and now nothing to see . . .

. . . Now I am lied on again and no way to prove it again. If only they had a polygraph here; they are dependable. I am not being punished for anything I did . . . But the more they punish me the more determined it makes me . . .

. . . I'm afraid I will never have the opportunity at my ghost writer or the book on this place I said I would write after I first was here. But I would gladly submit to a lie detector test, sodium pentothal, or any other truth medication known to medical science to prove every word I have told you where and when you visited me, is the truth. I have suffered and screamed but it has fell on deaf ears . . .

Constance

A young white social worker at Marysville who plans to make a career of corrections told me she had observed that I wasn't getting a "total random sampling of prisoners." She had accompanied me around the grounds and watched me talk with prisoners. "You are talking to women who are aggressive enough to come up to you—and the ones you seem to pick are aggressive, too. You are missing a lot of more meek people who have good things to say. These are the ones who are good workers and good citizens—while you were in the sewing industry, for instance, they stayed at their jobs and kept working. The ones with poorer work records who need closer supervision felt freer to come up and talk to you. There are a lot of passive people here who were scared to death when they came in—and many of them feel that prison has helped them."

She then accompanied me to the infirmary, where I met Constance Arlene Johnson—a small middle-aged black woman intently scrubbing and mopping the narrow hallway between the rows of tiny rooms for prisoners who are sick. The rooms had a bed and a sink in them and were dilapidated. Sick women walk to the end of the hallway to go to the bathroom, and I had heard complaints of how you weren't allowed to walk to the toilet unless you had the nurse's approval. ("If you're not sick when you go to the hospital, you're bound to get sick while you're there," one inmate had said. "It's the most disgusting place in the institution outside max.")

Constance Johnson said she works in the hospital every day of the week. "Most of 'em here, they ain't sick the way they eat," Constance said, never pausing from mopping the floor. "They mainly just don't want to go to work one day. But they get here, and they don't want to stay. This is less appealing than their rooms. Inmates are not allowed to run the hall here. If they're sick, they stay in their rooms the way they should.

Her small-boned face was hard set and bitter. "Look, they'll tell you this place is terrible now—you'd think the world owes them something. But life is what you make it. If you make a hard bed for yourself, you sleep hard. If you make your bed soft, you sleep soft. I was here from '64 to '66 and I liked it better then. There were more experienced women.

"Now there are too many teen-agers here—they be destructive, they be out to satisfy themselves. I know what people say about how it is here but it ain't the truth. Inmates do their own dirt. If they would learn to co-operate it'd be different. It's not the officers riding the inmates—it's the inmates riding the inmates. Officials didn't put 'em here—they put their own selves here.

"The inmates making rules is hurting themselves—it ain't gonna hurt the officers. It ain't gonna get 'em nowhere—they're still in the penitentiary, they still have numbers. There's just a lot of talk going around that ain't real. No inmate council gonna do no good. They don't have no power, they can't change nothin'. Anyway, it ain't my way. If they tell me to get down on my hands and knees and scrub, I will. If they tell me, 'Mop the floor again, Connie,' I will—'cause it's my job to do it. I'm liable to be here six more months. I have four more months before I meet the board—and whatever they ask me to do, I do it 'cause it's my job to do it. I made my own bed—I gotta sleep in it now."

Proud Mary

Proud Mary sold her soul for
50 grams of speed.
Then she sold her body,
To meet her hooked brain need.
She sold her brand new dress,
Her only pair of shoes,
Now Mary haunts the street
Dressed only in her blues.

The vulture came and ate her veins
Until there was no trace
Now hungry Mary kept shooting dope
Between tears on her face
No one mourned Mary's passing
There was no one to bother
But I sold my tears to buy her grave
Proud Mary was my "mother."

—IDA MAE TASSIN
Bedford Hills

Reprinted with permission from *Proud Mary, Poems from a Black Sister in Prison*, Ida Mae Tassin, © 1971, Buffalo Women's Prison Project.

Susan

Susan Moss* is a police statistic, a court statistic, a prison statistic. She is a murderer, by definition, and an ex-con who is now on parole. One night after she came home from four and a half years in prison, we had gotten together for supper to talk about her specific prison experiences at the state correctional institution in Niantic, Connecticut. Sue killed her husband, Marvin—a man she says she loved more than any other person in her life. With no urging on my part, she began to talk about the day she killed her Marvin. She wanted to share the horror of her act; she seemed to need to get it out.

"When I was pregnant with Kit, we had a five-room apartment," Sue recalled. "I was working and Marvin was working and we had saved money and bought a beautiful home at Sixty-second and Platte streets. We had got married and things were going really good. The day it happened, the twenty-eighth of June, Marv stayed home from work. He ran a filling station with two other guys. The week before we had celebrated our first anniversary. We went out to get some little things for the house and on the way home we got into a silly-assed argument.

"It started 'cause I told him I'd been sick in the mornings and for me that means only one thing. I was pregnant. He said, 'Oh no.' I told him it would be okay, I'd get a job again and save up the money, just like I had done with Kit. Then he came out with, 'I'll tell you what. I'll give you a hundred dollars and you can get an abortion.' I came up with things like I'm anemic and getting an abortion is laying my life on the line. Not only is there the danger of me bleeding to death, but the knife could be dirty or anything else. I said, 'You want to kill the baby, but you're not thinking about me and my life.'

"I've blocked so much out now—I hate remembering it all. But I remember going back to the house and Marv's sister and her man were there. Her husband was in Vietnam. I remember feeding the baby and Vicki. Marvin was mad at me and every time he was mad at me, he tends to take it out on Vicki. He was upset 'cause he just

* The names are changed.

couldn't see spending five hundred dollars for another baby, plus an extra mouth to feed and all. . . .

"Well, I guess Vicki sensed that something was wrong; she got to tearing up papers . . . and he went over and whipped her ass. I was always sensitive about his attitude to Vicki, because she was my child from my second husband. Her father had died from a liver disease. Anyway, I told him if he was mad at me to take it out on me, not on Vicki. Then I took the children up and put them to bed. Then I was sitting on the couch and he came into the living room and said, 'You're gonna listen to reason. You're going to have an abortion—it's not a life yet. You're not listening to reason, you're just talking from the heart.'

"I said, 'I'm not having an abortion and that's final. If you don't want the responsibility, I'll do it by myself and you can get out. But if you don't want it, you're not the man I thought you were.'

"He struck me across the face. I can't stand to be struck. I been struck too much. I said, 'You'll be sorry you did that.'

"I walked into the kitchen and started looking for the butcher knife. I looked everywhere but I couldn't find it . . . in the drawer, on the wall, I couldn't find it anywhere. Finally I saw it, sitting right on the drainboard over the sink. I walked back into the living room and he was putting an album on the hi-fi. I walked up and stabbed him. I didn't feel the impact of the knife going in . . . that's how angry I was.

"My sister-in-law was on the porch and she came running in when she heard the thump of the body. She said later she saw it all happen, but she didn't.

"I think when I knew I had stabbed him I would have stabbed him again—but what actually saved me in court was that I saw the stain begin to spread on his shirt. He was wearing this white polo shirt I had given him. He pulled it up and said, 'Oh, Sue, look what you've done to me.'

"I don't know who called the police. But it took 'em five to six minutes to get there. I thought that if I gave him mouth-to-mouth resuscitation he might live. But the air wasn't coming back into my mouth from his. I knew he had died. I knew I had hit the heart.

"I was sitting there holding him when the cops came in. I kept asking them if he was dead, but I knew. Then I went off. The sergeant grabbed me and told me that they'd have to put me into restraints if I didn't settle down. I knew that I'd go crazy in restraints and I couldn't stand that. Then they took me out. They took me out barefoot in shorts and a see-through blouse. I left my kids in the house and my husband dead on the floor.

"They told me they were going to take me to the hospital for sedatives, but they took me to police headquarters and booked me for willful murder. By then I was more under control, I was numb. The detective lied on me on the stand. He said I was composed and that I wasn't hysterical and that you'd never know I had just killed somebody. He said I'd even ate and that wasn't true. I had only had a cup of coffee.

"I was fingerprinted, and mugged and interrogated all night long in the homicide division and then was taken downstairs to a holding cell about four or four-thirty A.M. I was taken up at about five o'clock in the morning, still barefooted and in my shorts, for the arraignment. The magistrate asked me if I knew why I was there and said that one Marvin Moss, thirty-two years of age, had died of a stab wound at approximately ten forty-five P.M. the night before. I had signed a confession in front of a detective the night before and I gave a verbal confession into a tape recorder.

"After the arraignment I was taken to the House of Detention. I was numb—completely numb. I had no feelings, no emotion at that time. I felt very cold and very cut off. I felt like my life had ended. You must realize, Kitsi, that I had committed the act of murder.

"I didn't even think at that time, I wasn't thinking. I stopped right there. I didn't know where my kids were. I was going crazy about them. But I found out through the social worker at the prison a week later that they were at my mother-in-law's.

"At the House of Detention, I was pregnant and I knew it but they wouldn't believe me. They wanted me down on my knees scrubbing the cellblock. I was spotting and I told the nurse, but she said, "That's nothing unusual. Everybody spots." But I knew I didn't. I knew I was pregnant and they just didn't want to take me off my hands and knees on the concrete floor. Finally they gave me a rabbit test, and found out I was pregnant—but I was already spotting bad.

"Before I started bleeding bad, though, they took me down to a hearing in the police paddy wagon with my hands handcuffed behind me. It's just the bare paddy wagon, with no padding. I passed out with my arms behind me and fell off the seat. The cops were pretty decent. They stopped the wagon in the park and let me get out for air.

"When we got back from court I didn't feel very good and started bleeding. For ten days I hemorrhaged in the cell—and then I aborted right in the cell. I asked to see the doctor but he told them to give me an ice bag for my stomach. The girls took care of me. They brought me milk and extra vitamins, but the vitamins didn't do any good then—I had already lost the baby.

"When I passed the baby and called for the nurse, she wouldn't even come down until the next day. They wouldn't take me to the hospital until the end—and I was almost dying. Finally they took me to the hospital—but they didn't want to leave me there because it was a holiday weekend and they didn't want to put a watch on me since they were short on matrons. Since I had a murder charge on me and a detainer, they wouldn't leave me there without a matron to guard me. But the doctor at the hospital said I would die if they let me go out and that if they sent me back to jail, the hospital would take no responsibility. So they let me stay at the hospital. After they had given me a lot of transfusions and built me up enough, they gave me a D and C to clean me out. To be fair, I should tell you the doctor said I would have probably aborted eventually anyway from shock and the initial aftermath of the crime—even without the fall.

"Later, in the month of April, I had my trial. By that time, I had an indictment for second-degree murder, voluntary manslaughter and involuntary manslaughter. I pleaded not guilty to second-degree murder, so naturally I had to plead not guilty on the other two. I guess they figured if they didn't get me on one, they would get me on one of the other two. If I'd had my choice, I would have pled guilty to involuntary manslaughter—which carries a max of three years and you usually get probation on it.

"I was offered a plea of guilty on second-degree murder in exchange for one to eight and I refused it 'cause I didn't want no second-degree murder for my record. I didn't feel I was guilty of second-degree murder, not as the law defines it.

"I had a thousand dollars of my own money, so I paid my lawyers a retainer and after that took the pauper's oath and the state paid for the rest of it. They were pretty decent men.

"It was a two-week jury trial—I went through the whole bit again. My sister-in-law flew in from Albuquerque to testify against me. She did the most harm to me—she's the reason I got the guilty plea on voluntary manslaughter.

"I was put on the stand and had to go through the question and answer bit. The district attorney tried to make me out as a cold-blooded murderer but said it didn't rise any higher than second-degree murder. After my sister-in-law testified, the DA said he thought they could justifiably charge me with first degree. My lawyer said, 'Now, just a minute . . . there was no intent involved.' He said I was guilty of murder—but I was motivated out of fear and anger. My psychiatrist from the trouble center testified for me too. He volunteered to come to court from the street—I'd had a nervous breakdown the year before and had gone to the trouble center at the hospital, where they deal with people having problems dealing with everyday life.

"It was a nightmare. I don't even like to remember it even now It's too new."

Sue was found guilty of voluntary manslaughter. She served four and a half years in Niantic and is serving the remainder of her ten-year sentence on parole. One of the conditions of her release is that she not establish any relationship with a man until she consults her parole officer and receives permission.

Dessie

Dessie Kuhn is sitting on the edge of a prison hospital bed in Marysville, Ohio. Her thin, short legs dangle limply above the bedside stool. She is a little white woman, extremely thin, with wispy, uncombed brown hair. She is a picture of misery in her hospital gown. Her small-boned face is nearly hidden by a huge bandage covering her nose and cheeks.

I ask her what happened to her and she tells me she has just had surgery to straighten her nasal passages. But she wants to tell me why she is in prison; she wants to know, can I do anything about it? She has bigger concerns than surgery.

"I'm doing one to three years for fraud," she says. "I had food stamps from two counties, and it was my first offense.

"I offered to give them back or pay for them. They was a hundred and sixty dollars' worth, but they wouldn't let me turn them back in or pay for 'em. It was just a small hick town in Gallia County. It was the first time this judge had a chance to send someone to Marysville, so he sent me. He could have given me probation because I have no past record whatsoever.

"I have seven children and two stepchildren—plus over the years I've had five foster children. They're all with my husband now, but it's really hard for him working and taking care of them, too. I already been here nine months, and I could be here for another two years and three months . . .

"If I had ever had any idea that would happen . . . I regret having had those food stamps so many times. See, I signed up for food stamps in Meigs County—but that was before we moved to Gallia County. After we moved, I kept the food stamps from Meigs. So when they discovered in Gallia I still had food stamps from Meigs, they issued a warrant.

"I'd a gladly paid 'em back or done probation.

"This way breaks your home up. It's January now and I haven't seen my kids or husband since November. They tried driving up before Christmas, but the car broke down and now it's still broke down, so they have no way to come up. From a big city, I wouldn't have gone here for it. They wouldn't even notice it.

"I had a state-appointed lawyer. He told me if I dropped the jury trial and pled guilty, the judge would give me probation. All he done was prosecute me worse than the prosecutor. I got one to three for fraud because I done what he told me and pled guilty. I feel I was unjustly treated all the way through."

Martha

Turning left off of Route 411, about an hour's drive from Columbus, Ohio, you see a small sign which says, "Ohio Reformatory for Women, Marysville. Trespassers will be prosecuted." Driving up the long winding road, you pass a small guard's office and see two- and three-story red brick buildings which remind you of a boarding school or a closely constructed sanitorium where old folks walked around in bathrobes in 1940s movies. More than 280 women are prisoners here in the middle of a cornfield, in the middle of the state; a small community, not even served by a bus.

"It's a silly place to begin to get it all together when the root of many women's problems is with their families and loved ones in the city," said the institution's superintendent, Martha Wheeler—a dignified gray-haired woman in her fifties. She relaxed behind her desk and chain-smoked as we talked in her comfortable administrative office. "It's a big disadvantage for visitors to get to the institution without public transportation. You must have a car to get here—and since most of the families of the women are poor, few have this luxury or are able to get to Marysville easily."

Miss Wheeler said she agrees with the trend toward community-based systems—as opposed to rural prisons. "These community-based centers would have fewer women. It's important we concentrate on building newer facilities much earlier—as near as possible to the community where most of the resources are, where the women are and where the problems are. This way we can have realistic intervention on the first offense."

Martha Wheeler knew before she went to college she wanted to work in prisons and in the corrections field. Deliberately she charted her courses—studying criminology and social administration. She worked for eight and a half years at the state prison for women at Bedford Hills, New York, and then returned "home" to Ohio in 1958 to head up the women's prison at Marysville. She is currently president of the American Correctional Association, the first woman elected to that office.

"There are relatively few in my generation who came into corrections on purpose," she said, surveying the neatly stacked papers on her desk. "But I had exposure at an early age. I've known Marysville girls since I was eight years old.

"My parents used to operate an honor camp for the Marysville girls about two hundred miles from here. They ran it from 1929 to 1956. It was an old-age home—a small institution for elderly women. Specifically it was an honor institution for wives, widows and mothers of military personnel.

"Trustees from Marysville served as attendants, cooks and maids— and looked after the patients. When I was little, they got me up in the morning, fed me my breakfast and put me on the bus. They were older women, stable—and could handle the situation. They could make more money and feel useful. They lived in three dormitory sections—five women to a room. They were earning forty dollars a month when we phased out the program.

"We continued with that institution until a couple of years ago— but it had changed—housing retarded women and then being a halfway house for borderline mental defectives. As our programs here intensified, we hated to send them two hundred miles away to do laundry and clean. Also, the population was younger, so we didn't have the kind of women who were happy going there . . . it didn't have that much in it for them. It was giving the honor camp problems and not doing much for us. Plus sentences were shortened, so it no longer fed their needs or ours—so there's no more honor camp."

Some of the women who worked under the purview of Martha Wheeler's parents now have daughters serving time under the direction of Martha Wheeler. Two elderly women prisoners at Marysville knew Martha as a little girl and still refer to her as "Captain Wheeler's daughter." Now Miss Wheeler's parents are retired and live on the prison grounds with Miss Wheeler in a large brick house which sits majestically next to the administration building. "Marysville girls" still take care of the family—getting them up, feeding them breakfast, cleaning the house, serving dinners to family and company. They still do all the washing and ironing for all three residents and two dogs.

Barbara

"I'm twenty-eight—and it's too late for me to be rehabilitated," Barbara Baker says. "If I could get something out of this experience, I don't think I would mind.

"But it's not only the system that stops an effective experience, it's also the inmates. There's a lack of communication between the staff and the inmates—but there's just as much a lack of communication between inmate and inmate. We gotta start with unity from the inmates. It's impossible for the staff to regroup themselves without us regrouping ourselves right here . . . this is where it's at.

"Unity to me is first regrouping yourself and then coming together with a group. If you can't accept yourself, you can never accept anyone else. How can you talk about Janie's problems or deal with them without talking about yourself first—and really looking at yourself?

"It's gotta be something you do for yourself first; you have to examine yourself before you can see anyone else. Otherwise it's just like taking a mirror and looking at yourself—you never see the other person."

Barbara Baker knows a lot about people. A lot about institutions. A lot about people in institutions. She grew up in them. She is somewhat of a notorious figure now at Ohio Reformatory for Women in Marysville, where she has been incarcerated for eight years on an armed robbery charge.

I heard her name mentioned by staff members three or four times within the first six hours I was at Marysville. I had already been looking forward to meeting her because friends in Iowa at the *Penal Digest International* headquarters—a paper put out by cons and ex-cons—had told me she was prison correspondent for the paper. One staff member mentioned to the superintendent that Barbara had requested to see a friend from another cottage about to be released, and complained the precedent was already set—so she couldn't get away with denying Barbara's request even though she wanted to. "It would be a bigger headache than it's worth," she said. I also heard staff members exchanging passing comments about her as a "trouble-maker" and "a big mouth" and the superintendent, Martha Wheeler, said, "She ought to put her head where her mouth is. She's got a faulty connection between her head and her mouth." They had no idea I was aware of the person they were talking about—but even if I hadn't already been looking for her, their comments would have intrigued me.

Finally, on the third evening at the reformatory, I got into Washington "cottage," where Barbara lived. The women were all in the recreation room, talking to each other and playing cards before they were allowed to go back to their rooms and line up for showers, to be taken one at a time in tiny shower stalls. Bits of evening light were coming through the windows. As I started meeting the women and talking with them, I saw several women I'd met the day before in the garment factory. They introduced me to Becky Careway and to Barbara Baker—a tall, elegant black woman who shook hands firmly and directly. I gave her messages from her friends outside and we agreed to talk after showers. The matron blew her whistle and we started upstairs.

"Come on, girls," the matron said. "Step it up."

Following long conversations with other women, Barbara and I finally sat down to talk. She was in Marysville from 1962 to 1967 and came back again in 1969. She has a date to meet the parole board in 1975—having gotten a ten-to-twenty-five-year sentence for robbery.

"We've got a rotten system here," Barbara said. "Most people's dogs are treated better than the women in here. But the majority of the women don't carry themselves like women. If you want to be treated like a woman—you have to see: where does womanhood begin but in yourself? How can you expect them to treat you like a woman when you act like a child?

"I don't like Martha Wheeler or Dorothy Urn—I don't like things they have done in the past. They don't do their jobs. But there are two sides to every story. Martha Wheeler has one of the greatest minds you could ever come across. The woman's brilliant. She has an education—everyone needs it—but there are two classes of education. Education with common sense and education with refusing to use common sense. This has happened to Martha Wheeler—she doesn't use common sense along with her education. She has let her mother and father and two dogs be the circle around her life. It's impossible to pull her from those walls and let her see each woman as an individual. She's walled herself up into a prison that's tighter and more binding than most of us are in.

"It's like I said—if you look, you see two sides to every story. When women first line up to go through that gate and go into isolation for orientation to the prison—the first thing the matrons try to do is stamp out womanhood and respect. They treat us like children.

"But many women continue that child thing in here because they are *afraid*. Where's their courage? They've stood up to society some way outside or they wouldn't be in here. If their husband smacked them down and they were afraid to leave—they tolerated it up to the point of taking a gun and blowing his head off. But you don't have to go that extreme.

"Courage to stand up and speak is the beginning of your womanhood. You're going to be classified as a renegade—but who cares when you're speaking the truth and fighting for everyone? Just because you have a number, why throw away your pride? I'm in prison night and day but for twenty-four hours a day God has given me the courage to be a woman. When Martha Wheeler or someone says something I feel isn't right, I'm gonna stand up and let them know this. I'm not going to say, 'Yes, ma'am, you're right.' That's another ounce of pride from your womanhood. And that's basically all we have in here. I would rather go to room punishment or maximum security."

"But people sell their soul for artificial treasures," Barbara said, talking about "honor" status [the reward system at the prison symbolized by "moving up from a plain blue uniform to a print dress of flowered material made in shirtwaist style]. "You've got your 'prints' and that lousy JG [honor dorm]. The majority of the women in this prison never wore a print on the streets. They didn't know what a print looked like until they entered this institution. As for JG, I can go to my room right here in Washington Cottage and roll my hair up at six o'clock. The only real difference is they can keep their doors open or closed when they want. It's like telling your child, 'Honey, I'll roll your hair up and you can come out and watch TV.' Yet there are so many women here who would lay down their lives to get into JG for those simple little things—doors open, hair up when they want it up. I often wonder who is the real dogs—people up front or people in here. I would not sell myself for such small petty things. This is not human.

"I could run down this institution after eight years here—and I'm not institutionalized—but you have to look at the whole picture. Running the system down isn't gonna solve the problems.

"We gotta start here with the inmates. I don't mean to get up and rebel or carry signs saying we want this or that or rioting. This is silly. It would just prove to society that we're nothing but children. There's a way for a woman to do anything she wants. She can get anything she wants. Women get here in isolation and they forget women are blessed people. They are the gentle creatures—yet they are very shrewd. We know how to con from a little girl up—from the time we got up on our daddy's lap and got him to give a dime to go to the store.

"I believe each and every one of us is God—he created us in our own image. If we cast our womanhood aside, we are smacking our God aside, saying, 'We don't need it.'

"There are a few staff members here who are able to give some of themselves among the women. There are a few matrons who are open to people. And Mr. Kowalski, our psychologist, is open. For a long time I refused to talk to him or any of the rest of the staff. He was the first person I learned to trust after I learned to trust myself. Now I also rap with some of the matrons who are open. I found out if I tried to understand the world, the world would try to understand me.

"But there are many women in here who crave help but refuse help when it's offered to them. Mrs. King, the correctional officer who's our matron, is all for the girls. But some girls call her a bunch of names because she wants to help them. They cry out they want help —but it's a false cry for many of them—'cause when someone comes in here to help, they try to destroy her. Maybe it's a question of jealousy of her freedom. But you gotta be able to stand up like a woman and see the truth—good or bad. You have to look at yourself as a human being and look at your oppressor as a human being.

"With the system here—if inmates and officials would learn to cast out the past and look at each other with new eyes—it would be very different. It weakens you to rely on the past. We have to keep our feet halfway through yesterday and move on into tomorrow.

"This is a new day . . . it's got to be a new beginning. All of us have faults because we refuse to come up to date with what is going on around us in this big, bad world.

"It's a drag sometimes, sure it's a drag. We each gotta do time. We're the ones doing it, so we know what it's like. But I wonder if there were some way we could all get together. I don't believe in sitting back to wait, because there's only now. We move forward but together to unite . . . to look out at the world and face the world and be the world—not with black power or white superiority—but with power for all—calling out unity among the people.

"In order to survive, I must look at my people—not just black people, but all people. There's good and bad in all people. We need understanding from them. But they need understanding from us, too, evil as they are. I don't care what crime a person has committed —there's still some good in him. We can sit back and condemn them and we can say we know the reason why—but what good does that do without looking at yourself? There's an old story about a woman named Mary Magdalene. People were ready to stone her for being a prostitute. But this man named Jesus came up on the scene and said, 'Ye who have not sinned cast the first stone'—and nobody was sinless. No one could cast that first stone.

"I don't like to come on in a psychedelic world of fantasy. I like to say, 'Hey, man, this is it.' No matter how many dreams I try to dream to make it better or worse, it comes out the same way. I'm still here, man. I'm still in the penitentiary. I know why I'm here. No matter where you run to, the reality is still there with you. If I get out, I get out. If I don't, I know I committed a crime. There's a reason for everything.

"I was automatically found guilty of robbery this time—even without evidence—just because of my record. There are probably reasons I came back here January 15, 1960. I lay up there in isolation when I came back and said, 'Maybe there is a reason.' In the eyes of God all things are possible. But what the hell would that prove?

"But then things began to rolling—censorship was lifted and I could write my man at Ohio Penitentiary. And then I got a visit from Reverend McCracken—my first visit in three years. When I talked to Reverend McCracken, I found a *people*. He was sixty-five years old. And I myself was twenty-seven. He was white. I am black. But we found no gaps. There is no gap. It took me all these years to realize there is no gap when your heart is reaching out . . . There is no gap when you are open to understanding."

DEAR MOMMY,
    I got me a job so I don't have to steal till you get home.
    Ronnie ran away again but otherwise, everything is fine. How are you?

I love you,
XXXOOO,
      VICKIE

Aletha

They be callin us girl all the time. I ain't no girl. I got ten kids. That ain't no girl there.

"I be tellin my kids, please go to school and get me a diploma. But nobody's in school. My oldest one's in jail for A & B [assault and battery]. My one son, Johnny, who's next to the baby, is in the Industrial Home for running away from the foster home. I told him to stay in school but he didn't. One is staying with my sister. The oldest ones go where they wanna go. My three youngest is in foster homes. I tell them, 'Don't steal,' 'cause it's the only thing I ever did. I been stealing ever since I was seventeen. I got a letter from my little girl. She wrote me, 'Mommy, I got me a job so I don't have to steal till you get home.'

"I loves to steal.

"You can go out, and say you see something I want or would like. You think—I can sell this mink coat to her and get a couple bills. I didn't know how to do anything else but steal. I love to do it. I *loves* to do it! I wanna go around the world and steal when I get out . . .

"I would rather be in a county jail where you can holler out the window and contact people than be here. In county you can sleep all day. You don't have to work and you don't get paid no way.

"I guess I been in jail about ten times. I was here before, too. I been in Cleveland Jail, Akron Jail, Booster Jail and Toledo."

—ALETHA CURTIS
Ohio Reformatory for Women

Kathleen

The ombudsman at California Institution for Women is a woman who has spent her life asking, "Why?" Kathleen Anderson said her *whys,* in fact, are what got her into prison work in the first place.

She had been teaching in a school for the deaf in Riverside—and during one vacation some twelve years ago came up to CIW in Frontera to take a tour of the institution. "I was just curious," she said. "But when I got here they told me the only way I could get in would be to take the test and come in as a line officer.

"At that time, they didn't let outsiders in, period. It wasn't just because I was black—it was just the rule. I didn't think it was right the way they treated outsiders wanting a tour. I figured if they treated adults like that—other state employees like myself—how were they treating the women inside? I wanted to know. I wanted to know what made them tick.

"I guess I've always been a nosy person. Anyway, I took the civil service examination and I accepted the job. When I quit my job, the people at the deaf school were upset at my leaving—so I figured if I didn't make it through the six-month probationary period I could always go back to the deaf school. I thought I might want to go back if I didn't like what I saw here.

"At that time they had an ethnic quota. They had two blacks and one Mexican American working here and they couldn't see why they had to hire any more. I couldn't see why not—and I couldn't accept it. I wouldn't accept it until I got the job.

"I started out as a line staff. I worked in one of the cottages. After I had been here six months a supervisor came up and asked me what was wrong—I had been here six months and I hadn't written out a disciplinary report. I told her I didn't see any reason to be writing disciplinaries when I was talking to the individuals and we were preventing the problems from happening. They just didn't understand at that time that the best method of control is to know and understand the individual.

"I made it through that six months and worked my way up through custody rank to program administrator . . . that's through five levels of supervision. It took me three years to make my first promotion—that has a lot of overtones!!

"I have to admit I'm still biased against people in uniforms myself—why do they need them? Are they a crutch?"

Mrs. Anderson's job today is as ombudsman. That means she's in charge of self-help groups at the institution and of volunteers and outside activities coming in. Strictly speaking, she's liaison between inmates and staff.

"The possibility of hiring an outside ombudsman was defeated by the legislature," she said. "Our position was that if you'd worked your way through the ranks, you could see more things that are needed than a person from the outside."

As ombudsman, Kathleen Anderson sits in as an appeal officer at disciplinary hearings—in addition to her other duties. The programs she co-ordinates are centered around the community more than around corrections. "This is definitely positive," she says. "The problem isn't how to get along in the institution, but how to get along in the community you come from.

"There will always be prisons, because there will always be some people who need to be controlled. But there is another large group of women here who could go to community corrections centers and if they couldn't make it—they could come back here.

"Forty-five per cent of the women still here now could maintain themselves in the community if they had some kind of support.

"But then you have to talk about whether the community would accept them at all—and that's a whole different ball of wax altogether. Every person in prison was somebody's neighbor, somebody's child—that's the problem that should be looked at.

"We're working with society's rejects. You can get us to understand—but how do you get society to understand? We all have to deal with what society expects of a prison. And when you want to implement any changes—people tend to say No first—whether it's staff or inmates, or the public. I don't know why, but people just tend to resist change."

Nevertheless, Mrs. Anderson has followed through on a lot of changes since she came to Frontera. "When I came here twelve years ago, this was a holding center," she said, "and that's all. But now we really try to deal on a one-to-one basis. People from the community come in for programs and classes every day of the week—and if you look at the overall picture, you can see a lot of changes. Today our method of control is to know the individual.

"My main question here in every position I have been in is, Why do we do what we do—and what can I do to help it or make it a more positive experience? My whole cause is for positivity.

"When I leave here at night, I become a mother. The girls expect me never to leave. They seem to think I should be here twenty-four hours a day. I ask them, What, do they want me to lose my husband? He's in construction. He's a dry waller of inside walls.

"My three children are pretty self-sufficient. They're eight, nine and fourteen. Plus my husband's an excellent cook—probably in self-defense, because I'm also still going to the University of Southern California for my master's degree in business administration."

Ana

In the summer of 1970, Ana Lou Coelho and her four children left
Oakland, California, to go camping on the Yuba River outside Grass
Valley, California. "It was so beautiful and we all loved being on the
earth again. I asked them if they'd like to stay—and they said yes,
so after spending most of the summer there, we moved up permanently in September 1970.

"I had wanted to get out of Oakland and get the children out of
the city—so it seemed like a very good thing. We were all really
happy up there . . ." For Ana, who is three fourths Apache and one
fourth Chicano, being in the open countryside again was a realized
dream. She had been city-bound in the Oakland-Alameda area since
she was four, but had taken every opportunity to get outdoors from
the time she was small. She had always gone camping with her parents, her sister, ex-husband and relatives.

"Even with four children to raise, she's always managed to get outdoors every chance she got," her sister Dora Canepa says, "whether it
was for swimming, picnicking, camping at Yosemite, hiking or just
cooking out at home or the park. She just plain loves the fun things
of life. Ana and her children always just enjoy themselves. Just enjoy
being alive."

One year after moving up to the idyllic Yuba River outside Grass
Valley, life changed drastically for Ana and her children—Rhonda,
fourteen, Linda, eleven, Sherri, ten, and Ronnie seven. On September 25, 1971, Ana was charged with murder and held without bail
in Nevada County Jail. She was charged with killing a man she
didn't know in a barroom brawl. The man was stabbed to death. Ana
had been wearing a hunting knife in the bar the night of his death.

Ana's children went back to Oakland to stay with their grandmother and her husband. Ana sat in Nevada County Jail without
bail while stories and pictures of her ran on the front pages of the
Grass Valley newspaper. On December 6, her jury trial began. Thirty
witnesses took the stand against her, and, according to Ana, her
lawyer and court transcripts, they told thirty different stories—only

agreeing to one fact: Ana was wearing Levi's, T-shirt and a hunting knife when she came into Tip and Lindy's bar with her friends.

After fifteen minutes' deliberation, the jury found Ana guilty of second-degree murder on December 10, 1971.

Twenty-five days after she had been sentenced to five years to twenty years, Ana and I met in the Reception and Guidance Center of the California Institution for Women at Frontera, in southern California. Ana was CIW Number 8811.

"You gotta talk to Ana," several women told me after I had been in the "center" for less than an hour. "She's here for something she didn't do. She's innocent—and that ain't no jive."

Contrary to popular conceptions, prisoners rarely claim their "innocence" outside the courts. They usually admit, matter-of-factly, "If you play, you gotta pay," or say, "I don't object to having to pay for what I did. It's just that I object to being treated like this while I'm here." So I was curious—especially when I heard from several prisoners of another's innocence. I should also say I was skeptical, as well as exhausted from my traveling, and if it hadn't been for the insistence of the other women, I might well have missed meeting Ana— who, five feet tall with her shiny black hair tied in pigtails on each side of her small olive face, looked about seventeen years old, instead of thirty-two.

She wore a prison uniform covered by a beige prison jacket about three times too big for her. We sat down in the hall to talk—and then asked to have her door "popped" from the control center so we could talk in more privacy in her room. Her room, small and bare except for bed, toilet, sink and desk, was decorated with pictures of her children. Letters from them covered her desk. It was obvious they were as much the focus of her life there in that small barren room as they had been in their home on the Yuba River.

"I've never been in jail before and to be plunked down in prison is so heavy," she said, her hands shaking as she fixed coffee for both of us in a small automatic pot. "At times I get so close to losing my mind; I think I just can't take it.

"When I first got here, I didn't know anything. They just said, 'Here's your room.' Every time I asked a question, it was so stupid, I stopped asking anything. Like the first day I went back to my room and it was locked—so I went up to the control desk and asked if could have a key to my door. She just looked at me and said, 'No, we don't give keys.' I said, 'Well, how do I get in?' 'Just tell us and we'll pop your door.' I didn't know anything. I didn't even know I could go out in the yard for a week. So I just stayed in my room and went so close to going out of my mind—I was dangerously close to it. I knew I couldn't keep staying in my room and thinking about everything. But then I got a copy of the rules and read them and knew more what was going on. Then I asked if I could go outside—and they said, 'Of course—all you have to do is open the door.'

"It's so hard to write to my kids. There's nothing to write about but bad things. All I can tell them is someday justice will be done.

"I'm here for a crime I didn't commit," she said. "I guess if I wasn't innocent, it wouldn't be so hard—but I just can't accept that I'm really here for something I didn't do. All during the trial I was optimistic 'cause I didn't see how they could find me guilty of something I didn't do. My son Ronnie wrote. 'Those people must be mean to keep you there,' and I just told him. 'They can't help it—they're doing what the court ordered them to do.' It's hard for them to understand—I'm innocent, yet I'm still being punished for it. It's hard for me to understand too—and I guess I never will accept it."

Before we were able to talk any more, an officer came to Ana's room and said that we would have to go back to the dayroom to continue talking. "This is for your protection," she said to me. "We don't know what these girls might do. You could get physically attacked or propositioned and we don't want to put you in any kind of embarrassing or compromising situation." The fear that I was in jeopardy seemed ludicrous, to say the least, but nevertheless, we moved back to the dayroom, frustrated by the arbitrary nature of the order.

Ana began to tell me about the night a man named Billy Ray Cook was murdered in Tip and Lindy's, the small Grass Valley barroom which features rock music and dancing. She had gone to "Tip's" with several friends to drink beer and dance. "It's quite dark in Tip's and there was a band playing very loudly, making it impossible to talk and be heard without yelling. I may have been dancing 'wildly,' whatever wildly means—like they said in court—but I was only feeling pretty loose and having a good time. There were numerous altercations between people, but I wasn't involved in them, I was only aware of them.

"I had a hunting knife strapped to the side of me and somebody took it from the sheath when a big fight broke out. It turned into a brawl—like a free-for-all—with about fifteen or twenty people involved. I was pushed up-against the jukebox when the man was stabbed. I had never even seen him until the pictures of him were shown at the trial—I couldn't even see what was going on during the brawl. It was like a football huddle, only everyone was swinging, including myself, even though I was shoved back against the jukebox. During this brawl, a man I knew named Ralph handed me back the knife, led me by my arm towards the door and told me to get rid of it and don't let anyone see me. I ran down the street and put it in the back of the truck. During this time I heard someone yell, 'Someone's been stabbed.' I didn't even know anyone had been stabbed until I heard that. At this point I panicked because I thought someone had seen me put the knife in the truck. I knew something bad had happened and that Ralph was involved in it, because there were a lot of people outside yelling and screaming about a stabbing. I was yelling, 'Where's my knife?' because I didn't want anyone to know what I'd done with it. I know this was wrong, but I was trying to protect Ralph and I was confused. The crowd had already dispersed and we were standing outside when the police came. I was standing near Ralph and some other people. Someone told the police officer, 'Arrest them two, because someone's been stabbed and either one of them did it.' The officer told me to get in the car, which I did."

Ana said she was wearing the knife because she was going to join her children and another family on a camping trip when she left the bar. Ronnie, Rhonda, Linda and Sherri had gone ahead to the camping site with the other family, and their camping equipment, sleeping bags, extra clothes and food.

"I always wore Levi's, T-shirt and a hunting knife on these camping trips," Ana said. "The knife I used primarily in the preparation of meals, making sandwiches, cutting watermelon or cantaloupe—just general camping uses. I used it to help skin a rattlesnake once, but had a hard time as the knife isn't very sharp. . . ."

Ana had two Nevada County lawyers appointed to her case—public defenders. "The first one was put on another case, and the second PD told me I should plead guilty. He told me it was a cut-and-dry case anyway and if I admitted to it I would get off easier—like manslaughter and probation or something. He said, 'If you don't plead, they'll make it hard on you.' But I didn't want to plead guilty because I wasn't guilty—so he refused to take the case. Then my parents got a private attorney from San Francisco to go all the way up there. I saw him three times before we went to trial.

"I asked him to get it moved out of Nevada County because the case had been widely publicized and my picture had been on the front page several times. He said he thought the jury would be fair and wouldn't find me guilty. But he was wrong.

"First of all, the witnesses were so hostile. I wasn't an active member of the community in Grass Valley. We lived three or four blocks out of town. We had made friends with a family with seven children and apparently the community didn't like them. I didn't even know how unpopular they were until the trial. But there was a lot of emphasis on them—the Salazar family—all through the trial, as though just because I was friends with them, it must mean I'm guilty of something. It was also against me that I've been divorced six years and I was on welfare—all kinds of negative points. It didn't matter that I had been past president of the PTA in Alameda or active with the drug abuse council and the Alameda City Council. None of those things were brought up at the trial. They just said I was on welfare—but they didn't say that I had been working with a social worker and he was putting me on job training. I wanted clerical or secretarial work—although I'd like to teach roller-skating. [Ana took third place in the National Roller-Skating Meet in 1956 in Richmond, Virginia—representing the Bay Area and California.]

"Witnesses also said they heard me arguing and saying things in Mexican or Spanish but I speak neither Mexican or Spanish, so whatever I said was in English!!"

Ethnic background, economic status, marital status and association with the unpopular family seemed to be chief determinates against Ana at her trial. Apparently discounted was the testimony of the pathologist who performed the autopsy on the victim, Billy Ray Cook. The pathologist testified it would take an incredible amount of strength to inflict such a wound—because the victim was slashed from his chest to his waist and the stab penetrated muscles and tendons, going deep enough to cut the man's backbone. Ana, whose first offense came with his death, weighs less than a hundred pounds.

Another crucial point in the trial was testimony from an officer as to whether Ana's clothes and shoes had been sent to the lab for tests to see if there was any blood on them. The district attorney objected to admission of the report on the grounds that an officer could not read a laboratory report. The objection was sustained. Ana said that had the report been allowed into evidence, it would have proven she didn't murder the man, because there was no blood on any of her things. "In court, when they showed me pictures of that place, the floor was covered with blood and there was blood all over the wall and post. There was only one person besides the victim with a lot of blood all over his pants, shoes, hands, shirt and face!" Ana said. "He was involved in the fight, he had the knife in his hand, and I know he did it and he's walking the streets, a free man." The "star witness" against Ana cleared the man who Ana believes really committed the murder.

"I think I could have done a better job defending myself," Ana says, "even though I don't know the law. But the jury was incredible. One woman was knitting all through the trial and another was addressing Christmas cards. Can you imagine being a member of a jury at a murder trial and knitting or addressing Christmas cards? It took them such a short time to reach the verdict after five days of testimony. They'd made up their minds ahead of time. But all during the trial I was optimistic anyway, because I didn't see how they could find me guilty."

Ana's feeling that her association with the Salazar family prejudiced her case was substantiated by reading the pre-sentence report filed for the court by William L. Heafy, Chief Probation Officer, Nevada County. In the report, Heafy quotes the exact copy of the district attorney's version of the offense from the beginning. The second sentence of the report refers to the family—a fact that should be irrelevant:

"Ana Coelho has lived in Grass Valley Area with her children for more than a year. *During that time she has been known to be associated with the Salazar family, and some members of a loosely formed organization, "The Misfits," which is a kind of motorcycle club* [my emphasis]."

The district attorney's report also says: "According to a large number of witnesses who testified in generally consistent fashion, but *each to only a portion of the activities of the evening,* Ana Coelho wore her knife in the bar, acted rowdy, belligerent, insulting and threatening. Several people testified that she menaced Kenneth Haynes with her knife and engaged in a number of instances of disturbing the peace or fighting. At one point *Ana Coelho menaced Kenneth Haynes with her knife; several persons saw this although Mr. Haynes did not* . . . [my emphasis]."

"At the trial, there were a number of minor inconsistencies," according to the DA, "and one major conflict. Ana Coelho claimed she did not stab Cook or anyone. The jury resolved that question by its verdict of murder."

Mr. Heafy's probation evaluation states:

"The court is presently concerned with an attractive, diminutive thirty-one-year-old female of Indian-Spanish extraction who has been convicted of second-degree murder in the knifing death of a twenty-seven-year-old man. . . .

"Mrs. Coelho has steadfastly maintained her innocence of the crime for which she has been convicted. During several interviews with the Probation Officer, she has been polite and respectful and appears intent on making a good impression. During interviews she appears to consider her responses very carefully and seems intent on measuring their effect on the Probation Officer. At no time during her incarceration or in her contacts with the Probation Officer has the defendant displayed the vulgarity, hostility or threatening attitude attributed to her . . .

". . . Although it is contrary to the defendant's statement, there are numerous indications that the defendant becomes extremely hostile, belligerent, aggressive and profane particularly while under the influence of alcohol. Nearly every law enforcement report making reference to the defendant describes her as such and witnesses present in the bar, on the night of the offense, describe her as wearing a hunting knife in a sheath on her hip, and acting in a very wild and threatening manner.

"The defendant's impulsiveness, aggressiveness and potential for violence as demonstrated by the gravity of the offense for which she was convicted appears to necessitate that for the protection of society, future rehabilitative efforts be implemented in a secure, long term correctional facility.

"It is respectfully recommended that probation be denied and that the defendant be committed to the California Department of Corrections for imprisonment in the State Prison."

The day of her sentencing to five to twenty years, David Kogus, Ana's lawyer, filed an appeal. He says he made a grave mistake in not getting a change of venue. "The jury was unbelievable," Kogus said in a later telephone interview. They were so hostile to her—it was apparent from the first. Ana was disliked in the area because she was close to people in a motorcycle gang who had moved up to Grass Valley and terrorized the people. It's a conservative, white, older community of people who moved out to Grass Valley to escape the cities themselves.

"I was used to San Francisco juries and I didn't anticipate or see what a small time jury would be like. Ana had asked me to get a change of venue and she was right. I should have listened to her. I've been living with this case now and it's really rough. Ana has beautiful children and comes from a fine family. I feel so strongly about it I don't think I'd go back to Nevada County for another trial.

"There were allegedly two eye witnesses, but they didn't seem like much to me. And I don't think they're worth much . . . so I would expect that eventually we'll get her out. I'm confident we'll get her a new trial. I can't pick the county, but we will have a new trial. I just don't know whether they'll cut her loose or not. I don't know . . . I can only hope.

"I went to New York to talk to the guy who really did it, but he's scared—he's on parole—and not willing to confess to anything, let alone open his mouth. So that's not much help."

Nothing has been much help for Ana. Her brief was filed in January and her appeal was submitted in March. In April, the attorney general asked for an extension on his argument for denial of her appeal. In June, he asked for still another extension and her appeal was scheduled to be heard in August. If she wins the right to a new trial, it could be another year or two before her case goes to court again.

Meanwhile, thoughts of freedom are on her mind. In April, she wrote of being pulled out of CIW on a Superior Court subpoena to testify in a trial in Alameda County: "I was taken to Santa Rita Rehabilitation Center where I stayed until the end of March. What a horrible experience that was! Whew!!! While I was there, a girl kicked a hole in the wall and escaped. They still haven't caught her. It was a beautiful sight to see her leap over that fence to freedom. Being a few miles away from home myself, I was tempted to flee, too. I had the opportunity and I blew it. I hesitated because I felt that if I was to escape, it would be bad for my case. But if I could have escaped successfully, I'd be free. You just can't imagine what a hard decision it was that I made, to try and do this thing their way. But now I'm not so sure I made the right decision . . .

"At any rate, shortly after I returned here, I was moved from R.G.C. [Reception and Guidance Center] over here to the permanent prison side of this institution. They call it 'campus,' I call it 'prison'!

They call these buildings we live in 'cottages' but they aren't. I call them 'cell blocks.'

"The first day I was here they took me on what they call a 'tour of the campus.' What they did was show me the three work areas and the school building and that's all. The work areas include the laundry, industry and the kitchen. I have been over here for one week now and it's been a hectic week."

Ana spends her time now working in the kitchen of the California Institution for Women, scrubbing pots and pans. She's gotten her room fixed up "so that it is comfortable to live in"—with pictures of her children and letters from them still dominant among the decor, along with a "Leo" poster for her astrological sign. She has ten little guppies in a fish bowl and has acquired a drum, tambourine and harmonica. She's secretary-treasurer for the United Indian Tribes, a self-help organization for Indian and non-Indian women at the prison. The group discusses Indian history and culture and is cultivating arts and crafts—learning weaving, bead work and leather tooling. She's going to school to take a high school equivalency test.

Ana could be pointed to as a "model prisoner" getting "rehabilitated." But her personal turmoil would not be apparent to an outsider touring the prison "campus." She writes to her lawyer and to friends, going over and over the details of her case and the inconsistencies of testimony against her, hoping somehow to speed up the legal processes that may set her free.

"My hands are tied," she wrote in late June. "I'm so utterly helpless in here; I can do absolutely nothing. Where does a person turn for help?! And does help have to cost a lot of money? Is that what justice is, money?? There is no one here I can turn to for help, because in their eyes I am guilty because I have been found guilty. They don't know that in the eyes of everyone in Nevada County, the fact that I was arrested was enough to make them believe I was guilty, even before the trial. I keep calling it a trial—but it wasn't! You know that thing about innocent until proven guilty? Well, it's the complete opposite.

"Yesterday I was told by one of my fellow inmates that we are only allowed to keep ten letters when we leave here. I've got scads and scads of letters. I don't know what I'm going to do with them, but I do know that I refuse to destroy any of the letters I have received from my little people . . . For the whole of last week, I was at my worst. I was nervous about the fact that my little people were out of school and I didn't know what they were going to do . . . as my mom and her husband both work. This plus the fact that my lawyer hasn't written to me and I haven't seen him since February. I was in such a bad frame of mind that the doctor prescribed some heavy tranquil medication and told me I was on the verge of a complete mental breakdown. Wow, it was super scary. I've never been there before, and I'm hoping and praying I'll never return there to that mental condition.

"I work from 11 A.M. to 7 P.M. Some of those pots 'n pans are so huge I have to literally climb in them to get 'em clean. When I get back here to my room at night, I'm so completely exhausted I just fall out. I just don't know how much longer I can hold up to these terrific pressures both physically and especially mentally. I've been fighting very hard, with every ounce of strength I have, against becoming the kind of person you've got to be to exist here. And I feel my strength dwindling.

"Twenty four hours a day, you're being subjected to brainwashing, and they're constantly trying to get you institutionalized. Oh, it's really ugly. When Ma and Frank and the kids came to visit me during Easter break, I tried real hard to give the impression that I was doing O.K. But I'm not. It's been a long time and I was so sad to see them leave. I just can't take all this, it's way too heavy. I can't sleep, think or function. And these thundering headaches are killing me. But they have enough to worry about, without worrying about me, too. I am so hurt, confused and lonely. And what's worse, I am learning how to hate. The hatred is building up in me every second of the long days and nights. My hatred is centered on the person who's responsible for the crime I'm in here for, but it doesn't stop there. It includes the D.A., the judge, the jury, the probation officer and those witnesses who were either bribed or made some kind of deal to get on the witness stand and lie. I really used to believe in justice. Now I know there isn't any.

"God knows I am innocent—and if I can maintain my sanity, someday justice will be done. It has to be. I can't stand not being with my children."

Ana's Children

*A letter from Linda, eleven years old, to her mother on January 9—
the day after their visit in Nevada County Jail. Ana Lou Coelho had
just been sentenced to five to twenty years in the state prison.*

Dear A Beauitful (cp)
    Person,

Hi,
    I love you,
I cryed all the
way home. I am
going to write
Ralph and tell him
what he is doing
to us, keeping us
apart for all this
time, and beg him
to go tell the
truth. Tell Dee I
said hi.
      (over)
I think I am going
to go crazy with-
out you. I love you
MOM more than
anyone else!
I'v got to eat break-
fast now, give me
your new address,
I love you forever
ever, ever, ever, ever,

    Love,
      LINDA

From Rhonda . . . fourteen years old. (This letter was written two days before Rhonda's fourteenth birthday.)

Nov. 11, 1971
8:00 p.m.

TO MY MOM

I got your letter today. Thank you for the beautiful birthday card. It was poetic and sweet. I hope those people know they have made a sin putting you in "there"! Aunties house is nice. We went to Aunties house for dinner. Twart & and I were playing a game. When we went out in the kitchen to eat Laree told me that their going to have a skating party for me. She blew it. But their still having it for me even though I know. Peety died of distemper. Nothing is new at Better Way. Linda's Angel fish gets along with the other fish. She got them from "Doll." My rat "Persy" is so spoiled now by me and Grandma. She loves him. We don't even need a cage. Grandma lets him run around. She digs on him. She lets him climb on her.

I'm watching Flip Wilson Show the same time I'm writing. Last week the Jackson 5 was on it. We were at Auntie's house. She put the [TV] up loud and everybody danced even "Grandma" ha-ha. Bet when you get out you will be so fat I won't know you. ha ha. Don't get too, fat. Sherri & Ronnie will write as soon as they get their
_____ _____(censored) together. Well better go now have to feed my baby "Persy."

LOVE RHONDA

P.S. Persy says,   of course
"I Love Ya."   Miss   Love
P.S.S. I'll put Ronnie's   America   Happness
letter in here too, also.   Peace
P.S.S. Kick out the Jam   Persy misses you.
        M.F.

Poem by Rhonda—originally for Mother's Day when she was eleven (three years ago) but sent to Ana again at CIW.

DEAR MOM,

Deep in each heart, God puts the need of a love that is tender and strong. The need of one who can understand each sorrow and share each song. And to us all he grants one gift sweeter than any other, He grants us each a MOTHER,

By:
    Rhonda
      of
  course

Nov. 1, 1971

DEAR MOM,

We went trick-or-treating last night. It was fun. *I was a witch.* Linda was a hobo, Sherri an angel, Ronnie was a clown. Eddie had a fever so he couldn't go. Gloria was an Indian, Kathi was a hobo, Auntie had a pumpkin in the window with a peace symbol cut in it. This is Miss America speaking. I almost forgot the poem, I finished the poem and its time to go to school-baaaaa
I wuv ya
this much ———————————————————

LOVE
RHONDA
of
course

From Sherri, ten years old.

DEAR MOM,

   HI!!!!!
   How are you   I am fine?
I wish you were here NOW.
But your wish will not come true.
It will come true for you—and me.
I better go and eat.

        Love
        alway
        SHERRI
        Loose

Another from Linda . . .

I will
kiss me please

Feb. 8, 1972

DEAR MOM,

Hi,
How are you? I hope
you have been feeling O.K. Can Peggy
and Joshua use our Washer & Dryer?
They really need them know that the
baby came. I saw Randy the baby's
father. He is tall and strong. He swung
me all around in peggy's front room. It
was fun. Grand ma already said Peggy
could use the W & Dryer. It is no fun
when your there. I don't feel like I'm living
without you. Time to go.

Love
LINDA
Loose

Peace   Love
I LOVE YOU
13,1110,000,000,000,000 more even! ! ! ! !

And from Ronnie, when he was six years old:

11/18/71

TO MOM,

I Love you. I'm doing good in school. I don't have my school pictures yet. I miss you too also. I got my haircut ½ month ago. I hope you can get out for my birthday. Those people must be mean to keep you in there. Well time to go.

Love
RONNIE

After Ronnie's seventh birthday:

december 1971

DEAR MOM

I got some money for my birthday. We had cupcakes an brownies. I am 7 years old. I got a hat from Dorthy. I got a silly straw from Linda. I miss you. Will you be out for Christmas?

Love   RONNIE

Martha M.

"I've been here since November," said Martha Moore, a correctional officer at a state prison. "Before, I was a cosmetologist. I had my own shop. But now I have my shop up for sale. I thought this work would be easier; I've always worked with the public, plus my mother's a supervisor over at the prison hospital. She's been here ten years. I'm changing fields totally and I'm very happy about it. My mother always said I would like the work here.

"I work from seven to three, but I come in a half hour early. That's the way I do my job. I come in and check the log book to see what has happened before I came on. Very soon after I come in they start unlocking.

"I'm not teaching any cosmetology here. I'm mostly in supervision as a CO. I make sure to keep a schedule going—get the doors locked and unlocked on time. Write reports. Make sure the housekeeping's done. When the laundry comes in we supervise to make sure it's put away properly. The women come in and you check the pass for each woman. It has to be re-signed and marked with the time before she can leave the corridor. At lunch everyone comes back to the cottage. This is when food cards come back—and that's another roll call. We check them in and after the food cards are checked and roll is taken, we make two calls and say we have everyone. They stay on the corridor during this time. No one goes to their rooms except under very rare circumstances. They have to stay here so we can supervise. Then when the whistle blows they all go back to work. The AM's get back here at one P.M. They go to their rooms . . . but believe me, they're ready. They were up at six-thirty A.M. They get unlocked at four-thirty P.M. Sometimes they go shopping at the commissary or have a beauty shop appointment or hospital calls.

"I couldn't do anything with cosmetology training. Being responsible for fifty women at one time is enough. When the phone rings I know where they are. Each one of them. That's fifty people; that's a big responsibility!

"Today we have a cottage meeting and everyone has to be locked up—housekeeping and everything."

Anna

"I started to quit the first day I worked as a guard," Anna Hardy recalled. "I was taken into the mess hall and every face I saw was sad. I was sick inside. I developed a migraine headache. I didn't think I could go back the next day and see all that sadness. But my brother, he was a policeman, told me I had to go back and face it; that I had made a decision and I should follow through on it. Well, I went back the next day, and the next, and then it got to be a day-to-day thing.

Anna Hardy "went to jail" after coming back to the United States from four years in Europe as a correspondence specialist for the U. S. Army. In Europe she supervised one of the Army correspondence schools sponsored by the Department of Information and Education. "After I came to Washington, D.C.," she said, "I went to jail and I've been in jail ever since. I guess it would be nicer to say I hit the corrections field . . . and then the escalator moved me up."

After Anna became a prison guard, she moved up "through the ranks" to be an assistant superintendent of the Women's Reformatory, chief administrator of the women in the D.C. Jail and then administrator of the Women's Detention Center. Now she's the first woman to be a parole examiner for the Washington, D.C., Parole Board. Our interview was in her Parole Board office.

"The first year I was there I would cry. I would see mothers visiting their daughters and it would tear my heart strings up. I never got over it but I learned to deal with it.

"There were many times I did things I did not personally believe in. I was not asked to violate the law or be inhumane, but in my time we had many difficult things.

"There were times persons were put into segregation for reasons I thought they shouldn't be segregated for. There were too many minor situations they used major solution tools for.

"For instance, I believe a person has the right to talk. It used to be that the officer would feel offended and call it 'back talk.' Too often action was taken because of personal feelings or because the officer was short-tempered. There are many other ways to deal with the situation.

"I guess I was a nuisance. I was always asking *why?* It bothered me to see a person locked up for what I thought was minor. But I had to live with it. It used to bother me to take black coffee and a heel of bread for breakfast to a woman in a cell.

"Something else used to bother me. You'd have a woman in a control cell who was not allowed to take a bath. You wouldn't find it in the book—it was the exercise of power and authority that was overused. What could you do as a junior officer? You couldn't spare the time and sneak and give it. You had to live with that power and authority too.

"Among other things, what they were perpetuating was punishing the staff as well as the inmates. But I guess I stayed because I began to feel there was something about me that made me feel that I was somebody and there might be one of these somebody's who might want to be like me.

"I kept thinking—someday, if it's possible, I'm going to be a supervisor. There were so many things I wanted to change. I didn't get to change all the things—but I think I made a difference. And I know I've changed. I used to be more of a hard-liner than I am now. I had been orientated to regimentation with the Army to follow do's and don'ts. Out of that, if I was expected to do something at a certain time, I did it. But a lot of what I had to do made me sick. I just kept telling myself that someday I might have a chance to change things. But it wasn't easy.

"When I came into corrections, I was black. I'm still black. In the beginning it didn't look like I could by competitive examination come through the uniform ranks.

"But if you put your mind to what you are doing and believe in what you are doing, it can work. I made up my mind that I would never allow my black skin to keep me from being in competition by not allowing myself to be part of that competition. I'm very efficient and through efficiency, I did it my way.

"I remember, when it came time for the lieutenant exam, I had misgivings about it. I was afraid. Then another officer—who was also taking the exam—asked me why I was even bothering to take it. She was so sure she would get the promotion.

"I told her, 'There's only one way to lose the exam, and I'm not going to let it happen. You're the only other person taking it and in education, we're equal, so we'll score the same. In longevity, you've got it on me. In efficiency I'm better than you. There's only one way you can beat me out of it—and that's 'cause you're white, sweetie. That's why I have to get one hundred per cent on that examination. And I'm gonna get one hundred per cent.' I did get ninety-nine and a half per cent right—and I got the promotion.

"I'm not ashamed to say I've been a competitor all my life. I was one of nine children. I was in the middle, and I didn't want my brothers or sisters to beat me.

"Things have changed a lot since I first began. And, like I said, I've changed a lot. I've learned a lot. It was during my time when we began to learn the really serious impact of drug abuse. I had seen some of the late stages of withdrawal, but when the police women's building was closed, we began to receive a woman directly from police on arrest. This means taking them through line-up, fingerprinting and booking. We took over the precinct function for police women. Police started bringing us the women straight from arrest with no overnight in the district or a day in the court. We saw the whole works, straight from the street. I saw narcotics withdrawals that words do not describe. So pathetic that you couldn't look at it. It's total grief itself.

"We've had every kind of woman—women emotionally disturbed, women prone to go into catatonic state. Sometimes they're just one-shot situations; they come to jail just once. A number of fine people who just built up an emotional state—committed a crime once and not again.

"Then we've had some who are just bad. Not necessarily killers but ones who just have no respect for their bodies or the law. And who show neglect in terms of children. Occasionally we get someone motivated some way and it's rewarding to see a change of face.

"I like the women. I'm not telling you we sat up in each other's living rooms. But I don't have any biases. I do understand what is happening with these women. I know their children and I know their mothers.

"All of them have problems to face. Additionally a woman has to face coming out of jail. Some have feelings about it; some could care less about going back again. Some know they're gonna do it again, whatever their crime was, so it's a calculated risk and they don't put up a big protest.

"Eighty-five per cent of the women return—the figures kept creeping up—or *maybe they didn't creep up*. Statistics were not being kept for many years like they're being kept now.

"A considerable number of times there would be fairly affluent women eighteen and over arrested on a variety of charges. But once an affluent woman had gone to court we'd never see her again. I have every reason to believe her less affluent counterpart—on an identical charge—came back to jail. I can't vouch for what happened in court; I just know they didn't come back to jail.

"It's the same with prostitutes. There's no difference between one who prostitutes herself on the street and the one who lives in a luxurious apartment and pays for it in the same method. It's just that the ones in the luxurious apartments don't usually make it to jail.

"I'd personally like to see no woman arrested or prosecuted for prostitution. It would reduce the jail population considerably. We fill up the jails on prostitution charges. If there is to be a charge it should be against both the male and the female. If you're not going to arrest the man, then it's not fair to just arrest the woman.

"And believe me, not every arrest stems from the agent. Like these rich big shots from out of town who come in and want to pay for some fun . . . and they end up charging the women. They're led astray—tsk, tsk—the poor innocent men; no one thinks about what happens to the woman!

"So much of what brings about the prisoner comes from way back there in the community. There are serious ills that prevail in the early years that severely limit people from doing anything different. A lot has to do with family structure spread out into the immediate community and the schools. Not everybody is necessarily a victim in that sense . . . but so much of the responsibility for what brings people to jail lies in the general community frustration.

"So many of the women have been in juvenile facilities. What good's it do? Even if you're a hardhearted Hannah, you gotta realize that.

"In my time I've been around women who were motivated and had good thoughts of making it. Sadly enough, I've never had time to follow through. I did have one woman who served a felony term . . . and some years later she went to a reformatory in Maryland and went to school there. She sent me a high school graduation invitation from the reformatory. I had two of her daughters under my purview at the time, and two of their brothers were in jail, too. But in spite of all the things that happened to them—you had to admire their family spirit and unity. If one of 'em got sent to jail, they'd write faithfully to them and when it was time to get a box, they'd pack up a big box to send. In a way you can compare it to another family—when it's time for the kids to go off to college.

"These are the kinds of things that make people like me work in jail. I've gotten to know a lot of families—daughters, mothers, grandmothers. One family I knew for a long time. There were five sisters who came to jail at different times . . . and I'd met their mother first.

"I'll never forget one tiny kidnapper from Wisconsin who kidnapped a large man. I asked her how she did it. Her answer was, 'It was easy. He was scared. I wasn't.'

"There was one girl who escaped, and I felt a lot of personal involvement with her case. She was a beautiful girl with an IQ of a hundred and thirty-two. She was on trusted status and was attending American University. The psychologist took the girl to school and I'd bring her back when I was coming on to the midnight shift. Well, one night I went and waited for her in the same spot and she didn't come. I went everywhere looking for her and left the car unlocked so if she'd gone off for a beer or something she would be able to get into the car. Finally I had to call the institution and report that she was missing. It was not as if I had been responsible for her or she had escaped from me—it was just the disappointment of it all.

"About four months later we got a call from New Mexico, where she'd been picked up on a drunk and disorderly charge. She was brought back, and we didn't prosecute her. She got out on parole and went back to American University. She graduated and married a fellow student. She's living a very successful life right now. If she walked in here right now, you'd never know her from anyone else.

"Another girl had a baby and no place for him to stay at the time. She didn't want to give him up, so he lived in the cottage for more than a year. You can imagine, the girls loved him to death. After he was a year old, we were afraid of over-loving him, so he had to be placed in a foster home until she got out.

"When I had my first demonstrators out of the Pentagon, I had a whole new experience. I got accused of inhumane treatment, brutality, fantasies. The switchboard was flooded with calls. The complaints were made by white college-educated girls mostly, who had lived comfortable lives. Most of the persons arrested out of demonstrations are people either of very strong convictions or high academic qualifications. These are people you can't rehabilitate—and what are you gonna give them? After the first Pentagon arrests we had a lot of them for the first time. I felt so helpless then. It appeared to us nobody in the public wanted to believe we were other than inhuman.

"We established rapport with the demonstrators. They told us that part of their philosophy was that 'anytime we're in a situation we can't control is cruelty . . . we're in your jail and we don't have the key, so therefore this is a cruel situation.'

"During that time the contingent of women we had dealt with before were most co-operative with us. But often they got angry at the 'falling out' [passive resistance] and that sort of thing from the demonstrators. But I think after a while it was difficult for the demonstrators to see us as monsters.

"Part of my orientation to jail had been that there could be no newsmen near the scene of any trouble. Throughout the media was excluded; the idea was that newsmen make the situation worse. But then things started opening up. When we were getting all the calls after the Pentagon arrests, Walter Masterman from NBC came to interview me and after people saw me on the camera I think it changed things; it just wasn't what they expected. I think that's what stopped the calls. Usually more exposure is a good thing—but sometime it backfires.

"We had one woman come in—a reporter—and opened everything up to her, let her stay overnight. I'd like to spit in her face. She did me a great injustice and I'll never forget it.

"The things she wrote—the cold, barefaced lies. She wrote and implied that I was responsible for the death of a girl at the institution I had known for years. Why she didn't ask me about it, I don't know. It would have only been fair. She said the girl—Willa Mae Johnson— died in jail, but that was a lie. She died in D. C. Hospital.

"Willa Mae Johnson was the kind of person I'd save her life and I like to think I'm the kind of person she'd save my life. I'd known her for years and I never would have let her die. She came into the jail and was going through cold turkey. Eventually we sent her to the hospital and she died in the hospital four days later of complications —not the cold turkey.

"I can't tell you how that newspaper article affected me. I couldn't go to work the next day. I was really sick. I'm still bitter. But I just thought, what will my friends think, my neighbors? I couldn't call everyone I knew to dispute the article; I just had to live through it. I didn't know if I could.

"We all knew it was an imperfect institution. Not one of us would have wanted to be an inmate there. I know what people go through in jail. I always keyed the officers up to 'It could have been your daughter, or it could have been your sisters . . .' But I also have empathy for prison administrators.

"It's true—in jail a woman sleeps, eats, bathes by regulation. Everything she does is controlled and everything she doesn't do is controlled. Her flexibility and our flexibility can expand only to the walls of the jail or within the confines of the walls.

"Basically by philosophy I'm the same individual, but now the atmosphere provides for more use of my talents. I'm given great leeway in making decisions. I no longer have to respond to do's and don'ts.

"I've seen a lot of change in the corrections field. There are lots who'll never change until they die—some who are hard-nosed, but there are others who were hard-nosed who learned and are still changing. Even though I used to be so oriented to military thinking, I'm fully able to accept all kinds of programs the community has to offer for advancement of a person who needs it. I have no hang-up about a person serving a sentence to go to school or job training in the city.

"I think the Parole Board trusts me to use my judgment—and up to this time it's been pretty good. I give the full respect accorded to the board chairman and it goes beyond this to the people I am examining and making recommendations on. I have the satisfaction of feeling I am doing a good job. I've reached what I want professionally; I don't want to go any higher. I want to retire eventually—probably within a few years.

"Probably the reason I can sleep at night is that at the end of the day I feel I have not done an unjust thing to someone. My husband can worry—but if he does, he has to do that by himself. [Her husband, Kenneth Hardy, is Commissioner of Corrections in D.C.] It's a big picture to me. Even if I have recommended against a man or woman getting parole, I have to believe it's a justifiable recommendation—leaving the possibility open that I may not have put all the little screws together right. So far my batting average has been very good."

Suzanne

Q: Can you tell me about when you escaped from Alderson?

Suzi: Oh. I'll never forget that whole scene. Wheew. Well, my best friend had gotten himself into a jam in New York City. He had been arrested for the draft and not too long before that he had a really horrible jail experience in Wyoming. He had been beaten up and had almost died, and had not been in too good shape as a result of the thing and sort of was putting his head back together. And shortly after that he was arrested. He's into a lot of non-co-operating with jails; he feels pretty absolutely about right and wrong and stuff. And then he was picked up on his draft thing, and like I didn't know what sort of mental shape he was in, or how he was, or if he needed aid and comfort, or what. And I was unable to find out. They wouldn't let me call, so I figured, well, you know, like if he's in need of a friend, I gotta find out. I was just very worried about him. So I split.

Q: How did you get out? Did you just walk out?

Suzi: It's a little harder than that. First of all, you really can't hitchhike anywhere in the area, because it's in the middle of nowhere, and everyone knows what's down the road, and any strange unidentified females will immediately be picked up on.

And then this little matter of *counts.* Because their physical security is not that great they keep careful track of you, pretty much. They have nine counts within every twenty-four-hour period. So they count you up—at eight-fifteen in the morning, and then at twelve-fifteen in the afternoon, and at four-fifteen in the afternoon. Then they count you an hour after you come back from supper, then they count you when it becomes twilight. And then they count you at ten, and then at midnight, and then at three and then at six. Two of those were added while I was there on my '68–'69 bit. We call the eight-fifteen one the "Nancy Memorial Count." She skipped right around then, and then they put in that count. And the midnight one is the "Jo Memorial Count." They caught Nancy after about three years of her being out, but I'm happy to say that Jo is still at liberty.

Besides that, like you have your work assignment, and several of those counts are counted on the job, or else you're counted in the unit if you have a day off or something. But just generally, if you're not on the job, they want to know where you are. And if you're supposed to be in the unit, you got to be there. If you go anywhere that isn't on your regular schedule, then they will call up and say, "Suzanne Williams is on her way to the clinic." And if I don't arrive within five or ten minutes they try to track you down, and then they call back, you know, to my boss at work: "Suzanne Williams is on her way back from the clinic." So that most of your comings and goings are according to a set schedule. And things that are out of schedule, they will call you in and out.

There are ways to get around them. But generally they keep a close eye on people. And one thing which helps it a lot with the whole security thing is that women are generally trained that they can't do things, and to stay down and that kind of stuff. Plus most of the inmates there are from the big cities, and don't have the vaguest idea of what they would do if they were out in the sticks in West Virginia, or which way is north, south, east or west. So that's why they don't have more escapes than they do.

But what I did was, I went to the regular Saturday night movie, and I was dressed in warm clothes. In fact the cottage police remarked, "Oh, Suzanne, you're all dressed up warm tonight." You can't split from the movie because they have police right outside there and they take note of who comes and goes.

So I waited till it was over, and I wasn't the first one out, but I was about the fifth one out. I really walked quickly. At that time they weren't using Cottage Twenty-six. And so I walked over behind there, and climbed over the fence. And oh . . . as I was climbing over the fence, I had on this pair of sneakers that was a little bit too big for me, and I got up—oh, it's about a twelve-foot fence with three strands of barbed wire—and I had got up over the fence and very carefully over the barbed wire, and I was pulling my last foot up over, and my shoe fell off.

I wanted to die, I really did. I was going to say, oh the hell with it, and go on, but second thoughts told me that just wasn't practical, so back over the fence, inside, crawling around in all the leaves and crud, 'cause it was raining lightly, and scrub around for the shoe, finally I put it back on, retied the other one so it doesn't do a repeat number, and back up over the fence. I was worried 'cause that was like the most exposed part of the whole operation. If the car had happened to swing by and hit me with its headlights, that would have been it . . .

Q: When you finally got over the fence, what did you do?

Suzi: Then I walked on the railroad tracks for about twenty miles west. I had walked through a couple of little towns sort of holding my breath. But it was dark, and it was raining lightly most of the night. And I guess that damped out the dogs. There was one place where the tracks went through this tunnel, underneath a mountain. And it wasn't like a double tunnel, but it was two single ones, so there wasn't much room. And it was about a mile long. And oh it was scary, there was just this single little red signal light at the end giving a faint pink gleam on the rails, and I had never been so scared in my life. So I ran through the tunnel. Shortly after I got out of the tunnel the eastbound passenger train went zipping through. And every time a train came by, you know, you'd have to jump into the bushes.

I finally got to Hinton, and see, Hinton has a number of roads. Before that point like there's only the one highway. It's pretty obvious what highway it is, and any woman seen on that would be suspicious. But Hinton is a much larger town and there are a number of other highways going through there. So strange people would be much more likely. But I wasn't hitchhiking even from Hinton, because I couldn't think of any plausible reason why I would be out there at four-thirty in the morning.

So I just walked along, and I was walking up the mountain towards Beckley, and I got about four or five miles further, and some people that were going into town for a long trip, into Beckley, about fifty miles from Alderson, stopped and picked me up. They thought I had run away from home, see. And they came on all very sympathetic, and after the initial silence one of them said in a very fatherly type tone, "Did things get pretty bad that you had to run away?"

I said, "Oh yes." And he said, "Well, what was the problem?" And I said, "Well, uh, my boyfriend was in trouble and they wouldn't let me go see him." "They" being unspecified, but they thought I meant parents. And I kind of got into a rap, you know, "They were always telling me what to do," and "I didn't have much freedom." Every word was the truth. So they made sympathetic noises and I fell asleep. And then when I got to Beckley, one of the guys gave me a couple dimes. I made a couple phone calls and arranged some transportation. Then when I got business taken care of I went out . . .

Q: Did you get to New York City?

Suzi: Oh yeah. I spent a couple weeks there and found out that my friend was all right.

Q: Did you get to see him?

Suzi: No, I didn't. But there was a preacher that got to see him. But there was a funny thing on that, too. My friend was in jail and I would be down there like every day, asking to see him; they'd say, No, you can't see him, blah, blah, blah, blah, blah. And then one day they said, Well, Reverend So-and-So is up there seeing him, you can wait till he comes down. So I waited and he came down, some guy who was a Quaker, and the warden at the jail. The Reverend introduced me to the guy by my right name, and then the guy offered to drive us to the subway, which he did in his official bureau business car. I had walked by that car on the way into the jail and sort of shuddered at it, because it was just the same kind of official car they had at Alderson.

After I knew my friend was all right, I went up to my brother's place in Vermont, and figured they could come by and get me, 'cause with just a year's sentence it really isn't worthwhile to hide for the rest of your life for a short thing like that—even if you get more time tagged on for escaping. But yet and still, I'm not really geared to turning myself in, so I settled for something of a compromise. And they did come and pick me up.

Q: Did they just come by to see if you were there?

Suzi: Yeah.

Q: So how long had you been out?

Suzi: Oh, just three weeks. But when someone escapes from Alderson, they notify all of the police in the area immediately, and the radio stations and the newspapers in the area are notified immediately. Of course the first thing they do is they call the FBI. And then all the local police types, and they send male guards to beat through the bushes around the perimeter, and to go to certain crossroads of small dirt roads, and to run up and down the small dirt roads and main roads to see if anybody's there, at crossroads and railroad tracks, and different places like that. And they will hunt for you usually twenty-four hours, except if you're somebody they want real bad, then they'll search for you longer.

Q: Do they pay the local people for catching someone who escapes?

Suzi: Fifty dollars a head, which is a lot of money in that part of West Virginia. I think one reason why I had such an easy time escaping, once I had got out of the very immediate area, was that except for the people that work at the prison, I think all the locals believe that we all have horns and a tail, and are ten feet tall and smoke cigars regularly, and wear hobnail boots. So that you know, I was at the time twenty years old, had a short haircut, and I looked about sixteen.

It was funny, right after I was picked up, at my brother's place in southern Vermont, one FBI agent and one state trooper took me down first to the state police barracks, which was in the same town. And they sort of parked me in a back room while they were making phone calls and getting the stuff run through. And this off-duty trooper wandered in, just getting ready to go on the job, and he was charmed at the idea that they had a young girl in there as a prisoner. And he said, "Oh, what did they arrest you for, playing hooky?" And I wasn't feeling real talkative, and wasn't feeling real happy at the time and didn't want to get into a big rap with him, so I just said, "No."

But then he persisted. Had I been arrested for shoplifting? I said no, wishing he would go away. And he finally said, Well, what were you arrested for? I said, Escaping from a federal penitentiary. And his mouth dropped and he stuttered—You don't look old enough to even have heard of a federal penitentiary. What were you charged with to be there? And I said, Destruction of government property, destruction of public records, interfering with the Military Selective Service Act of 1967, and conspiracy. He shut up and went away, which was the desired effect. It's silly how that shuts people up.

When I went to court in Charleston to be sentenced for the escape, there were six of us altogether, from Alderson escape cases, staying in the Charleston jail. We stayed there for about four days while the thing was being run through. We came into the jail, with handcuffs and waist chains and all this hardware garbage, and the two older of the four of us were put in the second floor with the rest of the women, but then we created an overflow, so they took the four younger ones of us and put us on the third tier, and they put one of the local inmates up there to sort of tell us what the rules were and so forth and so on. She was what they call in that particular jail, a kick-out girl. Which is I guess trustee, or something. And she was their kind of person. Everything we said, she ran and told the police about. Yeah, we didn't care for this. And so we sent word to the police that we wanted her off our tier, please. She was gone in five minutes.

They were really afraid of us. They thought we were really going to do something to her. Of course a couple of the other people were making big bad threatening noises.

You know, and they had seen us being brought in in the chains and handcuffs and maximum security, escapees from the penitentiary, and we didn't really give a shit, because we had all had time, and we were going to get more time, so we were just goofing off. I got six months added to my sentence for the escape, so it ended up to be eighteen months total, regular procedure.

None of Us

In the dining room at Marysville, right after lunch, I'm talking to the "kitchen workers." All women that come to Marysville are assigned to work in the kitchen for ten to twelve weeks after they get out of "orientation." The institution's rationale for this is that since no one likes working in the kitchen permanently, everyone takes a turn at it this way. But prisoners say some women should be exempt.

"You got ladies carrying garbage cans and huge trays . . . and it don't make sense for us to have to do it," says one woman. "I'm three months pregnant," says another who is just beginning to show, "and she's seven months pregnant. There's another woman who's six months pregnant who works in here. I work in the dish room and I have to carry the garbage cans out full. We take 'em out once a day and they're so heavy it could really make me lose my baby—but the officers they won't let anyone else do it. You gotta wash 'em out after you get them out there and empty 'em."

"This work we're doing is a man's work. I done got a hernia lifting jugs and coffee," says a small, light-skinned woman in her late forties. "It's wet and slippery and too heavy even for a woman not pregnant. But at least they should let us old ones and the pregnant ones not hafta work here."

"Did you ever go to the state prison in Nashville, Tennessee?" asks another woman. "That place is something else. You should go there! I was there in '66—and they have the white girls on one side and the black girls on the other side. They got their coffee urn and we got our coffee urn. There it's a physical thing, here it's a mental thing . . . with all the petty rules.

"None of us don't like it here. We know if you play you gotta pay, but we just want to be treated like human beings. Back a dog up in a corner and keep yappin' at 'em—eventually they're gonna bite you . . ."

Although a caseworker and another staff member are standing nearby, about eight women sit at a table with me detailing complaints and grievances against the institution—including: "You gotta have a piece of paper everywhere you go and if you don't, you get restricted"; "You can take a shower at 6 P.M. but not when you want to"; You have to be sick at 5:30 P.M. the day before the clinic or you don't get to go to sick call because your name's not on the list"; "Only one box can come to each prisoner from the outside in one year"; "Men friends cannot come to visit" ("some of us don't have family come up—we need a friend to come up"); "The matrons don't know how to respect us—they treat us like slaves"; "Men get privileges at the penitentiary we at Marysville don't get—they get boxes with canned goods, visiting with friends, literature and college courses . . ."

As we are talking, another inmate comes up to the table and wipes it off with a wet cloth. The strokes of the cloth on the table are large, determined, seemingly angry. We all have to move our arms and back up. A few minutes later, the woman who has wiped the table leans on a mop and shouts from across the room:

"Why are you talking to her? What good's it gonna do? She ain't gonna do nothing!" The women at the table, and a few working across the room whom I talked to earlier holler back that I'm working on a book and that I'm gonna "tell it like it is." "She's okay," a large woman shouts back. "Leave her alone. Leave us alone."

"Well, even if she does write it like it is, people ain't gonna do nothing about it," she says, alternately shaking her head with anger, and wiping sweat from her brow. "They'll just say, 'Ain't that a shame' . . . and nothing will change. It'll be just the same. It was the same twenty years ago as it is now. Twenty years from now it'll still be the same. We'll still be here. And it'll be just the same."

The welcome to prison.

Getting booked: pocketbook emptied, medicine, rings, money, clothes, personal possessions taken. Fingerprints, photographs and numbers come next.

Cellblock in a modern jail exclusively for women now becomes
"home".

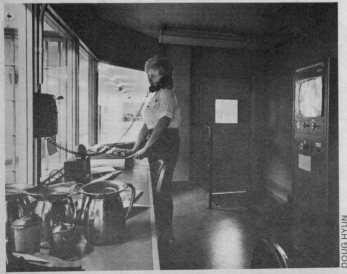

Push buttons replace large bronze keys in electrically controlled
prisons like this one in Los Angeles.

Cells are often left in disarray for the new arrival.

"Housecleaning" is an everyday affair for all inmates.

Visiting for the majority of confined women is touching glass, whispering into the phone and saying it all in twenty minutes twice a week.

EMIKO TONOOKA

Children are often only a memory, a scribbled note or a battered photograph to mothers behind bars.

In prison, there's little space between laughter and tears.

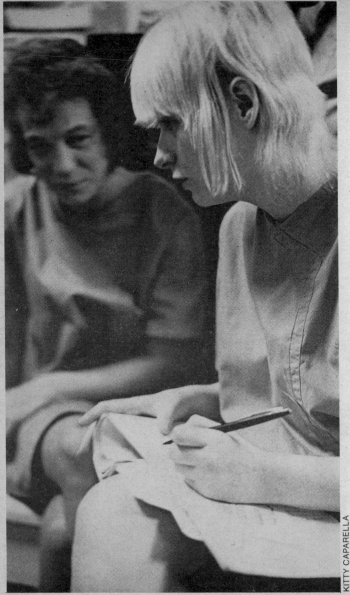

Prison time is waiting time.

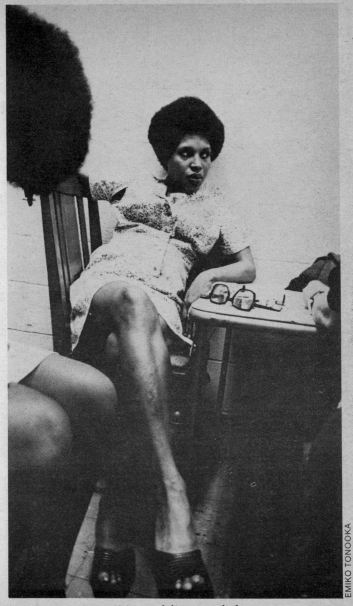

...waiting to deliver your baby.

. . . waiting to go into your cellblock.

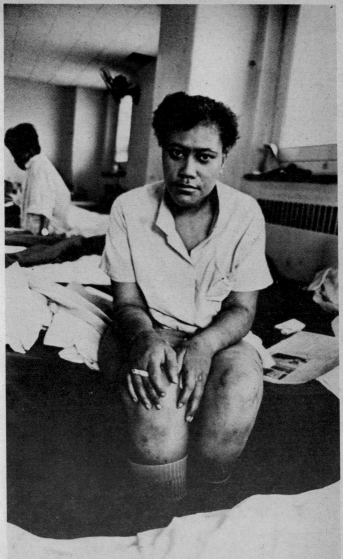

...waiting for treatment.

The "campus" at the Federal Reformatory for Women doesn't appear *to be a prison.*

Ninety-one women escaped from the California Institution for Women in 1971 despite the concertina wire. Armed guards now patrol the perimeters.

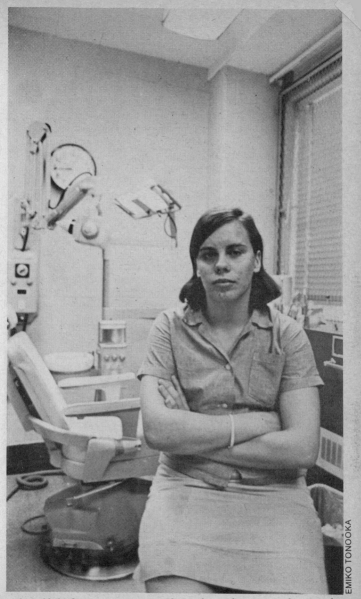

A handful of women prisoners throughout the country learn to be dental assistants, but they receive no official credentials.

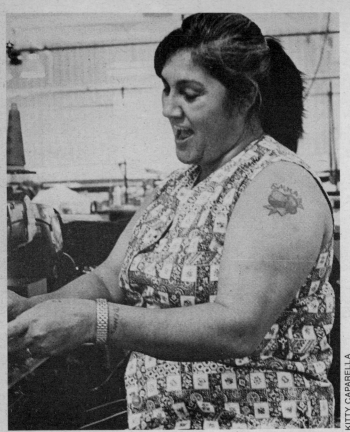

Sometimes a song breaks free above the hum of industrial sewing machines.

Factories run by prison labor are multimillion-dollar industries.
Most women earn an average of nineteen cents a day.

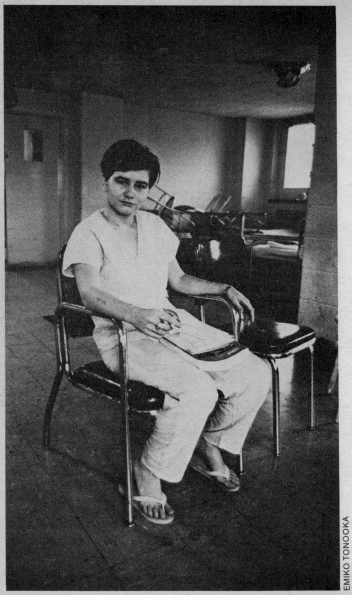

"I don't have much to say, but please take my picture".

EMIKO TONOOKA

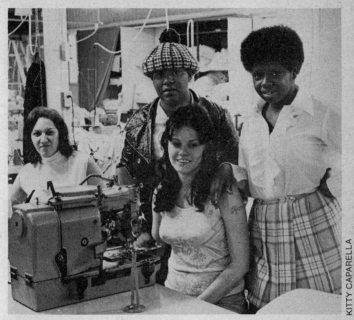

Friends are where you find them . . . in the factory, cellblock or work detail.

"We're rough, we're tough, we're sure enough".

During restricted hours, watching television also provides escape from routine.

Some women have spent their entire lives in institutions.

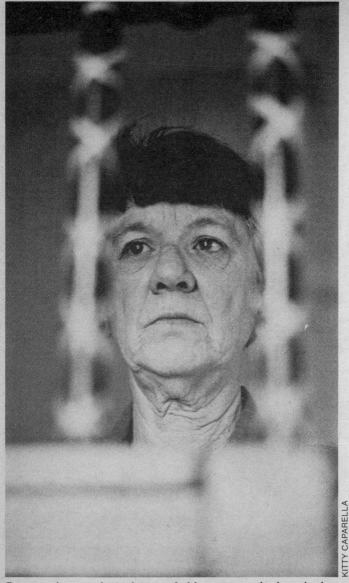

Prison enhances the isolation of older women who have had no families before their incarceration and no one to return to when they leave.

"The community wants us to do in six months what society hasn't done in the entire lives of these women".

–*Pat Taylor, superintendent*
Women's Detention Center
Washington, D.C.

Even after ten years, a mother's worries do not end behind bars.

Solitary confinement waits for any woman who breaks institutional rules, rebels or escapes.

The maximum security cell is also referred to as "solitary", "reflection", "peace and quiet" and the "adjustment" cell. Prisoners call it the "hole" or the "rack".

"There's no such thing as a good jail".
— Virginia MacLaughlin, superintendent
Federal Reformatory for Women
Alderson, West Virginia

Gathering in the rec room for a dance relieves tensions.

EMIKO TONOOKA

Up to 80 per cent of women in some prisons receive Thorazine, Librium or other drugs on a daily basis to keep them "manageable".

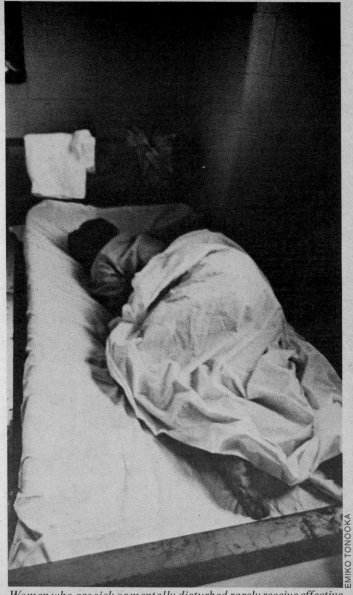

Women who are sick or mentally disturbed rarely receive effective treatment.

EXIT

A welcome to the world.

Part III   THE CONCRETE WOMB: "STAYIN' IN"

Chapter 7   ONE STEP FORWARD, TWO STEPS BACK

IT IS BOTH A CHALLENGE AND A DISADVANTAGE THAT INSTITUTIONS FOR WOMEN MUST BE ALL THINGS TO ALL PEOPLE. IN MOST STATES, IT IS POSSIBLE TO PROVIDE AT LEAST TWO INSTITUTIONS FOR MEN, ONE OF THE PRISON AND ONE OF THE REFORMATORY TYPE, PLUS VARIOUS TYPES OF MINIMUM CUSTODY HONOR CAMPS. BECAUSE WOMEN REPRESENT A SMALL PROPORTION OF THE TOTAL INMATE POPULATION, ONLY ONE STATE PROVIDES MORE THAN ONE STATE FACILITY FOR FEMALE OFFENDERS. EVEN THIS IS ON THE BASIS OF GEOGRAPHY AND POPULATION DISTRIBUTION RATHER THAN DIFFERENTIAL FUNCTIONING.

CAREFUL PLANNING, INGENUITY AND A HIGH DEGREE OF SKILL AT ALL LEVELS OF PERSONNEL ARE REQUIRED TO PROVIDE A DIVERSIFIED AND EFFECTIVE PROGRAM TO SERVE THE NEEDS OF ALL TYPES OF INMATES IN A SINGLE INSTITUTION.

WOMEN'S INSTITUTIONS HAVE MADE NOTABLE CONTRIBUTIONS TO PENOLOGY. THE PERSONNEL REQUIREMENTS HAVE ALWAYS BEEN REASONABLY HIGH AND WELL-TRAINED YOUNG WOMEN HAVE BEEN ATTRACTED TO LIVE AND WORK IN THESE INSTITUTIONS. SEVERAL OF THEM ARE RATED AS AMONG THE BEST INSTITUTIONS FOR EITHER MEN OR WOMEN IN THE COUNTRY. WOMEN SUPERINTENDENTS LIKE TO EXPERIMENT, TO TRY OUT NEW METHODS, AND TO USE NEW TECHNIQUES. WOMEN OFFENDERS DO NOT AS A RULE COMMIT ACTS OF VIOLENCE OR PRESENT A THREAT TO THE PUBLIC TO THE EXTENT THAT MEN DO. PUBLIC OPINION HAS THEREFORE NOT THWARTED THE SUPERINTENDENTS WHO WERE BOLD AND FEARLESS ENOUGH TO TRY NEW WAYS WITH OFFENDERS.

—"Facilities and Programs for Women," *Manual of Correctional Standards*, issued by the American Correctional Association, 1969

Captain Paul A. Strohman sat behind the chief administrator's desk at Sybil Brand Institute for Women in Los Angeles. A short, stocky man with a round face and receding hairline, Captain Strohman joked with the female deputy sheriffs who sat with him. A fat papier-mâché manikin dressed in female officer's clothing was propped against the wall behind him. On his desk was a yellow and black sign: "Behind this desk sits the sexiest executive in the world."

He seemed jovial as he greeted me. "What's the best jail you've been to?" he asked. I told him I didn't think I had been to a "best jail" yet. "Well," he went on, "*I think you're going to like this jail*. We think we have a fine place here . . . We think it's the best. Probably the best in the country . . ."

According to penal standards of architectural design, Sybil Brand Institute for Women *is* one of the "best in the country." It is a mechanically *perfect* jail; faultless in terms of security. From the "heartbeat of the jail," the main control center, a deputy sheriff can keep her eye on the entire prison without difficulty. At her fingertips are electronic detectors to monitor elevators and all entrances and exits. Television cameras throughout the prison monitor all "inmate traffic."

A two-way intercom system allows administrators to make public addresses in addition to tuning in on conversations in any part of the prison. The possibility of escape is infinitesimal.

Unlike most county or city jails in other parts of the country which are antiquated or where women prisoners are confined and forgotten in tiny cellblocks within the larger jails for men, this jail was built exclusively for women. No one in Los Angeles can complain that the 30,000 women booked in annually have been "neglected" or forgotten by the county jail system because of per capita cost. Sybil Brand Institute for Women was built with the sanction of a $6,315,-000 bond issue approved by the voters in 1960.[1] Typical complaints about physical conditions and understaffing just don't apply.

1. The bond issue was promoted by a woman named Sybil Brand and the jail was named after her. "She's a very active lady in today's society," Chief of the County Jail Division H. B. Creamer had told me in an interview. "She's active in civic affairs and especially in the area of corrections for women. She was highly instrumental in the building of this jail. She was the one that got the bond issue before the public."

"The rules and regulations and rights here will probably all be changed by the time your book comes out," Captain Strohman said. "There's lots of new Supreme Court rules and legislation. Also there's a lot of pressure groups lobbying for change.

"For instance, now we segregate or exclude active homosexuals from the rest of the population and group activity. If they come in dressed in drag or are obvious homosexuals, we call them *exclusions*. That will probably change because the Gay Liberation Front is getting stronger all the time.

"But the jail will still be run the same way—the only difference might be some rule changes. So I guess the basic facts won't change. Jails will always be the same, so your book will still be valid, even ten years from now or as long as jails exist, I guess."

Originally, segregated jails and prisons for women were designed to protect them and improve their lot. They were established as a benevolent move on the part of reformists.

Women had been detained in dungeons and almshouses and jails with men and children since the mid-1600s in the American Colonies. There was little segregation by age, sex or other condition. Women gave birth to children in the jails, and as one inspector said, "The early death of children is inevitable."

In 1838 men and women in Bellevue Prison in New York walked the treadmill together to grind grain for the almshouse and the city prison. After they labored, they ate the grain in a porridge. The work was long and exhausting and the diet inadequate. But as one author noted, "Women stood the ordeal better than men." At the same institution, he said, "Convicts could not lie down without mingling their limbs in one solid mass."[2]

In those years, prisons and punishments were in a state of upheaval. The 1787 Walnut Street Prison in Philadelphia had collapsed from overcrowding, corruption and rebellions. Everyone was looking for new answers to crime and punishment. New ways to establish law and order.

One new experiment was Eastern State Penitentiary in Philadelphia. It opened in 1825 after concerned religious people, including Benjamin Franklin, Dr. Benjamin Rush and Bishop William White, developed a theory of *penance* for sins through separate and solitary confinement.

2. Clifford M. Young, Chief Inspector, State Commission of Corrections, New York, *Women's Prisons Past and Present*, printed at Elmira Reformatory, 1932.

The penitentiary was considered a humane reform in comparison to the still common practice of corporal punishment for petty thieves and "criminals." Early Quaker idealists decried the policies of cropping ears, tying people to whipping posts and castrating or mutilating a criminal for adultery and other violations of the social order. They deemed public hangings of men and women suspected of stealing or treason intolerable and excessive. They also felt other prisons had failed because they were so chaotic, and believed imprisonment should be based on *repentance*, not retribution. This repentance could be established through strict order and constant silence.

Male and female prisoners were brought into the medieval, fortress-like structure with black hoods over their heads. They were blindly led to solitary cells, where the hoods were removed. Locked into individual cells behind two thick doors, they were left there for years with only a Bible for reading. Each prisoner had a back door and a tiny walled-in courtyard where he or she could step out for a glimpse of the sun and fresh air. Prisoners never left their solitary areas or saw anyone other than a minister. Guards would push bread, water or mush under the small opening under the bottom of the cell door.

Charles Dickens was one of many overseas visitors who toured Eastern State Penitentiary. He walked from cell to cell and talked with prisoners. Later he wrote in *Pictures from Italy and American Notes* (1867):

> The system here is rigid, strict and hopeless solitary confinement. I believe it, in its effects, to be cruel and wrong. In its intentions, I am well convinced that it is kind, humane and meant for reformation; but I am persuaded that those who devised this system of prison discipline, and those benevolent gentlemen who carry it into execution, do not know what they are doing . . . I hold this slow and daily tampering with the mysteries of the brain to be immeasurably worse than any torture of the body; because its ghastly signs are not so palpable to the eye . . . and it exhorts few crys, that human ears can hear; therefore I am the more to denounce it, as a secret punishment which slumbering humanity is not roused up to stay.

Nevertheless, the "Pennsylvania Plan" flourished. Penitentiaries built on the same model were constructed in other states in America and also in Europe. Eventually, when people continued to die and go mad in large numbers as a result of this isolation, society was forced to admit that thorough separation did not work. So they began to let prisoners mingle again and work at jobs to keep them busy.

Reform movements that began in the 1840s didn't seem to get anywhere until the 1870 National Congress on Penitentiary and Reformatory Discipline in Cincinnati, Ohio. By that time there was agitation over the unconscionable idleness and reports of brutality in prisons. Reformists started applying pressure to separate women and children from "hard-core" male prisoners. They felt that women "more nearly represent the residue of civilization's by-products than does the male group." The harsh environment of a male prison was considered unhealthy and corrupting for *dependent and weak* women and children.

The Congress also discussed poverty as a cause of crime, and its effect on immigrants, the majority of people in prison. One member of the Congress described the dilemma:

> The figures [of immigrants in prison] are so startling in their disproportions as to foster, and apparently justify, a strong prejudice against our foreign population. Foreigners crowd our almshouses and asylums, our jails and penitentiaries. . . . In the Albany penitentiary [alone], the aggregate number of prisoners during the last twenty years was 18,390, of whom 10,770 were foreign born. Formidable as such numbers are in their disproportions, we must not be hasty or harsh in taking up a reproach against "the stranger."[3]

Many people at the congress asserted that immigrants were in prison mainly because they were unassimilated into mainstream production. It was pointed out that four fifths of their crimes were against property; one fifth against persons. Twenty-eight per cent of the total prison population at the time could not read when they entered; 97 per cent had never learned a legal trade; 3.33 per cent were considered insane or feebleminded.

It is noticeable that most of these causes of crime are negative. They are want of knowledge, want of trade, want of work, want of a home, want of friends, want of mind and want of parents. It is not strange that a population from whom most of the natural and moral defenses are taken away, should be tempted and fall. Such helplessness borders on hopelessness, and nothing remains for its heirs but starvation

3. J. B. Bittinger, D.D., of Pennsylvania, "Responsibility of Society for the Causes of Crime," *Transactions of the National Congress on Penitentiary and Reformatory Discipline* (Albany: Weed, Parsons and Co., 1871).

or crime. Crime is the last resort of the helpless honest, unless society provides a refuge.[4]

It was resolved at the 1870 conference that the goal of prison should be *rehabilitation*—the act of restoring a person to useful life through education and therapy. The ambition was to educate prisoners and use work as therapy so they could go back out into society with altered values and attitudes.

Women were in the vanguard of putting this resolution into practice.

It was only three years after the Congress that the first separate prison for women was opened: Indiana Women's Prison. It embraced the revolutionary notion that women criminals should be *rehabilitated* rather than punished. Young girls from the age of sixteen who "habitually associate with dissolute persons" and older uneducated and indigent women were ushered into the model prison—apart from men and isolated from the "corruption and chaos" of the outside world. The essential ingredient of their rehabilitative treatment would be to bring discipline and regularity into their lives. Obedience and systematic religious education would, it was felt, help the women form orderly habits and moral values.

Four more institutions for women were opened during the next forty years; the Massachusetts Prison (Massachusetts Correctional Institution for Women at Framingham) in 1877; the New York Reformatory for Women (Westfield Farm) in 1901; the District of Columbia's Reformatory for Women in 1910; and the New Jersey Reformatory for Women (at Clinton) in 1913.

By 1917, fourteen states had established similar institutions. They were usually referred to as "reformatories" or "industrial homes" to distinguish them from penitentiaries.

The reformists seemed to have the fervor and drive of pentecostal preachers—decrying evil, exalting the divine. At the 58th Congress of the American Prison Association in 1928, reformists clearly expressed their conviction: "We must work for the regeneration, the cleansing of the evil mind, the quickening of the dead heart, the building up of fine ideals. In short, we must bring the poor sin-stained soul to feel the touch of the Divine Hand." They discussed the "moral turpitude" of the "poor creatures" and expressed the belief that in separate, home-like institutions women prisoners would have an opportunity, with as much time as they needed, to "mend their

4. Ibid.

criminal ways" and learn to be good housewives, helpmates and mothers.[5]

Today, as a result of their ardent efforts, there are thirty separate state institutions for women, including the Federal Reformatory built in 1927. In addition, there are twenty-four state facilities for women under the control of the warden of the male institution of the state, plus one federal prison on Terminal Island in California.[6] Five separate county or city jails have been built for women, and state statutes order that women imprisoned in some 3,325 local jails be segregated on separate cellblocks from male prisoners.

Another contribution of the time was the concept of the indeterminate sentence. An important part of the pioneer penal thinking was that women be detained in prison for whatever period of time it took to achieve the desired level of rehabilitation or "cleansing." Reformists, who included the Women's Christian Temperance Union and many other women's groups, believed that prisoners who demonstrated a readiness to return to the community should be granted an earlier discharge than would be possible under a set amount of time pre-determined by a trial judge. The possibility of release based on individual considerations seemed not only humane, but integral to the new concept of rehabilitation. To accomplish this, many states established special indeterminate sentencing provisions which applied only to women. Legislation establishing the separate prisons for women contained these sentencing provisions, as well as the requirement that all women over sixteen convicted of any offense be sent to these reformatories.

Theoretically, the "ideal sentence" would have no limits at all on the minimum and maximum terms an inmate was forced to serve. But most states put some limit on the sentence, usually setting the *maximum term prescribed by law* for the particular offense, with no minimum. For example, robbery might carry a twenty-five-year maximum sentence; burglary, twenty years; and prostitution, three years. Minnesota was one of the only states that met the "ideal" and originally passed a law requiring women to be sent to the reformatory "without limit as to time." Although the theory was that as soon as women were rehabilitated they could leave, in practical application

5. Maud Ballington Booth, "The Shadow of Prison," *Proceedings of the 58th Congress of the American Prison Association*, 1928.

6. The American Correctional Association, *Manual of Correctional Standards*, 1969.

the statutes resulted in women getting longer sentences than men for the same crimes.[7]

Today, indeterminate sentencing laws for women still remain on the books in several states. However in other states, legislatures have changed previously discriminatory sentencing provisions.

The courts have aided in this effort. In Pennsylvania, in 1966, Jane Daniel was convicted of simple robbery, an offense carrying a maximum penalty of ten years. The trial judge initially sentenced Jane Daniel to one to four years in the county jail. But because the district attorney drew his attention to the Muncy Act, the sentencing statute for women, the judge vacated the first sentence and gave her the maximum ten years to Muncy with no minimum, as the law provided.

A public defender, Carolyn E. Temin, took an appeal to the Superior Court on grounds that the Muncy Act constituted a denial of equal protection of the laws under the Fourteenth Amendment. It was clear from the first sentence that the defendant would have gotten a much lower term if she had been sentenced under the provisions relating to men convicted of the same offense.

The Superior Court found the act constitutional—passing their decision on similar challenges to the law in Kansas, Massachusetts and Maine. But Mrs. Temin appealed the decision and added another attack in the case of Daisy Douglas, which raised the same issue.

Daisy Douglas and her co-defendant, Richard Johnson, were tried together and convicted of jointly robbing a man. Miss Douglas, whose past record consisted of a number of arrests for prostitution, was duly sentenced to Muncy for the maximum term allowed by the law for aggravated robbery: twenty years. Johnson, whose past record consisted of six prior convictions for burglary, received a sentence of three to ten years in a state penitentiary for men. He would be eligible for parole after three years. Daisy Douglas would technically be eligible for parole at any time, but in practice would be eligible only after three and a half years. (In fact, Richard Johnson was eventually paroled after four years. Daisy Douglas served six and one half years before being paroled.)

7. Carolyn Engle Temin, "Discriminatory Sentencing of Women Offenders: The Argument for ERA in a Nutshell," *The American Criminal Law Journal*, Spring ——— 1973.

On July 1, 1968, the state Supreme Court declared the Muncy Act unconstitutional.

A similar result was reached by the U. S. District Court for Connecticut in the case of *U.S. ex. rel. Robinson* v. *York*, on February 28, 1968. That decision struck down a Connecticut statute relating to the sentencing of women misdemeanants which was the same as the Muncy Act. Since both courts reached the same conclusion independently of one another it seemed the constitutional issue of disparate sentencing statues had been laid to rest.

But two weeks after the Supreme Court of Pennsylvania handed down the decision in *Daniel*, the legislature passed a new version of the Muncy Act. The amendment provided that in sentencing a woman for a crime punishable by more than one year, the court "shall not fix a minimum sentence, but shall fix such maximum sentence as the court shall deem appropriate . . ." So the victory turned out to be short-lived. Although women would not receive a longer maximum sentence than men, they were still to be denied the right to have their minimum sentence set by a judge. Which was, basically, still a denial of equal treatment.[8]

This statute has never been challenged. And laws similar to the Muncy Act are still in effect for women in Massachusetts, New Jersey and Connecticut. Iowa law permits women to be confined up to five years for a misdemeanor, whereas men can only be confined up to one year unless the law states otherwise in defining the particular offense. In Maine, women between the ages of seventeen and forty can be sentenced to reformatories for up to three years even if the maximum punishment for an offense is less. Men in Maine are subject to the same law from age seventeen to twenty-six.

In practice, a much smaller percentage of women than men are sentenced to prison, as discussed in Chapter 3. But the discriminatory statutes allow for longer terms for the woman committed to prison.

Like other discretionary measures throughout the system, the indeterminate sentence also allows discrimination and bias in the setting of prison terms. At California Institution for Women during 1967 and 1968, for instance, white women with no narcotics history served up to two months longer than black women with no drug history for manslaughter, robbery and assault. But black women served from five days to eight months longer for forgery, burglary and theft. The

8. Temin, op. cit.

biggest differences in time served were for women with narcotics history, where black women served from two-and-a-half months to one-and-a-half years longer for the same offenses.[9]

The law, theoretically, is still designed to *protect* women. And it is bitter irony that the changes made by well-intentioned women of the late nineteenth and early twentieth centuries ultimately resulted in discrimination against women. It would seem that the vanguard reformists advanced theories that have ultimately discriminated against everyone. And it is a sign of great devotion to the theories of imprisonment that one hundred years after the 1870 Congress the goals of rehabilitation, treatment, discipline and regularity remain intact.

The words of the reformers of 1870 could easily be transposed to fit today's prison population with few changes. Poor people still go to prison. A disproportionate number of exiles from slavery have replaced the exiles from Europe and China. People in prison are without formal education. Less than 2.3 per cent have professional or technical skills. Many can't read or write. More than four fifths of the crimes they commit are still against property.

Currently it is popular, however, to allege that prisoners are "ill" or "sick" and need to be "cured." Although the talk of inherent evil and "moral turpitude" has mainly been left on library shelves and in churches, reformers today talk about "treating" offenders with the same pentecostal fervor of their predecessors. We still talk of making women offenders "well" by imbuing them with accepted moral standards and "cures"—as though they were diseased.

Increasingly, prison administrators are adopting the belief that therapy might be the answer to their problems within the prisons. They are experimenting with systems of rewards and behavior-modification models to help prisoners mend deviant or anti-social ways for the purpose of "more thorough rehabilitation."

These steps may *appear* to be positive and progressive—a further move away from punishment and retribution. But if we are to learn from history, we must be very careful about *humane* intentions. It could easily be said by looking at the track record that reformers often have good intentions but don't anticipate the effect of their actions. Nor do they realize the cyclical nature of their "progress."

When California adopted the treatment model for both men and women in 1959, for instance, their indeterminate sentencing statutes

9. Department of Corrections Memorandum, "Results of Study of Race and Time Served at California Institution for Women," June 17, 1971.

were considered a "giant step forward" in American penology. They
were credited with "pioneering" the indeterminate sentence for
felony offenders and a program for rehabilitation that would include
diagnosis, evaluation, classification and treatment. Excellent programs
of work, education, vocational training, medical services, group
counseling and therapy were part of the plan.[10] In fact, the concept
was not new. It was based on the same theory as the model for
women offenders established in the late 1800s.

And, as before, in effect the plan to grant earlier discharges based
on individual treatment and rehabilitation has backfired. Since California's "advance," the median time served in that state has increased
from twenty-four to thirty-six months, the longest median sentence
in the country. The number of persons incarcerated has more than
doubled during that same period of time. Thus during the period
when the treatment model was maximized in that state, more than
twice as many people have served twice as much time.[11] The percentage of prisoners released being convicted of new crimes remained unchanged—leading to the obvious conclusion that people are not
being "helped" any more by three years in a *progressive*, rehabilita-
tion-oriented prison than they were by approximately two years in a
punitively oriented prison. The public apparently is not protected
from crime by these new measures, nor is the offender "corrected."

"Yes, I'm one of those people who was sent away from society to learn
to adjust to society," said Fran Chrisman, now a member of Fortune
Society in New York City. "Yes, I was there. Even though I'm from a nice,
white, middle-class background, I spent fifteen years in prison and in crime.
I started at sixteen and lasted in that life until I was thirty years old. My
first crimes were not violent . . . but after two or three times in jail, I put
a gun in my hand.

"Yes, I was one of those people who learned to survive in jail. I was
happy in there. It was out here I couldn't make it. While I was down, I was
head cook in the prison—and made two dollars and fifty cents a month.
But there were advantages to working in the kitchen. Extra desserts, sandwiches—I could trade them for cigarettes. I learned how to prey on the
weak.

10. Jessica Mitford, "Kind and Usual Punishment in California," *Atlantic
Monthly*, March 1971.
11. American Friends Service Committee. *Struggle for Justice—A Report on
Crime and Punishment in America* (New York: Hill & Wang, 1971).

"I was guilty of every crime I was sentenced for . . . and more. I'm not hollering about going to prison. I'm hollering that nothing happens there except that you are giving your money to make people so bitter that they will come out bigger and better criminals who can rob you more efficiently. You can't stop with changes inside. We gotta change it out here—start opening doors for people. *You gotta change yourselves*—offering to help us live out here, with you, not against you."

Can one seriously doubt that if Charles Dickens were to visit *correctional* institutions for men and women in America today, that he would not be dismayed at the uncanny resiliency of our attitudes regarding imprisonment as a "cure" for crime? Dickens said he was convinced imprisonment was "cruel and wrong."

If he went into our new and modern jails for women today or looked at the therapeutic and treatment models of rehabilitation and talked with men and women confined about their responses to behavior modification, chemotherapy and psychotherapy in other institutions, he would probably say, once again: "I hold this slow and daily tampering with the mysteries of the brain to be immeasurably worse than any torture of the body; because its ghastly signs are not so palpable to the eye . . . and it exhorts few crys that human ears can hear; therefore I am the more to denounce it, as a secret punishment which slumbering humanity is not roused up to stay."

In spite of the Supreme Court rulings and administrative changes in prisons that now allow inmates to have books and newspapers and magazines, visitors and mail, prisoners essentially remain wrapt in isolation from the world, in self-contained cities.

"When you're watch commander, it's like being mayor of a city," the control room officer tells me. "We don't travel around away from the city like Mayor Yorty does. We're here and we have to be responsible and take care of business. Everything that happens in the street—fires, accidents, fights, traffic tie-ups, emergencies—happens in here."

The interaction, the nuances inside these cities can never be fully known by outsiders. State inspection teams visit jails only once or twice a year, if that. Their focus is mainly on physical conditions. Selected groups or individuals are sometimes allowed to come into the institutions to conduct classes (charm and body dynamics courses are the most common, outside of religious instruction), and on occasion tours are conducted for the prison board or judicial authorities who request a visit. Prisoners rarely have the opportunity to talk with visiting authorities—and often visitors are steered away from disciplinary cells or "sick" prisoners. Whether or not the press is allowed in to talk to prisoners is up to the discretion of the administration in most cases.

Family contacts have changed considerably in the last decade, but they still remain limited. At Sybil Brand Institute for Women, for instance, prisoners can have "visits" twice a week, for twenty minutes each time. Even these visits—through glass—are isolating experiences. Women can't touch their men, mothers don't hold their babies. Children under eighteen are not allowed to visit at all.

"We've found it's too traumatic for the child and the mother," said Lt. Audrey Lehre, a deputy sheriff who has worked with Los Angeles County's women prisoners for twenty-four years—first at the Hall of Justice and now at Sybil Brand. "The child can't understand why they can't touch their mother. We're not unfeeling, but we can't bend for everyone. It's a problem thing for a nine-year-old to want to hug mommy and can't get any closer than a glass window. We've had a couple of exceptions. One fourteen-year-old who was in trouble because she couldn't see her mother . . . Another was a little baby which was newborn. The court wanted the mother to be able to hold the child, and that couldn't cause any harm. But the regulation protects everyone from unnecessary traumas and problems."

Records are kept on every visitor that comes in to visit a prisoner.

"We wouldn't allow some people in here," Strohman said. "It's not written in the rules. But we want to know who's coming in. We're not going to let just anyone into our jail. We search purses because a lot of people are trying to blow up jails these days. We only keep a record of visitors, not letters."

Visitors can bring in wool yarn for knitting, money and three sets of panties, slips and bras to the women inside. The money is put on the woman's "books" and she can use it for commissary items. Visitors cannot bring food or cigarettes. "Nothing else except eyeglasses or a hearing aid," said Strohman. "We don't accept packages. There's too much possibility of contraband or bombs. They can buy what they need in the commissary: candy bars, cigarettes, magazines, toothpaste, papers, cosmetics . . . no douche bags or powders. I talked to our doctor and he said, if necessary, a douche can be prescribed in the medical department."

Even in state prisons, which are generally more open and treatment-oriented than local prisons and where visits are often allowed now in a living room type environment or face to face over tables, the exposure is still controlled. Women in state prisons usually are not allowed to greet or talk to anyone else's visitors, even if they know them from the outside. The effect is that visits, both in jails and in state prisons, are often excruciating periods of time.

My old man got cut loose from San Quentin. Two days later he came home and came to see me. We wanted to hug, kiss and have that physical thing. He was told he couldn't visit me if we touched. We couldn't so much as hold hands. If you took away my clothes and gave me a county dress [jail uniform] and let me visit through the screen it would be easier. My man and I are sitting together on the couch and we can't touch. My daughter hugged me and the staff said, "You can't do that." I told her to send me to lockup if I couldn't. Before my old man came to visit, I had to say into a tape recorder that if we are allowed to visit, we will not have any physical contact in the visiting room . . .

—Mary Vangi

In state prisons—where women are sent for two or more years, they are usually allowed visits from their children. At the majority of these institutions mothers are allowed to hold their children.

When you're in that visiting room, you have to turn off so much. Your people, they say, "What's the matter?" You can't show all your feelings because they're carrying that out with them and it eats them all the way home. You hurt, but that's your fault, and you shouldn't put it on them—especially not your children.

When my children come I can hug them and hold them—but I can't fall apart and let them know how important it is they're there. You gotta give them strength to walk out with. You hurt but you don't impose it on them; you don't force them through your ordeals about them coming and going. When they go they're not gonna cry and I'm not gonna cry . . . not until after they're gone, anyway. What crying I do, I do alone.

—Pearl Waters

At Sybil Brand visitors see their loved ones through screen or glass. Although there are more than 700 women at Sybil Brand, there are only twenty stools for visiting. Visits here and at similar jails become sad circuses—with everyone shouting to be heard, talking through telephones to one another over the loud din of urgency and confusion. Visits are short to allow each woman a chance. The same amount of time is allotted to each inmate—whether she is "innocent in the eyes of the law" awaiting trial, or already convicted and sentenced to a year or less in jail.

This quarantine can have devastating effects, especially on mothers with dependent children. Most of them, it might be safe to say all of them, are arrested unexpectedly. They can't predict when they are going to be arrested—although for many, arrest is an occupational hazard. They are picked up at every time of day or night. It's not uncommon to talk to a woman who was waiting to meet her children after school at the time she was picked up by the law. Thus her child comes home to an empty house and no mother.

In detention, a woman is allowed one dime, one telephone call, to arrange for bail or a lawyer or a friend to take care of the children. In addition to the unpredictability and uncertainty of when she will have a hearing, when she will get bail or when she will go to trial, women who are locked up have the immediate and constant anxiety about their children—where they are, if they're safe, if they're being well fed, if they will be taken by the county and put into a children's shelter or a foster home. Women cannot receive incoming calls or make calls out.

> If it's an emergency
> they can receive messages
> through my office,
> like if it's a death
> or someone's dying
> I will take a message
> and then let them call out.
> If she's trying to sell me
> a bill of goods,
> we'll listen in
> to try and keep her
> honest.
> But usually you can tell
> by listening to one end
> of the
> conversation.
>
>   —Lt. Merle Hess

"I'm worried that my sister has run out of cereal to feed the children," Judy Jacobs said as she sat in York County Jail in central Pennsylvania. "I don't even know what they'll have to eat today. My mother said she would take care of the children if I was sentenced to prison but I'm afraid they'll take them away from her 'cause she's on welfare." Judy, who had a newborn child, a one-year-old and a two-year-old, was a small, pale girl with long straight blond hair. She pulled at the skirt of her county prison dress and rubbed her hands —crying and looking as vulnerable as a four-year-old with the weight of a woman's responsibility. "I don't want my kids to end up in a home. I was in two foster homes before I got married and it's really terrible. They put us there mainly because my father was drinking and they thought he couldn't take care of us. There were eleven of us; two of my sisters have been in foster homes since they were born. I wish I could just stay right here in York. The state penitentiary's so far away, I'll never get to see my kids. But then, I'm not allowed to see them here at all . . ."

Often the same problems plague a woman who has been convicted and sentenced to prison. The bureaucracies surrounding her life and the lives of her children, through inefficiency and bumbling and sometimes outright lack of concern, leave her in the dark for days or weeks. Welfare departments are notorious for their inability to keep mothers informed about their children's placement.

When Pat got to prison, she didn't know the whereabouts of her children. On top of everything else, she said she was asked when she got to the prison if she wanted to make out a last will and testament.

After two weeks in isolation, she was moved to a cottage and she asked to see a counselor about her children. Her counselor said she would write a letter, but Pat still didn't hear about what had happened to her three children: Johnny, seven, Heather, five, and Toni, eighteen months.

All she knew was that a family court judge decided where her children should be placed. Pat had wanted the children to stay together with her two aunts, but the court did not grant her request. She was never given an explanation as to why.

Nearly a month after her visit with the counselor, Pat found out where her children were located from the County Welfare Department. Toni was in one foster home, and Heather was in another.

Johnny stayed with Heather for a while and then was transferred to a children's shelter.

"My son began to have emotional problems in February of 1971," Pat said. "I was not notified of this until October 1971. I was never asked about solving anything. I was merely informed of what they had done about it. Also, my son broke his arm in the spring of 1971 and I wasn't told until three weeks later.

"I haven't seen my children . . . and it seems like they're using 'not seeing mother' as a form of punishment for the kids. I resent being kept in total ignorance and not having any information about them.

"They haven't been able to visit me. It must be a welfare rule because my counselor thought it would be all right for them to visit. She contacted the caseworker, who said she would have to think about it—that was in October 1971. Welfare says it wouldn't let Johnny come, but it should be all right to see Heather or Toni."

When Pat couldn't communicate directly with her children, she protested, and received the right to correspond with Johnny and Heather. She still has to send letters to Toni through the welfare services.

"I keep asking about seeing my children, but I'm told to wait; I'm always stalled.

"It's the kids who suffer for our crimes.

"It's the children who are punished the worst."

Incarcerated women are also isolated from legal assistance as a general rule. Women have no opportunity to assist in their own defense when they have no law books, legal materials or access to legal advice.

At Sybil Brand, Strohman said, "We don't have a legal library. If a person is designated to act as their own attorney, they can have law books *if the court decrees it*. On rare occasions, they have the qualifications to act as their own attorney. But generally there's very little in regard to fighting their own case. They are entitled to law books. If they have money they can buy them. If they're acting as their own attorney, they can borrow law books from the central jail. But most of them aren't interested . . .

"We can't become involved in getting legal consultants or providing appeal papers or that sort of thing. We would not be doing our duty if we got involved with legal questions."

Administrators and officers in the prisons and jails I visited said that the women "aren't interested" in legal questions. "They wouldn't know how to read it, what to look for—or how to prepare a brief." An officer in Washington, D.C., pointing out meager library facilities for the more than 100 women confined in the Women's Detention Center, said, "It wouldn't make sense to keep law books here—they abuse everything so badly." Another administrator, who was accepting a donation of law books for her state prison, said, "I would think when women take one look at the law books, they will go back to writing the boys in the penitentiary. I may be surprised, I often am, but I've never seen women who take to law books."

"It doesn't occur to anyone that since legal materials never have been available, they could be now," said one inmate. "If you ask any of the staff if they know how you can get a form for appealing your case, they look at you like you're crazy. They don't know any more about it than we do."

Although it has not been the prison's *duty* to provide legal forms, law books, advice or assistance, some administrators do seem to feel a *duty* to be involved in police functions at the other end of the system's spectrum. They provide information to police agencies as a matter of course and have a developed relationship with state, local and federal police agencies. The records kept on women in jails and prisons—including their work records, medical records, disciplinary procedures and legal data from the court—are readily accessible to police and other law enforcement officers, upon request.

"We keep a record of everything they do," Captain Strohman said. "Some are complete, some are not so complete. This has no bearing on their case, but their records *can be subpoenaed by the court* [my emphasis]."

"The records are confidential, but if somebody asks—like the police, the FBI or the probation department—we tell them undoubtedly. If I found out something bearing to a heinous crime committed outside or a planned escape, I'd call our detectives. . . . We're law enforcement officers . . . it's our *duty*."

Strohman said that a woman's "jacket"—the file containing all her personal history and jailhouse records—is kept at the prison until she's released. After that, her records are sent to the archives of the central jail's record section. "Presently it's a manual thing," he said. "Ultimately all this information will be on computer tapes and even at a station house they will be able to get all the information on somebody they arrest."

In many jails, and at some prisons, a woman is limited to writing five to ten people at the most, or only her immediate family. Names of these people, or those of visitors, are usually kept in her record. Theoretically, when all the information in her jacket is available at the time of a new arrest, all of her associates' names and family's names could be available to the police.

At Sybil Brand letters are not kept on file. "They can get an unlimited number of letters in here," said Strohman. "It's the same for sentenced as unsentenced. We examine all the mail that comes and goes. A lot of the case law says we can examine it. There's too much mail to read. We only skim it—but if we need to, we read it.

"If it's bad news, we can alert the inmate personnel so the woman doesn't go off. If it's a death or sickness in the family or one of her children is hurt or she gets a Dear John letter, she might get hysterical and start trouble in her dormitory or something. This way we can help her. We can take her aside and tell her the news and let her get out the tears in private.

"Also, there are certain things just not allowed in jail. If it's unacceptable coming in, if it's inflammatory or talking about the overthrow of the prison system we just return it. If the mail going out is unacceptable, we destroy it. They can't discuss anyone else's case or prison business or be lewd. If letters coming in are too lewd we return them to the sender."

Once a friend of mine sent me
one of those postcards with an artists' reproduction
of a classic painting.
There was a naked woman on it.
The censor marked out the tits on the picture.
I wouldn't have even noticed it
except for it had a black magic marker bra.

—Woman inmate at CIW

Once my boyfriend wrote me a fifteen-page letter. They sent it back to him, telling him it was too long. He sent it to me in sections, two pages at a time, twice a week, and got it in that way . . . You can't take any letters out with you when you go—but I'd like to keep that one, even though it took so long to get here.

—Woman at San Bruno County Jail

As U. S. District Court Judge J. Doyle wrote in an opinion on the prisoner's right to correspondence: "State governments have not undertaken to require members of the general adult population to rise at a certain hour, retire at a certain hour, eat at certain hours, live for periods with no companionship whatever, wear certain clothing, or submit to oral and anal searches after visiting hours, nor have state governments undertaken to prohibit members of the general adult population from speaking to one another, wearing beards, embracing their spouses, or corresponding with their lovers. There has been no occasion to test the constitutionality of such measures as applied to members of the general population. New ground must be broken, therefore, in deciding which, if any, of the individual interest, affected by such requirements and prohibitions are to be characterized as fundamental [to prisoners] . . ." (*Morales* v. *Schmidt*, [U. S. Dist. Ct. W. Dist. Wisconsin], Opinion 4/6/72, Doyle, J.).

Like Captain Strohman said, "The rules and regulations and rights here will probably all be changed . . . but the jail will still be run the same way. The only difference might be some rule changes. So I guess the basic facts won't change. Jails will always be the same . . . even ten years from now or as long as jails exist . . ."

It seems ironic that it is prisoners *innocent in the eyes of the law*, people awaiting trial, who often live under the most punitive and physically primitive controls of all the people incarcerated in the country. More than thirty-five times as many people fill county and city jails in one year than are in state and federal prisons. More than half of them have not gone to trial. The operating costs of these jails alone are more than $324 million annually. Over two million people are locked in local jails in one year just for drunkenness, and many of these people are women. Administrators usually are frank enough to admit they only are running holding facilities.

"We don't have time for rehabilitation here," said Captain Strohman. "We see our job as locking up those people society has decided should be out of the general population and we're doing it as humanly as possible.

"These people awaiting trial aren't criminals. They're innocent within the eyes of the law. Sixty-five percent of the women here are unsentenced."

My memory focuses on the single-file line of two hundred women

I saw earlier walking into the dining room to eat during their twenty-minute food shift. They wear blue uniforms. They are not allowed to talk on the way to the dining room, inside, or on the way back to their maximum-security cellblock. They work without pay. They are not allowed to see their children. They are all *innocent in the eyes of the law*.

My mind searches for an irreverent parallel I can't quite get hold of. Later I remember that it's from Lewis Carroll's *Alice's Adventures in Wonderland*:

"Let the jury consider their verdict," the King said, for about the twentieth time that day.

"No, no!" said the Queen. "Sentence first—verdict afterwards."

"Stuff and nonsense!" said Alice loudly. "The idea of having the sentence first!"

"Hold your tongue!" said the Queen, turning purple.

"I won't!" said Alice.

"Off with her head!" the Queen shouted at the top of her voice . . .

"We can't rehabilitate them when they haven't even been found guilty," Captain Strohman continued. "With sentenced people we would like to rehabilitate them so they wouldn't do the same thing. But I couldn't point to any single individual or percentage of success we have had.

"Anybody that thinks they are rehabilitating these people are fooling themselves.

"We're responsible for their conduct, care and safety. Of course, if they had learned to obey the rules of society, they wouldn't be here in the first place. But some functions we can't assume. We try to give them something in the way of vocational training, but we can't follow up on it. Once they leave the jail we're no longer responsible.

"Certainly I would like to rehabilitate these people and I realize we'd save a lot of money to put them back on the street. If I were convinced we could rehabilitate them, I could be for it—but I'm not convinced. . . . It becomes a problem of money. It's not my problem in operating a jail—it's all our problems. My chief problem is too few deputy sheriffs. I'm eighteen people short of what I'm authorized. If I still have to have security here, I need ten male deputies . . .

"Maybe we're trying to do too much rehabilitation here. Maybe we should strip them of everything and their human dignity when they come in and let them out sooner and they wouldn't want to come back. I've heard that in France the prisons are terrible and brutal but they don't keep anyone in them for long. Maybe that's what we should be doing. We only know what we're doing sure isn't working."

"We're only teaching them how to live within an institution," Audrey Lehre added. "We're not rehabilitating them. They can learn to get through here to do easy time, but this may not necessarily help them on the outside. It only helps them to know how to live in jail."

The most important thing is security. That's my problem in operating a jail, security.

There's NOTHING that interrupts the count in a penal institution. It's *the most important thing* in a penal institution. It's the difference between going home and staying here. All activity stops during head counts. *Count has to be official.* All counts have to balance with head counts. We call our count in to the chief security office.

—Capt. Daisy McLendon, House of
Correction, Chicago

Work release is a positive thing. But you have to have facilities for it. You have to have the money for it. I've always dealt with people and with businesses, so I like this field. I would like to expand the work release program and also get rid of all untried prisoners. It will be a long time, though, before we could have any work release for the women. We have problems with some of the women banging on the walls and calling over to the men. It irritates the men a little bit.

There's a lot of complications, but as long as you keep 'em fed—give them some milk and sugar and cigarettes—you usually don't have any problems.

—Warden L. V. Roth, Jr.,
Montgomery County Jail,
Jenkintown, Pennsylvania

We have no room for counseling, attorneys, public defenders, no separate room for clergy. We don't even have one large room to run classes for rehabilitation purposes. We do the best we can but it's impossible because of space. The jail was built for eighty-five people. There are a hundred and ninety-three here today. They have to meet with their attorneys in the washroom. You can see in conditions so crowded, communicable disease can spread quickly throughout the whole institution. We have to be careful of epidemics. The conditions are the same today as they were in 1958. The overcrowding is not in keeping with minimum standards. When they're brought in, we have to have space to process, classify and keep. We don't want to put traffic violators in with hardened criminals, but we have no choice.

It's very costly. A false economy.

This jail reflects many of the disadvantages of jails built on top of courthouses or office buildings. If there was a catastrophe, an explosion or a fire or an airplane hitting the building, or even a bomb scare, I just wonder how we would get a hundred and ninety-three prisoners out. Where would we move them to?

My purpose in my job is what they bring in with a warrant. I do what the law says. I keep 'em in custody. I keep 'em as human as possible with proper custody . . . I recommended a regional thing for female offenders a while back and never heard nothing about it. It would be a better way of dealing with females because it would be a savings to all three counties who kept the females in one place.

—Sheriff Martin Segal, Camden County Jail, Camden, N.J.

The vocational shops and the school are empty because there isn't enough staff to supervise the women going and coming from their dormitories or cells. These people have to be supervised . . . that's why correctional officers must accompany them wherever they go. What if they got into a fight? . . . There could be a sociopath undiscovered and then we would have a disrupted institution. If we weren't understaffed the women would be freer to go to school and to programs. As it is, we don't have enough staff to accompany them.

—John Walsh, of the Corrections Department,
New York City Correctional Institution for Women

We get about seventy-five per cent recidivist rates here. Most of the girls who come in here are about twenty-one to twenty-five years old and are addicts. So we see them back. No, there is no drug therapy or treatment here.

There are some girls who get rehabilitated as they get older. When a girl begins to reach forty, she rehabilitates herself. Not the institution, she does it herself. She gets tired. About twenty-five per cent rehabilitate themselves somehow—they get jobs or they stay out of here. We don't know how, but at least we don't see them back.

—Lt. Dorothy Zeno Day Officer in
Charge, Cook County Jail Women's
Division

Jails are not conducive to women being good mothers. Mothers in jails are not conducive to bringing up good citizens. We have about seventy per cent recidivism. Yes, they come back, and their daughters come back, and their daughters, and their daughters' daughters.

—Lt. Audrey Lehre, Assistant Warden,
Sybil Brand Institute for Women

They changed the hanging law way back when Eva Dugan was de-
capitated because they miscalculated her weight . . . She was ex-
ecuted February 21, 1930. The last hanging we had was August 21,
1931. The reason we went to lethal gas was basically Eva Dugan.
Death by lethal gas was made effective October 28, 1933.

Out of sixty-three executions, Eva Dugan was the only woman.

—A. E. "Bud" Gomez,
Business Manager,
Arizona State Prison

Eva

Eva Dugan was hanged at 5:02 A.M., February 21, 1930, in Arizona
State Prison's death house. She was a convicted murderer.

Seventy-five people, including seven women, viewed the execution. They watched as Mrs. Dugan plunged through the trap door
and hit the end of the rope with a bouncing jolt. Her head snapped
off and rolled into a corner. There was an immediate horrified and
widespread demand that a "more humane means of execution"—such
as a gas chamber—be substituted for the "unreliable gallows." It
should be emphasized that the cry was not for abolition of the death
penalty, but for a more reliable, more antiseptic execution—one that
would not shock the sensibilities of the spectators.

Eva Dugan was convicted of killing an elderly Tucson rancher
named A. J. Mathis in January 1927. Mathis's skeleton, encrusted
with lime and a gag still in its teeth, was found almost a year after
his death by a camper from Oklahoma who accidentally discovered
the rancher's shallow grave while driving a tent stake into the ground.
Police arrested Eva Dugan for the crime and said at her trial that
after the slaying she had "fled with a mysterious drifter," a young
man known only as "Jack," who was never arrested. She maintained
her innocence from the beginning.

The day and night before her beheading, Eva Dugan visited with friends and newsmen. According to one newsman she made small jokes, "some of them a bit macabre"—and from time to time glanced at the clock. She told a reporter for the Arizona *Republic:* "I am going to my Maker with a clear conscience. I am innocent of any murder and God knows I am."

Until she left the women's cellblock at Arizona State Prison for the death house within the same complex of buildings, Eva Dugan said she was sure she would be spared because she was innocent—and that "the attorney general is probably on his way here now." But no pardon came to stay her execution.

According to the newspaper reports from 1930, a rumor on the prison grapevine spread the news shortly after midnight that Eva Dugan would "cheat the gallows"—or cheat the spectators—by taking her own life. Guards searched her cell and found a hidden bottle of raw ammonia. They searched her body and found three razor blades in the collar of her dress; they charged her friends in the women's cellblock with attempting to aid Eva's wish to die privately.

A veteran guard called "Daddy" Allen led Eva Dugan's small procession to the death house. The tiny fifty-two-year-old woman was flanked by two other guards and followed by the prison chaplain, who in later years became chairman of the state parole board.

"Don't hold my arms so hard," she told the guards as she mounted the scaffold. "People will think I'm afraid." The noose was placed around her neck and she swayed slightly as she stood on the trap door. She closed her eyes and shook her head "no" when the warden asked her if she had any last words.

Eva Dugan was buried in a Florence cemetery in a beaded, jazz-age silk dress she had sewn by hand while awaiting execution. She paid for her own coffin by selling handkerchiefs she had embroidered in her cell.

FOOTNOTE

When I visited Arizona State Prison, I procured a single piece of paper documenting "the death penalty in Arizona." The list reports the prison numbers, names, race and time of death for four Chinese, twelve black and forty-seven white persons executed since Arizona became a state. Of the forty-seven whites listed, nineteen appear to have Spanish or Mexican names—which would make the list read: four Chinese-Americans, twelve Afro-Americans, nineteen Mexican-

Americans and twenty-eight Anglo-Americans executed. The "fact sheet" has been so stark and haunting to me that I felt others should also have to see it in its total form. Notice that the death penalty was abolished in Arizona on December 8, 1916, and restored December 5, 1918.

In June 1972, the U. S. Supreme Court banned the death penalty on the basis of erratic and arbitrary enforcement. Will it be so easily restored under new guidelines within the next few years? Pre-meditated executions by the state can be "reformed"; legal murders can seem "cleaner" and more efficient by the changing of technical methods. But whether executions are performed with the aid of an ax, a guillotine, gallows, electric chair or gas chamber, the fact of death remains the same.

DEATH PENALTY
IN ARIZONA

An initiative measure effective December 8, 1916 deleted the provision for the death penalty as punishment for first degree murder.

The death penalty was restored December 5, 1918. The method of execution was by hanging.

Death by Lethal Gas instead of by hanging was made effective October 28, 1933.

Last execution by hanging was 8-21-1931.

First execution by Lethal Gas was 7-6-1934, at which time two brothers, Manuel and Fred Hernandez were executed.

Highest number executed in one day were four Chinese on June 22, 1928.

28 have been executed by hanging since statehood.

35 have been executed by Lethal Gas since statehood.

1 commutation of sentence by death to life imprisonment has been granted since 1934.

EXECUTIONS BY HANGING ARIZONA STATE PRISON

3094	Jose Lopez	White	10:23 AM	1-5-1910
3327	Cesario Sanchez	White	10:30 AM	12-2-1910
3326	Rafael Barela	White	11:10 AM	12-2-1910
3497	Domingo Franco	White		7-7-1911
3582	Alejandra Galles	White	10:40 AM	7-28-1911

4436	Ramon Villalobo	White	3:20 PM	12-10-1915
3566	Francisco Rodroquez	White	5:10 PM	5-19-1916
3479	N. B. Chavez	White	3:20 PM	6-9-1916
3814	Miquel Peralta	White	3:20 PM	7-7-1916
5400	Sinplicio Torrez	White	10:10 AM	4-16-1920
5597	Pedro Dominguez	White	5:30 AM	1-14-1921
5565	Nichan Martin	White	5:01 AM	9-9-1921
5693	Ricardo Lauterio	White	5:00 AM	1-13-1922
5699	Thomas Roman	White	5:20 AM	1-13-1922
5826	Theodore West	White	5:00 AM	9-29-1922
5979	Paul V. Hadley	White	5:00 AM	4-13-1923
5981	Manuel Martinez	White	5:25 AM	8-10-1923
6367	William Ward	Negro	5:00 AM	6-20-1924
6193	Sam Flowers	Negro	5:00 AM	1-9-1925
6621	William Lawrence	White	5:20 AM	1-8-1926
6824	Charles J. Blackburn	White	5:09 AM	5-20-1927
7046	B. W. L. Sam	Chinese	5:16 AM	6-22-1928
7047	Shew Chin	Chinese	5:42 AM	6-22-1928
7048	Jew Har	Chinese	6:06 AM	6-22-1928
7049	Gee King Long	Chinese	6:33 AM	6-22-1928
7435	Eva Dugan	White	5:01 AM	2-21-1930
7748	Refugio Macias	White	5:11 AM	3-7-1930
8149	Herman Young	White	5:03 AM	8-21-1931

EXECUTIONS BY LETHAL GAS

9299	Manuel Hernandez	White	5:00 AM	7-6-1934
9300	Fred Hernandez	White	5:00 AM	7-6-1934
9250	George Shaughnessy	White	5:00 AM	7-13-1934
9391	Louis Sprague Douglas	White	12:30 AM	8-31-1934
9924	Jack Sullivan	White	5:05 AM	5-15-1936
10021	Frank Rascon	White	5:10 AM	7-10-1936
9880	Roland H. Cochrane	White	5:00 AM	10-2-1936
10094	Frank Duarte	White	5:00 AM	1-8-1937
10540	Ernest Patten	Negro	4:00 AM	8-13-1937
10580	Burt Anderson	White	4:00 AM	8-13-1937
10252	David Benjamin Knight	White	4:00 AM	9-3-1937
10853	Elvin Jack Odom	White	4:15 AM	1-14-1938
11163	James Bailey	White	5:00 AM	4-28-1939
11253	Frank Conner	Negro	5:00 AM	9-22-1939
11506	Robert Burgunder	White	5:00 AM	8-9-1940

12409	J. C. Levice	Negro		1-8-1943
12410	Charles Sanders	Negro		1-8-1943
12411	Grady B. Cole	Negro		1-8-1943
12609	James C. Rawling	White	6:15 AM	2-19-1943
12334	Elisandro L. Macias	White	6:00 AM	4-27-1943
12964	John Earnest Ransom	Negro	6:00 AM	1-5-1945
12988	Lee Albert Smith	White	5:00 AM	4-6-1945
13306	U. L. Holley	Negro	5:05 AM	4-13-1945
14854	Angel B. Serna	White	4:05 AM	7-29-1950
16003	Harold Thomas Lantz	White	5:04 AM	7-18-1951
17659	Carl J. Folk	White	5:00 AM	3-4-1955
18392	Lester Edward Bartholomew	White	5:00 AM	8-31-1955
18320	Leonard Coey	White	5:00 AM	5-22-1957
17337	Arthur Thomas	Negro	5:05 AM	11-17-1958
19169	Richard Lewis Jordan	White	5:00 AM	11-22-1958
19795	Lonnie Craft	Negro	5:05 AM	3-7-1959
20414	Robert D. Fenton	White	5:06 AM	3-11-1960
21245	Honor Robinson	Negro		10-31-1961
21598	Patrick M. McGee	White	5:00 AM	3-8-1963
23773	Manuel E. Silva	White	5:00 AM	3-14-1963

Father Charles

Father Charles Repole, a Capuchin priest and Franciscan monk, sits down in his little office, folding his floor-length brown robes around him. I have met him in the hallway of the women's jail on Riker's Island and he cheerfully welcomes me into his office to talk.

He offers me a piece of peppermint candy and a cigarette and tells me he has worked at the women's New York City jail for six years.

"The girls here are eighty-five per cent addicts and eighty per cent prostitutes," he says. "They will open up to me because they know my lips are sealed.

"I've seen 'em all. I even had Angela Davis in for an interview. I wanted to see her even though she was not Catholic. I wanted to know what I could do."

Father Charles ruffles through three-by-five cards in a little box which he says contains the names of the women he has interviewed along with his comments about them. "I've seen Weathermen, Black Panthers, a doctor, a psychiatrist, a correctional officer from another institution and a lot of Colombian girls. I call the consulate for them. I speak Spanish, so much of my work is bilingual. Twenty-five per cent of the population is Spanish-speaking.

"Some of them are in here for bringing drugs into the country. All the heroin comes from Turkey to France to the U.S. Some comes in from Colombia. They get a poor farm girl and give her fifteen thousand pesos to come to America and all she has to do is bring this 'package.' In all my years, I had one gypsy, three Chinese and three redskin Indians.

Father Charles has many opinions and anecdotes:

—A girl tried to cut her wrist, she tried to commit suicide . . . it didn't work and when she came in here, I said, "Why'd ya do that: *Why not come in and sit down and have a cigarette?"* [my emphasis]. I always give the girls cigarettes free . . . you know, a little extra treat.

—After the baby is born, a girl can give it to her parents or family or put it up for adoption. *I leave it up to them* [my emphasis]. It's a hard thing for a lady to give up her own flesh and blood. But if they keep on drugs and are an unfit mother, I say, "You can't take proper care of your baby . . . you should give it up for adoption."

—I think pimps should be castrated and put up in front of firing squads and shot!

—In all my experience inside and outside, psychology withstanding, lesbians are made, not born. Homosexuals, yes, some are born that way.

—Visits for children would not be very rewarding. Most of their children are placed with foster families. They can see them again when they get out.

—Prisons are not as bad as people make them. It's "a priori"; they wouldn't be here if they hadn't done anything.

—In the case of the death of their baby, the girls can go to the funeral if they get the proper papers from court. They can write to anybody they want . . . and they talk on the phone in case of serious sickness or death.

"I never divulge what they tell me. I meet with staff, but I never divulge unless it's public and I have their permission. Or unless it's something like an insurrection that would affect the institution. My role is different . . . instead of being in a parish on the street, my parish is here. I get them lawyers, I call their mothers, sometimes I let 'em talk on the phone to their kids. I keep candy and cigarettes in this drawer for them. See, look at all the candy . . . and in that file cabinet I have cards they can send out on special occasions.

"I am the link between the girls and the authorities and the outside world. When there was trouble here last year, they were going to take me and the Protestant chaplain as hostages. But I know they wouldn't have hurt us—they probably chose us because they knew we could speak to the administration for them."

Chapter 8   INDUSTRY: THE
KEYSTONE OF PROSPERITY

WORK:

1. Every woman has a job to do which she is assigned. You are expected to do your work properly and to accept willingly and cooperatively the supervision of the person who is in charge of the work group.

2. If you have any question to raise about your assignment, take it up with your work supervisor first. If there is something further which you have to discuss, take it up with the assignment committee by putting in a pass to see your caseworker.

3. Remember that you are always in a better position to ask for a job transfer if you have a good record on the job you already have. Failure to do well on a job may result in *demotion* or *punishment*.

4. Each woman is paid four cents per hour for the assignment which she performs (except flat-timers who receive two cents per hour). Each assignment carries a pay scale based on the number of hours worked on that assignment during the month. One half of the pay is placed in a savings account and given to you when you leave the institution. The other half is placed in your commissary account and you may spend it, if you wish, while you are in the institution. In the case of flat-timers, all the pay is placed in the commissary account.

From rulebook for inmates,
Ohio Reformatory for Women
Marysville, Ohio

Prisons are big business.

Usually the only figures we see in relation to prison are the tremendous costs of operating institutions. We know that imprisoning a man, woman or child in an institution costs from $3,500 to $7,400 per person per year, and that *corrections* operating costs run over a billion dollars a year. Budget breakdowns show us that tax dollars go for administrative and custodial personnel, salaries and travel, institutional maintenance and construction, transportation of prisoners, custodial equipment, security devices, arsenals, and food, uniforms and medicine for prisoners. Less than four cents out of every tax dollar spent on prisons (and usually less than one cent in county jails) goes for *treatment* or *rehabilitation* . . . education, recreation and vocational training programs.

What most of us do not realize is that most prisons are self-sustaining through inmate labor. And aside from employee salaries and administrative costs that come from tax money, prisoners contribute undetermined sums to the state economy through their work in big prison businesses. The Federal Reformatory for Women at Alderson, West Virginia, for instance, runs a more than $2.5-million-a-year industry for the federal government. What the services would cost the government at minimum wage scales could make that figure multiply several times.

Many of the "state goods" we use every day are made by prisoners who work six or seven days a week. They are "rewarded" for their work with only a pittance (up to fifteen dollars a month), and the incentive of a good work record, which may contribute to their release on parole. In some state prisons and in all federal prisons, certain jobs earn inmates "good time" off their sentences.

Road signs, license plates, benches and tables in state parks, garments for patients in state hospitals and state schools, state and national flags, clothes for state children's schools, linens and pajamas for veterans' hospitals, mattresses, sheets and blankets for state institutions—all these things are made by prisoners in state and federal institutions. In addition, prisoners make the cloth from which they sew their own uniforms; they make the shoes they and other prisoners wear; they sew uniforms for state troopers and prison guards. Women at Alderson make prison uniforms for all the male prisoners in other federal institutions. Prisoners do printing and computer printouts for government agencies; they raise and harvest their own food and run canneries. They make soap for state and county jails and produce furniture that is used both within the prison and in the offices and homes of correctional personnel and government employees.

The network of diversified industries is run by corporate penal industries contracted to the department of corrections in various states and the Federal Prison Industries, Inc., for the federal government. The industrial goods are not sold in competitive trade because of labor laws restricting unfair competition. The goods and services are contracted out from the prison to other parts of the state and federal government. They are considered inter-agency commerce.

We know that state and federal agencies benefit greatly in costs saved from cheap prisoner labor. But we don't know how much the state actually makes or saves because government agencies don't account for funds in terms of profit. Figures are additionally difficult to locate or analyze because prison commerce is so matter-of-fact that administrators themselves seem vague and uninformed about transactions.

I had been aware of the exchange of goods and of the "business traffic" from prison to prison, but it has always seemed an immense impenetrable maze. Wardens had told me their institutions were "self-sustaining" and I had met foremen from penal industries in various prison factories that talked of their tremendous output and profit. But it wasn't until I visited Arizona State Prison and the Los Angeles County Jail Division that the reality of prison production cut through my resistance to economic details. It was in those two places that I first began to realize the extent to which prisoner labor is used and depended on by the state for the maintenance of state agencies, the maintenance of prisons and the control of prisoners.

In Arizona I was having one of those disastrous before-it-even-begins type interviews with the superintendent of the state prison, Frank Eyman. Eyman's word has been law at the old territorial prison for more than eighteen years.

When I came in and sat down opposite him, he was sitting at a large walnut desk in front of a wall of small framed photographs documenting his eighteen years of receiving awards and shaking hands with various Lions and Kiwanis Club presidents, state officials, military officers and movie stars. He shuffled papers on his desk and snorted through his nose occasionally, not looking up once. His face was red and splotchy and the veins on his nose were swollen. He wore a yellow flannel shirt buttoned tight around his throat with a turquoise bolo tie made by Navaho Indians. He looked like he might have been an old cowboy from O.K. Corral.

Finally, after nearly five minutes of uncomfortable silence punctuated only with his coughs and snorts, I introduced myself—even though I had already been introduced once by the secretary when I first walked in the door.

He glared at me for a minute and then demanded in a raspy voice: "What are you doing here?!"

I handed him a copy of the letter he had sent granting me permission to visit the prison, and told him, as I had said in my original letter, I was doing research for a book on women in prison.

He looked at the letter and then wadded it up and threw it in the wastebasket by his desk.

"I was going to tell you you couldn't come in," he said.

"What changed your mind?"

"Nothing. Nothing at all. Nothing changed my mind."

I felt my initial anger dissipating and laughter erupting at the Alice-in-Wonderland statement, but the potential for getting thrown out of his office before I got my foot inside the women's division made me twist my face into seriousness and scramble through my brain to look for questions that might get me through the barricades.

"If you're doing more than one year, you have to be in prison, you can't be in county jail," he volunteered out of the blue. That was a contribution. Now it was my turn for a question.

"We have 1,263 men here and forty-five women," he confirmed, after making a telephone call to check the figures. "We've been up to as high as seventeen hundred men and seventy-some women. It fluctuates. There's more crime now than you ever had before. The reason my population is down is because of the conservation camp and the halfway houses for pre-release in Phoenix that have been taking people out. We have six or seven women up in Phoenix taking the drug cure. They *belong to us*, but they're up there for the drug cure [my emphasis]. Women draw the same rations as men."

Each of these sentences was drawn out by questions—some of which I had to rephrase more than once. It was a painful process, like trying to draw water out of a cactus, but I kept going, trying to

get somewhere. "Hell, I don't know how many employees I have."
It looked hopeless.

But finally I sparked his mind. I asked him about the prison industries, and his response continued for nearly fifteen enthusiastic
minutes.

"Hell, this is a big industry we have here. We just sell to state institutions and to the children's colony and university. Yes, this is a
big business. [He smiled!] A *damn big business.* We have four farms
within a distance of seven miles, worked by male population. There
are trustees living on ranches under the foreman. I don't know the
number. We also manufacture innerspring mattresses and make all
license plates for the state and all the street signs. We have a printing
company, a cotton gin mill, a dairy farm, a swine farm, beef cattle
and a big chicken ranch. We also make the barbecue grills and big
picnic tables they put in rest areas all over the state. We also have a
cannery for fruits, vegetables, potatoes and tomatoes. We feed 'em
fresh seasonally and then can all the excess. We raise all our own
food; everything they eat comes from here. Everything they wear
comes from here. They even make the mattresses they sleep on.

"Hell, yes, running a prison is running a big business," he continued, bragging about how the prisoners at Arizona State did all
the printing of documents, legislative reports and studies for the
state—as well as printing prison manuals and contracting for business with the state universities. He said the prison had its own
draftsmen and construction crews and that prison labor had been
used to build every building on the grounds—including the gas
chamber, a minors' division and the $275,000 women's division. They
also built fifteen prison residences on the grounds for correctional administrators and officers and had completed a twenty-three-apart-
ment housing project in Florence for correctional officers, paid for
by state general funds. Prisoners pick cotton and process it through
cotton gin mills and then make state garments with the cloth. Prisoners work as plumbers and electricians and masons, in addition to
doing all repair work and upkeep of prison facilities.

The prison is more than self-sufficient. It's a moneymaking proposition. Yet the week I was there, out of the 1,263 men and 45
women at the prison only 107 were on the payroll under a "wage
incentive pay plan" started six months earlier, in July 1971. Those
107 prisoners in "key positions" were paid twenty cents an hour. Six
of the paying jobs were held by women inmates.

The majority of prisoners at Arizona State work only for time off their sentences. If prisoners have a "two-for-one" job, they get two days' credit for every one day of labor served under state law. In addition, with a good work and behavior record, these men and women can get two months off their sentence after the first year; four months after the third year; and five months are cut from the sentence every year after the fifth year as long as their employment record is consistently "successful" and their behavior record "clean." Anyone in segregation or in the "adjustment center" cannot get two-for-one status and can lose time already earned. Inmates can try to earn money for commissary by selling crafts in the prison hobby-craft shop—or by selling blood in the Cutter Blood Program. They get six dollars for each bleeding, and can do this once a week.

"There are no work furlough programs here and no work release for men or women," Eyman said. "I don't see that ever happening here. I wouldn't allow it. I just wouldn't be in favor it. There's plenty of work to do right here. There won't be any work release from here. I just wouldn't like it. We don't have it, let's put it that way. And we don't expect to have it—not as long as I'm here."

When I asked Eyman what he thought of conjugal visits, he said, "I'll never have 'em, I just don't want 'em. If they want that, they should have stayed in the free world. If they chose a criminal way of life, why should they enjoy the privileges of tax-paying citizens?"

The thought that prisoners pay more taxes in labor than any citizens in the "free world" was totally foreign to Eyman's thinking. Just as the idea that sex and affection are "privileges of tax-paying citizens" was foreign to my thinking. He, like many others, openly disdains the concept of rehabilitation, and rather believes that prisoners are in *his* prison to be punished and to *pay* for their crimes. They do *pay*—not to victims of crime, but to the state general fund.

Under the Slave Emancipation Act of 1865, slavery and involuntary servitude were abolished for everyone *except* convicted criminals; so it is perfectly within the law to force prisoners to work for no pay. Whether it is right or wise or just is an entirely different question. Even at prisons that emphasize treatment and reintegration into the community, prisoners still literally pay the state with their labor and the *effect* is the same . . . even if a strict custody approach like Eyman's is abhorred.

Although it is legal to force a sentenced prisoner to work, it is illegal to force a detentioner, someone jailed while awaiting trial or sentence, into involuntary servitude. Thus, county and local jails offer detentioners work as a *privilege* to pass the time. In many places the alternative to the privilege of having a job is being locked into a cell twenty-four hours a day. The difference between force and coercion or "incentive" becomes a very hazy legal question. Work by pre-trial prisoners is also often encouraged by the privilege of getting "unlocked" an extra hour a day or being *paid* with a couple of packs of cigarettes a week.

"I'm a hall girl," said Barbara, at Cook County Jail. "That's supposed to mean I'm a trustee. Trustees get to stay out one hour later at night [in the dayroom] and get extra food. We work in the beauty shop, do the corridor and sweep and mop. That extra hour means a lot to me; I don't like to be locked up. Usually the job is appointed to someone. Most ask the matron, but I got the job different. A girl got shipped to the penitentiary. So I just picked up her mop and started mopping and I had the job."

At Sybil Brand Institute for Women, no woman is paid for her daily labor in the institution. A few women can earn a little money for commissary items by washing or making blouses for officers, or washing cars on occasion after they have finished their regular industrial and maintenance jobs in the institution. Officers pay prisoners through their employee fund: three cents for washing and ironing a blouse. Two of the three cents is divided up between the laundress and the ironer and one cent goes to the soap fund since the officers aren't allowed to use county soap to wash their blouses.

Prisoners who are selected by officers to do the job are also paid three cents for making blouses on a piecework basis. The three cents is divided up between the cutter, the sewer and the buttonholer. This would mean that the three women would have to make nearly fifty blouses to buy one pack of cigarettes. They don't make money individually for the things they make in hobby-craft shop programs. That money goes into the inmate welfare fund—which allegedly pays for the different activities in L. A. County jails and provides occasional cigarettes, soap or toothpaste for destitute women who don't have anyone to bring them money from the outside.

Profits from commissary sales in prisons and jails also go into an inmate welfare fund—again, allegedly for the benefit of the inmates. But inmates say they rarely see any benefit other than perhaps candy, cookies or free packs of state cigarettes at Christmas parties. They have no say in how the profits are spent. In New York City, the commissary fund of over $1 million from combined jails somehow filters into the general fund for the city. In San Francisco, Sheriff Richard Hongisto said that before he took office, "No one seemed to know where the money had gone to." Hongisto said the commissary profit from San Francisco jails alone totaled at least $18,000 a year. He planned to track down the money and start using it to improve direct services for inmates who live in what he called "outrageous and inhumane conditions." Hongisto said that he could only figure the money had been funneled off into private gain, because certainly it hadn't been used for inmate benefits.

Some of the women at California Institution for Women said that if they really could determine the use of the profits from their purchases each week at the commissary, they would use the more than $21,000 in the fund to build a swimming pool and install several pay telephones.

The way the law works often seems incongruous to its intent. More than 65 per cent of the women at Sybil Brand are awaiting trial, as we pointed out before. Legally, they can't be made to work. Yet nearly everyone confined there works, cleaning their living areas, working in a large garment factory, the laundry or kitchen. Women do all the janitorial work, including trash collection and disposal. The garment factory makes shrouds for the coroner's office and gowns for the county hospitals.

Inmates—sentenced or unsentenced—get no pay for their work.

"The inmates get no pay except at our camps," said Chief H. B. Creamer, Chief of the Jail Division, after telling me about the division's budget, the 2,800 acres of beef herds, a dairy, produce farm and bakery run by inmates. "They work for reward. They get five days off for working and five days off their sentences for good conduct.

"Everybody who's sentenced is automatically figured at a twenty-day month. If they refuse to work, or have bad conduct, the time gets recomputed. It makes the time go much faster for them. I'm not saying we're rehabilitating them, but in many cases, they're adding a skill to a field of knowledge they can perhaps use someday.

"Constitutionally, we can't work unsentenced inmates unless they volunteer. We are merely a detaining agency until the court decision. Prisoners who are not sentenced are not getting time off. Once a person is sentenced, she starts earning her good time and her work time. [As of March 1972, the dead time became part of the sentence served.]

"*Reward is an excellent means for us to gain compliance to rules* [my emphasis]. If you want to gain time you comply to our rules. That's the greatest reason why we've had so little trouble here."

Capt. Paul A. Strohman repeated Creamer's statements about "work incentive and rewards." He said quite frankly that, "The good time and the work time is a great help to custody. It gives us an incentive to get them to work . . . . There's been a lot of talk about paying people in jail, but it gets back to the budget. There would be a taxpayer revolt to that."

Perhaps Captain Strohman is right—taxpayers might "revolt." But consider this. If prisoners earned fair wages for their labor, they would be able to support their familes—and that alone would take thousands of people off welfare roles. As it is now, dependent families are forced to go on welfare when their wage earner goes to prison. Children become dependents of the state and the costs don't make sense—especially when prisoners are actually paying more than their share of taxes in terms of physical labor and profit to the state. In addition, if prisoners earned even minimum wages, they would be able to pay court costs, fines and restitution. They would be able to save some small sums of money to help them get readjusted upon release. It seems more than reasonable that the profit they earn for the state should be returned to them rather than transferred to state coffers.

But the fear that people would *want* to go to prison if they could earn a decent wage or live in less-than-sterile conditions still seems to exist, irrational as it is. One of the notions seemingly inherent in the concept of imprisonment in America is that prisoners should get no reward or sense of gratification during confinement; i.e., if they were comfortable, being separated from society wouldn't be so much a punishment. In 1870 William Talleck openly acknowledged what we still seem to believe today—that forced labor with no rewards will reduce people's temptation to go to prison for an easy life. Mr. Talleck, secretary of the Howard Association in England, was addressing the National Congress on Penitentiary and Reformatory Discipline in Cincinnati, Ohio, on a model prison in the United States that enforced "in a most prominent degree, the great principle of restitution, at once punitory and reformatory":

It makes the inmates pay handsomely, by their labor, for all the expenses of punishment, for their board and lodging, and for the salaries of the officers. In addition, they earn a new profit to the state of from $24,000 to $28,000 per annum (Upwards of £5,000). Thus, after all, an honest outsider is not likely to be very strongly tempted by the fish hash and corned-beef (diet of the prison), if he knows that for it he must be shut up for several years and "sweated" for the benefit of his chastisers to the extent of $220 (£40) per annum.

In many ways, the work program Mr. Talleck described sounds much like the "progressive" work release programs initiated in Wisconsin twenty years ago and becoming increasingly popular today. The *low-risk* prisoners in these programs are allowed to work during the day at jobs in the community and return to the institution at night. In most of these programs—as in Franklin County, Pennsylvania, and in Marin County, California, people in the work release program pay room and board to the jail out of their wages. The employer usually deposits the person's regular wages with the prison authorities—who in turn charge costs for housing, fines and family support against the prisoner's account. "The more money you make, the more they take." In some counties, like Franklin County, court costs and restitution to the victims of crime are also deducted from the prisoner's account. Some prisoners leave jail with few debts and some savings left when finally released from confinement.

It was also noted at the 1870 Congress by a man from Pennsylvania that "those prisons were best that paid best; therefore it would be necessary for every prison manager to make his prison pay, or else he would be pronounced a failure. It would also be necessary to introduce trades and manufactures, and in order to make these pay, it was necessary to employ all the modern machinery and improvements, so that they could get the same amount of labor and of the same kind, that private individuals, companies and firms did outside." The man said, "The result was that the inmates of our prisons were turned into machines."

It is clear that the use of prisons as a dominant sanction for crime was greatly a product of the Industrial Revolution, which created a need for cheap labor in economically expanding America. The view that labor was "therapy" was both economically appealing and fit the Puritan moral heritage which viewed idleness as the root of crime.[1]

1. American Friends Service Committee, *Struggle for Justice—A Report on Crime and Punishment in America* (New York: Hill & Wang, 1971).

But even in 1870 there was much dispute as to whether "moral and religious improvement" was compatible with industry on the part of the prisoners and economy on the part of the prison officers. Several people were vehement that "The desire to make a prison a source of revenue or even self-sustaining, should never be allowed to supersede those more important and ever-to-be-remembered objects—moral and religious improvement."

These beliefs led to great dispute over the labor contract system—under which prison labor was contracted out by state legislatures to private individuals and contractors. This practice, especially in the South, meant that slavery was perpetuated under a contract system. Supposedly free black people could be virtually kidnapped back into slavery as punishment for a "criminal offense" in lieu of payment of fines or taxes or civil judgments. Vagrancy statutes were commonly used to enforce criminal sentences—so in spite of the recent abolition of slavery, thousands of black people who had committed no real criminal offense were kept in involuntary servitude on farms or road gangs through this system. In urban areas, European immigrants were rounded up for vagrancy and violation of drinking and "morals" laws. At the 1870 Congress a Mr. Cordier of Pennsylvania opposed the contract system. He said there were two things essential to a prisoner's reformation. "The will to live honestly and the power to earn an honest living." Both must be given him in prison, Cordier said—the one through moral agencies, the other through industrial training. He believed the contract system, which utilized prisoners for hard manual labor, did not teach a trade and was an obstacle to getting a trade.

It is interesting to see that, even then, opponents to the contract system in general still considered the people in prison "criminals" or a "type" who needed reformation, and did not view them as victims of an expanding economic system, although the facts would seem to contradict that view. Only Judge Carter of Ohio said that if prisons were to continue to exist (he believed they should be abolished), there should be "some system of co-operative labor, by which the prisoners would receive the wages they earned just as if they were at work outside."

It was not until the 1920s that pressures from competitive businesses and unions curbed the "unfair competition" of the labor contract system, so prison production became an intra-governmental matter with products confined to use only by state and federal agencies.[2] The free labor was simply too much competition for union labor, because it could naturally under-bid anyone, and still make a profit. It's curious that today it's considered "radical" to suggest that as long as prisons still exist, prisoners should be able to join unions and make union scale wages for their work. Administrators say there isn't enough money in the budget—but if outside unions were allowed in or the profit was returned to the people who earned it, the wages wouldn't come from "the budget."

In 1870, the annual net earnings from prison labor at Ohio Penitentiary, where women and men were confined, were "over and above ordinary expenses from $40,000 to $50,000 profit." During World War II, prison industries boomed and produced war goods valued at over $138,000,000. Where does that excess go today—a hundred years later, thirty years after the war? Who controls it? How is it distributed?

It is beyond the scope of this book to analyze the figures today, but it seems that if the profit-making trend continued—that what was $50,000 profit for one institution in 1870 would well be millions of dollars in today's economy. Since the number of penal industries has increased, not decreased, it seems that estimates would be multiplied even further. It seems that the real profit-making from prison labor is an area worthy of detailed investigation. And if in fact there are hidden profits, the figures should be made public—and taxpayers inside and outside prison should be able to evaluate them. If there is a real interest in cutting recidivism rates and the destitution that stimulates so much crime, perhaps profits should be returned to people who have labored for them.

As it is now, profits apparently are turned over to state general funds on the state level and into the Justice Department on the federal level. Industries at federal prisons are run by Federal Prison Industries, Incorporated—a private company. But the commissioner of FPI is also the director of the Bureau of Prisons. The two jobs go to-

2. The abuses of the contract system of leasing out prisoner labor were curbed with a series of restrictive federal laws, beginning with the Hawes-Cooper Act of 1929, effective in 1934. These laws practically put prison contract industries out of competitive business. Road gangs and work projects still continue (with men still wearing shackles and iron chains in some states)—but not for private contractors. In some ways it could be said the contract system of prison labor still exists, but now prisoners are contracted to the state, which is not in violation of labor laws.

gether, but the accounting is separate. This means separate payrolls for civilian employees of FPI and separate budgets. At the Federal Reformatory for Women at Alderson, the two divisions of FPI are the garment factory and the automatic data processing. The women in the garment factory make clothing for other federal prisons—khakis and denims for the men prisoners and shirts for guard uniforms. They have other federal contracts—like making linens and pajamas for veterans hospitals throughout the country. They have a tremendous production output annually—even though the industrial sewing machines they work on are out of date for commercial use. ("Even if you wanted to get a job in a garment factory on the streets, you wouldn't know how to operate the machines," one woman at Alderson said. "And your speed isn't up because you've been working on such old machines. It's a real sweatshop and the superintendent of industries is a real ogre about production, production, production . . . All she cares about is production . . .")

The automatic data processing is smaller-scale, but women with a certain level of education and manual dexterity work at computer keypunching jobs for the Bureau of Prisons, the Army, Navy, Veterans and other federal agencies. They keep statistics for the Bureau of Prisons with extensive personal backgrounds on all federal prisoners, which the women say includes even the most lowly misconduct report form.

The majority of women working in these industries are paid nineteen cents an hour. A very few women make top-grade prison industry wages of up to fifty-two cents an hour. They all work eight hours a day, sometimes six and seven days a week. Most women who have no funds from the outside depend on the work for their essential commissary items—from toothpaste to cigarettes to underwear. The biggest advantage to working in industry—besides the meager commissary income—is the reward of "industrial good time."

In institutional jobs other than those under industries—such as dining room, maintenance jobs, office jobs, paint crew, landscape crew, laundry and hospital and storehouse—women at Alderson are eligible to be given MSA—meritorious service award—which is meritorious pay. After a woman works on the job for three months, she's eligible to get ten dollars a month and this amount can be increased. But according to prisoners, most people don't get it at all. They are also eligible for "meritorious good time" allotted to those who get it at the same rate as industrial good time. But meritorious good time and meritorious pay are not given to long-timers (five years or more) until the last three years of their actual sentences.

"To get paid you have to be really really good at what you're doing," Suzi Williams said. "You can't goof off at all and you have to put in a lot of overtime, particularly in the dining room, where they're very hard on people. And they will give you like two people's jobs to do on your shift. They'll make you be the beverage girl and at the same time carry trays from the dish room, when you're only supposed to be doing one of those. We ran into somebody who had been washing pots and pans seven days a week for over a year, because she just didn't want to do anything that would mess with her parole. She was basically a straight housewife type who was very easily intimidated and didn't know much about bucking bureaucracies or making a stink.

"In all of these things people who can buck bureaucracies or who are hustlers just have a much easier time. It's the people who aren't hustlers who have it so hard . . . and there are a whole lot of them there, because prisons are for people not who committed bad crimes, but who committed crimes badly. You know, the fuck-ups and the bumblers. And the people who could be led around by the nose by other people and influenced and then left to take the rap when the smarter people cut out or have enough money to buy their way out afterwards.

"It's hard to get paid and most people just don't know how to get around it. And then once you're getting paid, then this is an excuse to load everything on you, call you up at five and say, 'Hey, report at six,' and all this kind of stuff. Or they'll threaten to take it away. Because you're getting paid, you should do thus and thus. And, 'Hey, wow, remember you're getting paid and we can stop that!' You have to earn your days in pay. And you're also subject to take away your days in pay for things that have nothing to do with your job—for instance, if you're messy around the cottage, or loud—'We don't consider you an exemplary person'—or untidy in your dress, they can say, 'We can't give you days in pay and you're not eligible for the next three months.' "

Economic and utilitarian aims still seem to dominate the work ethic in prisons—in addition to the emphasis on keeping everyone busy and under control for the smooth functioning of the institution. It also relieves any "idleness" that would lead to "trouble" or slothfulness. The *Manual of Correctional Standards*, a current publication issued by the ˜American Correctional Association, outlines "elements essential to the successful operation of a woman's correctional institution" and includes the following criteria for vocational training and work assignments:

> A realistic vocational training program which is divorced from the maintenance needs of the institution and under qualified instructors; training should be in as many as practicable of the varied industrial, commercial and service occupations in which women are engaged today. A work program to provide upkeep of the institution will also provide an opportunity to teach good work habits which are essential.

The manual specifies that vocational training should teach skills "salable in the community" but gets back to reality when it states: "Perhaps the largest number of inmates are placed on work assignments necessary for maintaining the institution; by-products of such placements are the development of improved work habits and attitudes."

When I first visited several county jails where women were confined, I was appalled at the rules that demanded "ladylike" conduct in the midst of meaningless make-work such as scrubbing floors an excessive number of times each day and scrubbing bars on cells. Mainly the women were locked in their cells or kept from being idle by "keeping the place clean." Male prisoners were assigned to heavier work details that contributed to prison maintenance—and the women remained cramped into the small, segregated areas of these jails. It was only after I visited more state prisons that I realized what heavy "male role" work women at all-female institutions do for the prison economy. The view that women should "learn their roles as mothers, housekeepers and wives" and that their work should contribute to their reintegration into the community as "whole women" seems even more ludicrous when you see women working as butchers, truck loaders, janitors and "maintenance men."

"How many women do you know that work on garbage trucks or repair cars or lawn mowers or drive tractors or lift hundred-pound bags of potatoes and whatnot for a living?" asked Sheila "Terry" Dunnigan, an inmate at Frontera. "How many people do you know that make six dollars a month working at an eight-hour-a-day job five days a week? If you're lucky, you may make up to nine dollars a month . . . if you're lucky.

"How many women do you know on the outside who drive trucks and how many women plumbers do you know on the streets? The women here are wasting time and energy on these type of jobs running the institution when they could be in some kind of training program and making something of themselves, but there are little or no training programs that would benefit these people when they get out.

"There is a cosmetology course that is sixteen hundred hours long—but after spending all this time, there is no guarantee that you will be able to get a license, because they don't give licenses to felons or ex-convicts. So here you have wasted sixteen hundred hours or a year that won't do you any good at all on the streets.

"Society talks about rehabilitation and rehabilitating the criminal. I guess one of the things that impresses people the most when they come here is the grounds and our surroundings. The campus has trees, flowers, shrubs and looks really nice when it's green and the sun's out shining or when it's wintertime and it snows in the mountains and looks really pretty. But it could never make up for all the mental pressure that people undergo. There is no rehabilitation here . . . they offer nothing. And not only is there no rehabilitation, there's no communication. If you want anything, you have to fight for it and even then you usually get nothing. You get a good runaround from people who can't give you even a few minutes to rap and that's about it."

Besides the complaint that jobs of lifting and loading from trucks, acting as butchers and other jobs women do are not salable skills for them on the outside, women complain that the heavy jobs "break them down." In addition, they say the health standards and safety conditions in the factories and work areas are often hazardous.

When state prisoners at the Detroit House of Correction went on strike in the fall of 1971 in an attempt to get better conditions, chief among the women's complaints were the hazards of the laundry and the canning factory. Included in their list of grievances was a demand for a state health inspector.

They said the jobs in the laundry and the canning factory were the hardest jobs and pointed out that women:

—use presses that are outdated and break down frequently.

—lift 100- and 150-pound bags of soap chips, etc., to pour the contents into barrels.

—load washers by lifting anywhere from 25 to 100 pounds each into old machines that have dangerous washer doors.

—unload and sort approximately 100 bags of 25 to 100 pounds of laundry which comes to the institution from the general hospitals. The sheets "are stained with blood, fetus and other forms of contagious germs. This institution provides no masks, head-dress, gloves or protective clothing for these women to wear while doing this."

"We as women would like to leave here still able to have babies and our bodies as healthy and productive as when we entered this institution. Are we wrong to feel this way?"

Suzi Williams, who did time at Alderson for interfering with the Military Selective Service Act of 1967 and destroying draft records, said the keypunching program there was probably the "only worthwhile vocational training program" salable on the outside. But she pointed out that not too many people qualify for the program because of educational requirements. Those who do can go only so far.

"I had a friend who was doing a ten-year sentence for bank robbery," Suzi said. "She was a very intelligent person and wanted to learn computer programming instead of just keypunching because it's more interesting, plus it pays better. So she begged and pleaded with them, but they were not at all interested in helping her learn programming. Finally she decided she was going to learn it whether they helped her or not. She had to fight with them a couple months for permission to even order the books and pay for them herself. They were quite expensive, but finally she got them paid for and ordered. But the people who censor books held them up for another couple of months and then they were transferred to her boss. After another month or so she heard a rumor that there were these books sitting around and she squawked, and sure enough, they were hers, the ones she had paid her own personal money for. She studied them hard, but she suffered continuously because authorities threw stuff in her way. Neither her boss, the head of her department, her caseworker nor the education department people who had a hand in it were helpful. Nobody was really helpful. So they talk about all this rehabilitation stuff, but when you get it together to do something, they will not help you. You have to do it in spite of them."

Suzi said that despite the rhetoric, production always comes before individual considerations. I have also found this to be true no matter how good the intentions of some administrators are. Women have a hard time getting out of work for a dental appointment or educational programs when they are available. At Alderson, most of the Spanish-speaking women work in the garment shop because most of them don't have any money and depend on the income for their commissary. Suzi said a lot of them would like to learn English, but they can't if they have to be in the garment shop all the time. "Most of the classes are during the day and when there are night classes, they're too exhausted." There are a few isolated cases where women with an incredible amount of will get certified as laboratory technicians or earn college credits through correspondence courses, but usually they have done it in spite of the prison, not because of it.

Even the most conservative penologists admit privately that jobs in prison don't have any significant relationship to rehabilitation. They admit the production methods are obsolete and that besides keeping the prisons functioning, keeping the prisoners busy is necessary for the operation of security. Jobs also have a way of helping the prisoners forget about the immediate oppression they are experiencing and where they are. But petty details fill the day along with tedious time schedules and block meaningful programs that women could set up for their own education or enlightenment if given an opportunity.

Alice Evans has been at Ohio Reformatory for Women since 1965. She will be eligible to meet the parole review board in 1977, although her actual release date is 1985. She's doing a natural life sentence of twenty years for being an accessory to first-degree murder. We met in the basement of one of the living units of Marysville when Alice was hauling a huge beef carcass across a table. At the institution, she's a butcher.

A small, pale-skinned woman, Alice doesn't *look* any more like she could be a butcher than Julie Nixon Eisenhower does. But she hauled around the beef carcass with skill and nonchalance. "We do lifting but usually two or three of us help each other. We get five beefs in at a time," she said. "We unload truckful after truckful. I come to work at eight-fifteen A.M. and we have orders to fill and get on the cart for the truck girls to deliver to the central food and diet kitchen. If it's on milk day we sit around until nine or nine-fifteen and unload the milk truck, which comes from Marion. Then if we have beef, the chief butcher does the breaking down and I do the sawing on the power saw. I cut it in steaks and get it ready to go out. If we don't use it that day we put it in the freezer for later on.

"We get off at eleven-thirty and go to lunch. We sit up on the corridor after we get back [twenty minutes later] until twelve forty-five. They crowd fifty-some women in the corridor—and it's the source of real tension. We have to sit all crowded up on those benches and can't go to our rooms. All of the women are trying to yak after lunch and it's a lot of tension because you don't want a bunch of women sitting on you. Officers say this and that and don't do nothing . . . hush. A lot of fights—practically every one I can think of—has started from that corridor sitting. Even if it erupts later, you can know where it started. There was a bad fight last night that had started in the corridor in the noon period. Three women jumped another one and beat her bad. The staff knows who did the beatings, but they're not doing anything about it. You would think they should move the three who beat her up to the adjustment unit—but oh no, they moved her out. None of what goes on here makes much sense—but they keep us working.

"I'm confined to this building only. The only time I get out is for dinner or to go to the hospital for clinic—which doesn't do any good. I really get the feeling of being confined. I live in this building and I work here in the basement.

"The BVR [Bureau of Vocational Rehabilitation] thing don't help lifers and about all vocational things run here are by BVR. They say they have just so much money and so far it only goes for short-timers. I think it only takes three years of butchering to get a license— and I started working here in 1965. But I don't have a license—and I doubt if I could get a job if I did.

"There are so many jive rules here and so many things to hold a person back . . . We go through hell and there's nothing we can do about it. I'm cottage rep for the corridor and elected rep to the communications group, but we have no power. Our suggestions are always just 'taken under consideration'—they don't move on them. I don't know whether the outside world don't believe this hell or whether they don't care.

"There are so many things we should change—I don't know where to start. You gotta do manual labor for six dollars a month—that oughtta be changed . . . but it's really hard to get the women together. How can we get anything from Congressmen when we can't even get our problems together here on the farm . . . There's all sorts of petty shit . . . like we can't go into the TV room, for instance, unless two officers are there. And there are only two officers on duty at a time, so we can't go in. Or if you forget to turn in your food card or forget to pick it up, you get three nights' early bed. That means if you don't want to eat, you still have to walk over with your food card and check back in here. There's a hundred more things like that. So there are all these petty things forced on people's minds and it's hard to get organized around bigger issues when these little ones keep you worrying all the time.

"We've talked to the administration about our pay—but they say, We can't do anything about it—not us or Miss Wheeler or Governor Gilligan unless you get state senators to pass a bill."

It's funny how so often rumor is accepted as fact. When I was at Marysville, everyone I talked to, including administrators, said they thought the pay scale should be changed—but it could only be done through legislation. The top salary for inmates was ten dollars a month. Six dollars were put automatically into the woman's commissary fund and four dollars into her savings account—to be given her on release. That's five cents an hour—with three cents for commissary and two cents for savings. The pay is purely a book transaction; women never see the cash or benefit from interest accrued on their savings. When they leave the prison, they leave with a minimum of twenty-five dollars and up to a maximum of three hundred. At the time they reach the maximum amount, they stop earning that extra two cents an hour; it stops going into their savings fund. From that point on they get only three cents an hour.

"The twenty-five-dollar floor and three-hundred-dollar ceiling is established by legislation and departmental directive," Superintendent Martha Wheeler confirmed. "We have no idea why or who decided. But it would have to be changed by the legislature. Back in 1966 we wrote a proposal for pay to be raised, but we never got any response on that. If the person has another source of income, the ceiling has nothing to do with that. Money that comes in from the outside is considered personal. If someone gets a pension, for instance, we'll open a savings account in a local bank for her and she accumulates the interest.

"Some people make less than ten dollars a month. People who are in school are not presumed to work full time, for instance, so they don't get full pay. They get $4.95 to spend on their personal account a month and $3.30 in savings. This is if they're not docked for absences."

When I talked to Bennett Cooper, Commissioner of Corrections for the state of Ohio, he said that the department planned to raise the pay of inmates; that there was money in the budget to do that and it wouldn't take legislative action. When I asked him about the floor and the ceiling on inmates' savings, he said he had been told it would take legislation to change that. I told him I thought it just didn't make sense—I'd like to see the statute that set it up. It would take a woman nearly seven years to earn $300 and if she was there for twenty years, she theoretically should be able to take $960 home with her—at an abominable savings rate of four dollars a month.

During the interview, he asked his assistant to check what legislation stipulated the floor and ceiling. Before I left, his assistant had returned with the information that the "ceiling" of $300 and "floor" of $25 was not legislation—but was an administrative directive from 1952. It would only take another administrative directive to change that condition. No bill had to pass through the legislature.

Cooper said, "It just shows what creatures of habit we are," and noted that many of the unquestioned rules and procedures were going to be thoroughly re-examined. Administrations have changed many times since 1952—and I have no reason to doubt the sincerity of any of the administrators who believed it would take legislation to change this situation. It just reaffirms my belief that the more these vague and hidden procedures are given light, the more changes can be made simply and easily through directives, which were originally made in the economic interest of jailers, not inmates.

What appears to me even more direct exploitation than the indecent wages prisoners are paid for their labor is the use of prisoners in the personal service of prison administrators. Women prisoners often work as housemaids and cooks for the families of prison superintendents, and men work as cooks, in lawn crews and as maintenance men at the homes of superintendents. It may be that my indignation at such arrangements is excessive since I have been a live-in maid in years gone by—and carry vivid memories that make me overreact. Certainly administrators generally don't see anything wrong or try to hide the fact that prisoners cook and clean, wash and iron for them. It is an accepted custom and the household servants come hand in hand with the administrative position. I'm sure in their minds they are just providing more jobs for prisoners who otherwise would be idle. Nevertheless, my sensibilities are grossly offended when I hear a woman tell me about the long hours she spends cooking for the warden or experiences she's had "serving" at a party or dinner in the superintendent's home. I can't hear about it without feeling the vibrations of my own rage. It's usually humiliating enough to be a house servant when you're being paid meager wages see no alternatives—but to have it be involuntary servitude gives me the plantation shudders. Nevertheless, it's a common practice.

"Leslie Simms" said after she had recovered from a miscarriage, she was working in the staff dining room at a detention center I am not at liberty to name when the superintendent of prisons, a man I'll call "Mr. X," needed a "house girl." Mrs. Williams (a lieutenant) put Leslie's name up for the job: "He interviewed me and asked me about doing housework and what I was there for. I only told him 'I'm here for homicide,' which he already knew—he was just asking.

"Close to September I went to work there. Their house is set off from the actual prison itself. They have two bedrooms on the third floor and four on the second floor with two bathrooms. Downstairs there's a real big L-shaped living room and dining room, a den and recreation room with a place behind that for an extra stove and refrigerator. In the basement was the actual kitchen and laundry room and storerooms and bathroom for the help.

"They had a girl, Carol, already working there as head house girl. She did the cooking and I did the laundry and cleaning shit upstairs with another girl. They always got three black girls and one white houseman nobody would want to fuck. I went over and helped Carol with dinner one night and helped serve dinner. I guess he liked the way I served. He fired Carol as head house girl and shifted her upstairs to do housework and then later fired her because she was 'sloppy and incompetent.' I don't know about incompetent but she was definitely sloppy in appearance. We wore our prison uniforms to work in.

"Then I was head house girl. I went in at eight-thirty in the morning and did the laundry—washing, drying and ironing, every day. They had a lot of laundry—six people—Mr. and Mrs. X and their four children. The kids would leave their dirty laundry laying all around. Then I left around ten or eleven A.M. and went back to the jail for lunch and count and all. Then around five a car would pick me up to go and do dinner. I'd be there till around nine or ten every night, even weekends, yes. There was always somebody home for dinner—even if Mr. and Mrs. X went out, which was almost never.

"I'd fix supper in the basement and put it on the dummy and then go up and pull it up from downstairs—'cause they ate upstairs. I'd have already set the table up before they sat down—and I would put the food on the table. He did all the carving and serving of the meat. Then I'd bring water and coffee and during the meal they'd call down and tell me to bring up milk or juice—or somebody might want mayonnaise or mustard, so I'd take it up. Sometimes somebody might want tea, so I'd have to find a damn tea bag and heat water and up the stairs I'd go again.

"Mrs. X complained about everything. There was a houseman—he was white, get that—and he was supposed to do the breakfast dishes. When I got there I was supposed to go up and gather up all the laundry—wash, dry, iron it and hang it up and put it away. One day she told me about the stove being greasy—and I told her it was from breakfast and was supposed to be for the houseman. We got into a big hassle. She also complained that on Thursday, when they got the new groceries, the refrigerators weren't straightened up properly— that I hadn't gotten rid of the old stuff first and washed them out well.

"I told her that I wasn't a black maid and furthermore I was going to ask for a change of jobs. She said that was fine because 'I wouldn't want anybody working here that didn't want to.' I told her, 'I'm only working here because I have to, not 'cause I want to.'

"That night I came back to prepare supper and she had told Mr. X what I said. So he waited till after I served dinner and cleaned up before he came downstairs to talk to me. He came down then and said he understood I had told his wife I wanted to change my job, so I said, Yes, this was very true. Then he went into his act. 'Nobody's irreplaceable,' he said. 'I can replace you in five minutes.' I said, 'That's what I want you to do—replace me.'

"He said he could confine me to the wing for refusing to work— which means I would be locked in my cell. He told me I had a homicide and I was bound to get some time on it—that I'd have at least two years and my behavior record would count. He told me to think about what he said—and that the only reason he wasn't gonna lock me then was 'cause he felt I was upset. Yeah, he didn't want me to quit; that's what he was saying in reality—but he didn't say it in words. But evidently he wasn't too keen about replacing me. He could have locked me in my room—I didn't care. So apparently my work wasn't as bad as she was pretending it was.

"Anyway, the next morning I refused to go to work. Mrs. Williams called the warden and he and the major came over. He talked to me

for about an hour or more—with Mrs. Williams and the major present. What he did was talk me into going back over there. He couldn't
go over the superintendent's head, he said, but he said he didn't feel
I should be put in the hole—and that was the alternative to not
going back to work. The warden said I should understand that
Mrs. X was a sick woman—she has a heart condition—and evidently
X didn't want to fire me. He said I should go over to avoid being
put in the hole for 'extreme disobedience.'

"It was a whole dressed-up thing. I was refusing to work—that's
disobedience. But I was disobeying the goddamned superintendent
—and that's *extreme disobedience*. I was thumbing my nose at them
all until I started digging what it would do to me mentally to go to
the hole. I could have handled the concrete floor and one meal a
day. What I couldn't dig was the solitude. I thought I'd better let
well enough alone. I didn't feel that mentally I would be able to cope
with the hole right then—in fact, I probably would have gone crazy
at that point.

"So I went back to work after I talked to the warden. I got very
upset, so they sent me upstairs to the dispensary for a tranquilizer
before I went back over. It wasn't any good, but really I had no
choice. Really an untried prisoner doesn't have to work unless they
choose. I think that's the law. But I cooked supper that night and
stayed on the job. They weren't going to listen to anything else."

Reliable sources from the same institution told me that two years
later, at the same institution, another of Superintendent X's "house
girls" had a more severe crisis. "Sonya," an inmate awaiting trial, was
also working as a daily maid at X's home. When she became pregnant, five months *after* she had been admitted to the jail, a matron
performed an abortion on her in the cell block. This incident was
hidden even from the warden until Sonya developed complications
from the abortion and had to be put into intensive care in a local
hospital.

Records are kept in such a way that it is very difficult to find written substantiation of such events. But I was told by involved persons
that the superintendent's eldest son was the man who impregnated
Sonya. Details were arranged in such a way that if the truth ever
came out, a guard would take responsibility for the pregnancy to take
X's son off the hook.

Leslie's and Sonya's jobs were considered "trustee" status because
they had to be "trusted" to work in the superintendent's home. Many

trustees have been taken advantage of in similar ways because of their literal lack of independence. They depend on their jobs for meager income but are unable to "quit" if they find the job distasteful, degrading or worse.

Many "trustee status" jobs (message carriers, "count" assistants, staff helpers and low security jobs on the grounds) are held by people charged or convicted of homicides. One warden told me, "They're our best people. They're the most stable. They flipped out and killed somebody after a long and pressured situation—usually their spouse —and they'd never commit another crime. They know they got a lot of time to do and they don't want trouble 'cause they've got to live with it."

Work at old-fashioned industrial sewing machines isn't much better. In summertime, women in these shops often pass out from heat asphyxiation and lack of air ventilation. More than one woman has told me of the tremendous production pressure put on them— broken only by two ten- or fifteen-minute cigarette breaks in the morning and afternoon. Silence rules are still rigidly enforced in some of the factories.

"I worked in the garment shop work with all the hassles just because I wanted that twenty dollars a month to buy my coffee and cigarettes . . ." said a woman who had been confined at Terminal Island, a federal division for women in California. "I did it even though I used to pass out from the heat. Just bonk—I'd pass out. They'd give me smelling salts and bring me some water and I'd go back to work. It's so insane when I look back on it—I just can't believe I did it. But it was some kind of need; I had to do some of those little extra nice things for myself since I didn't have no outside source of funds. Not many people did have any outside source of funds.

"The people there that really needed a trade or skill besides the streets, something useful, are the same ones who go into the garment shop to work because they don't have a source of funds. But they can't learn anything useful in there—it's just a way to survive inside. Then they go back out in the street and hustle some more.

"I had to hustle a lot at prison—you know, like do people's ironing or cleaning for them. For about two dollars' worth of commissary a week you can do their laundry and that kind of thing. Even though cigarettes are cheaper without federal taxes and all, you can't earn enough money to support even smoking—let alone all the other little things you want, like extra food or goodies. People do all sorts of things—like maybe you knit sweaters or blankets for people or you do their hair or that kind of thing. If they get money from the outside, that's the way they can share it and get helped out at the same time themselves. It's all like a constant hustle between the women—but there's a lot of co-operation, too."

In the women's garment factory at Ohio Reformatory for Women, as in other places I have mentioned, prisoners make dresses and undergarments for patients in the state mental hospitals, for children in agencies supported by public funds and for ORW prisoners. They also make flags—United States flags and Ohio State flags. According to the superintendent, ORW got into the flag business in 1963, under what I would consider a male power play on a woman's prison. "The old governor, James Rhodes, discovered that the wonderful world of Ohio didn't make state flags—we had to buy them from out of state," Miss Wheeler said. "He was quite upset by this state of things, so we found ourselves in the flag business."

Both the flag and dress makers work in the same industrial building at the prison six to eight hours a day for ten dollars a month under the auspices of Ohio Penal Industries.

YOU TAKE A STRIP OF RED MATERIAL AND WHITE MATERIAL AND SEW THEM TOGETHER. THEN YOU SEW THIRTEEN STRIPES. THEN YOU SEW IN THE BLUE PIECE WITH STARS. ONE WOMAN SITS AND DOES NOTHING BUT DRAW STARS ALL DAY. SOMEBODY ELSE CUTS OUT THE STARS. THEN YOU SEW THE LINING ON THE BACK AND THEN YOU PUT THE BAND ON THE SIDE AND KNOCK THE HOLES IN IT. THEN IT'S HEMMED AND IRONED AND STARCHED AND YOU HAVE THE NATIONAL FLAG OF THE UNITED STATES OF AMERICA. WE FOLD THEM AND PACK THEM AND THEY'RE READY FOR THE PUBLIC.

"They don't really teach you nothing in here," said Venartha Graham, a small, mature woman with a long Afro, deep brown skin and a devil-may-care attitude about the supervisor watching her. "If you don't know how to sew, they don't teach you. You just do one specific part of a job and that's it. You never get a sense of overall production or real training.

"They say the production we put out is for the overall payroll.

Our work pays the whole institution's six-dollars-a-month salaries—but we're the only ones who get docked for being absent or taking a break. Like for talking to you, I'll probably get docked about four hours off my pay—even if we only talk for twenty minutes. But I don't give a damn any more. The thing they hold over our head is that if *we* don't work, *they* [the other inmates] don't get paid. That's what we're told every time we begin to think about organizing or stopping work or anything. Everybody depends on that six dollars a month, so it puts added pressure on us."

Venartha and several other women, including myself, were standing around a table where finished products were folded—flags put in plastic bags and dresses stacked in piles for packing and delivery. An opened record book lay on the table in front of me. Two figures caught my attention from the orders completed that week: $1,260 sales to Gallipolis State Hospital; and $4,995.50 total for 690 regular jumpers at $2.45 each, 360 regular jumpers for $3.65 each and 1,050 white blouses at $1.90 each. Thumbing through the pages and seeing orders for $1,739; $2,620; $2,162; $2,220—it was even more amazing to think that the workers were earning four cents an hour.

Anyone at ORW who refuses to go to work is locked in her room or in maximum security; the same is true in other state and federal prisons. When I have asked administrators about this, they have said frankly it's because people refusing to work are potentially disruptive to the institution; plus prisons cannot function without inmate labor.

The many work strikes we have and haven't heard about in institutions throughout the country reflect an increasing awareness on the part of prisoners that their work is also their chance for a demonstration of power. Stopping work is one way to be heard, one channel to the authority usually blocked by "red tape."

Most Americans have been conditioned to believe that a reasonable protest will bring a reasonable response and, despite the evidence of the Atticas past, many women and men in prison still believe that if they organize in a nonviolent and adult manner, they will be treated accordingly. But the needs for control and security as seen both by the public and by prison administrations don't always allow much room for "reasonable" response to a reasonable protest. Even when the administration resists pressure to retaliate with physical violence or force, it still deems it necessary to punish "insurgents."

Some of the women at Marysville attempted a reasonable protest, as many have in other women's institutions—too extensive to document. I first heard about it from the women working in industry, and later from Becky Careway. Becky—with short blond hair and a cherub face that reminded me of Campbell soup girls—had been at Marysville since 1968. She is serving a one-to-twenty-year sentence on seven counts of forgery, breaking and entering and grand larceny. She was supposed to meet the parole board in October 1972, but figured her chances of getting parole were slim since earlier in the year she had walked off her job in the sewing industry with fifteen other women—including Venartha Graham, Annestine Roper and Barbara Baker.

"The prison offers nothing," Becky said. "The school books are out of date, the IBM machines are outdated and the teachers aren't there half the time. Where would a woman get a job on the outside as a trash collector? Or on a chicken farm? A lot of the women worry about what they're going to do when they get out—and want to change the situation. We decided to try to do something about it before it became a whole blown-up thing; the tension was getting really bad.

"Sixteen of us women walked off our jobs in industry to see the superintendent. I led the walk. We had put in pass after pass to see her—but she does not call passes. So we walked to the administration building and demanded to see her. We got to see her and we actually got some things accomplished, even though she avoided questions we asked her. Two immediate things we accomplished were getting to smoke when we were with our visitors and getting to visit for longer hours when our people come to see us once a month.

"But for walking off our jobs and going to the administration building to see her, we all got six months' probation and had two weeks of recreation time taken away from us. She threatened if she ever seen us with another group of women within a six-month period she would send us off the farm and we'd be given new charges for inciting a riot. We didn't disturb anybody, beat up nobody or anything. We went as ladies and conducted ourselves as ladies—and then she called us renegades."

The sixteen women carried twenty-nine grievances to the superintendent and later to the "communications group" (the inmate council). They also carried a written explanation of their actions and initiative:

"First of all we want it known that our overall grievance does not come before the Communications Group. Neither does it come against the way that the inmates are conducting our complaints . . . We trust their representation of their fellow inmates, but we also know that they are not the solution to our problem, they can only serve as a source of relaying what our problem is. The solution to our problem lies in the hands of our staff members but mainly our superintendent. As we believe, it is under her jurisdiction to assist us and converse with us on a woman to woman basis and help us relieve unnecessary mental strain. We are not here to be discriminated against due to a staff member's personal evaluation of us, or to be discriminated against because of the nature of our crime, but to be helped! We are here not with our individual problems, but with our overall problems that affect us as an individual.

"Surely it is no oddity that people protest a certain system, it is done every day and permitted if it is conducted in an orderly manner. The reason that it is done is to bring forth what a particular group feels is best for the general welfare of the people concerned, and to reach either a satisfactory compromise or solution to whatever the problem is.

"We know that changes will be made. The newspapers tell us that, our outside communications with people tell us that. The system will be changed. We are not interested in the system right now, we are interested in the things that affect us just because there seems to be a lack of communication between the inmates and the staff, or a lack of concern for the inmate as another human being . . .

"We did not assemble to be disorderly or to be destructive. We are seeking help from the source that we know a solution can be derived from. We are presenting things that need to be solved in our community *now* TODAY in this institution. Not things that will come before the system sometime in the future. . . . We are only trying to solve our own problems in a conducive manner, as ladies. We are seeking 'help,' understanding, compassion. We do not want any trouble, this is not our purpose; we want to unite together with the 'superintendent and her staff' to solve problems we are faced with NOW in this institution. Problems that we must live with and is important to each of us as individuals."

The administration's response to sixteen women walking off the job was as follows. The letter was received personally by each of the women who wanted to effect change *now*.

OCTOBER 5th, 1971

To: (Venartha Graham)

From: Disciplinary Committee

On Wednesday, September 22, 1971, you and fifteen others left your assignments without permission in order to confront the Superintendent with demands regarding institution programs and procedures. In so doing, you were in violation of institution rules by being out of place. You also interfered with the function of the Communications Group which was scheduled to meet that very afternoon. Subsequently, the Communications Group agreed to include you in their meeting so as to hear you out on your concerns. You were so included for three meetings including the final one in which the Superintendent responded. At the end of the third meeting, it was apparent that the one remaining matter to be decided was the penalty, if any, to be imposed upon the group of sixteen. The Communications Group felt it was not appropriate for them to make this decision but that it should be made by the institution Disciplinary Committee.

The Disciplinary Committee has reviewed the total situation and the following decision has been made:

1) No report will be placed in the permanent case folder.

2) You are suspended from all extra-curricular activities for two weeks. This does not include Catholic Mass, Protestant Services, Muslim Study Group or Church of Christ Communion Services, all of which take place on Sunday. These are the only exceptions.

We must point out to you the other natural result of the kind of behavior you displayed when you walked off the job. If there is any more of this kind of group behavior, it will be firmly handled. Once, the group was given every chance to talk the situation out. Now, it has been made clear that this kind of talk is to be channeled, in an orderly fashion, through the Communications Group. If there is any more of this "Walking Off" behavior within the next six months and any of you are a part of it, you must know that you will be identified as leaders and will be promptly separated from the institution community. You can avoid this by being where you belong, carrying out your assignment at all times.

The women involved said the response was considered relatively "reasonable" by the Disciplinary Committee. From what I have seen, this probably says more about how the sixteen women conducted themselves than about the usual reasonableness of the Disciplinary Committee. A less organized protest would have ended almost before it began—with all sixteen locked in maximum security—and more to follow.

Allegedly, women work to earn money for the essentials they can buy from the commissary. But the greater reason for working in a prison, just as it was on plantations, is the power wielded over prisoners' lives by the systems of control. Prisoners know administrators have the potential power to lock them up physically, abuse them, kill them if taken to an extreme. The power of the parole board is almost as ominous a power. Indeterminate sentencing predetermines behavior to a large extent because parole means spending perhaps four years in prison rather than twenty. And only a good work record and clean behavior record will earn parole. So the parole board and the institution have control of your future. It is fear of this power unleashed that allows so many people to be effectively controlled by so few. Prisoners' attempts to reduce this power, to gain more control over their own lives, are a threat to the power balance and therefore, the perpetuation of prisons as we know them.

CIW RULES*
SECTION I

CAMPUS PRIVILEGES:

1. Unless otherwise restricted, those who are off duty are permitted campus privileges between 8:00 A.M. and 5:00 P.M.

2. After the morning and noon meals, except in foggy weather, residents may remain in the Circle until scheduled for work or other appointments.

3. After the evening meal, residents off duty may visit in the Circle or in the areas directly in front of the cottage recreation rooms until campus is cleared for the evening count or until dusk, whichever is sooner.

4. Residents may sit on the grass in the Circle, but not lie down or use the grass for a pathway. Sidewalks will be used in going from place to place.

5. Shift workers who are off duty from 8:00 A.M. to 4:00 P.M. Monday through Friday, may go to the Library but must have a pass issued by the Cottage Supervisor. Residents will present pass to the School Secretary.

FOG PROCEDURE:

1. When fog procedures are in effect, campus privileges are not authorized. Women will return to their cottages until time for work release or for regular authorized appointments.

* Rules governing behavior and dress are generally more relaxed in state and federal institutions than they are at the county level. Some of these rules may seem repetitious of those reprinted after Chapter 4, but I have included them to emphasize the similarities of regulations throughout the county.

UNAUTHORIZED AREAS:

1. The following areas are out-of-bounds *at all times* except to those on official business . . .

    a. . . . Adm. Building (including outside area)

    b. . . Bakery

    c. . . Clinic (including outside area)

    d. . . Canteen

    e. . . Commissary

    f. . . Counseling Center and outside areas

    g. . . Hospital and outside areas

    h. . . Industry

    i. . . Laundry

    j. . . Maintenance

    k. . . PTU and RGC

    l. . . School Building and outside areas

    m. . . Walker Detention and outside areas

    n. . . Vocation Sewing

    o. . . Areas behind Cottages

    p. . . Areas around CFF

VISITING:

1. Women may not visit supervisors or residents in cottage other than their own. This prohibition includes the opposite side of the cottages in which they live.

2. There will be no visiting from the outside through the windows of any building at any time.

3. Visiting areas are restricted to the Circle during week days, and to the Circle and the areas directly in front of the cottage recreation rooms in the evenings and on weekends.

SECTION III
PERSONAL APPEARANCE

A. *STANDARDS:*

1. Women in CIW will dress appropriately to the occasion and activity in which they are engaged. Each resident will be held fully responsible for her appearance.

2. Clothing will be neat, in good repair, and of proper fit.
   a. Dresses and skirts will be moderate without extreme of length or fit.
   b. No open or revealing patterns are permitted with regard to blouses.

3. Brassieres and panties will be worn at all times, unless the resident is alone in her room.

4. Knee socks may be worn as appropriate. Mid-calf or masculine sox are not permitted.

B. *CLOTHING:*

1. *General:*
   a. Alteration of clothing, whether state issue or personal is not authorized except for shortening or lengthening of dresses and skirts.
   b. At no time will there be any cutting or restyling of wearing apparel.

2. *Work Clothing:*
   a. Dresses, skirts, blouses, sweaters and special uniforms issued for the particular assignment will be worn for work. Approved sweaters may be substituted for blouses when worn with a skirt. Sweaters and blouses are not to be substituted for work uniform tops.
   b. Work uniforms will be worn for work *only,* and only for the assignment for which they are issued. They may not be worn on days off. Work uniforms will not be altered.

    (1) They may be worn to breakfast and the noon meal on work days but not the evening meal.

    (2) Work uniforms may be worn to school only if the person is going directly from work to school or vice versa.

    (3) CFF uniforms may not be taken or worn by any worker to her cottage.

3. *Leisure Clothing:*

  a. Dresses or skirts and blouses will be worn for:

Church	Special Programs	School
Movies	Receptions	Dance Nights
House Parties	Evening Meals	Adm.

  b. Leisure pants may be worn at the following times:

    (1) Breakfast and noon meals *on days off.*

    (2) After evening meals.

    (3) When attending athletic events; for individual sports; and for sunbathing.

    (4) To clinic or mail room appointments.

  c. Leisure pants may *not* be worn:

    (1) On house party or dance nights, whether participating or not.

    (2) For work or school.

    (3) To Adm. Building at anytime.

    (4) Any evening meal.

    (5) To entertainments, movies, church, or receptions.

4. *Shoes:*

  a. High heeled pumps or sling pumps may be worn during leisure hours, or for work except when safety or health requirements prevent. All high heeled shoes must have plastic or rubber capped heels. No steel caps or stiletto pointed heels are permitted.

  b. Rubber thongs may be worn during off duty hours only. They may not be worn for active recreational activities.

  c. Bedroom slippers and scuffies may be worn only in the house when off duty. They may not be worn for house parties or on dance nights.

  d. Shoes for work areas are governed by safety requirements. (See Procedure B-7 Resident Clothing).

5. *Sweaters:*
   a. Only approved sweaters may be worn. Low neck, or loosely knit, revealing sweaters are not authorized.
   b. Sweaters may be substituted for blouses with skirts and leisure pants, but may not be substituted for work uniform tops.
   c. Sweaters may not be altered or restyled after being received or approved.
   d. Sweaters may be worn with uniforms.
   e. Sweaters knitted by residents while at CIW may be retained if:
      (1) Yarn was obtained legally.
      (2) Garments do not exceed the authorized allowance.
   f. Knitted shells will be counted separately—not exceeding 4.

6. *Clothing Permitted in Medication Line*
   a. Gym suits may be worn to clinic only if a woman is coming directly from or going to any recreational activity where gym suits are authorized.
   b. Hospital aides may wear the hospital uniform to the clinic but not the white apron. Aprons are to be worn *only* when the aide is on duty.
   c. Kitchen uniforms may be worn to and from the clinic if a woman is *on duty* at the time she is due at the clinic. She may not linger on campus but must go directly to and from the clinic.
   d. Work uniforms may be worn on work days only.
   e. Leisure pants may be worn only when a person is off duty and is not scheduled for work or other appointments after clinic.

7. *Gym Suits:*
   a. Gym suits will be worn only:
      (1) While participating in athletic events.
      (2) Going to and from the athletic field or athletic activities.
      (3) While on athletic field or in the gym.
   b. Neither the shorts nor the blouse of the gym suit will be worn with any other outfit. Gym blouses and shorts may not be altered.

Margaret M.

The day I met her she was sitting in the lobby at Marysville waiting for an appointment with the voluntary attorney to start the process of a divorce. Leaning forward on her cane, she called me over to talk with her. She was a short, extremely heavy white woman who appeared to be in her fifties.

Margaret L. Morris told me she was graduated from a vocational high school in 1947. When she was arrested in 1970 she was charged with insufficient funds and intent to fraud. "I just signed the checks to get medical care. My husband wouldn't help me and I didn't have any other money. I wasn't getting proper medical care until I came here. There's a lot of things wrong with the hospital here, but at least I'm getting attention. I've had polio and don't have complete control.

"They've done a lot for me here. I weighed three hundred and five pounds when I came in and had had two mild nervous breakdowns due to medication. Now I've lost more than fifty pounds and I'm going to lose more. I weigh two hundred and forty-seven right now and it's because the nurse is giving me water pills. I'd been through the big hospital in Cleveland and they never gave me any water pills.

"Coming here has done me a lot of good. This was the best thing that could have happened to me 'cause now I have the chance to start a new life. People here have helped me. When I first came in here I was scared of my shadow. When I leave here I'm gonna start a new life to prove to the people here they've helped me."

Margaret Morris got tears in her eyes as she talked about how much she had been helped—and about how it was a big thing for her just to talk to me. Before, she said, she would have been afraid to open her mouth. The water pills were the main thing that had helped her, she said, and getting on a regular schedule that was helping her organize her life. She said she worked in the sewing industry, making American flags.

"I'm an official flag starter. I take the blue field and I dust this with a pattern—leaving point marks. You take a star and follow the pattern, but you have to be careful. When I leave, I would like to work with people and help others, like I've been helped."

Chapter 9 HEALTH CARE: WHO PLAYS DOCTOR?

We had had a food strike and the next day I was called out to the warden. He told me I was here before, and I knew the rules, so it was up to me to see there were no more kinds of actions. I said, "I'm not responsible for those women. They make decisions for themselves." Anyway, he sent me up to the hospital and kept me up there for punishment, in spite of the fact they couldn't do anything to stop the food strike by removing me.

To tell the truth, I didn't mind too much being sent up to the hospital for punishment because I was in a lot of pain. The cops had kicked me in the head and handled me pretty rough putting me in the paddy wagon. Somebody else had kicked me in the side. I'm not sure who did it at the time, but I sure was sore for days. And in jail I figured out I was pregnant, too. I could feel it in my body. They didn't give me any tests, but I know my body pretty good and I can tell. So then I was worried about whether the kick in the stomach had hurt the baby.

Anyway, in the hospital, I was between two mental patients. One who laughed all night, and another who would scream if you touched her bed. It was hard not to brush against her sheets if you moved 'cause the beds are so close together and I had to be really careful. I was also across from a heroin addict who cried and screamed all night. She was going through cold turkey and she was really sick. She was shackled to the bed.

I was ready to flip out . . . because of the pain and all the hassle. One day there was a big cockroach on the wall and a woman hit it with her shoe and it screamed. I swear it screamed. That was about it for me. It was really a mind fuck. I think it was 'cause of the physical pain. I had got the shit beat out of me—and then in addition, the male guards had thrown us in the cells and maced us, closed our windows and took our mattresses and blankets after they put Marsha in the hole. They came back a couple of hours later and gave us the rules of the jail.

Really, most of the younger black and white guards are pretty nice and pretty human. It's the older matrons who are on a whole macho trip about power and authority . . . but they're run by men, so they ain't shit either. They're all either vying for power or so intimidated *by it themselves. So you can't expect decent medical treatment when everything else is so fucked up. They don't have time to be concerned about your health. You can't expect anything less than indifference and neglect.*

I mean, it was bad in the hospital being between those two women who were so out of it and listening to the laughing and screaming all night long, but it could have been worse, I guess. If you're really sick or dying, they take you to Cook County Hospital from the jail for treatment. There you're shackled to the beds in the hospital prison ward and you can't move around. A woman died there of pneumonia while being treated for a bullet wound of the hand. You can't expect anything less than neglect, but you know, sometimes the neglect is like really criminal. You just can't afford to get sick when you're already down . . .

—DEE PETERSON, *a prisoner at Cook County Jail, Chicago, after she was arrested at demonstrations at the Democratic Convention, 1968*

In December 1970, prisoners in the old Women's House of Detention in New York refused to lock themselves in their cells in protest against the unconscionable conditions they were living in. They were sprayed with water hoses and forcibly locked in their cells for nearly two weeks as punishment for protesting.

Their grievances were reprinted and circulated to New York residents by the Women's Bail Fund, a group of politically active women who had been helping provide bail and legal support for women awaiting trial at the House of D. The inmates had addressed an open letter to *the concerned people of New York*:

We the prisoners of the Women's House of Detention wish to inform you of the barbaric conditions we are subjected to by the correction officials here in the House of Detention. The system breeds mental degradation and physical deterioration. The majority of us are Black and Puerto Rican. We cannot afford the ransom the courts call bail. It is apparent to us that you, the public, are not aware of the barbaric conditions that exist here.

Our grievances are:
1. We do not receive adequate medical attention. We do not have a doctor on duty twenty-four hours a day although there are seven hundred and fifty-four women in here. [Maximum capacity was 457.] The doctors we do have are old and senile.

a. We ask that all doctors practicing medicine here be required to take a medical Board examination at least once a year.

b. We ask for a doctor to be on duty twenty-four hours a day.

c. We ask that it be a requirement that any inmate suffering from any medical problem be permitted to see a doctor at any time of the day or night, and that it not be left to the discretion of the officer on duty or the nurse in attendance.

d. We ask for first rate medicine. That it be labeled properly and after it has lost its potency, it be thrown out.

2. We do not receive an adequate diet. We do not get any fresh vegetables or any fresh fruits. Our diet consists of beans, rice, potatoes, and powdered milk. We get hot cereal twice a week, one boiled egg once a week.

The rest of the days we get cold cereal and powdered milk. The meats that we eat are as old as the building we must live in.

    a. We ask for our meats to be inspected.

    b. We ask for at least one glass of fresh milk daily.

    c. We ask for fresh vegetables and at least one piece of fruit a day.

    d. We ask for citrus juices once a day.

3. The House of Detention is infested with mice and roaches. They roam the building freely, carrying filth and disease. We are often bitten by these germ-carrying rodents. There is no extermination system.

    a. We ask that an exterminating company be allowed to come in twice a month to eliminate these health hazards.

4. There are four punishment strip cells where we are put if we receive an "infraction." The cells do not have any toilets, sinks, or mattresses. In them we are stripped of all our clothing. We do not receive any bedding for the cold tile floor. We are allowed to shower only every five days. We ask that these cells be shut down immediately.

5. We are beaten by the male guards. We ask that male guard brutality be stopped immediately. We are harassed and threatened with an infraction by the female guards. We ask for the harassment to be stopped.

6. Our funds which are sent and brought to us are misappropriated. We ask for an investigation.

7. We are unable to purchase in commissary bras, panties, socks or stockings. None of these are given to us by the state as long as we are being held in detention. We ask that we be allowed to purchase bras, panties, socks, stockings, bobby pins for our hair, hair rollers, makeup, large rubber combs for the sisters in here who cannot comb their hair with the very small combs we can now buy, creams for our faces, lotions for our bodies so that we can care for ourselves as women.

8. We are two in a cell. The cells are 5 feet by 9 feet. Out of a fifteen hour day, we are locked up eleven of these hours. We ask for longer recreation periods.

9. The adolescents are separated from the adults as long as they are on detention floors. Once they have been sentenced, they are put on the same corridors as the adults. We ask that the adolescents be kept separate from the adults after sentencing.

10. When we are appointed a legal representative by the courts they do not come to us to discuss the facts of our cases. We ask that the courts require a visit to be made by the court appointed legal representative to us, the accused, before we go to court.

11. We are often brought to court and required to wait in the bull pen five or six hours in order to see a judge only to be told our cases have been adjourned. We ask that when we are brought to court that we see the judge.

12. There are some of us who have been here twenty months and still have not gone to trial. We ask for speedier court dates. We ask that our court dates be made known to us.

13. We have been raided at five-thirty in the morning, made to strip off all our clothing and to squat down, our personal belongings being thrown on the floor. The adolescents have been made to go into the kitchen and strip off their clothing in front of everyone.

   a. We ask that the stripping of inmates be stopped immediately.

. . . We the oppressed women of the New York House of Detention humbly seek your support and help. We who are your fellow human beings need you, the public, to help us in our struggle to eliminate these injustices.

Captive Sisters in the House of D.

All the grievances listed affected the physical and mental health of the women. Their greatest concern was medical attention and the need for adequate medical staff on a twenty-four-hour basis. Although no practicing medical doctors are required to take a medical board examination once a year, their demand expressed their doubts about the professional qualifications of their medical personnel.

Fear of death natural to most people is heightened considerably in confinement. The women are afraid for themselves, as well as being additionally burdened by their responsibility for one another. "Home remedies," smuggled vitamins, extra glasses of milk and long hours, are involved in women inmates caring for one another. Women usually have to "steal" the remedies they use. When a sister prisoner is denied medical attention or called a "malingerer," the other women try to nurse her to health with the only resources they have available. Sometimes women say they are afraid of going to the medical staff because it often means risking the wrong prescriptions or diagnosis and the fear is that incompetent medical attention will lead to death.

The many other pressures of prison life—such as knowing court dates, talking to a lawyer, worry over children's well-being—relate to the tension and pressures that contribute to the breaking down of both physical and mental defenses.

The grievances and requests of the women at the House of Detention were never really rectified. Less than six months after the protest, prisoners in the House of D were transferred to the new correctional facility for women on Riker's Island and the old House was closed down for good. It had long been condemned as excessively overcrowded, antiquated and inhumane. It was a mark of pain, a "nuisance" at Eighth Street and Avenue of the Americas in Greenwich Village.

It is interesting to note, however, that when the twelve-story H-shaped building was opened in 1932, it was considered a "breakthrough in prison design." The 1931 Annual Report of the Department of Corrections said it was "undoubtedly the best institution of its kind in the United States, if not in the entire world." They considered it luxurious because each cell had an outside window from which the inmate had a "clear and unobstructed view of the sky, the street, the changes in the weather." Early observers praised the "clean, new sanitary glass block construction, good ventilation and light." Having hot and cold water in the cells seemed almost revolutionary. But somehow this "humane" and "best of institutions" had become nothing more than a filthy rat-infested warehouse for human beings. Sanitation could not change it. Friends and families calling to inmates at the windows from the streets below became an irritant to Village residents and to administrators.

The House of D had to be removed—something like removing the pain from sight so it won't hurt any more. So women detentioners and sentenced inmates, the guards, administrators, medical staff, psychiatric staff, social workers and reams of paper documenting each woman's criminal record, background and institutional behavior, were transferred to a new red-brick institution called the New York City Correctional Institution for Women.

What had been cramped into a twelve-story building that cost $1.2 million to build on one third of an acre was relocated in an enormously spread-out two-story building costing $24.2 million on fifty-five acres of ground. Corrections Commissioner George F. McGrath called it "New York's newest and perhaps best hotel." It was praised for its clean, new sanitary red-brick construction, good ventilation and light. A New York *Times* article quoted officials praising its single cells, brightly colored decor and lack of obvious prison "hardware." It was built to house 679 women. The day I first went there, the population was 723. Instead of four punishment cells, there was an entire cellblock for solitary confinement. The medical department had a section to itself on the second floor, as did the psychiatric and social work departments.

But it seemed that the transfer from an antiquated, overcrowded facility to a modern, overcrowded facility had just been a relocation of the same problems—especially the medical and psychiatric problems. In fact, some of the problems were worse. In a petition to the mayor, in the early fall of 1971, correctional officers at the new institution voiced their grievances:

"The female officers at the House of Detention for Women waited in vain for your concern and promised alleviation of our poor working conditions. The Deputy Commissioner asked us to wait until we moved into the *new* institution before we actually looked for an alleviation of our burdensome situation. We have moved and our situation is 10-fold more cumbersome," said the petition in part.

The officers complained that they could not possibly function effectively because of the tremendous size of the physical plant. They said that the only job they were accomplishing was *custody*—and that real care or control were impossible. They said the telephone was not being used because of a lack of personnel to make calls out to the inmates' mothers, husbands, children or lawyers. They asked the mayor, "How would you feel if, after five or six days after you were arrested, you had been unable to contact your family?"

"The medical services are under-staffed professionally as well as custodially. As you know, sir, approximately 80 per cent of our inmate population are drug addicts . . ." The officers asked the mayor to imagine that he had been arrested, had been in court all day and was put into a receiving room to await processing . . . now experiencing the pains of drug withdrawal. Getting sick and then being told you will be isolated, not examined—and that "tomorrow after you give your medical history and are examined—then you will be given medication."

The petititon continued: "You are then put in a large hospital-like room with the other women to await tomorrow. But in your sickness and pain you look around. There are 20 women in this room with you and one of them is having a seizure. You call, 'Officer.' No response. You call again, this time joined by some other women. Still no response. You get up and start banging on the glass in the door. Finally the officer comes. You tell the officer, 'There's a woman having a seizure in here.' The officer turns away saying, 'I'll be right back.' You think the officer doesn't feel a thing? You are wrong. The reason she can't come right in is because she is alone and has been alone all night. That is also the reason she did not hear you before—she was on the other side of the hospital making rounds. She is responsible for the entire floor. She must open doors with 20 girls inside to allow one to go to the bathroom in another area that houses 15 to 20 other inmates. Before this officer can help this inmate, she must call her superior so she can provide another officer to assist her.

". . . Finally after what seems an eternity, the woman with the seizure is helped. But not before you realize that if time was a factor, that woman could be dead! . . . You question [why inmates are] potentially hostile? . . .

"We have worked under these conditions for too long. We are petitioning you, sir, Mayor Lindsay, the Board of Correction, and our union for immediate redress of these long-standing grievances. Must we have happen in 1971 what happened in October 1970? Is this the only way to get relief?"[1]

"Beauty is only skin deep . . . like what you see, baby, is not what we're getting," an inmate said during my second visit to the new institution. She pointed to the freshly painted walls and empty vocational shops. "They used all their money to build this place . . . now they don't have enough money to run it. It's so cold here. Everybody has colds and is sneezing and coughing. There's no heat and no water to bathe with half the time. There's no recreation, no training and not even enough to eat. We get the same old diet—no fruits or vegetables, just starch and more starch.

"Pregnant women can't even get milk to drink, or vitamins. Girls come in here four and five and six months pregnant and conditions are so bad that they have miscarriages. We're treated by medical rejects here; they're so old they can hardly walk. They don't consider us human. To them we're human robots. If you want tranquilizers,

1. "Guards Petition Mayor," *The Village Voice*, December 2, 1971.

you can get them—unless you're a junkie. Women walk around here like zombies from all the tranquilizing.

"I was injured on my job and I was in the bing for six days for refusing to sign a medical statement saying I was attended by a doctor. They wanted me to sign it to relieve the institution of any responsibility for the accident here because it hurt my back and was fairly serious. I hadn't been attended by a doctor and so I wouldn't sign it. In the bing, I was given nothing. No washcloth, haircomb, towel, soap or item to help you keep good hygiene. Toilet tissue was rolled off and shoved under the door. The food was shoved under the door, too.

"During my six days there, I saw a girl attempt to kill herself. She set fire to her mattress and burned the bing and herself. The smell of human flesh is still in there. While I was in there, I didn't get nothing and I didn't ask for nothing because that's what they want—for you to beg. I just wanted to maintain my mental freedom."

I had seen the burned cell the first time I had been to Riker's Island, and remembered the stench of it as she talked. This time I had come to the prison because there had been a rumor that two women had been badly beaten by male guards—and that one of the women may have died. I had called Jack Newfield from *The Village Voice* to come along. He brought his wife, a photographer, and a friend. A radio reporter, my photographer Kitty Caparella, and John Walsh, of the Corrections Department, were waiting when we arrived. Both John Walsh and Essie Murph, superintendent, assured us the rumor was false. They said they knew nothing about any incident at all until they started receiving calls from families and reporters. They produced one of the women allegedly hurt, who said, "Nothing happened to me," and seemed frankly baffled by the report. The other woman was unavailable for comment. We never received confirmation as to what really happened, or what might have caused the rumor.

Since we were already there, we toured the institution. Because of a New York law allowing access to the press by prisoners, we were able to speak with imprisoned women at random, but only briefly. Mr. Walsh instructed us not to be "personal" or "talk too long" with any one inmate.

As he ushered us through the long, shiny corridors, Walsh talked about the "excellent psychiatric and medical set-up" at Riker's. One full-time doctor makes $15,000 a year for a forty-hour week, he said.

One psychiatrist makes $16,500 for a twenty-hour week and another makes $16.50 for each hour he works in the institution.

We asked to talk to the chief psychiatrist, who makes the $16,500. Granted an interview, we walked into his small, barren office. He was sitting behind his desk, stiff and expressionless when we walked in. When I reached out my hand to shake hands with him, he pulled back. The gesture seemed to frighten him. His shoulders pulled together as if in an effort to protect his chest. He clasped his hands tightly together and pressed them until they were white-blue throughout the interview.

"You can't quote me by name," he said. Why? "Well, if you did, I would get millions of telephone calls. Just refer to me as the chief psychiatrist, that's all.

"I work fifteen hours a week. I have to screen emergency problems as they come up," he said when asked about his work. "I've worked here fourteen years. I don't particularly do diagnosis. I mainly treat emergency cases that are *'acting out'* [my emphasis] and *medicate them.*"

The chief psychiatrist said he had a staff of six, including one part-time psychiatrist, one intake worker, one social worker and a psychologist for each "intake area" who do the initial background interviews of the women coming in each day. He said he and one other psychiatrist do all the "therapeutic" work with the more than 700 women incarcerated at Riker's. (Theoretically, if each of the psychiatrists devoted his entire attention to consultation during every minute he was at the prison, each woman could have a psychiatric session less than four minutes long once a week.) But in addition to "therapy," the psychiatrists have administrative duties, staff co-ordinating and reports to write. Thus what little time they do spend with inmates stems from emergency cases.

"I've never had a suicide in the fourteen years I've been in this department," he said. "I think that's because they know they can see a psychiatrist if they have a problem. They know that help is available. I think it's also because this place is run like a family. The officers know them and they know us. The ones who don't come back we don't see, so we don't know what our success rate is."

He said he "couldn't say" how many inmates he "did therapy" with each week, but conceded he rarely saw more than fifteen at the most in a week's time. He said these were all "situational cases" of women "acting out." "Besides seeing inmates I see staff with administrative problems," he said. "Today I saw three inmates. They were 'situational cases.' For instance, one of the women was upset because she is facing seven and a half to fifteen years of prison. She was just sentenced. You don't tell her to face it—you just give her a feeling of sympathy. I medicated her." He said there really wasn't any time to do follow-up work with cases; usually if there's more "acting out" the medication is just continued.

The chief psychiatrist at Riker's "excellent psychiatric department" was not unlike other psychiatrists I'd met in other prisons. His time is chiefly spent as an administrator and chief disperser of "nerve medications." He didn't seem to have the time to deal with the causes or roots of problems behind *nervous conditions* or symptoms of *acting out*.

Certainly at some jails, women greatly in need of help are not even given tranquilizers when they need them. I remembered Captain Daisy McLendon in Chicago's House of Correction saying matter-of-factly: "Emotionally disturbed women are locked in their cells twenty-four hours a day." And the memory of a gaunt, bleary-eyed woman methodically banging her head against the wall between "argghhhh" sounds is something I can't forget. "She's emotionally disturbed," was Captain McLendon's explanation of the woman. "She does that all the time."

Lack of medication does not seem to be the usual problem.

More often, it seems, both at Riker's and at other prisons, women inmates walk the halls in what seems to be a dazed, zombie-like state. Their words are slurred, their eyes are glazed, their clothes disheveled. Some women I have seen on one day having to be supported by other inmates even to walk look like totally different people a day or two later, when they said they "got off the medication." Some women complain that they are given Thorazine and Millaril against their will when they are upset about something; others complain they are unable to get tranquilizing medication when they want it. Administrators estimate that between 50 and 80 per cent of the population in most institutions are given some kind of tranquilizers on a daily basis. Only at the state reformatory in Iowa were a minority of women taking any tranquilizers—less than 10 per cent of the population.

"The psychiatrist here is an ex-inmate of a concentration camp," said one state prisoner at another institution. "He's Jewish and he should have a bet-

ter understanding of us because of his own experience—but he prefers to
operate as a Nazi in his attitude.

"He's very authoritarian and rigid on the outside. But underneath all that
authority he's a very frightened person. Really he's scared to even talk to a
lot of the women. Women put in slips to see him and he just avoids them. If
they come up to him and ask for an appointment or say they've been trying
to see him, he'll either tell them to go away or say, 'I'm busy. I'm busy. Can't
you see I'm busy?' He'll tell them to send him a slip. He sometimes just runs
away if he sees someone coming he doesn't want to talk to.

"He suggested to me he'd put me in the state mental hospital for a year.
I told him he was crazy. He said I'd never get out of here until I learned
to keep my mouth shut."

The medical department at Riker's Island is *quantitatively* better
than most other prison or jail medical departments I have seen.
"Better" because a medical department with nurses and doctors and
hospital beds actually exists. The second-floor medical department
has a ward for women sick or recovering from surgery and two
large wards for addicts recently arrested and going through withdrawal; also a pharmacy for dispensing medication and methadone
to heroin addicts, a real nurses' station and a glassed-off section for
women with communicable diseases. It looks like a small, clean,
white-tiled hospital.

The group of us *on tour* at Riker's were standing by the nurses'
station talking with a nurse when the chief of the medical department stormed into the room followed by three little old ladies with
white jackets on. The leader of the three was a tiny woman in her
sixties at least, with silver hair, a white jacket over her dress and
a stethoscope around her neck bobbing up and down with each
step she took toward us. She came in shaking her finger at us and
shouting, "I won't answer any questions. I work under Health
Services Administration and I don't have to talk to you. I don't
want to talk to no reporters." She turned around threateningly to
my friend and photographer Kitty Caparella, and shook her finger
at her as she hollered, "You better not take any pictures. No pictures. No pictures. I'll sue! I'll sue!" The three little women behind
her also started hollering, "We'll sue. We'll sue. . . . No pictures,
no pictures!"

I still hadn't said anything, I was dumbfounded. I didn't even
know who the woman was. "No tapes, no recordings. I don't want

anything," she continued. "Yes, we're always misquoted," one of the little white-haired women standing behind her said. Just as quickly as they had appeared, they disappeared back out the door, still shouting. John Walsh followed them, hurrying to catch up with their pace. It was only after they had left we found out that the angry little lady was the chief doctor at Riker's Island. The others were her medical staff; all certified doctors.

Meanwhile, I noticed a memorandum on the nurses' bulletin board. It was titled: "Subject: Sanitary napkins" and addressed to the staff from the "superintendent-in-command":

1. As of this date sanitary napkins are not to be issued indiscriminately due to the severe plumbing stoppages caused by dispensing sanitaries in the toilets.

2. All officers are required to instruct the inmates to use the trashcans for disposal of napkins.

3. If this problem cannot be resolved, it will become necessary to place strict controls on the issue of sanitary napkins and take disciplinary action against any inmate who causes a toilet stoppage by disposing the sanitaries in the toilets.

By the time I had copied down the communiqué on toilet stoppage, John Walsh had apparently talked the medical staff into having an interview with us. The agreement was that we would not quote any one of them by name from the interview—we could use only their titles as doctors. We could use the chief doctor's title, but not her name. We were ushered into a bare-walled conference room to sit around a rectangular, linoleum-topped table. The four doctors pulled their chairs close together at the end of the table nearest the door.

The first question we asked was whether heroin addicts were forced to use methadone when they came to the prison. More than 80 per cent of the prisoners are estimated to be addicts—and certainly many of them show no real effort or desire to give up the habit. But the arrest forces them to give it up and go through excruciating pains of withdrawal.

Several women at Riker's told us that they didn't want to take methadone because they thought it was "addictive" and harder to withdraw from eventually than heroin. They said, however, that they were refused any alternative to methadone but cold turkey.

"No one has ever forced a girl coming in here to take methadone," the chief doctor said. "They are only detoxified. We give them up to a total of eighty milligrams of methadone until they go to court, and no more. If addicts don't want methadone, we don't give them anything else.

"If you believe the inmates and don't believe us, then you don't believe us. Don't use my name . . . it's a violation of my rights," the chief doctor said vehemently, looking as though she would bolt for the door any minute. Her three staff members nodded and murmured in agreement.

There was a surreal quality to sitting at the table looking at the four white-haired women—all of whom had been identified as certified medical doctors. The chief doctor had worked at the Women's House of D since 1940, and the other three, all past sixty, had come to work in 1957, 1960 and 1965 respectively. One of the oldest, who was very thin, sat rocking back and forth smiling. Her eyes seemed somewhat glazed, and when she spoke her thoughts came out in half-phrases. Sometimes she would repeat the same phrase over several times and then sit and rock, nodding her head in agreement with what someone else had said. I thought she looked as if she just might fall out of her chair if she tipped to the side—like a pantomime of "Laugh-In." As seriously as I felt about the horror of being treated by one of these women myself if I were sick—and what it must be like for the women who fall sick at Riker's—I kept being flabbergasted by what was being said and the great surges of hilarity that swept through me. This was real, they were really doctors, this wasn't a scene from a Kurt Vonnegut, Jr., novel or Dr. Strangelove somewhere else in time or space. Nevertheless, they reminded me of four little girls with stethoscopes around their necks playing doctor.

The chief doctor punctuated the air with her fists and her statement that, "In my experience with inmates over the past thirty years, a great many—I would say at least half—are malingerers. The first day they have a pain in the head. The second day they have a pain in the stomach. The third day they have a pain in the wrist. The fourth day it's a pain in the knees. *They come on purpose to trick us.* They want medicine, that's all. Some are legitimately ill. They're the ones we take care of."

"How do you know the difference?" I asked.

"You can just tell," she said. "You get to know them. We just tell them, 'Nothing's wrong with you.' Some just do it for attention."

The doctors said that they give the rectal and vaginal searches to all the women going and coming from court every day, in addition to seeing about a hundred women a day for sick call between 9 A.M. and 12 noon and again for one hour in the afternoon. "Yes, yes, half of them are faking," the older doctor murmured several times, nodding her head up and down.

"We also give a venereal disease test to every single woman who comes in," the head doctor continued. "We've seen a sixty to seventy per cent increase in syphilis." When pinned down to specifics later she estimated that about twenty women had syphilis, out of more than 700, which was in fact, a startling increase statistically compared to ten years ago.

Women at the prison had complained that the vaginal searches given them on return from court—ostensibly to look for heroin, weapons or other "contraband"—were not only humiliating and painful, but caused infections and bleeding later on. At the same time that these vaginal exams are given indiscriminately to all the women, they said there is no Pap smear given—a preventive test for cervical cancer.

The head doctor confirmed the charges with irritation: "We don't do Pap smears unless it is indicated. If we notice anything on the vaginal exam—like a lump or anything—then we do a Pap smear."

I pointed out that there was a basic medical contradiction in what she said. A Pap smear is a precautionary, diagnostic measure women are urged to take every six months or at least once a year; if there were any "indication," it would be too late for a Pap smear.

"I don't understand what you're saying," she said. The other doctors shook their heads in agreement. "If we need a gynecologist, we send them to Bellevue. If it's an acute disease—something inflamed or distended, we may not want to treat them."

"I saw sixty-two women yesterday," another of the doctors volunteered. "Half of that was faking. But everyone who was really sick was taken care of."

Q: "Is it true that you don't give pregnancy tests here?"

"We don't have the frogs and all those other things—but of course we examine for pregnancy," the chief doctor said with irritation, lightly pounding her fists on the table. "We do it by a simple vaginal exam. By the old method, the simple old-fashioned way. We look inside the way we used to do it before they had frog tests and all these things you don't need. If we examine them and if we don't think they're pregnant, we tell them to wait. If they still think they're pregnant in a couple of months, they can come back for another exam."

We started asking more questions—such as, "Why couldn't they use the simple slide technique for testing pregnancy that takes less than five minutes?" But the tolerance level of the doctors was diminishing as they defended the "simple old-fashioned method of feeling or looking inside" for pregnancy—and they abruptly ended the interview by getting up and leaving, saying, "This is enough. This is enough . . ."

John Walsh also seemed in a hurry to leave the institution. I wonder if he will ever again tell outsiders about Riker's "excellent medical department."

The medical conditions at Riker's are about equal to those at most state prisons—and better than some. Many county jails have no doctor available to prisoners, period; if someone is severely injured or dying they are taken to the hospital. Progressive administrators say that it is almost impossible to get qualified medical staff into institutional work, even with a concerted effort on their part. Not only is the pay quite low in relationship to other, outside medical positions, but state prisons are generally located in isolated out-of-the-way places. Additionally, routine institutional work is most often quite uninteresting to skilled physicians. So administrators who care just have to do what they can. James Murphy, the new superintendent of Muncy prison in Pennsylvania, for instance, has cut back on the custom of tranquilizing the majority of the population. Before he became administrator of the institution, the majority of women in the general population were on high dosages of Thorazine. Now a relatively small number are medicated. With an overall change or environment that allows the women more personal freedom, there is also less immediate pressure from strict custody to cause the intense repression and nervousness women felt under the old punitively oriented administration.

But because of the insulation of most institutions, many practices regarding the medical health of women go unquestioned and unchecked. At Ohio Reformatory for Women I was also told that young women are given Pap smears "where there's any suspicion or suspicious history." Older women are given Pap smears by a gynecologist, the nurse told me, but younger women have to show "indications."

One strange medical custom at Marysville was giving small white pills to newly admitted prisoners three times a day for ten days. When I was in the "reception and orientation" unit, the women were taking the medication and asked me if I knew what it was. I had no idea—and neither did they, but they had to take it. Some said it was making them nauseated and dizzy. Barbara Tennon had just been "processed in" three days earlier and was still in shock from getting a ten-year sentence and was worried about her husband trying to work, go to school and take care of their three children. She said she had demanded to know what the pill was before she took it. "They told me it was an 'internal douche,'" she said. "Whoever heard of an internal douche? It doesn't make any sense at all."

I decided to try to find out what the pill really was. I was sent from the officer-in-charge of the unit to the superintendent to the floor caseworker to the doctor. None of them knew; each one sent me to someone else. Finally the nurse in the Adjustment Unit told me it was Flagyl—a drug given to women who have trichomoniasis—a vaginal infection caused by a protozoan and resulting in inflammation and discomfort. (Once when a doctor gave me the medication, she said, "If this doesn't knock it out of you, nothing will. It's really strong, so don't be surprised if it makes you nauseated or light-headed—but it *will* get rid of the infection.")

When I asked the nurse why *all* the women were given such a strong drug, she said, "So many of the girls have *trick* when they come in that we automatically give it to all the girls rather than wait until all the slides and cultures come in. It does get rid of the organism. It would take a week before we got the slides and cultures back —and this is much easier since the majority of them have it anyway."

In an environment where security and management are controlling factors, regulations naturally become more important than individual concerns. One day when I was at Marysville, I met three women who had been sent out of the clinic and told they couldn't come back until the next week to see the doctor. One was told her earrings were too big and the other two had been told their dresses were hemmed too short. Women say they are often "banned" from the hospital for whispering to a sick patient or violating a dress code deemed "proper" by the staff member in charge—circumstances which don't seem to have any relationship to a person's health.

Becky Careway at Marysville told me of an incident that demonstrated a clear example of priorities in a prison setting: "I had passed out in my room, and a guard carried me from here over to the hospital," Becky said. "I was unconscious over there and one of the girls got scared when she seen I wasn't breathing. There wasn't no doctor on duty, so she picked up the phone and called Miss Arn [the assistant superintendent]. Miss Arn came over and pinched me.

"I had a big black and blue mark on me later, I didn't know where it came from. They told me it was from where Miss Arn pinched me. Anyway, they took me to Memorial Hospital and put me in intensive care. They fed me intravenously and gave me oxygen. The doctor said later if they hadn't gotten me there when they did I would have died. *But, you know, the girl who picked up the phone and called Miss Arn got punished for it. She got room punishment for three days because inmates aren't allowed to use the telephone* [my emphasis]."

Becky, like many other women, said, "You almost have to be down on your hands and knees dying to get into the infirmary," on an average day. And when women do get in, they often meet with unprofessional attitudes and treatment, such as the time when Becky broke her foot at baseball practice.

"The doctor looked at it and said, 'You'll be all right, girlie, just take a couple APCs [aspirin].' They never set it. I walked around on it that way for four months and the only reason I had something done about it was because I contacted my parents and my father came up here to see Miss Wheeler. I was walking around with my foot turned in. My father saw my foot and went storming into the administration office. The officer tried to put him off and say, 'Make an appointment,' but he busted right through the visiting room and into her office.

"When it comes to one of his children, my father doesn't play around. He means business. So four months after it had been broken, they broke it and set it. A doctor from town—a specialist from Columbus—was the one that set it. It's pretty good now but it gets stiff easy, that's all—and sometimes it still pulls in a little."

Women at Sybil Brand Institute for Women and at other prisons and jails told me that if they were sent out to a hospital for treatment of a serious injury or illness, they were often sent back to the prison for the remainder of their recovery. Because of neglect, lack of treatment or the wrong treatment in jail, complications set in—some that affected them permanently. In some cases, the wrong medication is prescribed—or wrong quantities—by the doctor in the prison.

"Most of the trouble comes from when they send you back from the hospital and don't bother to follow the doctor's orders," said one twenty-nine-year-old woman in a county jail. "When they're going to do that, why send you over there in the first place?

"I've been here one and a half years approximately. I was eleven months waiting trial for forgery, but a lot of that was bedridden because I had to go to the general hospital for removal of bilateral ovarian cysts. Two days after surgery I started bleeding again. The first time I came here was in 1967—also for forgery. I got sick and had to have a partial hysterectomy. Later I got a blood clot in my lungs, and I've had a reoccurrence of blood clots ever since.

"The first time, after I got out of the general hospital, I had to go back due to the doctor here switching medications around. He gave me an overdose of Coumadin—an anti-coagulant. It started internal bleeding. Another time he discontinued my medications and within a month I got another clot. I understand that the head of the hospital wrote a letter over here that was pretty threatening. Since the doctor from the hospital and my mother got on their case, the institution hasn't been giving me any trouble; I've been getting my medicine on time. I also go to the outpatient clinic periodically for checkups ordered by the outside hospital doctor.

"Another thing I think helps is that I told them here I was writing for hospital records to send to the judge. This messing with medication puts my life on the line."

Because of the inattention of some matrons and the prevalent attitude that women are "faking" and "malingerers," many serious problems are not detected until too late. I've heard many stories such as one inmate from Albion, New York, told about a woman from Buffalo, who died at Albion in December 1969. "She was kicking and couldn't get any medication," Geraldine Lucas said. "Nobody would believe her or help her. She committed suicide and I'll never forget that day." Geraldine told of another woman on her floor who had hepatitis. "She was put in lockup because she got too weak to work. They said she was just trying to get out of work. After the other women refused to go to work until she got attention—she got some attention. By then she was almost dying and so she was rushed to the hospital."

Prisoners who work in hospital wards of state prisons have told me of incidents they have personally witnessed that still haunt them. Although there is no way to confirm many of these stories which would be a strong indictment of medical and prison personnel, the pain, the tears that come with the telling are convincing of the truth.

"Mary had a kidney operation," a prisoner working as a nurse's aide at one state hospital said. "She kept complaining of pain and they didn't give her nothing. 'You're a dope fiend—we're not giving you medication,' this one nurse told her. 'We're not giving you heroin to stop your pain. You'll just have to learn to live with it like the rest of us do.' Three days Mary asked for help. Then one day I stopped by her bed and asked her how she was feeling. She looked real calm and cool. She told me all the pain had stopped. By some miracle she didn't hurt any more. She was dead within an hour. What had happened was the abscess inside had ruptured and the poison had spread through her whole body."

Prisoners and staff alike say that the prisoners sometimes have to "literally fall out" before they get medical attention. "If you don't go off you don't get attention . . . there's no way to win," said one middle-aged woman. "It's really humiliating to try to prove you're not bullshitting. I have a slipped disk and a chronic bone disease . . . and the doctor she tells me, 'Learn to live with your pain.'"

Addicts, who are already involved in a system of self-destruction, usually are arrested more frequently, locked up more often, given longer sentences and have a harder time making parole. When they are sick in prison they are often suspected of "just wanting to get high." "When I ask for something for nerves, they just say, 'You drug addicts always ask for something for your nerves,'" Deloras Neely said, at the House of Correction in Philadelphia. "If you're on drugs, you get nothin', just nothin'. You're just physically sick. They say, 'I can't help.' And they don't."

Mary Vangi was nine months pregnant when she was arrested for possession of narcotics. She started labor at county jail and was taken to Los Angeles County Hospital for delivery.

"When I woke up I was shackled to the delivery table," she recalled. "Then I was shackled to the stretcher and then taken back to this locked ward where there were so many women they had two in a bed. I kid you not. I had just delivered my baby and I was put into the bed with another woman there from the jail.

"I didn't get to see my baby. I almost got out to see her at the hospital. You can see your baby on the way out only if a deputy sheriff will take you from your locked room down past the nursery to look in through the window.

"Three days after I had delivered I was in a wheelchair. They weren't sure whether I was to stay at the hospital prison ward or be returned to Sybil Brand—so I was going to be allowed to make one phone call. A deputy sheriff was wheeling me along and I told her, 'Hey, I haven't seen my baby. The nurse said I could see her if you would stop the elevator on the nursery floor and if you call ahead, they'll hold her up to the window.' She said, 'If you wanted to see your baby you wouldn't have gotten arrested. What kind of mother are you?' We got on the elevator and went past the nursery floor straight to the thirteenth floor. So I was sitting there in the wheelchair on the thirteenth floor, waiting for the phone, and there was this little black dude on a stretcher—bleeding all over the place from bullet wounds. He was moaning and his face was all twisted up. When some people came by I said, 'What are you gonna do for this dude? He's bleeding to death.' This one cop said, 'So what. He's a nigger. He shot a deputy sheriff.' I went off and told him where his mother came from. I was hollering at them and cursing them out. I was crying by then.

"The little dude on the stretcher looked at me and said, 'It's okay, little sister.'

"Then they took my cigarettes, Kotex and dime and put me in the prison ward again. I was taken back to the jail that night without having made a phone call—stitched from stem to stern. They searched me for contraband and put me in general population. Do you dig that? My baby wasn't three days old and they gave me a vaginal search for contraband. I got an infection and three and a half years later had to get a D and C from it.

"I never saw my baby until it was four months old—and that was Christmas Eve of 1968. The judge ordered the foster mother to bring her to Sybil Brand for one twenty-minute visit."

Some prison personnel, including nurses and doctors, are repulsed by what they see and experience. But to fight the status quo means risk of not only losing their jobs, but losing what good effect they do have by being in the institution. Like so many of us, they feel powerless to change bureaucratic procedures that cripple our humanity.

One such staff member was a registered nurse I met in a state prison.
I first met her when she was standing behind a table—pouring pills
from a cup into each prisoner's mouth. The women were lined up
behind the table with their hands behind their backs. Mrs. Brown
[not her real name] stood behind the table and a matron sat on a
stool next to her. As the inmate stepped to the front of the line with
her hands still behind her back, Mrs. Brown would find that particular woman's medication and pour the pills onto the back of her
tongue, then pour a small cup of water into the woman's mouth, too.
The guard would watch the inmate's mouth—to make sure she
swallowed the pills and didn't keep them "under her tongue" to give
to someone else or get high on later. The inmate would then step
away and the next inmate would step up, mouth open, for her medication. (This is the common procedure in most prisons—whether the
pills are given whole or crushed into powder as an extra precaution
against "saving" medication for a high.)

Several inmates had told me to find Mrs. Brown; she would "tell
it like it is," they assured me. The next day after she had punched
out on the time clock, Mrs. Brown met with me in a private place.
I felt like a spy keeping a visit, covering my tracks and her tracks so as
to minimize the risk of her getting into any trouble.

"I'm frustrated," she said. "More than anything else, I'm frustrated. I'm primarily a psychiatric nurse. I need to have a job where
there is more communication, more involvement. Primarily now they
have me working as a robot. I'm a robot. That's my frustration. I'm
not being a nurse standing in that little place popping pills into people's mouths.

"Let's face it. It's a cold world out there . . . and the women
need somebody to talk to in the first place. All the procedures you
have to go through before you can accomplish anything . . . [she
shakes her head]. My biggest problem is being tied down to a
mechanical job and not being able to rap with the girls when I think
it's needed. Any rapping I do is on my own time.

"I believe we need more staff with empathy. Everybody thinks I'm
crazy because I say they need to hire more people for the girls to
talk to. If a girl needs someone to rap with right now—she's in
trouble. She has to break a window to get attention or get sent to
jail [maximum security]. She has to throw a fit or have convulsions
on the floor. If they tell me, 'I need to talk to you now,' I still have
to distribute medicine first. I can tell them to wait until the end of

the line. But most of the nurses don't feel that way. They say they don't get paid for it—plus they don't want to get involved.

"All the rules reinforce their not getting involved. The staff can't give their telephone number or address to the women here. We're not allowed to communicate with the girls after they get out. They can call or write us here . . . but we can't answer unless they get special permission from their parole officer. It's irritating to me because I know a lot of girls out there need help. The reason given for the rule is that if you get attached and then they come back, they would get preferential treatment. But by being able to communicate we might be able to prevent half of 'em from coming back.

"A lot of staff members like that rule because it lets them keep their distance with no questions. Just as in any staff, there are some that are very institutionalized . . . so if a narcotics addict complains of pain—the nurse says she's just looking for a fix. They won't give her the medication she should have—or she'll be steered away, deterred from getting to the doctor.

"As far as realistic nursing care—if you get surgery, you get damn good nursing care here. But with everyday things . . . because of a few, they categorize everybody as malingerers. If you come into arrival and orientation and state that you are an epileptic and state you are on medication, they take your medication and put you in the hospital for thirty days. It is true some do it to get out of work for thirty days—but a true epileptic has to have a couple of convulsions to be diagnosed through tests before she gets her proper medication. For a true epileptic, it's awful. For a malingerer, they just lay around and get chubbier; they don't realize they're really harming themselves. But for the epileptic, as soon as we find verification—with a couple of seizures—we can give medication."

Mrs. Brown said that one of the biggest complaints is that sick call is at 6:30 A.M. and the women who are sick have to sign the slip the night before. This is also a "routine" procedure at most institutions. If they call into the clinic at 2 P.M. and say they have a rip-roaring headache, they're told to get on the list for the next morning.

Women in nearly every jail I've been in say, "Don't get sick at night. Whatever you do, don't have any sort of attack or seizure at night because you'll die before you get any attention." Barbara, an inmate at Erie County Jail in Buffalo, New York, was operated on for gallstones after being acquitted of charges of larceny and released from prison, where she had awaited trial for nearly two months. She said she was in constant pain during her incarceration, but she was only given Maalox and aspirin. One night stood out in her mind. "The pain was killing me and my body was beginning to swell with the poison from the gallstone infection. I started calling for the matron to get me some medicine and finally she came by my cell. She told me I was faking. 'Faking at three A.M.?' I told her. 'What the hell for? I'd like to be sleeping too!!'"

Mrs. Brown said that night care at the institution she worked in was virtually non-existent. "After five o'clock in the afternoon, there's only one nurse in the whole institution," she said. "She'll have about twenty patients in the hospital and three or four surgical patients she's taking care of plus any psychiatric patients there . . . and there are usually three or so at a time. Then calls start coming in from the cottages and she has to log them in and chart them and decide whether to send medication to the cottages. If she decides to send medication over to the cottage, she has to package it. She gets so busy she can't even get to the hospital patients; she hasn't been allowed to, really. I've suggested they get a two-to-ten P.M. nurse. If you get sick in the middle of the night, forget it! You have to stick a towel out the window. It used to be you were locked in your room during the day if you were sick, but that's changed now, at least here.

"I used to break the rule. If a girl was sick at night, I would leave her door open so at least she could stagger out in the hall so I could see her. And I would make hall visits every thirty minutes, but I'm sure many staff don't do that. They say they do, but many do homework and have no knowledge of what's going on.

"There's another rule that hangs over new staff's head—and I know I'd break this rule. I don't know if I'd get fired or what . . . but if a girl is hanging in her room or on fire after ten o'clock at night, a staff is not allowed to open the door unless another staff is there. This is allegedly to avoid a trap. But nobody can tell me— 'cause I'm a nurse—I can't open a door or cut a girl down who may still have a chance to live. A new staff without medical background would think—should I open that door or would it be my head? This rule has been broken twice I've heard of, where staff cut them down . . . but I don't know what happened to the staff.

"Since I've been here there have been attempted suicides, but no deaths. There are several slashed wrists or arms periodically . . . or overdoses from bluing from the laundry or cleaner. We get a lot of overdoses here.

"Some staff knock themselves out for the girls. They really do care. But like with any staff, you have good ones and bad ones. My question continues to be—'Why do you still tolerate the bad ones?' Their answer is, 'What are you going to do? You have to have *somebody* here.' I maintain we'd be better off with no one.

"The dentist here is an example of that. We'd be better off with no dentist. Once he gets around to it—he does a fair job. But he's pretty cruel and sadistic. If someone comes in with a toothache and he doesn't like her, he often tells her to go away, or says he won't treat her. We are always treating his abscesses. And abscesses can be pretty dangerous, in addition to being miserable.

"There's a lot of sadism here and it really does wear you down if you let yourself see it. I don't know how long I will stay here. It depends on what other offers I get—and also on whether I can really do something here without robot binders on me.

"I did work for a while with the psychiatric treatment staff here—but it was a lot of political games between staff. I got to do a lot with staff, but not much with the women. I was always being frustrated. They wanted me to be more assaultive towards the staff . . . in encounter sessions with staff you're supposed to get out gripes . . . say, 'I feel like I don't like you,' and all that. I feel like if I don't like you, or something you do irritates me, I'll tell you personally. I don't believe you have to do it in a group in front of other staff. I don't feel it was a very good or successful program.

"I think all the women here have problems and could stand therapy. But the treatment unit played games with them out there. If you played games with them, you'd get out of prison. If you didn't, you got kicked out of the unit and would have a big confidential psychiatric report filed in your jacket. What good is that?"

There has always been a lot of confusion between medical *treatment* for illness and *punishment* for crime. A *New Yorker* cartoon a couple of years ago showed two Pilgrims talking to each other as a woman was being hanged after a witch trial. One Pilgrim said to the other, "When will society learn that floods, lightning, earthquakes and disasters are not caused because they are *witches* but because they are *sick?*"

Since the early 1900s medical doctors have been called upon to identify mentally ill prisoners and to classify and treat other prisoners. They have often unwittingly been used as part of a custodial process to justify discipline or punishment in the name of *mental illness*.

In a letter to the State Board of Charities in 1918, Miss Helen A. Cobb, Superintendent at New York State Reformatory for Women at Bedford Hills, wrote: "As soon as the assistant physician has caught up at her work, we hope it will be possible for her to make mental examinations which we appreciate are needed for classifying inmates."

The assistant physician, Dr. Orie M. Grover, testified that she had "no qualifications for such work." Dr. Grover wrote about the *treatment* of women she witnessed while she worked at the institution from January 1914 to March 1918. Prisoners were "strung up with handcuffs," she said, "toes barely touching the floor. Young women many of them psychopaths, were handcuffed to cell gratings so that only their toes touched the floor . . . and then their faces were dipped into pails of water until subdued."

She wrote in her notes of August 14, 1916, that on one occasion she was "sent by Miss Cobb with Miss Julia A. Minogue (assistant superintendent) to Elizabeth Fry Hall to help discipline two girls . . . they were handcuffed to cot and spanked, one 25 blows, the other 20 . . . they were then gagged and hung up for one hour each . . . [male guard] helped to hang them to the grating by the handcuffs, standing on their toes. They were also gagged. Miss Minogue and Dr. Grover present." Two months later the two girls were transferred to a state hospital for the criminally insane. Excessive treatment for mental patients was much the same.

Today "moral forces, organized persuasion and scientific treatment" are relied upon as the norm for prisoner management, with as little dependence on physical force as possible. More and more, penologists and society in general are looking to the medical profession for answers to problems such as crime. The emphasis is on mental behavior—psychiatry and therapy. There is a great deal of discussion about *mental disorders, pre-psychotic* or *psychotic conditions* and *personality disorders*. Medical doctors employed by institutions serve the dual role of advising the correctional administrator and directing medical services and medical staffs.

We see the emphasis filtering into the courtrooms—where judges tell people they sentence to prison, "I'm doing this for your own good. I'm sending you to prison for *rehabilitation/drug therapy/ psychiatric treatment*." Although programs for such treatment are rarely in effect or even in existence in the institutions judges sentence defendants to, the judge who has not himself been to the prison can feel he is acting in a constructive or humane fashion.

We also see the emphasis on therapy in the current euphemisms for prisons, with *correctional institutions; correctional officers* and *correctional counselors; inmates, residents, patients*. Isolation units for disruptive prisoners are *Psychiatric Administration Units* and *Adjustment Centers*, and prisoners locked into solitary confinement are in *administrative* or *punitive segregation* for *treatment*. Systems for control through rewards and punishment are called *behavior modification models*.

On the surface, the emphasis on *rehabilitation, treatment* and *therapy* is a commendable thing. It advances the idea that the lawbreakers who have been caught have committed crimes that are really just symptoms of deeper problems. It disclaims the notion of the inherent evil of individuals and advances the concepts of self-improvement, *cure* or change.

But it is possible that just as the establishment of the penitentiary seemed a humane thing in comparison to public hangings and corporal punishments—that therapeutic controls or "psychiatric punishments" might ultimately be even more insidious. The concepts of free will and emotional freedom might well be even more in jeopardy under therapeutic control than they have been in the penitentiary.

This is true because it is deceptively easy to equate non-conformity with mental illness. Traditionally, criminal law in this country has enforced the dominant culture's standards on deviant behavior. The advancement of psychiatric labels as a justification for sanctions against different values or moral systems is a frightening thing.

It is already common for prison employees to use psychiatric terminology to justify their treatment of various individuals. I've often been told that so-and-so prisoner is a "sociopath" or a "psychopath" or that she behaved in such and such a way because of a "personality disorder." When I have prodded the speaker for definition of these terms and the specifics of an individual's behavior, I have more often than not discovered that the individual in question has been defiant of institutional rules or has tried to organize other prisoners in some kind of protest or has "talked back" to staff members.

Thoughtful professionals would be horrified at the careless use of terminology and the mystique surrounding these terms.

Traditionally we have a high regard for members of the medical profession because we understand that they employ their knowledge for the good of other people. We adopt their terms and philosophies often without question. Because the average person knows so little about psychiatry, psychiatric labels and sanctions can easily be used to legitimize actions and the imposition of controls within prison settings. Since they are "scientific" or "medical" terms, they have a way of fooling us all—as a substitute for a subjective feeling. Moral and value judgments are not a reliable measure of mental health.

In prisons we see the merging of two views of medicine. The first view—which is the view we hold in general society—is medicine based on a voluntary contract. When we go to see a doctor or a therapist, we willingly put our lives in their hands and suspend our rights —trusting that the doctor will take over and take care of us. When we are sick we voluntarily allow the doctor to say, "Take this pill," or, "Have this operation," or, "Follow this diet," or, "Change this specific action." We trust his judgment enough to willingly suspend our rights and know that as a doctor he will do his best and eventually give us our rights back by making us well.

The other view of medicine, in a total institution, is the situation where our rights are forcibly taken from us and things are done to us regardless of our wishes. Our lives are in someone else's hands in spite of the fact that we have not made a voluntary contract, and we are often treated against our will.

We can see this in the many situations where prisoners have been used for experimentation. In the past, prisoners in Texas and other parts of the country were subjected to sterilization when scientists believed that a chromosome factor in criminals would be passed on to their offspring. Aileen Adams and Goeffry Cowan in World magazine, December 5, 1972, reported that according to the federal Food and Drug Administration, 90 per cent of all first drug testing has been done on prisoners.

In the *Manual of Correctional Standards* section on health and medical services, the authors write:

"There is a vital need to implement and enhance our knowledge in the field of deviated behavior. Toward this end, penal institutions offer *unparalleled resources for research*. For instance, the prison community is an excellent setting in which to test the thesis that deviated behavior results from underlying mental disorder. Studies of offenders can add to our knowledge about maladaption or failure in adaptive capacity. The practice of medicine in penal institutions affords unique opportunities to gain increased understanding of medical psychology; to improve administrative skills and to participate in behavioral research."

Some of this "experimentation" is being carried on now in California. It has been carried out in the past when prisoners have been subjected to lobotomies—and basically used as guinea pigs to see if the "aggressive impulse" is located in one part of the brain. The controversial prison in Vacaville, California, which is called the Maximum Psychiatric Diagnostic Unit is said to be considering several types of research, including aversion therapy, electroshock, psychosurgery, sound-wave control, sex hormone injection and electrocauterization brain surgery on what it calls *aggressive*, *destructive* or *irrational* inmates.

In many states, prisoners can be transferred to state mental hospitals by administrative order with virtually no appeal. On the recommendation of the prison superintendent and psychiatrist, with the approval of the department of corrections, a woman or man in prison can be sent to a mental asylum for an indefinite period of time. They have no opportunity to be heard or to challenge "scientific" conclusions about them, often based on no more than one interview. There is no hearing and no requirement for consultation with their families. It is considered an administrative transfer and remains immune from criminal law. This is possible because legal criteria have not been delineated for such transfers. The lack of established safeguards and imprecise standards for commitment to psychiatric treatment leave open the possibility for excesses and abuses, as well as misuse.

If we examine the reasons for the lack of procedures which would protect the rights of individuals being treated or transferred, we can only conclude that when mental hospitals were established it was assumed there was little fear people not suffering from mental illnesses would be committed. There was little fear that people who were mentally healthy would be subject to forced or coerced psychiatric treatment. This assumed that medical professionals would act without bias in the interest of the individual—honoring the contract between doctor and patient—and safeguard his interests on the basis of scientific expertise. The view of psychiatry as an established field with measurable medical definitions required no need for legal definitions to protect the rights of individuals.[1]

But because the study of human behavior, the conscious and subconscious, is still developing, the standards used for defining mental health are based on value judgments, not facts. We can see already that many of the assumptions regarding mental health and treatment were not realistic; they were *theory* without regard to possible *effect*.

When prisoners are transferred to *mental hospitals* or *adjustment units* or *psychiatric centers* without opportunity to challenge the commitment, the criteria for transfer should be questioned. This is not to say that some of the women transferred might not be disturbed and in need of mental therapy, but just as a transfer can be used in the interest of an individual, it can be used against her in total violation of her rights as a human being. Standards and procedures should and must be established to protect the rights of the individuals whose lives are in the total control of others. Imprecise standards and lack of safeguards often allow security considerations of the prison to dominate therapeutic considerations of the individual.

A case in point occurred at Ohio Reformatory for Women, when five "difficult" women were transferred to Lima State Hospital. The five had escaped from ORW's isolation unit one cold night in November 1968. They tied up two officers before leaving. They were all captured within twelve hours and returned to the prison, where they were kept in solitary confinement from November 1968 until February 1969, when they were transferred to Lima.

The women said they were given no prior warning about their impending transfer. They had no hearing. One woman was transferred to Lima in December and the other four remained in solitary confinement until they were taken away in waist chains in February. (See Mary Wilkins' account, p. 63.)

Martha Wheeler, Superintendent at ORW and president of the American Correctional Association, as noted above, said the staff had decided to prosecute the women for the assaults on staff and the escape. She said they were locked in solitary pending the indictments from a grand jury. "They threw food and raised all kinds of hell in there," she said. "They had welded close together. They threw

1. See Nicholas N. Kittrie, *The Right to Be Different*. Baltimore and London: Johns Hopkins Press, 1971.

things at us and hated us, so we had to separate them from each other and separate them from us. We can make an administrative transfer to Lima as we did with the four women—it's the only facility available. Male prisoners would be more apt to be transferred to one of several other prisons in the state.

"They were transferred on the recommendation of the psychiatrist, the psychologist and myself, with the approval of the department of corrections. Their sentences continued to run while they were there."

Miss Wheeler said that the procedure has been used before and since: "Usually they recover and are returned here for the remainder of their sentence. The review is in Lima—they decide when to send them back."

All five women remained at Lima until March 1970, when they were transferred to Union County Jail, and sentenced to six months in the Dayton Workhouse for their escape. In May of 1970, four of the women were returned to ORW. The fifth was returned to Lima, "cleared," and returned to ORW about five weeks later for the remainder of her sentence.

"What they did at Lima was think that we sent them up together to be punished," Miss Wheeler said. "They kept them as a group and sent them back to us. Since that time we have moved away from the close custody approach, so we moved them to a psychiatric adjustment unit. Lima has been less and less satisfactory. We figure we can do a better job here.

"The adjustment unit is not all for punishment. We started it as a psychiatric alternative to Lima. They can work out of there and then go out eventually to recreation and activities. They don't go out to eat. They are served their meals in there."

The possibility of compulsory psychiatry is ominous—especially in cases such as this one, where it seemed the "only alternative." It is also ominous when it is used for determining when a person will get out of prison; under indeterminate sentencing laws in Ohio and California, psychiatric "adjustment" is often the measuring stick for parole denials or release on parole.

I think that there is a lot of confusion about what psychiatry is —and this is especially true in an institutional setting. For clarification, I consulted physicians and psychiatrists and gleaned the following basic understanding. Psychiatry is the branch of medicine in-

volved with matters of the mind. The field of psychiatry can be
roughly divided into three categories:

—Medical psychiatry, where the psychiatrist remains in the mode
of a physician, a healer, whose basic interest and responsibility lies
in the emotional area of his patients;

—Academic psychiatry, where the emphasis is on the understanding
of disease entities or clinical patterns as abstractions, not necessarily
related to individual people, but rather to theses and theories;

—Administrative psychiatry, where the emphasis is on the management of behavior, triage (the methods by which individual patients are referred to appropriate facilities for treatment, etc.), the
business or financial affairs of psychiatric institutions and management of such matters as staffing and personnel direction as might be
found in any organization.

It should be clear that *incarceration* could plausibly be defined as
psychiatric when it is viewed in the realm of administrative psychiatry. This is, however, obviously incorrect. It is incorrect because
we view psychiatry as a tool related to individual treatment, not as
a matter of institutional management or administration. And as far
as is known today, effective psychiatric treatment can only exist
where there is a *voluntary contract* between patient and therapist—
a contract which *must* include the patient's willingness and desire to
change.

People in prison are, by definition, forced into confinement; they
are there because it was so ordered. It is not uncompelled; there is
no voluntary contract—so a relationship between a prison doctor and
a prisoner is by definition already limited.

And when a prisoner is remanded to psychiatric treatment, he or
she is actually being handled by *administrative psychiatrists*—which
is contradictory to what we know as effective psychiatric treatment.
Although it is true that tranquilizers, for instance, may be used as a
part of psychiatric treatment when they are included in the voluntary
contract between a patient and a therapist, their use in a prison situation can constitute a subtle form of chemical straitjacket.

It is feasible—even within a prison—for a person to make a voluntary contract. If a prisoner says to a therapist she has a problem and
would like his help, she is initiating a contract with him. She is willingly putting herself in his care. She may tell a psychiatrist or psychologist, "I would like to do something about my temper. I don't like the
way I go off. If you think behaving in a new way or taking a certain

drug will help me, I would like to take it—but I don't want to change my mind or my intellectual capacity." At that point, the doctor does the best he can to help her, because he knows she is in his care and he acts in her best interest.

But his part of the contract requires that his role cannot be dual. He must be loyal to the concerns of his individual patient. He cannot force medication on her because of his concern for the institution. And it is essential that he protect the professional ethics of confidentiality.

The situation where the person approaches the therapist and they have a trusting doctor-patient relationship is a situation different from being forced.

Unfortunately, voluntary contracts are rarely found in prison. Public and penal emphasis on prison security and custody violate the ethical relationship which would allow growth and change to people who choose it—and, in fact, make it nearly impossible. Medical records and therapeutic reports are accessible to the institutional staff and parole board. The use of the psychiatrist for recommendation for or against parole reduces any effective therapeutic interaction to a game—another device for control and behavior modification beneficial to the *institution*. *Therapy* becomes a misnomer and in effect becomes just another hurdle women must try to leap or sidestep in an attempt to get out. Any effective process which prisoners might choose if given the opportunity, is invalidated before it even begins by the dual nature of treatment within a custodial institution.

"Real treatment or therapy will never work in the traditional prison setting," the superintendent of Iowa Reformatory for Women told me, "because whenever there's a choice between rehabilitation efforts or custody, custody wins out."

"We can't make people change unless they want to change," was the comment of Lieutenant Shaw at the Women's Detention Center in Washington, D.C. "If it was 1984, we could give pills and change them into robots. Until then, we can't change anyone unless they want to change. We can influence them, that's all."

There are some ways prison administrators can provide inmates with their own vehicles to change. For instance, when support is given for prisoners to form treatment groups of their own choosing, through their own initiative (whether they are "group therapy" sessions, drama workshops, poetry readings, etc.), the administration has begun to provide the imprisoned person with the option of forming a voluntary contract toward effective self-help, i.e., psychiatric treatment. However, such opportunities are all too rare.

As one state prisoner put it: "If I ask you for a pair of shoes, don't give me an overcoat. If I'm ready to ask for something—don't try to force something else on me, don't tell me I'm spoiled. Give me the tools and I'll fix my own carburetor."

A lot of men and women in prison would like to change. They want to develop; they want to grow. But when they ask for the tools, they are denied them. Their initiative is stifled. Sometimes they are told someone else will use *their* tools on them against their will. Some people in prison have no interest in changing—no desire to be any different than they are or lead any kind of life different from what they know. But often the values and needs of other people, people in control, are forced on them. They are called "sick" and told to change, whether they want to or not. None of this makes sense if we are really involving ourselves with the needs and realities of other people.

So much energy is focused on control and forced change (which has never worked and probably never will) that often the few people in prison who truly have severe problems are totally ignored. These are people sometimes dangerous to others or dangerous to themselves; in need of intensive security and care. But as Mary Vangi said, ". . . We end up taking care of them and trying not to get hurt by them while the administration concentrates all its attention on women who break rules . . . or refuse to work. They [the administration] deal with political women in a psychiatric way while women who really need psychiatric care are just given Band-Aid care, drugged up or left to rot . . ."

Her observation seems to be the reality of what we call *administrative psychiatry* in prison. It has everything to do with management and nothing to do with effective treatment.

One night when I was at California Institution for Women, one of the institutions considered most progressive and *treatment*-oriented in the country, a woman I'll call "Jane," was taken to the Psychiatric Treatment Unit for "flipping out." The other inmates were accustomed to watching out for and taking care of her, so they were not surprised when she "went off."

Marguerite Ferrante—an inmate whom Jane trusted—was assigned to sit with her through the night as an "inmate sitter."

"Jane is very paranoid," Marguerite said. "And there are some

cruel people who play on a person like her who has no controls, no
defenses. They told her there were guns here . . . and there are,
along with some saws for escape . . . but they're very well hidden.
This one gal told Mary, though, that someone was going to come
in and kill her. She couldn't handle it. She flipped out.

"I got into the *quiet room* to see her and sit with her. She had
the windows toilet-papered so the man who was going to kill her
couldn't see in. When I walked in she was down under the steel
bunk pounding on the supports to see if a gun was there. The room's
bare—the toilet's not covered. And there are bars across the front of
the room, so she has to reach through to the sink. I was asked to go
down and sit with her—I didn't volunteer. The whole thing really
blew my mind.

"I was sitting in the open passageway from eleven P.M. to four-
thirty A.M., and she'd say, 'A man just walked by you.' Then she'd
tell me again and again, 'They put recorders behind the air vent.'
It's so hard . . . I can relate better to someone functional.

"Then she wouldn't take medication unless she was taken out of
the quiet room. So two guards and a regular rack staff and the
surveillance were going to hold her down and give her a needle.
She screamed and hollered when they came because the guards were
men. I told them, 'Look, give me a chance.' I got her to put the
sheets down and put the blankets on the bed. She calmed down and
went sound asleep. After she had been asleep for quite a while, I
went to get a cup of coffee. I had told her before she went to sleep
that if she woke up and I was gone, I would be right back. That I
would have just gone for a cup of coffee. But just as I started pouring the coffee, she woke up and started screaming again and shaking
those bars. They came instantly, held her down and gave her a
needle.

"The whole thing puts me through so many changes. I think they
should have qualified personnel instead of inmate sitters."

Lady, You Don't Know Me

"The Lady" is reading the paper
My record is on,
"And she say" she know all about me
Right on, right on.
"And she say," I'm one of the hardest
criminals, that she has ever known.
That I've almost been a criminal
since the day I was born.
Right on, right on.
"And she say" my mother is tired of
sticking by me,
I be away too long,
That it seem I've made this place
my second home.
Right on, right on.
"Now I say" you don't know me
No you could never guess
for it's you and your kind
That has kept me oppressed
"Now I say" I have been forced to
live in poverty, and never had an
equal chance,
To be a free thinker or to advance.
"Now I say" my mom was a hustler
She had to survive
And all the things she wanted for me
She had to put aside.
"Now I say" she sort of got used to
looking for herself.
And she truly forgot about how I felt
"Now I say" you didn't know since
I was twelve
I've lived on my own

and been through hell
"Now I say" you finally recognize
I was born in the slums?
And it's you and your kind
that has kept me a bum.
"Now I say" all the things you don't know
about me,
would make a new world
so lets start again
and see if you said what I thought
I heard

—IDA MAE TASSIN
Bedford Hills

Chapter 10   WHAT'S THIS ABOUT SEX?

There's a difference between what I feel like when I do something with a girl from what it felt like outside when I did something with a man. When I was with my man outside, I felt big and strong and like a woman . . . and, you know, I was aware of being a real woman. My man's loving me really makes me feel like a woman. And like soft and full. But inside this place, when I do something with a girl, usually I feel like a little girl and someone's comforting me and just making me feel good. It's not really a sex thing, even when it's sex . . . because in here you feel so damn little and alone. And you don't feel like a woman, because when you feel that little, you don't know anything about sex. All you know is it feels good.

—WOMAN AT A STATE PRISON

It seems that sex is considered dessert in our culture—too special and rare a treat for bad children.

When the topic of sex for prisoners comes up, people seem shocked and curious. They've never considered before what people do with their sexual and emotional needs when they've been confined behind bars. Some seem to think that if you've been caught for breaking a law, you somehow lose your sexuality or your right to physical contact.

Although little has been written on women in prison, the few sociologists and psychologists who have written major pieces generally have focused their energetic research efforts on one aspect of life for the female prisoner: sex.

At public gatherings about prison conditions or prison reform, people from the community often ask ex-prisoners, "What about homosexuality? Is there homosexuality in women's prisons, too?"

When people are in a homosexual, unisexual world—heterosexuality isn't easy to come by. You are locked up with people who are all the same sex as yourself. Is it then so shocking that there's homosexuality in prison?

People restricted to a total environment of people of the same sex still have the feelings, emotions and needs they had when they came in. We forget how long they must live in that environment: one year, three years, ten years, twenty years. No matter what their crime—however long ago it was—the circumstances that dictated imprisonment do not turn them into automatons. It isn't realistic to expect people to survive without intimacy or affection for long lonely months or years. If anything, inner life becomes more intense in this strange world. The need for warmth and identification is greater.

"Almost all the women who come to prison have husbands or children," said the superintendent of Frontera's CIW, Virginia Carlson. "It makes a tremendous impact on life style. If a man goes to prison, the wife stays home and he usually has his family to return to . . . and the household is there when he gets out. But women generally don't have family support from the outside.

"A woman who has a husband and children is in a different

situation. Very few men are going to sit around and take care of the children and be there when she gets back. So to send a woman to prison means you are virtually going to disrupt her family. She knows that when she gets out she probably won't have a husband waiting for her. It will really mean starting her life over again."

A woman in prison knows she is basically powerless and helpless in an attempt to keep her real family together. Whatever happens to her will happen—no matter what she does or how she worries or how much she writes. A woman can know her husband is going through traumas on the outside but she can do nothing to help. He may be having a new relationship—he may have lost his job— he may have broken his leg or been in a car accident. What can she do? Her oldest child may have run away from his foster home or be having problems in school. Her children may be lonely, upset, hurt or sick—but she is unable to mother them or be there for them when they need her. Friends and loved ones die. Time marches on outside prison walls with all its usual chaos and disorder—but if she worries and concentrates on events she is unable to affect or change, she goes crazy doing "hard time."

"You just can't afford to worry all the time," Shelley said. "You just have to tell yourself there's nothing you can do and/then try to put your mind on other things. The old-timers tell me, 'Baby, you just gotta learn to do easy time. You're gonna kill yourself with the hard time you puttin on yourself.' But I worry anyway, I can't seem to help it."

If you're going to remain "sane" in prison, you have to make adaptations—unless you choose to escape and face what that will mean. In a thousand little ways, prisoners have perfected the art of survival in a sterile environment where few outlets or possibilities for self-expression exist. They "make do" with very few resources. They make dressers for their clothes out of boxes. Bags are decorated and used for wastepaper baskets and ashtrays are made from tinfoil from cereal and cigarette boxes. Women in Cook County Jail in Chicago charge batteries for their portable radios on the lights in the top of the jail cells and make their own tampons out of strips of Kotex. They make hangers for their clothes out of rolled-up newspaper and alter worn prison uniforms to fit.

Women who know *the life* or who have made the trip before try to help newcomers learn the ways of "coping" with the prison environment. They show them how to split a match into three sections to make them last. They show them by example workable methods of self-preservation. Games and humor are perhaps two of the greatest tactics for survival. "If you don't got a sense of humor, you just can't make it, honey," said one woman who had just done a splendid imitation of *police* sniffing around to smell out homemade hooch. (She strutted and searched till she found the hooch—and made everyone around crack up with laughter at her pantomime.) "Takin' things with a sense of humor is the best weapon we got to live through this shit."

"I find that even flat timers [who know when they're getting out] can't cope with all the pressures," said Alice Evans at Marysville. "I tell 'em, 'Hey, look, you can't always think about yourself. You gotta think about other people.' I sort of serve as a backbone for them—and here I am doing life."

It seems we human beings have endless ways of making terrible circumstances seem natural and authentic.

When we live in an insufferable or destructive environment— whether it is with brutal parents or in a concentration camp—often we adapt by creating a world of our own, a fantasy world that allows us to survive. The further the fantasy is fostered, the more secure a delusion it becomes. It doesn't necessarily have to have a connection with reality—but it usually does. And certainly, every detail within prison reflects forces and contradictions at work in the society at large.

Women who face the emotional deprivation of imprisonment have to face the world in which they live some way. One of the ways they have chosen is modeled on the real worlds they come from outside, a world we all know at least to some extent.

This is an affectionate world of families—people we relate to as though they were our mothers or fathers, children and sisters or brothers. In prison there is a world that has often been referred to as "a family system."[1] Any family we traditionally know includes men. So in prison some women play the parts of men—fathers, husbands, boyfriends, sons, grandfathers. A lot of these women actually model themselves after men—cutting their hair short, wearing slacks, walking and talking in a masculine way. Some of them show a lot of machismo—reflecting the sense of power, authority

1. See Rose Giallombardo, *Society of Women. A Study of a Women's Prison.* New York: Wiley, 1966.

and unrelenting strength expected of a man in this society. Other women play the traditional role of mother or wife—roles that allow some degree of security and support. The whole family system is characteristic of adult female institutions. Women don't necessarily set out to build families. Rather, they wander into relationships and adopt those friendships which have meaning to them. The friendships are much like friendships we have on the outside— where, for instance, you guide and counsel a friend as though he or she were your own child.

The difference in prison is that you most often call that friend your "child" or your "mother" openly. It is a family that allows a sense of belonging—and eases the loneliness of feeling isolated and small. It creates a common bond that eases the pressures of doing "hard time." The world of prison is a blend of real friendships and fantasy world that gives the women mothers, fathers, husbands and wives—but more than anything else, comfort and security. Although it may sound strange, this world is natural, somehow, in the unnatural world of prison.

In the context of prison society, it is not shocking to meet someone's institutional *wife* or *grandfather*. On several occasions while visiting prisons, I met a woman's entire prison "family" and saw the interweaving of wife, grandmother, son, wife-in-law, daughter. The conventional interaction of people in these different roles in general society is followed in the prison family. For instance, a father looks out for his daughter's welfare—advising her who she should spend her time with, warning her not to involve herself with so-and-so because it would be a bad relationship. The family actually becomes a substitute family even though the relationships are formed by choice, not by birth.

It is easy to understand how the family system has evolved if you look at the history of women's prisons. As we know, women's prisons were created as a reform measure in the 1920s. Women sent to prison were considered dishonored and disgraced creatures who had violated the moral and social code of their sex.

Architecture for state prisons for women and for the federal reformatory at Alderson followed the reformist philosophy that women prisoners need sexual morality and sobriety to resume eventually their predestined roles as homemakers, mothers and wives —the roles that had been *misguided* or *sin-stained* through a *life of crime.*

Women just weren't considered as dangerous or as violent as men. They weren't expected to rebel. The assumption was that women would accept imprisonment with less resistance than men. Being basically docile and dependent creatures, they could conform to a more open and less punitive environment with fewer difficulties.

So rather than the mass penitentiary housing used for men— with high walls, guard towers and armed guards—women's prisons were designed in a domestic model—with each woman having a "room of her own." Often no more than stretches of open fields or wire fences separate women prisoners and the "free world," and armed guards are rarely visible. Just like women outside, a woman prisoner would be confined to "the home."

"The home" planned for women was a cottage that was built to house twenty to thirty women, who would cook their own food in a "cottage kitchen." Several similar cottages would be arranged in quadrangles on green, tree-filled lawns. The cottages in most states were built to contain a living room, dining room and one or two small reading rooms. The idea was that a domestic atmosphere would help the women learn the essential skills of running a home and family. The geographic isolation of the prisons in remote country areas reflected the belief that it would be "good for the women to be close to the earth and growing things." The environment was designed to nurture the domestic instinct of a lady. Reformists theorized that on nice days women prisoners could do gardening or pick flowers to be close to the earth. They could grow their own tomatoes and vegetables and then cook and serve the food they had cultivated. This would give them a sense of satisfaction and completion.

Originally quarters for women officers were provided in each cottage. The matrons who lived in the cottage and supervised the women were expected to instill moral values and the knowledge of the essentials of cooking, laundry, proper speech and table manners. Local housewives were as well equipped as anybody else to take the jobs of matrons under this requirement. They only needed the knowledge of ladylike conduct and the essentials of housekeeping. They directed the work of women prisoners, who originally spent almost all of their time confined in their cottages sweeping and washing floors, doing laundry and ironing and cooking. When they were allowed outside it was for working on "the farm"—planting crops, milking cows, picking tomatoes. This is also how so many state prisons came to be referred to as "The Farm."

Although many changes in the format of programs for women in prison have taken place, the same architecture exists. In California, New York, Connecticut, Pennsylvania, Florida, Ohio, Texas and Washington—and in most other states—women live in cottages or "residences" that house from twenty to sixty women each. Although industry has been introduced into most prisons and cooking has been transferred to a central dining room, women still "keep house" in their own cottages. Outside of work or school hours, when they are allowed to walk across "campus," they are confined to the "cottage." Some prisons have abandoned their farms—but in others women still raise chickens and crops that provide the majority of the food they cook and eat. It also still holds true that superficially, at least, women are expected to conduct themselves in a *ladylike manner*. The "Missouri Inmate's Guide to Institutional Living" clearly states the institutional expectation carried on today in its "Social Rules" for prisoners in Missouri:

1. Be sure you are using acceptable language. No profanity or obscenities.

2. Keep yourself clean, well-groomed and attractive.

3. Always be considerate of those about you.

4. Be careful about telling tales and spreading gossip.

5. Do not appear off your Dorms unless you are suitably dressed. Reasonable modesty is expected on the Dorms.

6. On Sunday wear dresses until after 3 P.M.

7. No loud arguments which disturb others are permitted.

8. Improper personal behavior between two women is a segregation offense.

The language of the Christian ethic for socially acceptable women underscores all such instructions. As the Missouri guide cautions, "We like to see generosity among the women but we dislike having them use material things to buy favors or affections. Beware of the girl who says, 'I like you, can I borrow a cigarette?' Chumming too closely with any *one* person is strongly discouraged" [their emphasis]. "Saving the souls" isn't out of date, either. As the Reverend Ann Altergott, who "has her ministry" at Cook County Jail in Chicago, said, "The only hope I have to save lives is that the girls be saved and know the Lord."

The model still exists to create a new morality for "fallen" or "erring" women. Theoretically, the aim of the environment is still to establish the roles of "lady," housewife and mother. Simply put, the setting is perfect for "playing house."

And it is only logical that in playing house, one needs all the players—including husbands and children. The architectural model is there, the emphasis is there. Only missing are the real relationships with men and children and real blood relatives. So the *family system* has developed naturally—an evolution of the *model* for rehabilitation that reformers first conceived—but had no real conception of.

As Marguerite Ferrante said, "We are just like a small community except we don't have any men. So there are women who take the place of men . . ."

"It just happens," one woman said. "Just like on the outside, you get close to certain people. It's the same in here—but we probably get even closer than a lot of families because of how lonely it is otherwise.

"It also becomes sort of a game between us and the staff. Because the staff places so much emphasis on our relationships, they're responsible for getting a lot of women interested. It gets back to the old game of cops and robbers—when they set down rules about relationships and contact—you're gonna try to break them."

"Families, at least in this penitentiary, come in all sizes, shapes and colors—black, white and brown," said Ruth Kelly, at Ohio Reformatory for Women. "Some are a result of 'playing'—a form of homosexuality—and some are the result of having no one for a real family outside. For the remainder it's just a penitentiary thing. But just like in free families, there are sisters, mothers, grandmothers, fathers or *pops*, brothers and children—like 'my kid' or 'my child.' You'll notice I make no mention of aunts and uncles. I attribute this to the fact that aunts and uncles are not as close as immediate family.

"Women may not be old enough to really be *mothers*—but they're disciplinarians or they take care of their *child*. *Grandmother* goes for the elderly or older woman who fits the role—but when a woman of this age is not in your family, out of respect to her you refer to her as "Miss" whatever her first name is—married or not.

"The father or brother's role is usually assumed by the stud broads, who take the part of the masculine role in an arrangement—like marriage, going steady or that sort of thing. This is where the term 'players' or 'playing' comes in. The true homosexual doesn't fit totally into this category. He's different from a player. A player is usually a person who is married on the outside and has children—along with the annual visits from her husband and family. For some strange reason when they're in isolation in here, they put a *hump in their backs* [this is an expression for a type of masculine walk], get their hair cut and assume the role of husband, father, brother. It's possible there may be some signs of latent homosexuality here, but it's usually a game, and they return to their proper roles at least once a month for visits and again when they're released.

"The true homosexual looks down on players like these with disdain and disgust," Kelly continued. "In this situation in prison, a gay person from the free world usually takes his or her time before getting involved with anyone and once she takes a partner it's usually for a duration of time and only one woman. The player has many women and they are usually referred to as wife-in-laws and take their place in the harem—first, second or third. The player also uses an association for commissary reasons, which can become dangerous, because it's just one person taking advantage of another. But I suppose the most dangers of the situations is the unrest in the harems. Everyone wants to be first wife—and this results in fights."

Kelly said that it's her feeling that there are very few "true homosexuals" in any penitentiary. "It just doesn't have that much to do with sex," she said. "And it's almost silly to call them homosexuals—especially here in this penitentiary anyway. The behavior of the players tags the true homosexual with much unhappiness and reflects poorly on people who are truly gay. The gay persons feel they are made to look worse than animals to the world at large from people who are just playing games.

"I've discussed this with both gay women and players quite thoroughly . . . and the gay women say, 'A woman likes a woman because she looks like a woman'—and 'nothing is prettier than two pretty women together.' They don't believe women need to dress up like men and act like men. They think that women who dress and act like men are sick. The player, on the other hand, says, 'Variety is the spice of life'—and she gets involved very quickly with people she's attracted to. A lot of it is just experimentation.

"The families here usually have a strong bond and find some pride in it. But I can't honestly say you can depend on your family. They are quite open with their family names and don't hesitate to use titles in front of the staff. But it makes me honestly believe that families are made up a lot out of defiance to the police because they strip us of so much. And since *family* means *unity*, it's a form of uniting against them—against the staff."

What Ruth Kelly said about the family system and "playing" seems to be prevalent in most of the institutions I've been in or talked to women about. Women "play" the part of husband, lover and protector—and women "play" the part of wife, mother, comforter. The term "playing the part" is perfectly appropriate because it is much the same as acting and role playing. Often we hear professional actors say they became absorbed in the role they played; that they become confused as to whether they are speaking for themselves or the role outside the part. They often feel they have become that role or that the role has taken them over.

Some women who *play the role* in prison become absorbed in the role they play. They get to believing the role more than themselves. They become what they pretend to be—and at least for a while they *are* the part and it is real. This suspension of reality, this believing is real in its own way—and thus valid. It is often taken very seriously—and the roles between "man" and "woman" often lead to a copy of the traditional marriage ceremony and traditional marriage role, where the man is "domineering" and the woman is "docile" and "dependent."

While I was in one prison, a couple got *married* by another inmate in a small service they had planned in their dormitory. They had attendants and flowers and rings. The staff thought they had had an escape because the "count" turned up one person short. But it turned out that B. and P. had got themselves locked up in the same room for their honeymoon, unbeknownst to the guard. When the honeymoon was discovered after a search was started for the "escapee"—both women got sent to individual cells in solitary confinement for two weeks. A lot of other women say they think this kind of ceremony is "silly" or "going a little too far with the game to justify what you're doing"—but they can understand how it happens and the process that leads up to the serious acceptance of the roles.

The roles are so "normal" to prison culture in fact, that inmates constantly refer to a woman playing the masculine role as "he" and "him." The habit is catching, even when you know *he* is a woman.

Sometimes there is real emotional turmoil and confusion created by relationships that become destructive, but in general, the family system seems to have a positive role and provides a sense of belonging and personal concern. It's a system that allows for a sharing of goods that come at a premium from the commissary. Cigarettes, supplementary food, clothes and yearly "boxes" sent in from families on the outside are shared by family members. When a woman is sick, she has someone to mother her. If a woman is being bullied or threatened by someone, she has brothers and father to come to her defense. If she hears bad news from the outside, she has *people* to confide in. Women rely and depend on their family members to varying degrees—depending on how tight they are.

Some women say the relationships provide role models—for instance, what a mother *should* be like, as opposed to what your own mother has been. For some women who have grown up in institutions or orphanages, their prison *mother* is their first *real* mother. A real mother who pays attention to you and instructs you and guides you and helps you set limits—not one who is neglectful or withholds her love and comfort.

Women say that the only real problems in the family system involve competitiveness between wives-in-law or when a woman changes relationships or "drops her belt"—in other words, goes from playing the male role back to her female role. There is a shortage of women pretending to be men. So when someone *drops her belt* and goes back to being feminine, she not only reduces the number of available men, but she is breaking her contract with the prison hierarchy and is considered fraudulent. She is also "messing with" the game—and this is threatening. Some women who play the male role also become overly *macho*—and order their women around, demand to be waited on, have their laundry done and rooms cleaned. Usually in this kind of relationship, though, the woman has accepted subservience as part of the role she plays and the conditions she accepts from her "man." She has put herself in his care on the basis of long-standing conditioning.

Women say there definitely is a difference between women who have been gay on the outside and women *acting* gay in prison.

And in spite of what many people have theorized in the past, a woman who has been gay on the outside *doesn't* necessarily have an easier time of it in prison. These women have just as difficult an adjustment in prison as anyone else. It is just as hard for them to leave the person they were living with on the outside as it is for women who left a significant or meaningful heterosexual relationship. They are as lonely and as frightened and confused by prison as anyone else. Some gay women, like some straight women who have close communication with and support from their loved ones on the outside, don't get involved in an intimate or physical relationship while in prison.

"It's just like with anybody else," said "Roc." "Just because I'm gay doesn't mean I only like to be with women. I have friends that are men and women on the outside; in fact, several of my close friends are heterosexual couples."

Roc is a lively, attractive woman. She doesn't *play* the masculine role or dress like a man. She is a "butcher" at the penitentiary and works in the kitchen. She is one of the women on "campus" who cheers people up with her infectious laugh, lively spirit, and humor that seems boundless. She happens to be Italian and belonged to a club for Italian women in the prison she was in. I met her "family"—her *mother*, who was black, her *grandmother*, also black, and one of her *children*—who was white. Another of her *daughters* was Chicano.

"I'm very comfortable being gay," Roc said. "And because I am —I have respect for myself. I wouldn't expect you to put your hands on me or my hands on you any more than you would anyone else. Relationships are meaningful to me and they're deep—based on a lot more than physical attraction.

"There are a lot of girls here who just want some cheap thrills, or a quicky experiment and then they go out and forget it. Or they *drop their belt* for a while and then curl up their hair again. To tell you the truth, I wouldn't have anything to do with any of them. No, I don't think being gay makes prison life any more bearable . . . especially when your woman is gone."

Prison administrators estimate that less than 5 per cent of the women who come into their institutions have had lesbian relationships on the outside. Prisoners estimate from 5 to 10 per cent at the most. Several administrators commented that women who had lesbian relationships established outside the prison either seemed to be very stable in a new relationship within the institution—or remained loyal to their mate on the outside.

Nevertheless, women classified as homosexuals when they enter jail are often discriminated against—especially in county jails, where they are often segregated from other women and not allowed to "mingle." At Sybil Brand Institute in Los Angeles, for instance, there is a separate cellblock for women who are considered gay. It is cellblock "4000" but it is referred to by inmates as the "Daddy Tank." I was told that "obvious homosexuals" are put into the Daddy Tank. Authorities make the decision as to who is an "obvious homosexual." Women in the Daddy Tank are locked into solitary confinement cells twenty-four hours a day unless they are allowed out to work. They are rarely allowed to attend institutional functions—such as monthly entertainment that comes into the prison. They are also barred from the few outside programs that come into the institution. Several of the women who had been in "4000" told me they had gotten humiliating treatment by deputy sheriffs in charge of the area.

Terry Dunningham said she spent three months in the Daddy Tank at Sybil Brand before going to court. "They said I couldn't have my fingernails showing. One day when I came out of my cell they said, 'We're going to cut your fingernails.' I said, 'Oh no, if anybody cuts them, I'm going to cut them.' I went to my work assignment and when I came back this police said, 'Come here, Terry.' I thought she was going to open my cell, but she took my wrist and proceeded to try to hold me down while she cut my fingernails. I proceeded to break her nose. They took me to court for it, but I won because I was in the right." Women in other parts of the country also related incidents of being labeled and segregated when they were booked into prison.

"When I got to Riker's Island, the guards asked me right off if I was a butch or a fem," said Guillermia, a short stocky Cuban woman from New York. "I didn't know what they were talking about. I had very long hair . . . down to here. But they took me down to the beauty shop and cut my hair and right away I was called a 'butch.' People started calling me 'he' even though I have four children. It was a very confusing thing."

When I met Guillermia after she had gotten out on bail awaiting trial, she still had her hair cropped short. She wore pants and shirts that gave her a masculine appearance. In restaurants, waitresses often called her, "sir." Although she had been in jail only three months, the experience seemed to have affected her sense of identity as a woman.

The focus of many matrons and staff members on "homosexuality" often exaggerates problems considerably. They often gossip about "who is going with whom" and make notes of relationships on their records of the prisoner's behavior. These records are put into the woman's prison file and become part of her "personal history" accessible to other staff members and the parole board. Often they create situations through their own distortions that women claim never existed. "The first thing my counselor asks me when I see her is, 'Who are you going with? I know you are going with someone— you might as well tell me about it,'" one woman in Pennsylvania said. In Iowa ten years ago, staff members at the state prison would single out anyone they thought to be a homosexual and make them wear a yellow uniform. The uniform was a form of "punishment" for anyone accused of playing around with another woman. Everyone else wore blue uniforms, so when they saw another prisoner in yellow, they would know she had been singled out. If two women were friends and one was visiting another in her room, the matron would slam and lock the door and then both women would be sent to solitary confinement. When they were released from solitary, they were given the yellow uniforms.

"You might as well have been going down on each other," said a woman who had been at the prison during that time. "The matrons were just looking for things to bust you for. Now, with the new administration, they don't bust you for homosexuality and they're not as nosy as they were then. So there's not many serious problems any more, hardly any at all."

Mrs. Baum—her hair pulled neatly back from her face into curls at the back of her neck—sat at a desk in the hallway of Cottage B on the first floor of a state prison. "I'm responsible for the first corridor," she said, when I asked about her work. "I start unlocking at quarter of eleven. There are a couple of women who are idle because they are not able to go to work. They can't be out in the recreation area while housecleaning's going on. But most prefer to be in their rooms anyway. They write letters or crochet. They stay here in this cottage until they get a promotion or until they go . . . unless they get a disciplinary action and have to be transferred. They get disciplinaries and such if there's fighting between the two or if they're caught in a homosexual act. They can't go into each other's rooms or that kind of thing —and they don't have much of an opportunity because we keep a close eye on them."

The warden at the Federal Reformatory for Women at Alderson, Virginia McLaughlin, also says that one of the biggest problems with homosexuality is the "staff's preoccupation with it."

"My personal attitude is that what goes on between two consenting, discreet adults is their own business. I like to think we're not moralistic about it—but some attitudes are difficult to change. I get quite a bit of criticism for my philosophy."

Mrs. McLaughlin doesn't get upset at seeing two women walking around the prison grounds holding hands or sitting and talking quietly together in close proximity. But she doesn't approve of kissing in public; she expects the women at least to be discreet. Unlike many administrators, she isn't adamant about trying to keep women from wearing pants or walking with "a hump in their backs." She says rules against such behavior often only push people into breaking them.

She attributes much of the role playing to genuine friendship and says, "Who knows how much of it is real homosexuality? Or how much of what seems to be homosexuality is actually consummated? I would suppose that about 80 or 90 per cent of the residents here are involved in some kind of boy-girl play. But in our culture, if you ain't got a man, you ain't got nothing. And that model from outside carries into this institution.

"People play roles, but a lot of it is just to fill out the public image the culture says women are supposed to project. And a lot of it just has to do with people needing to be close to another human being . . .

"I don't like jails. And I'm not going to defend them or everything that goes on here. There is no jail in the world that's any good. They're bad places and you're in them against your will. If you're black, poor or a woman in twentieth-century America, the dice are loaded against you. But I believe that you can learn and grow in any experience . . . in Nazi concentration camps, even, people survived and learned.

"I tell the women in here that they're each a unique individual. Every human being hurts. No one has a corner on that market . . . every human being hurts and every human being dies . . . and we all end up in a pine box somewhere. But the important thing is to accept people as people and not for the role they're in. Life is lived by yourself, and there are some things no one shares with you . . . so it's important to live with yourself. I tell the women—

'You can spend all your time here fighting the cops and the system —or you can reach out for the things in this system which can be of benefit to you. I just want you to do your best here so you can go out and not spend the rest of your life in these joints.'"

Mrs. McLaughlin says she knows there's no way prison can be "fun" or "good." Even if women had the finest conditions possible, there would still be the pain of incarceration, the pain of being separated from their children and the world and the people they love.

So she says it doesn't make sense to her to guard against close relationships between women or struggle to control personal or physical interaction that doesn't cause friction. Relationships and friendships, she says, are only natural in the prison environment and indeed for a sense of identity anywhere. Besides that, "precautions just don't work—because women will manage to do what they want to do."

Mrs. McLaughlin says she doesn't believe that what she considers basically "role playing" inside jail will carry over for most women when they leave prison. "If a woman comes into this joint heterosexual, she'll leave here heterosexual. She may play games here to make her time easier—and you gotta remember how much time women do—but darn few women who have developed real patterns on the outside get turned around permanently in here."

Women at Alderson are locked into solitary confinement for fighting or refusing to work—but they're not often locked up for homosexuality unless they're caught in bed together. At many other institutions where there is more overt preoccupation with homosexuality, women are locked up for only sitting in another woman's room or combing her hair. Before the new administration was installed at the state prison for women in Muncy, Pennsylvania, the institution used to send out letters to the families of women inside whenever a woman was sent to maximum confinement for homosexuality. "Can you imagine what your family thinks when they get a letter stating that their daughter is a homosexual?" said one woman from Muncy. "How could I expain that one to them? Those disciplinaries had more to do with the staff's fantasies than with any reality. I mean, like two girls holding hands would get letters sent home to their mothers. And these are *grown* women!"

One of the long-termers at California Institution for Women pointed out that despite the fact that there are women on the staff at many institutions involved in homosexual relationships, women prisoners are the ones who pay for the "crime" of homosexuality—real or imagined:

"One of our CCs and another staff member have been living to-gether for seven years and that's okay," she said. "They can meet in the snack bar and touch feet under the table, but oh, no, not you. You're a convict. You have all that playing around with homosexuals on the staff . . . and then the married ones going with other staff members. And then they're the ones who tell us how to live our lives. Don't set standards for me when you're worse than half the women here.

"There's a couple now who been together for quite a while. Re-cently they got loaded and were in one of their rooms when they got busted for making it. So now the staff is saying their relationship is destructive. It's giving them more determination and strength to keep their relationship together. The staff says the one in Psychi-atric Treatment Unit is doing all right. She's so doped up she has to be. They dope you up legally, you know. The other one is in the rack.

"There's just so much double standard. And there is a lot of dis-crimination against the stud broads here, especially. It would be hard for someone with T. or B.'s appearance to get a job up front in the administration building, for instance. Evidently they think no one in the free world has ever seen a gay woman. Last year if you had short hair and dressed masculine, they wouldn't give you minimum time."

Staff and administrative attitudes vary—from total fantasy to rel-ative realism and enlightenment. A matron at Muncy who had been in charge of the "punishment cottage" for more than ten years told me she usually took care of twenty to twenty-five "disciplinary prob-lems" at a time—usually sent to her for fighting or homosexuality (referred to at Muncy then as "ducky" or "bulldagging").

"A girl has to have friends," she said. "But when they get to a point of getting to be homosexuals, we try to separate them. You have a good idea when they've gone too far. Some are born that way and can't really help it . . . or maybe if they're not born that way they just acquire it at an early age. It's funny though, that a lot of women who came in as homosexuals and are attached to a woman on the outside they lived with won't get involved with anyone here."

Her attitude was mixed with her reservations about male visitors, mail and the proposal for weekend passes and home furloughs (which were later instituted by the new prison administration under the auspices of a state law). "It might be all right for the men, but it's going to make a whole lot more work for the state nine months later if they allow women out," she said. "I worry about the dope involved and that the girls would get pregnant."

Some staff members see more "trouble" in women being allowed home on twenty-four to forty-eight-hour furloughs than the advantages of their being able to maintain contact with their husbands and children. Often they are upset about men being the "source" of women's problems and rebel against new administrative regulations that lift rigid mail restrictions or allow for home furloughs. They feel this way even though the women given furloughs usually only have a few months to go before they are released from the institution anyway."

Sometimes people who have worked in prisons for a long time have a difficult time changing old views in certain areas of their thinking—even when they are progressive in other areas. They resist some changes vehemently. When the Ohio Department of Corrections put out an administrative order for open correspondence for *all* state prisoners in August 1971, for instance, staff at Marysville threatened a walk out. Open correspondence would mean that women could write to anyone anywhere—and anyone anywhere could write them. Letters were no longer to be censored; incoming letters could only be inspected for contraband. This meant that women at the institution would be able to write the men in other penitentiaries and vice versa. ("If you're going to have open correspondence, that means no censorship," says Bennett Cooper, Commissioner of Corrections. "Any limitations are naturally a form of censorship.")

"Since August 1971, the division has an open correspondence policy," said Martha Wheeler, Superintendent at the institution. "It's unlimited and the women can seal a letter and mail it, so she can encourage a man she wants on her visiting list and tell him what he should do to get it. We have always wanted the man to make the first move—a letter or a phone call saying 'This is where I am—and I want to be involved with this woman.' He has to give his evidence. It's a pretty reliable way to find out what he feels about her.

"If she is free of impediments [another relationship or a marriage], we ask the parole authority to check the man out . . . his standing

in the community, police record and all. If they say, 'Yes, this is
a relationship we approve,' we okay it. If they say, 'No, we wouldn't
want them to associate,' we go along with that. So a man who
genuinely cares about the woman and is her boyfriend can sometimes get permission to be on her visiting list. That is only if he
is a community resource and not a drawback.

"If he goes out of his way and tells us he genuinely cares about
her, then we explore the possibility.

"We have one pat rule: one husband to a customer. Our responsibility is to help a woman understand as long as she's married
it's her responsibility. She has to get rid of one before she can get
another.

"People are inclined to say we're keeping men out—on the
assumption that men are lined up waiting to see the women. This
isn't the case. It's just that we have a responsibility to these
women, to help protect them.

"The psychiatrist is concerned about this open mail policy because these are quite dependent women so in need of an expression of concern. So many have been manipulated all of their
lives by someone who tossed them a warm bone. With the open
mail policy, they can get false encouragement, plus they can
initiate the contact and tell people what to try to do to get on their
visiting list. It all reminds me of a card I saw: 'I'd climb the highest
mountain, I'd swim the deepest river . . . I'll be over if it doesn't
rain.' They have gotten empty promises, empty words.

"I feel that in the mental hospital at Lima they have a good
policy. They feel the women need thirty days cut off from other
people—without seeing the people who were part of their breakdown. The same is true here.

"But with this open correspondence policy we have a hot correspondence between the women here and the men in the state
institutions. A good forty per cent of the correspondence now is
between the prisons. I didn't think it was a good idea to begin with.

"I'm well aware of the need for women to stand still and get ac-
quainted with themselves. But they have such a need for acceptance
that they want to please everyone. They don't distinguish between
opinions that are important. They seek warmth and acceptance. We
feel there are troubled people everywhere—so we need to decide
who I am, what do I believe in . . . and if it pleases me, that's what's
important. If the focus is changed, they are battered around and
can't get direction. These women are frightened, lonely and de-

pendent. They'd hate me if they heard that. They think of themselves as tough, independent and strong."

Miss Wheeler doesn't see a real connection between visiting policies or correspondence limitations and homosexuality in prison. "The whole ramification of homosexual behavior is very difficult," she says. "There are some confirmed homosexuals, some confused as to whether they are boys or girls, and some experimental. They run the whole gamut.

"The most serious ramification is that the relationships give rise to fighting. There are very volatile emotional situations over jealousy and separation. Some idiots are like a moth to a flame—if they see a warm or close relationship forming, they have to get in between them and break it up.

"We deal with homosexuality in different ways—from counseling the women—to punishment or separation if it's necessary. For instance, when someone gets parole, the women fall all over each other and this is natural—we don't do anything about it. But when we find people hiding behind bushes and french kissing, they get max.

"Some are seduced into relationships or bought for protection—like, I'll buy you commissary. A lot of the relationships are exploitive like that. But they are not attacked or raped—we have no problems with that. Sometimes there are mature adults who seem to care about each other—and if they're consenting adults and are discreet about it, there's no problems. I have the attitude that if you can handle it, fine—as far as we're concerned, they're good friends. But if one partner is terrified and not allowed to go here or there or not allowed to see this or that person or do this or that—it's not good. Then we like to intervene."

TO ALL RESIDENTS
MEMO FROM: Miss Wheeler
FOR: ADDITIONS TO VISITING LIST: HOW TO REQUEST ADDITIONS TO VISITING LIST.

Please talk to your case worker. The following kinds of questions are asked about the requested additional person or persons; name, address, age, sex, marital status, employment, relationship, community adjustment, does your family know and approve of the person, will the Adult Parole Authority approve, in what way would visits from the person be of help in your future. The person may also be requested to complete a questionnaire. Your requests are forwarded in writing, by the caseworker to the superintendent for decision.

Even when a woman can get permission for her man to visit her, visits are difficult and infrequent anyway because women's prisons are usually centered in remote areas. The Federal Reformatory for Women in Alderson, for instance, is more than a hundred miles from any urban center. There is no public transportation to Alderson; the closest bus or train stop is more than twenty miles away. The six hundred residents of the prison come from forty different states and more than two dozen of the women are from South America or Europe, arrested usually at borders and convicted for smuggling drugs into this country. The majority of all these women come from poor families and few of them see even their families during their incarceration, let alone the men who may have been important in their lives outside.

The cost of travel is prohibitive if nothing else. Loved ones die, husbands drift away, children grow up without their mothers.

"The only way I can deal with it is just to cut myself off emotionally," one prisoner at Alderson said. "Like I haven't seen my daughters for five years. I know I'm their mother, and I guess they know I'm their mother—but what kind of mother is that? It can't really be real to them.

"Thinking about it makes me feel dead inside. Sometimes I just want to forget everything and not have to feel anything else inside."

"The staff creates their own monsters," said Chatta Mercado at California Institution for Women. "They worry about homosexuality and then they keep men away. We're only allowed one adult male on the visiting list. Mary had one man on her visiting list and her eighteen-year-old nephew wanted to come and visit her on his leave from the Air Force. It was denied because he was a male, eighteen years or older, and single. And he's her nephew.

"My nephew brings my daughter down to visit—but he's not allowed in because he's twenty-two and single. He has to wait outside. It's really ridiculous. It tends to make you feel dirty and unclean— like you're a threat to anyone in pants."

"It's hard for people to understand how you get into what they call homosexual relationships," said Theresa Derry. "But they forget how powerless people feel, how alone they are in here . . ."

Terry said she had gone back to Muncy recently and was talking to James Murphy, the new superintendent—and the first male administrator of the prison.

"A lot of things have changed up there—and he has a pretty open attitude," she said. "But he was upset about the girls going together. I was telling him he has love—he has a wife and children to go home to every day. But I told him, 'Just imagine you were without them and isolated away from them with only people of the same sex. You still need that reassurance in the *here* and *now* of your own identity, your own emotions and worth that somebody cares about you.'

"Most of the girls in here don't have anybody that cares. Nobody. And even if you do, it doesn't help to know you have a mother a thousand miles away that loves you. You need somebody now.

"It doesn't start out as a big sex thing. Actually, it doesn't have anything to do with sex. People see girls holding hands and they just think sex. But it starts out as just a need to know someone cares about you now. I told him, 'You don't give any real alternative.'

"People need to be needed—just be warm—have somebody to care about you and recognize you as a person.

"It's a thing everybody needs—a thing of feeling and touching and reassuring you that you're somebody. And you are. You have human needs. I love my daughter—but I need to hug her, let her sit on my lap to let her feel my love. It's the same thing with homosexuality in prison."

"If you're friends with somebody, homosexuality is always suspect," said Janet, an inmate at Marysville. "There is so much emphasis on it. You have all those petty rules and that ain't what it's all about. If you and another girl do something, you're gonna do it anyway.

"But as it is their petty rules just create tension and resentfulness. You be combing somebody's hair or sitting in somebody's room filing your fingernails and it's a maximum offense. Anything can be a maximum offense. We have two latrines on our floor—but only one person is allowed in at a time. We're supposed to be here for rehabilitation—not to see who's a homosexual. We couldn't possibly function in society as we're made to function in here. You're not going to go out there and be afraid to go into somebody else's room!

"So we did something—committed a crime, and the judge gave us time. We come here to do our time—not for more punishment, but for rehabilitation. And all we find is punishment and folks sneaking around looking for homosexuals. We leave here bitter and hostile . . . thinking when we're gonna get out we're gonna get even with society. It's not the right attitude. But it's a natural result of this place."

"There are a lot of homosexuals in prison," wrote Pat Singer, a former inmate at a state prison.[2] "It's only logical. A group of human beings placed into a given situation will act like human beings—with emotions, feelings, desires and needs—the need for someone or something to relate to. And that's what I am doing . . . relating to someone. Have you ever really related to an animal? Sure. Why, then, do so many people get so uptight when one human being is relating to another human being? God, society is so fucked up. While I was relating to this woman a whole bunch of people were uptight about it. What was a nice middle-class white college graduate girl doing relating to another woman? A total freak out. Some of the women were, of course, lesbians during their pre-jail days. Others, like myself, were not. I was never forced into anything. I guess there's a lot more of that in men's prisons. The whole thing in this case was my choice. I just kind of slid into it. I didn't sit down and think—should I or shouldn't I? In fact, I try to stay away from that as much as possible —sitting down and trying to logically come upon some sort of decision about something. I just sort of slide with it. So I slid into this relationship. And I was really overcome—by beauty and dreams and good vibes and new awareness."

Pat said she went through many changes in jail and participating in a lesbian relationship was just one of them: "We all grow every day. I grew in jail while others were growing in the 'free world.' A part of me grew that I never knew existed. Now I know that wonderful part of me exists . . .

"What many folks fail to realize is that one of the hardest things to deal with about jail is the sudden complete absence of males. In fact, it is rarely brought up. People ask me whether I ever got to eat ice cream, could I watch any television, could I get newspapers. But no one asks me—did you have any sex? And the choice between ice cream and sex is a heavy one. Being taken away from sex like that for a said period of time is a heavy reason why I had relations with women. The first time I felt a love for a woman I realized that love can happen between me and any number of things: women, men, fathers, cats, dogs, trees, stars. . . .

2. Reprinted with permission from *Off Our Backs*, A Women's News Journal, Vol. 2, No. 8. Washington, D.C., April 1972.

"It was a beautiful sense of awareness. We are all capable of experiencing love feelings which we really never dreamed of. I knew that to love a man was beautiful, but now I know there are all different kinds of love. I loved two women in jail, both very differently, and I still love them. One of these women was my first female lover. It was beautiful. Sexually she turned me on like no one else had. It was a heavy mental thing because being in the situation we were in, we had few opportunities to physically make love. And those few opportunities always turned out to be sneak previews. But we did the best we could, as lovers do, and thrived on those sneak previews. I felt good about having a relationship with a woman. I was all wrapped up in it. Totally into it. A relationship between two human beings. A love relationship; a mental love and a physical love. Heavy. Light. Fun. Ugly. New. Old. All those things. I had no hang-ups about it at all—and I still don't. I love another human being.

"Many of the committed gay women would tell me that once I had sexual relations with a woman I'd never be able to go back to a man. As for my own experience, this has been proven false. I did go back to a man. Am I gay? Am I bisexual? What am I? I'll die not knowing the answer to that question. I'm a million things. I try not to think too much about the Whys of life. Deal with the facts; I went to jail for two years. While I was there I had homosexual relations with women. What the hell differences do the Whys make?"

"The staff is always asking you, 'Is homosexuality forced on you?'" said Alice Murray. "That's ridiculous. If you want to play the game, you do. Nobody forces anybody else. The only people who get any pressure are the stud broads. What happens is there are a lot of sick bitches here who are inmates . . .

"They see an aggressive-like woman come in and *they're* the ones head-hunting.

"You see a poor little pretty stud broad come in and everyone's after him. It's like everything—there's good and bad. But homosexual pressures are on the stud, not the bitches. Women look up to the masculine traits and want to identify with someone tough or strong. They feel like they're not right somehow unless they have somebody to walk around with.

"Some women do make homosexuality ugly—but that's all the staff looks at. Most of the women are just doing their time—and it's no big deal. The staff really create their own monsters."

When women consider getting out of prison—integrating them-selves back into a heterosexual world—they almost have to "choose" worlds. The world they've lived in for months or years—or the world outside.

Leaving any role or fantasy behind is a hard thing to do. But per-haps even more painful and confusing is forgetting what's real about yourself—what part is you and what part isn't. Often masks have be-come a part of your face and you don't know where the mask stops and you start. And a lot of times the role and the delusions are safer and more comfortable than painful reality.

The paisley-papered apartment is musty, dimly lit. Fran's lying in a narrow couch-bed that seems to crowd the tiny room. Her fever has reached 102° and she's crying and moaning with the despair of someone in mourning.

Both her wrists are wrapped with tape and she has an old navy-blue bandana wrapped around her thin forehead to keep the sweat out of her eyes. Her stomach bulges slightly under the covers. She talks rapidly, then falls asleep. Her eyes are glazy, but each time she begins to talk again she returns to the subject of the woman she left in prison.

"I love that girl, I really love her. I know it's wrong by society's standards, but I can't help it—I love her. I don't know why I ever did this to her—I don't know why I gave her up for him. Please tell her for me I love her; I want her back. Will you write her for me? If I was sick, she was there with me. She gave me strength. And now I've done this to her. Oh God . . ."

Fran—a thirty-two-year-old woman who has spent the better part of her life in jails and prisons for crimes of violence—was out of state prison four months before she met Hank. Hank had spent nearly twenty years in prison for a homicide. He had killed a man in a fight. Fran's last bit, eleven years long, was for manslaughter. She had killed a man in a fight.

The night they met, Hank said to her: "You need a man, I need a woman. We can grow together—we can give each other the strength and support we need. We can understand each other; we both have done time 'n' we both done hard time."

Five days later, Fran moved in with him. "Why not? We know marriages aren't made in heaven. They're made of hard work and commitment. We both need somebody. Neither one of us have nobody in this world." Within eight months, she was pregnant with his child.

This afternoon, Fran's face and eyes carry the look of an abused child. She has been sick a lot since she moved in with Hank and he can't tolerate it. "You're not sick if you tell yourself you're not," he says. "It's all in your head. Sickness is a sign of weakness . . . and who the hell wants a weak woman?"

"I ought to be able to read what I want to read," she tells me in whispered tones when Hank is out of the room. "But he won't let me. If I want to read detective stories or murder novels or whatever, I have the right. I'm not ignorant. But he rips up the books if he doesn't approve of them. See my face? This didn't just happen yesterday. It happens once a day.

"I gotta get a place of my own. I hate him. I really hate him. But I loved him once. It's just I can't live with him this way. I killed a man once—I don't want to do it again . . . I just don't want to do it again. But I can't let him beat me . . ."

Flat on her back and unable to move, Fran seems to have no alternatives. She seems totally helpless. She says she doesn't have the money to get an apartment by herself. She is on heavy medication because four days ago she tried to kill herself by slitting both wrists. "I was so desperate. I just want to die. I just want to die. I don't want to live this way. It seems like it's been this way all my life.

"And now I've given up the only person who ever really loved me and I don't know if it's too late to get her back. I am mentally ill, I know I am. I need help and there's no way to get it. I don't have money for a psychiatrist. But I'm sick. I've been spotting for three weeks and I know I'm going to lose the baby . . ."

After prison, the agony of trying to function in society again is more than many people can take. Hank's way was to imitate the power that had been used against him. The powerlessness of twenty years in prison has made him copy the very things he hated and resisted behind prison walls. He is afraid of his smallness, he is afraid of losing power. So he cannot afford to have his authority challenged. "In this house, I am the law," he says. "I will not have any outside propaganda brought into this house. If you're going to try to fill *her* head with that think-for-yourself shit, you are not allowed to talk to her. You'll corrupt her mind. . . ."

Fran, her face cut and bruised, her wrists and abdomen taped, looks like she is an accident victim. And she is, in a way. By accident of birth, she was born poor and small and helpless—and she's never gotten past the helplessness of those early years. She's still looking for the mother she never had—for the comfort she never had. The only kind of caretaker she's ever had has been a powerful one. She has grown accustomed to being powerless, to being helpless. While Hank chose one path, Fran chose another—both essential to the pattern, almost without conscious choice on the part of either of them.

As Fran spoke of death and her longing for her woman, she said, "This is the only dream I have left. I don't have any other dreams. I don't have any other hope." The only person she believed really understood her and cared for her in the loneliness of prison was the one she turned to again in a time of need. But her companion was behind bars and wouldn't be out for another two years. In the meantime, Fran wasn't allowed to write her or vice versa. The prison would let them correspond. But Hank wouldn't. He intercepted and censored all incoming mail. "I wish I could go to her," Fran said. "I'd do anything to be with her."

I Am a Woman

I am a woman.
I know.

I know everytime I see,
   through the glass of this cage,
      a child, playing—laughing
   and my heart aches to see my own child.

I know everytime I force my chin up,
   smile,
     and cry inside for home.

I know everytime the hunger
   for male companionship
      overwhelms me,
   and I pull the covers over my head,
     hug my pillow,
       try to sleep.

I know everytime I remember
   the sunrise
     or the stars
   and force myself to forget.

I know everytime my soft and gentle spirit
   comes up against the steel,
      the barbed wire,
        of living in this place,
   and the tears flow from the pain
     from the frustration.

Yes, I am a woman.
I know.

by JOANNE "FRIDAY" FRY
California Institution for Women

Dora

Dora Grey* says the worst thirty-six days of her life were spent in a halfway house in Des Moines, Iowa. It was a relief for her to come back to the Iowa Reformatory for Women in Rockwell City on a probation violation.

"That halfway house was worse than I could believe. I had to share an apartment with a woman I detested and vice versa. Everybody knew it. She ran off with my good suede coat as a last measure. I was out on bond to Model Cities and they put me in the halfway house. I worked at a cleaners for some really good people. But my probation officer was uptight and one day my roommate escaped and she thought I had escaped, too. She figured I wasn't at work so they called work and asked for me. My boss just said, no, I wasn't there. He didn't think it was anybody's business that I was out making deliveries and they didn't tell him why they were asking. So I was sentenced for a probation violation on a 30-day indictable misdemeanor. The probation officer had no right to violate my probation, unless I was convicted. I was found innocent of the violation but I got sentenced here anyway. If they don't give me parole in July, it's all over. I'm not gonna stay around here. I'm not gonna do no two and a half years on a ten-year sentence—I'll run."

Dora is little and wiry. Her voice is small, but her words are big and ferocious. When she's really talking angry, she talks out of the side of her mouth, reminding me of Woody Allen doing a takeoff on Humphrey Bogart. Her blond wispy hair also reminds me of Allen. But humor doesn't come quickly to Dora. A laugh is a long time coming from her, as are tears.

Dora's first husband was killed in Vietnam. Her second husband, Lee, was a bricklayer. "Lee treated me like a queen and I treated him like a king," Dora said one night as she sat on her bed in the reformatory. "He was a bricklayer and he always earned good money and took good care of me. I woke up one morning and he was laying there waiting for me to come back from the bathroom. He looked upset and he was sweating . . . and he told me about this dream he'd had a few nights before. He told me he had dreamt that I was pregnant but that he died. He told me he knew I was pregnant—he could tell. And that same morning I had realized I was preg-

* Not her real name.

nant. He was crying. I told him one part of the dream could be true without the other part being true. But he said it was all true. He made me promise to take care of myself and the baby. That same day he went to work and he was knocked off a scaffolding. He fell from seven stories in the air. They took him to intensive care in the hospital and called me. He held out six days even though the doctor said he wouldn't live overnight. I visited him every day and stayed with him every hour I could. On the seventh day, the bus didn't come on time and I was late to the hospital. When I got there, they told me he was dead. When I was leaving the hospital, I fell down the steps and had a miscarriage. I lost my baby and my husband on the same day.

"Lee had this cousin Darrell he'd told about his dream, too. He told Darrell to marry me and take care of the baby and me. So Darrell forced me to marry him. He threatened to kill my baby sister if I didn't. My baby sister is my heart—I raised her myself. He beat me so bad. I lived with him one and a half years and then we were married for four and a half months. He used to come home and he would have been drinking and he'd beat me. He wouldn't let me go out of the house or go anywhere alone. If I wanted to buy a soda, he would go with me across the hall and put the dime in the machine himself. He never gave me a penny. He wouldn't even give me a dime for a soda.

"This one night he had been drinking as usual and when he came home he started beating me with a glass ashtray. Then he passed out on the bed. I just flipped out, I couldn't take any more. I tied him up in the sheets with his legs tied to the bottom and his arms above his head and I beat him with a baseball bat. Then I went to the hospital to get my head and cuts checked from where he beat me. When I came back, he was still tied up. I got all his money and the keys to the car. He had never given me a thing. His one mistake was that the car was in my name because he had a record and he couldn't get it under his name. He woke up and said, 'Untie me.' I told him, 'Motherfucker, you got yourself in there, untie yourself.' He got himself loose. When he came through the door into the living room, I gave it to him with the baseball bat again. I knocked him out and kept beating him. Then I left and I haven't seen him since. I heard he was looking for me, but he'll never find me."

Dora got in the car and drove—first to Chicago, then to Iowa. She has one daughter by her first husband. But when she got busted and came to prison, she said for the prison record she had no children. "I have a little girl, but I'd never tell anybody here I had her. They give you so much hassle. My sister on the West Coast has her and is waiting till I get home. I don't want any child of mine in a foster home or in the courts, ever."

Dora continually referred to her daughter her "heart," and talked about her youngest sister, also her "heart." She showed me pictures of both. She is used to raising children. She was the oldest of sixteen children in her family —"twelve by my father and four by my stepfather.

"My mother's biggest disappointment was that I was a girl. She was only seventeen when she had me, so she couldn't understand. One time when I was sitting down by a chair where they couldn't see me, I heard her tell my father she would never forgive me for not being a boy. She forgave my brother for having one leg shorter than the other . . . but she never forgave me for being a girl. She didn't love me. I guess I knew it but I never admitted it. I guess I just wanted her to love me so bad that I just kept trying to win her love. And I kept trying to believe she loved me. The last time she ever hit me was when I was sixteen. I was in the front yard, and she lifted my dress up and beat me in front of the neighbors with a board. I was wearing one of those summer dresses with spaghetti straps, I'll never forget it. I was so ashamed. I was so embarrassed. That night I snuck up behind her and she jumped when she heard my voice. I said, 'Don't you never touch me again, Mommy. Don't you never touch me again in front of the neighbors or no one.' She never hit me again."

Chapter 11   GETTIN' OUT:
A LONG WAY HOME

When you get out, it's like being all alone with no one around. You have all these things on your mind with no one to talk to, not really, about all the things on your mind.

That's what pushes you to go back with the same crowd and the old drag, because those people don't care what you are or aren't. You got decisions and then you got your own identity to deal with. Whatever identity—artificial or not—you had before you came in here has been stripped from you and you just feel so small and exposed . . . You come out feeling guilty and down and like nobody. Just a small nothing. And everything was fucked up when you came in, but now it's really fucked up.

The hardest thing to face getting out is the decisions. For months, for years, you haven't been able to decide anything for yourself. Then all of the sudden, you're supposed to be able to decide everything, make every kind of decision. It's just too much.

—"EMMA GREEN"
Parolee from the state prison
for women in Lansing, Kansas.

"Would you believe—when I was in the county jail last time and found out I had got bond, I cried. I fell back and grabbed hold of the bars. I didn't want to go out in that street. It seems like a big dark pit out there."

Cynthia Evans, a prisoner at Ohio Reformatory for Women at Marysville was talking about going out again—in a matter of weeks—from the prison she'd been confined in for more than two years. "I guess I'm a little scared about going out again. It still seems like a big, dark pit. On the one hand, I want to go out—and on the other hand, I'm scared. It's a big cold world out there.

"I don't want to turn tricks no more. I want to go straight. I guess I'll live with my mother when I get out. But I can't talk to my mother about anything. My grandmother was the one who raised me till I was fourteen, and then I went to live with my mother. I couldn't talk to her about menstruation or pregnancy or anything. When I asked her about menstruating, she slapped me. So I tried to help myself. When I got pregnant, she was so angry, she kicked me out. So I did what I could. I didn't know anything—but I didn't quit school. I went to a home for unwed mothers. I was trying to do something halfway decent anyway.

"I just don't like to be around my mother. She leaves me alone and I leave her alone. It don't bother me. It's always been this way. She never wrote me while I was in the institution; she never came to call. In fact sometimes I think she's glad I'm here . . . she's happy I'm here. I think she wants me to stay here. It's like this: I could be in a room with fifty other people and if she came in, I'd want to leave. I'd want to get out of there before she even knew I was there.

"I don't know. I don't know what I'm going to do. All I know is that when I get out I'm just going to try to raise my son and stay straight. I want to make it."

Cynthia didn't know at the time how she could support herself. She hadn't received any training at Marysville that would assure her of work or give her any future means of support. She didn't feel she had any alternative to living with her mother until she got herself together. She had no friends outside her prison friends inside and the world of pimps and whores and people she was involved with on the

outside when she was arrested—and she said she didn't want to see
them again. Going back to Toledo promised nothing but loneliness
and frustration.

"You're so sure you're not going back to the same crowd," Theresa
Derry said. "But pretty soon you be hanging out with the same ol'
crowd again—just to feel like you belong somewhere, and even
though you can't get all the things off your mind, you're not quite so
lonely.

"I know when I got out of there—after nearly four years away
from civilization, I felt like I was walking around with a big tag on
me: LOOK AT ME. I JUST CAME OUT OF PRISON. They take
a city girl and put her in prison and she picks tomatoes for four
years—it's oblivion—and then they send her back to the city as
'socially adjusted.' Even the bus ride back to Philadelphia scared
the shit out of me . . . the noise and the people talking and moving
around. I just shut my eyes and prayed to survive the trip.

"After I didn't see my family for so long, everything seemed so
strange to me . . . and it was so hard to adjust. I really wanted
to be a totally different person from when I had gone in. I had
studied so hard. I had decided I wanted to be a registered nurse and
I wanted to be a good mother. I could tell you every bone in the
body by name, and exactly how the circulatory system works. I came
out with all these dreams . . . and then started getting doors slammed
in my face.

"Sometimes I just get so tired, I'd actually think about going
back to prison. I guess I still do . . . just to rest, just to forget all
the hassles out here. Like sometimes I just feel like I can't take the
pressure any more. But I've been lucky. I have my daughter to think
about and her future. She needs me. And I'm determined to do right
by her."

Theresa did her six years on parole and worked as a court-prison
administrator for a release on recognizance program for women in
Philadelphia jails. She still wants to enter nurse's training. It hasn't
been easy. It never is.

People getting out of prison have an affliction something like bat-
tle fatigue. And a hundred thousand people are released each year
from state and federal penitentiaries. They are filled with the numb-
ness of alienation, rage, guilt. Some people call it "impacted grief"
in epidemic proportions.

"You just come out BAMB," said Marian. "And you don't

know how to deal with it. You don't have a family to go to half the time. You don't have a home or a job. All this time you've been fantasizing about the way things are and the way things are going to be when you really have no way of knowing how they *are*. You can imagine the shock. A lot of times the only thing left for a person to do is commit new crime.

"Besides that, prisons really help produce crime. You take away any human being and put them out of contact and take away all their responsibility and you're denying them an opportunity to grow. So to expect a person to leave here being grown and responsible —you're making an impossible demand—because all her sense of responsibility and her ability to interact has been brutalized . . .

"To deal with society you have to interact with society. We only know how to interact with one society—and that's prison society."

Ninety-eight per cent of all the people sentenced to prison are eventually released. Although I could find no nationwide statistics on women returning to prison or jail—reliable estimates on recidivism vary from 50 to 85 per cent. In Los Angeles, officials say the recidivism rate exceeds 75 per cent on the county jail level. At New York's Correctional Institution for Women, it's 85 per cent for misdemeanors. Some officials at state prisons for women say their rehabilitation programs are working for felons because recidivism rates are from 10 to 25 per cent. But they are only counting the return to their particular institution from their institution. They don't count the county jails or other state prisons women have been in before or return to afterwards, so I don't consider the estimates valid.

There is no established method for the prison to keep track of what happens to women after they leave—unless they violate parole or return to the same prison on a new conviction. "We can't write to them and they're not supposed to call us," said one officer. "I really worry about a lot of them. If they could just call us up when they feel like putting a needle in their arm—or if we could help them someway or just know somebody was helping them . . . But I know they're just out there in the middle of so much chaos, and they're just so alone . . ."

Ninety per cent of the women at the Federal Reformatory for Women at Alderson have histories of prior arrests. The majority have been incarcerated before. Little or no attention has been paid them before when they got out of jail, out of the reformatory. The main attention paid them is police attention. There are few services in the community for the readjustment and re-entry of prisoners. Some groups of ex-convicts have formed self-help groups that have been very successful in terms of reintegration through a supportive community. Groups like Fortune Society, Connections, Barbwire Society and other prisoners' rights councils and organizations have made a great difference in the lives of many individuals. But they don't reach the great majority. They can't begin to touch the lives of the thousands of people who are out of contact and basically alone when they leave prison gates with one dollar—or twenty-five dollars or maybe even sixty-eight dollars with nowhere to go and no one to go to.

For Cynthia and Theresa and a lot of other women facing release for the first time or second or fifth or tenth time, the fantasy of real freedom is tantalizing. And the fantasies are far from outrageous. They include talk of fat juicy cheeseburgers, milk shakes, abundances of milk and sugar, pizzas, wine, comfort, a double bed and a lover, sleeping late and doing what you want to do when you want to do it. After institutional food, starches and food quotas as a steady diet, prisoners spend a lot of time stimulating taste buds with visions of delicious, well-prepared and favorite foods. Chitlings, beans and rice, tacos and other home cooking can be scintillating. Also the thought of opening your own mail, wearing what you want to wear, going where you want to go, and living each day without foghorns, bells, buzzers and matrons giving you orders is wonderful.

But the reality of being on your own, and being thrown back into a big, hostile and threatening existence where you are totally responsible is at the same time overwhelming. Taking a bus downtown can become a frightening thing. Walking into a store to buy something you need. Signing up for welfare or looking for a job. Seeing your children again. Wondering if a man you care about will reject you . . . Fear makes each event monstrous. Where will you live? What will you do with your freedom? Do you remember how to open a door? Being on your own "should" be easy—but it's not.

Getting free from prison regulations is more pleasant as myth than reality. The disappointed expectations make reality just so much more painful, the experience more bitter.

People have come out of an environment where they've been stripped of the autonomy of decisions, leadership, self-determination. Judges have sent them to the environment to "adjust" and be "rehabilitated." Rehabilitation is by definition "to restore to the original state or form." It could be said that prison does reinforce the original state or form that has been normal to a person: the state or form society alleges it doesn't want them to return to. For many people that form, that state, is one of real chaos and disorientation wherein it is normal to be involved in illegal activity; it is normal to be without resources or self-direction. It is normal to get in trouble again and it is normal to go back to jail. In that state, staying out and making decisions based on a sense of self-worth are abnormal.

At Iowa Reformatory for Women, Superintendent Laural Rans invited me to stay over in the cottages with the prisoners. During the time I spent at Iowa, locked into a room at night along with everyone else, I felt like a prisoner. Although Iowa's state prison was the most progressive and open institution I had visited, where more than half of the women are going out of the institution daily for work release or to school, I could understand for the first time in prison terms the concept of *the concrete womb*—the security of being taken care of in a place you don't even like—and how hard it is to break out. Especially when you're trying to break out of a situation and a culture that have become normal to you.

"I don't know why I've been so depressed this week except maybe because I'm getting out so soon," Shirley Temple said the last night I shared her prison room in Rockwell City, Iowa. "I've been here so long—fourteen months now—and I keep wondering, how much have people changed and how will I act? Will I be able to get myself up for school, feed myself and make it to work on time? I'm really afraid.

"I'm just so scared of going out there. I don't know. I'll have to wake myself up in the morning and get up and carry myself to work and make all my own decisions. I'll have an apartment of my own. I just don't know if I can make it. It's been so awful for the last two months. I've been thinking about things I never thought about before."

Looking at Shirley, a bouncy, smiling black-haired woman with tattoos on her body—including a devil; a hummingbird perched over a rose and her name on her arm—you wouldn't think she could be so vulnerable, so afraid of being helpless. She would probably appear to the average person who saw her as fun-loving, carefree—almost a bon vivant.

But Shirley Temple was contemplating living a new reality. A reality that involves responsibility and self-concern and thoughtful decisions. This new reality is not normal for her. It wasn't normal before she came to jail—and naturally it is not normal *in* jail. Her models in life—the people she loves and cares for—are part of the prison culture. Her mother is on parole, her boyfriend and stepbrother are serving time at the men's prison in Newton, Iowa. Shirley has had a life that might seem devastating from a different perspective—but to her, it's what life is. Hearing her talk about old trips and highs and disastrously overlapping marriages made me cry, laugh and experience the despair and joy of her chaotic existence . . . and my own.

"You talk about minorities—well, I'm a minority of one—don't tell me about minorities," she had joked with Gloria Diggs, a close black friend, the day I met them both. You could tell it was a common topic between them. "Let me tell you, my people were suffering before your people even knew what continent they was on."

Shirley was the only Jewish woman at the prison. Her mother before her had been the only Jewish woman at the prison. She talked a lot about her mother—who ten years before had lived in the same cottage, on the same floor, in the same prison. "She ran around scrubbing floors, working on the farm. They all did farm work then. Now there's no farm. Then it was hard physically—but now it's hard mentally. She's on parole now—she'd send me anything, but she doesn't have any money herself. But I know if she had it, she would—and that's what counts."

Shirley was convicted of "receiving stolen property." "We'd broke into a factory and took the payroll. I was lucky for just getting the receiving property charge—it could have been for breaking and entering, forgery and the whole geschmier.

"I know how to commit crimes badly—it's doing things straight and staying out of here that scares me. I want to be a beautician when I get out. That's what I'm in school for now. I guess I want to be one, but not really . . . it's just that that's what's available. What I would really like to do is just travel . . . travel everywhere.

"I was talking to the cottage supervisor the other day about getting my own apartment and being out on parole and she said, 'Shirley, just remember that if things get too hard to handle, you can always call up the institution and come back until you get a hold of what you want to do.' I mean, it was like a mother saying to her daughter, 'Don't worry if things get too rough. You can always come home.

This is your house.' That's what she was saying. I thought maybe she was saying she didn't think I could make it out there and that really upset me. I can always come back here, but this isn't my home! It's not! It's a prison. I gotta keep telling myself that. I really want to make it. But I really don't know what making it's all about."

In relation to many women getting out of prison in other states, Shirley was *luckier* than most. She was in a prison with a population of only fifty-seven women. The staff at Iowa actually spend a lot of relaxed, undirected time with prisoners. The administrator is young, friendly and comfortable—and is most accessible to the inmates. Women are as involved with the community as possible, considering their remote location—and disciplinary cells are not in use in the institution. They're used for storage. Women can make telephone calls out from the prison on pay phones every night in order to maintain contact with their friends and families. Shirley herself was going into town daily—driven by another inmate in a state car—on a study release to learn a trade. She would be able to continue her cosmetology studies at the same school when she got out—so she had a *link*— somewhere to go and something to do that had a purpose. With the training and a license that was assured upon graduation, she'd be able to be self-supporting, self-sufficient.

But emotionally—going from one secure reality into another separate and unknown reality was just as frightening for Shirley as going out with no link at all. Just the challenge of living with all that responsibility and possibility of self-power—staying away from the ever present temptation of retreat into drugs is something like facing a pit of hungry alligators with no visible way out.

I'm sure most people can make comparisons in their own lives: the decision to leave a marriage that is unhappy and unhealthy but that has somehow become comfortable; the decision to take a new job or move to a new community; the decision to begin to live a new way you know little about—is all frightening. And the biggest stumbling block to doing what you feel you want to do is *fear*.

For the majority of women in prison, the outside world has always represented hostility and chaos. Disorganization that seems normal. Imagine yourself facing the possibility of finding a place to live and a way to earn money when you have thirty-five cents subway fare in your possession. And all your worldly goods in a paper bag. You have no more money; no home and nowhere to go. And you're let out of a bus in the middle of New York City at four o'clock in the afternoon.

This is the reality for many women getting out of jail in New York City. Or imagine that you have been in prison in California for eight years—and you leave the prison with sixty-eight dollars to support yourself until you can find a place to settle again. You might leave some penitentiaries after fifteen years with twenty dollars savings to help you start your life again—and don't forget you have no salable skills nor more than a ninth-grade education. In addition you have a prison record. These are common realities to people getting out of prison—women and men alike.

Even with the rare blessing of financial security or the support of family and friends, adjusting to the outside again is no easy thing.

I had not expected that when I came out of jail I would feel so exhausted mentally, physically, and spiritually. The impact of the world and its problems is crushing, numbing and painful, at the same time. It is hard to rise in the morning to the "duties of one's state in life" . . .

One comes out from jail into a world where everyone has problems, all but insoluble problems, and the first thing that strikes me is that the world today is almost worse than jail. Looking at newspapers, listening to the radio, even watching the activities of children, and fearfully thinking of what they have to look forward to in the way of education, work and war, I am appalled.

If we who think are sensitive to this the average exprisoner is sensitive in a different way. He comes out a marked man, with the eye of the law upon him . . .

—Dorothy Day, "Thoughts
After Prison," *Liberation*, September 1957

Three days after her release from the North County Holding Facility in Palo Alto, California, Angela Davis was drinking coffee in the home of a friend in the Bay Area, and feeling the exhausting impact of her release. "It's hard to believe how tired I am," she told me. "But I'm just physically exhausted from moving around in spaces bigger than a cell—let alone everything else. I really forgot what it's like. I guess it will take me a while to adjust to being able to move around freely—and even to get used to seeing the sunshine again.

"The last three days we've just been moving so fast . . . I can't take it all in at once. I really can't believe that it's all happening and that I'm really here."

Angela had been in jails for sixteen and a half months waiting trial on charges of murder, kidnapping and criminal conspiracy in tenuous connection with the deaths of a judge and two prisoners in a Marin County courtroom. The state of California pressed charges on the basis that the guns used in the incident had been registered in her name. At her trial she was found innocent of all charges. But the effect of her arrest and imprisonment without bail reflected the belief that she was guilty until proven innocent. During her long months of imprisonment she was transferred to different jails and usually confined to one cell during the day, where she had her books and legal materials. In Palo Alto there was barely room for me to sit down in the tiny cell. During the night she slept either in the same cell or in an adjoining one. She wasn't allowed to go outdoors for exercise or sunshine, nor was she allowed to "mingle freely" with other inmates in the institution. Only a court order won her the right not to be locked in solitary confinement under armed guard—even though she was *innocent in the eyes of the law*.

She shared with other detentioners throughout the country the anxiety and uncertainty of when she would go to trial; the jolt of unexpected transfers from one jail to another and the lingering, unsettling possibility of not being released on bail.

The day before she finally got out on $102,500 bail, she sat in a gray sweater, pink prison smock and warm woolen socks in her cramped, antiquated cell packed with her books, cartons of papers and legal materials. The squalor of the physical conditions was in sharp contrast to her dignity and profound calm. The loneliness she had experienced in spite of so much overwhelming support from the outside seemed apparent.

"I don't want to get too excited about the possibility of getting bail," she said. "They say they're sure this time, but they've been sure before. I'm hoping, but it's too disappointing when it doesn't happen—so I can't afford to count on it." She was released the next day, February 28, 1972, five days after the California Supreme Court ruled the death penalty unconstitutional. Bail had been denied her up to that time on the grounds that persons accused of capital offenses are not entitled to bail.

Until Angela's imprisonment, many people in the general society weren't even *aware* that women were jailed in this country. Many more people weren't aware that so many people accused of breaking a law are imprisoned as though they were guilty *awaiting* their trials. The support, and of course the counterreaction to the support, came in massive proportions.

Angela knew, for instance, that literally thousands of letters were coming in for her every day from people in this country and from other countries throughout the world. "The mail I get overwhelms me," she said. "It's really moving—I want to answer each letter, but I can't." (She didn't receive most of the letters while she was in jail because officials said there were "too many letters for such a limited staff to sort and censor.")

But even with love and support and understanding through sixteen and a half months, her sudden victory of being released on bail still entailed adjustment—physical, emotional, mental. Lights, colors, space, conversation, interaction, friends, demands; they all required reorientation. And the scars of those many nights, and many nightmares in shared human experiences and frailty, can never be measured by her acquittal.

Ericka Huggins, a close friend of Angela's, touched on many nuances of imprisonment so difficult to verbalize, when she wrote from Niantic Prison in Connecticut in 1970:

> noises
> sounds
> unspoken words
> feelings repressed because
>   the prison walls are also
>   soul walls
>   barriers
> if only all barriers could be removed
>   and we could walk/talk/sing
>   be . . .
> free of all psychological, spiritual
>   political, economic
>   boundaries
> all of us all the freedom lovers of
>   the world but especially
>   right now—prisoners[1]

1. Reprinted from *If They Come In the Morning*, Angela Y. Davis and other Political Prisoners, © New York: Signet, 1971.

"Getting out isn't easy for anyone. But it's not just getting adjusted to the world again, it's getting adjusted to the people you care about," said "Yvonne Williams," a woman I spent many hours talking with at the state prison for women in Iowa. She had served two sentences at the prison, and this time she was back on a parole violation for starting to use narcotics again. "No matter how much understanding you have, two years later, it's different. The stem of love might still be there, but it's branched off in different directions.

"Like with Ronnie and me, we loved each other deep for more than eighteen years now. He's a pimp and I'm a whore, but we love each other our own way and that counts. But to put it simple, we're victims of a system. If I'm ever gonna get out of here, I have to get a divorce from Ronnie to get out of here. The parole board they think he's a bad influence on me and if it wasn't for him I wouldn't have started using drugs in the first place. Before I got out the last time I filed for a divorce to satisfy the parole board. He's in Iowa City and he wanted to see me, naturally. But we had to sneak. I didn't think I should have to sneak to see my husband.

"They gave me a furlough once to see my kids and they asked, 'Is Ronnie going to be there?' Of course he was there. But we had to get a hotel room and sneak, 'cause I'd had to say I wouldn't be seeing him. Meanwhile the police had seen me get off the bus and they called the institution to say Ronnie had been there to meet me—but I didn't know that until I got back. The police can do that; they know who we are.

"Anyway . . . I hadn't been to bed with any dude for fifteen months and I didn't know how to react. He didn't know how to react to my not reacting. We had got a hotel room and I had to go up after he did. We just sat there . . . we didn't know what to say. I wanted to make love to him and he wanted to make love to me but we didn't know what to do. We finally did make love, but just did that. I could have done better with a trick. We talked about it afterward, but we couldn't figure it out. When I got out on parole, we still had to sneak to see each other. Imagine, having to sneak to see your own husband. So I got out there on parole, shot up and forgot everything.

"It seems like if they cared, the institution would have involvement in relationships—like provide marriage counseling or home furloughs together—not like just split up the whole thing. I don't know how I'm going to keep from seeing him when I get out this time—unless I move to a different state. I guess that's what I'm going to have to do if I want to make it. I love the dude too much . . ."

"Association" is one of the most deadly of parole restrictions placed on people released on parole from prisons. "Association" means that the parolee is not allowed to communicate with any person who also has a prison record—nor with any person specifically named "undesirable" under conditions of parole. A violation of the rule means return to prison on a parole violation for the duration of the sentence. For many people this restriction means they are not able legally to associate with any of their old friends and buddies. Not only is this an ominous rule that spells loneliness if followed, or risk if violated, it is another implicit sanctioning by the law of mistrust toward all ex-prisoners, whether law-abiding or not. This parole restriction, along with many others—such as the denial of the vote, curfews, restrictions from going into any establishment where alcohol is served—discourage the newly released person from participating in normal community life by restricting him or her from activities routinely performed by other people involved in the life around them. If anything, parole restrictions are often counterproductive—a liability to adjustment because they deny natural access to the norms of community living which foster involvement and acceptance and reduce the feelings of alienation that often led to crimes in the first place. People meet other people in bars, at political or community meetings, at parties—but these experiences are unavailable to the parolee. Plus the parole officer—who has the dual roles of counselor and policeman, the person with power to return you to prison—is ineffectual in many cases, except for the enforcing of violations.

I have met many people in prison who are there for having spent time with another ex-convict on the outside. Perhaps the most ludicrous example was a man who had gotten married and started farming after he got out of prison. He bought a horse from a seller who came by with a "fine horse." "I'd always wanted to have a horse, and it was a real dream come true," he told me. When his parole officer learned who he bought the horse from, however, he wrote a violation which sent the farmer back to prison for "association." The seller also had a felony record. "The deal was aboveboard," Number 37846 had said, shaking his head in the prison corridor. "I had no idea he'd ever been in the rack before. I don't s'pose I had talked to him more than two or three times total." Records substantiated his story—also the stories of women returned to prison for living with a man they weren't married to, or "associating" with the "wrong" crowd or getting pregnant when they weren't legally married.

The conditions of parole speak for themeslves:

PAROLE ELIGIBILITY FOR CONCORD-FRAMINGHAM HOUSES OF CORRECTION

No inmate shall be considered for parole other than the time indicated according to Parole Board rules except in the cases where extenuating circumstances are presented in writing and the Parole Board by a four-fifths vote may hear the inmate as a special case.

The Parole Board shall not entertain the parole of an inmate from any correctional institution unless *detailed, factual information* is available and furnished to the board within thirty days prior to an inmate's eligible hearing. A decision will not be made until such time as sufficient information is available to permit the parole board to make a considered judgment in the case.

Parole Conditions

1. I will remain at liberty without violating the law.
2. I will be honorable in all respects, work diligently at a lawful occupation and support my dependents, if any, to the best of my ability.
3. I will abstain from the use of intoxicating liquors and narcotics of all kinds and will not frequent places where they are dispensed. I will receive permission from my Parole Officer before working in a place where liquor is sold.
4. I will not associate with persons of questionable character, nor with anyone on parole, nor with any person having a criminal record.
5. I will not leave the State of Massachusetts without permission of the Parole Board.
6. I will not leave my employment nor change my place of residence without permission of the Parole Board.
7. I will make a full and truthful report to the Parole Board, State Office Building, Boston, Mass., once each week for the first month, and thereafter once each month until the expiration of my sentence.
8. I will submit to medical treatment if ordered to do so by the Parole Board.

9. I will not marry without the permission of the Parole Board, nor without informing my intended partner of my parole status.

10. I will not live with any person of the opposite sex to whom I am not lawfully married.

11. I will not make application for a license to hunt, or to drive a motor vehicle without the permission of the Parole Board.

12. I will not correspond with inmates confined in any Correctional Institutions without permission of the Parole Board.

HOWEVER, THE PAROLE BOARD RESERVES THE RIGHT TO MAKE EXCEPTIONS TO THE ABOVE RULES OR TO IMPOSE ADDITIONAL CONDITIONS IN ANY OR ALL CASES.

"Making it out there ain't no easy thing, honey," an older woman told me, her hands shaking slightly as she lit her cigarette with the burning stub of her last smoke. "We're as good as lepers out there. Tell somebody you just got out of the joint and they run like hell. 'Fraid you'll grab their wad or something. Tell you the truth, tell you like it is—it's a hell of a lot easier in here. At least I know when I'm gonna eat. The most for real people you gonna meet are right in here with me. That's the truth, that's the truth. They'll admit they're nobody. They'll admit they're scared, they're just what they are. And that makes 'em somebody in my books . . ."

The onus of a criminal record seems haunting, never ending. When Fran Blackwell asked to go to Florida on vacation from Pennsylvania, for instance, her parole officer required that she give him the exact time she would enter each state as she and her mother drove south. Parole stipulations required that each state and city she passed through be informed of her entry. She had to carry papers showing her "criminal status" at all times. "It would be one thing if you could do your time and be finished with it," Fran said. "But they never let you out, it's never really over."

One of the most painful stigmas attached to being in and then getting out is that of having been a "bad" mother, if for nothing more than being separated from your children. At least 80 per cent of the women in prison have children—and while they are incarcerated, their children either live with relatives or are dependents of the state—placed in foster homes, juvenile shelters and, in some cases, put up for adoption. Their mothers carry a lot of guilt and anxiety—often because of the lack of emotional security the child or children had prior to the mother's incarceration and then again during her absence. Children who feel they have been abandoned or disappointed, have their own resentments and adjustments to life without their mothers. The separation causes anxieties and fears in both mothers and children.

"It really knocks me out to realize that I'm actually afraid of my own children," Victoria said. "I'm really afraid of them. I don't know what to do. I don't know how to act. I'm literally afraid of being a mother. Here I am, thirty-six years old with four beautiful children and one day I realize I'm afraid of being a mother. I don't know what to say to them when I'm with them—what to do. I feel paralyzed and helpless. Really, sometimes I feel I don't even like them. Like I resent them being my children."

Little is done within the prison or without to help women deal with motherhood—with reacquainting them with their older children, or having to sever the bond with tiny babies. Two state prisons in the country, as far as I know, allow newborn babies to stay with their mothers until they are one year old. Others allow a stay of one month. Even then, the babies stay in the nursery, until they are old enough to be released to a foster home. When a woman gets out of prison, she not only faces the trauma of finding a place to live and suitable work or economic support—she faces the trauma of being reunited with her children.

Some women who were deeply into *the life* before they went to prison neglected their children because of drugs, alcoholism or prostitution. Many had their children stay with friends or relatives because they didn't want their children exposed to the life they were in. Many never had good mothering themselves, so they really have no "mother model" to return with from jail even if they love their children deeply and want to be effective, responsible mothers themselves. And the complications of bitter prison experience obviously don't help. Any more than do the uncertainties of what is going on in the foster home or happening to the child while the mother is imprisoned.

For "Geraldine Johnson," who was at Muncy for more than two years, and in jail for a year waiting trial, the reality of being with her children was overwhelming. She came home on a four-day furlough to visit her children and was afraid and angry. Angry at the foster parents she had met only once—after more than a year of trying to locate them—angry because it would be so hard for her to get her children back and to find a place to live and a job. Afraid of what she would find. But she was excited to see her babies again; her love for them was deep. But again, the expectations didn't match reality.

"They didn't even know who I was, Kitsi," she said. "The foster mother had them calling *her* mother. She hadn't told them anything about me. When I got locked up Kathy was three months old and Linda was eighteen months old. My in-laws had kept the kids, but they didn't want Linda, so they had her staying with a friend and they kept Kathy. So while I was at the House of Correction, I had them removed from my in-laws and put into a foster home. Linda's my heart; I've been through some hard ups and downs and my baby came through it all with me.

"I wrote letters to them through the DPW [Department of Public Welfare] caseworker. But I didn't find out where they lived for more than two years—and when I did it was only because my friend Terry started hooking things up for me to come home on furlough—and she traced down where they were.

"The woman in the foster family has tried to instill herself as a mother figure—but she can never be the true mother figure 'cause she's not their mother. I resent her because she lets 'em run around and call her 'Mommy' . . . She *could* say, 'I love you, but I'm not your mommy.' It's not fair to me.

"Nobody else could do the divine act of bringing Kathy and Linda into the world. There is no other Kathy and Linda and there is no other me. I'm their only mother . . . I can't tell you how much it tore me up for them not to know me when they saw me."

Geraldine ended her furlough of four days by slitting her wrists. The suicide attempt was unsuccessful, though, and she returned to the prison to face a staff and parole board who felt she was too unstable, after this incident, to be released on the date she had been previously given. At the present time, she is out of prison—and has had custody of her children for more than a year. She's had her share of troubles readjusting, but she was finally able to get her children back by getting a job and proving she was a "fit" mother. Often because women are arrested in the first place, the court declares them "unfit." Women say the legal processes they have to go through with the court to prove they are "fit" mothers are usually as excruciating as their original trial.

The lack of counseling or concern available for prisoners re-joining their families is indicative of the low priority given by society to their struggles as individuals. And the onus of a criminal record makes it only that much more difficult for a person who's been imprisoned to find work or fit back comfortably into any legally and financially secure life. Often when they do come home they see their children have gone through traumatic changes. Sometimes children of prisoners have been the target of teasing by schoolmates aware of their mother's background. "Your mother's a jailbird"—or, "Your mother's a you-know-what." Children have great fun "playing the dozens" on other children's mothers. The stigma of being a "criminal" is carried into every corner of society—no matter how *normal* going to prison is. But no matter the amount of understanding or awareness a child may have—the reality is that mother's *been gone* and the child has been left alone and "rejected"—no matter whose fault that is. Perhaps one of the worst hurdles is the woman's own internalization of societal disapproval, the disappointment of self-expectations plus abuse and mistreatment through the years which reduce her to feeling like "nothing," or, worse, a misfit . . .

Things had happened to me that no amount of time could change or heal. I had gone to jail when I was ten because a forty-year-old man had tried to rape me. Sure, they had no more business putting me in that Catholic Institution than if I'd been hit by a damn truck. But they did. Sure, they had no business punishing me, but they had. For years I used to dream about it and wake up hollering and screaming. My God, its terrible what something like this does to you. It takes years and years to get over it; it haunts you and haunts you.

Getting booked and busted again didn't help, either. I might explain the first rap was a freak accident. But the second was tougher. For years it made me feel like a damn cripple. It changed the way I looked at everything and everybody. There was one chance I couldn't take. I couldn't stand any man who didn't know about the things that had happened to me when I was a kid. And I was leery of any man who could throw those things back at me in a quarrel. I could take almost anything, but My God, not that. I didn't want anyone around me who might ever hold this over me or even hint that on account of it he was a cut above me . . .

—BILLIE HOLIDAY, from *Lady Sings the Blues*[2]

Theresa Derry said she's seen many women accept guilt for things they never did—but rather were done to them.

"It's like—if they treat me this way, I must be bad—or there must

2. By Billie Holiday with William Dufty (New York: Lancer, 1969).

be something wrong with *me*. They don't stop to wonder if there isn't something wrong with the people who are treating them this way! You'd be surprised how many of the women were raped by their fathers, their mother's boyfriend or their uncle when they were young," she said. "I was shocked by how many had either been raped or got vicious beatings a lot when they were young. It cut across all classes—upper class, middle class, lower class. It wasn't just people from ghetto areas, like some people might think. It was all classes. I had known from friends of mine what happened to them— but this was across the board. I kept interviewing women at the House of Correction and I kept being shocked at the numbers.

"What's even more shocking is that they seem to accept the guilt for what happened to them. Take 'Bodine'—you know her. She was raped by her father when she was twelve. And look what she went straight to when she got out of jail—a pimp. You'd think that would be the last person she'd go to. But she's putting her daughter in the same situation she was in—where the same thing could happen to her daughter as happened to her. You'd think that's the last thing she'd do. But she assumes the guilt for her father having raped her . . . and then she goes straight to a pimp.

"It doesn't make sense—but people seem to go back to the same thing that messed them up in the first place. They seem to create the same environment they came from—sort of like to keep themselves fucked up so they'll be comfortable. I don't understand it—I just know it works that way. They ought to want to change conditions— but they'll do their damnedest to maintain it."

I also saw many many examples of these truths—women whose grandparents raised them were now giving their own children to the same people to care for; drug addicts whose fathers or mothers had been addicted to alcohol; people who were neglected neglecting their own children. It seems a vicious cycle—a chain with few broken links.

"I think it's much easier for a man to get over the stigma of being a con than a woman when she gets out," said Fran Christman. "A man has broken a law—a social law. But a woman has violated both social and moral laws in the eyes of the public, and sometimes in herself, and the stigma is there. Granted, we have some advantages. Like when I filled out job application forms I could put 'housewife' to explain where I'd been for the last fifteen years—where a man can't get away with that. But that stigma, once people know, is always there. When we go out speaking, a man who is a former murderer or armed robber can get through to the audience, who accept him because now he's made it or it's part of his past he's overcome. But when I get up to speak, you can cut the hostility with a knife. They hear I was a prostitute and they project, 'There goes that tramp'—they just won't cut it loose. It's like I've committed a moral crime against them as well as a social crime."

"When you forget all about the stigmas—it's still a hell of a thing to just plain come out of a prison, out of captivity, into society," Theresa said. "Even if you had a model prison in every other way— you still have three basic elements that are destructive. You're in captivity, you have a laid-out system and lack of freedom. These three things will destroy anyone and you can't get around it. I've tried to imagine a model prison. But no prison can be made right. The only way is no prisons at all.

"You take the wildest beast in the jungle and put him in a cage and then take him out and put him back in the jungle and he can't survive. You've destroyed his automatic defenses."

A lot of ex-prisoners just never make it back. Like old prize fighters, they keep punching but never really get on their feet again. A lot of addicts never learn to love themselves or stop destroying themselves for what's been done to them. There's some kind of invisible line, though, where a person leaves the environment that so mutilated her and takes up the task herself. She has been victimized and then continues the process; it's true to some degree in all of us. Prison is another suicide trip for some people—who for so many reasons have given up their will to struggle for freedom.

But like anything and everything else, we don't look for alternatives when we don't know they exist. We all need to examine and explore other realities, especially other possibilities to get ourselves out of the bondage we find ourselves in.

More than anything else, prison is America's vast wasteland. It's a wasteland for human energy and creativity and growth. I only have to think of the life of one individual—and there are thousands—to know the enormity of the human tragedy we call the criminal justice system—and its effects. Katie Haley, whose life was laced with the mutilating process of institutionalization, is one of those people I think of often.

Katie and I met at Sybil Brand Institute for Women in Los Angeles, just one month before her release from jail after a stay of one and a half years. She hoped this time would be the last. She had tried to make it on the outside before. She wanted this trip home to have a different ending.

"The first time I came in here was for eighteen months—November '67 to May '69," Katie Haley said as she sat in a visiting booth across from me in the "attorney room." "When I was here I was schooled in work, the illegal kind. It was the first time I'd ever been to an adult jail. I was hearing all these stories . . . I learned about the streets and how to survive without legally working. I didn't have a trade and I couldn't get a job . . . so when I got out I couldn't seem to adjust after doing all that time. I didn't know the first thing to do when I got out.

"I didn't know I had to lie on questionnaires or anything like that. I was super naïve. I still had a little of the home training . . . and it never occurred to me to lie. The questionnaire would say, 'Have you ever been arrested?' 'Yes.' 'What for?' I'd write it down and there went the job. So I started doing what I had learned in here to survive. This time they gave me one year for second degree robbery."

Katie—a tall and attractive twenty-nine-year-old woman with deep brown skin and curly black hair held on top of her head by a bright yellow bow—studied my face and her hands for a while. "Now I'm getting PBX training [telephone switchboard]. I just want to go to work somewhere. The main thing, I don't want to go from place to place getting turned down. I'm afraid that if I go job hunting the rejections will tear down the defenses I'm trying so hard to build up and I'll eventually just say to hell with it. It would be easier if the institution could get jobs for you so they'd know already you'd been in jail. Then I wouldn't have to be worrying about if they'll be running a check on me, or how long I can work before they find out."

More than just worrying about a job and financial future, Katie also had to worry about her five children. Presently, her sons, nine and ten years old, were staying with her mother. Her three daughters —ages four, five and six—were in a foster home together.

"In '67, they were all together . . . they found a home for all five of them in Altadena. That was the only way I'd have it. I wouldn't sign the papers for them to go to a foster home unless they guaranteed they would be in the same home. I didn't want them separated. It had just been me and the kids. All they had was each other. When I got out in '69, the first thing in my mind was I wanted my babies. So I go out and get 'em. Then I went down and applied for welfare.

"The welfare department said I would have to fill out an application and wait ninety days for the papers to be processed. I said, 'Hey, what will my babies eat for ninety days?' They said, 'Sorry, it's just a lot of red tape.' I said, 'Well, hey, my babies can't eat red tape.' So I called my mother and asked her if she could keep them. She said she could keep the boys . . . and then I called the foster home where they'd been and asked them could they keep my girls till I got on my feet. It kind of tore me up to have to get rid of 'em. I started tripping—and all different forms of escape. This time I have definitely decided my kids are gonna stay where they are at least until next summer. I get out in March and I'm not going to try to take all the responsibility at one time. I'll build up slowly. I'll have the kids once a week. Then I'll try to take them over the weekend and build up that way.

"The foster father has got awfully attached to my baby. She was only six months old when she went there. They wanted to adopt her. No. She's the last child I can have. Those are my babies, that's me. That's a part of me.

"I got a pretty good idea of what direction I want to go in . . . but I always had strict schedules to follow. Now I'm afraid I've built up so much resentment against having to do certain things at certain times in certain places that I won't want any routine. Sometimes I have mixed emotions about going home. At times I can hardly wait. Other times I'm a little scared. Plus I'm afraid to live with my mother. She pressures me too much, and I just go off. My mother's the kind, she's over-possessive. She stifles me. She's the 'I told you so' kind—always putting my past up to me.

"But I have to live with her. The county says so. If she wasn't here, the county would provide a place—but as long as you have a relative, there's some kind of rule that you have to live with them. It was when I was under that pressure before, with all those disappointments, that I started using dope. The main reason was to forget . . . to escape. I'm not worried about using it again, though. The thought of it makes me sick. I wasn't even aware I was addicted until I was busted . . . 'cause I was with people who was dealing, so it never entered my mind since I always had a supply. I really didn't know what was happening until I was in that jail cell getting sick. For five days and nights I kicked cold turkey. It really turned me off. I don't think you could pay me to get down. When I listen to broads talk about highs I can only relate to the sickness. I can't stand pain. That's a funny thing about me. In 1960 I had a nervous breakdown and tried to kill myself. Yet I don't like pain."

One of the things that haunted Katie was what kind of relationships she would have with women and men when she got out. In jail, she found warmth and comfort with other women . . . the kind of comfort and affection she hadn't found with male lovers on the outside. The only places she had had homosexual relationships were in all-female institutions—starting as a youngster.

"The first time I was ever in an institution since I was grown was 1967. As a teen-ager I was in and out of Juvenile Hall. The first thing I wanted to do when I reached age was to get married—I didn't care to who—and have a baby. What this was—and I didn't figure it out until last year—was I was afraid I had homosexual tendencies. I didn't want to admit it. This wanting to have a baby was my way of saying, 'Look at me, World, I'm normal.'

"I had only had affairs with other women. Actually I didn't start having bisexual relations until I was nineteen . . . and then when I started having relations with men, that was only 'cause I wouldn't admit I dug women. So I was walking down the street pregnant—with a big belly, saying, 'See, I'm normal.'

"Now I completely accept my likes and dislikes but I got my kids to consider. I've been married twice. The first time it was a big love thing, but it turned out later he was already married, so our marriage was annulled. The second time it was an older man. A forty-two-year-old disabled veteran. He loved my kids and he was one hundred per cent government compensation. He was also supposed to be divorced. Would you believe . . . he was married, too. Time and time again I tried working out a marriage thing and it just didn't work.

"Then the guy I was going with before I came in here this time . . . Eddie. I had told him I knew he'd have to sleep with someone while I was gone, but please to go to her house or to a motel—not to my house. I didn't want them fucking in my bed or in my room or in my house. Well, he was coming up here every week and everything was just fine. Then one time for about four weeks he didn't come up or write. Then this broad came in who kept looking at me. Finally she said, 'Those pictures in Eddie's bedroom are yours, aren't they.' That was kind of a mind blower. She told everyone about how she had been living with Eddie, and I just about went off. What got me was that he lied to me . . . not so much he had done it. 'Cause when he had started coming up again, I had asked him if he had stayed away 'cause he was seeing someone else . . . and he had lied to me.

"This is another reason I have more feeling for women than I do for men. They're more understanding. They can hurt, too, but you can trust 'em more than men. Eddie still comes up and brings me money for cigarettes . . . but it's not the same. I really had thought I was in love with him.

"The most for real people I have ever met are broads in here. They're not shallow, they're not surface. There are so few people that know where their head is and where they're coming from. When I'm in here I keep wondering, where they be hiding in the free world? I'd like to find their hiding place.

"There are good people here—but at the same time, jail can make a person so vicious and so violent. It's nauseating. Sometimes I lay in my bed and think about how I've changed. It's unbelievable. But it's mandatory to survive. It's dog eat dog. It's a true statement.

"If I could have any wish I wanted I'd have money on my books and take off in an opposite direction from anybody I know. I wouldn't have my mother or Eddie come pick me up. I dread them being here when I get out. I'd leave by myself, if I had the money, and stay clear of them."

Katie realized most of her problems started as a young girl. "I was mostly runaway and incorrigible," she said of herself. "Here the majority start getting in trouble when they're older.

"But I wouldn't really be running away. My mother was so strict on me, the only way I could get out was to crawl through the bathroom window. Naturally she'd call the police and they'd pick me up and take me to Juvenile Hall. She used to gamble quite a bit . . . she'd leave the house and I'd wake up and she wouldn't be there. At first I was scared. Then when I got older, I took advantage of it. I'd go to a football game or to my girl friend's or to a party. She'd come home and if I wasn't there, she'd call the police."

It never ceases to amaze me how we accept the horrible, primitive things our parents did to us as *natural*, as normal. And how so many of us live out our lives as adults never understanding or examining the total process; never looking at how we are affected today by what happened yesterday. It is horrifying to me that if your mother can't deal with you or doesn't know how to relate to you—that she would call the police. But to Katie's mother, I'm sure it made perfect sense. It was as natural and as real a response from her perspective as it was for the mother of another friend of mine who told me she feels "safer" when her son is in jail. "At least I don't have to worry about him," she says. "I don't have to wonder where he is or if he's all right. I know he's getting fed."

Katie wasn't criticizing her mother at all. She was just relating what had happened; accepting the reality of it as part of life. Just like everyone's world—no matter how "different" it is—is matter of fact; it's tradition.

As we talked, and as the hours went on, it seemed that somehow Katie and I were old friends—finally getting together to talk after not seeing each other for the last five years, or maybe the last five weeks. It was a real sharing. Our time came abruptly to an end, though, when the deputy sheriff in charge of visiting told us we had to discontinue talking because visiting hours were up.

Neither one of us wanted to stop. But there was no real choice. We promised to write and keep in touch. "I wish we didn't have to stop," Katie said as we parted. "This is the first time since I've been here that I've been able to say what I feel and get so much out . . . maybe it's the first time ever . . ."

After I came back to Philadelphia, Katie and I exchanged correspondence a few times. Her letters were bright, brief. She said she wished we could get together and talk again—she didn't really have anyone to talk to. The exchange was mainly an attempt to touch base and say hello. When I didn't hear from her for three or four months, I figured she had gotten swallowed by chaos again. But I *hoped* things were better for her, that somehow she could stabilize.

Then one summer day, I got a small envelope in the mail from East Eighty-eighth Street in Los Angeles. Before I opened it I knew Katie was dead. I expected what I saw. It was a note from Katie's mother, along with a funeral program from Paradise Baptist Church, where Katie Haley's obsequies were held June 24, 1972. Katie was dead. I don't know how she died—someday maybe I'll hear the full story. I only know the rage I felt. The pain of "just another death" in another culture . . . as foreign a culture and as foreign a death to most Americans as the abstraction of death in Indochina.

I know that few people knew or cared that Katie Haley was dead. And I know that her life was part of a process that kills millions of Americans emotionally and physically. Katie died a prisoner of herself and a prisoner of her world—never really knowing alternatives to the inner or outer tyrannies that shaped her reality.

It Used to Be So Beautiful Here

The man, more than fifty years old, is standing outside the front entrance of the Control Center at Riker's Island, New York City's penal colony. His eyes seem alert to movements and nuances in the scenery invisible to me. His brown face is full and gentle, and his neck bulges out above his tight-fitting military gray uniform, which looks like it has tried to mold his body but failed.

His name is Tim Davis—and he has worked on Riker's Island as a guard for more than twenty years.

"You see this over here," he says, waving his arm horizontally over the island. "That used to be a mountain, but we expanded so much they had to clear it away. Now we have buildings there, and there and there . . .

"We used to have farms here twenty years ago. This was a beautiful place to work those days.

"That's the new Woman's House of Detention . . . where you want to go. There used to be trees there, and a mountain . . . but they chopped the mountain down and put in the Women's House of Detention.

"We used to call it a nursery out here because there were thousands and thousands of trees. But they took the trees one by one to plant along the highways. The Park Department took them.

"And see that over there"—his hand goes up to shade his squinting eyes in the sun—". . . there used to be thousands and thousands of chicken coops and the inmates used to take care of them. Now look at the place. It's fantastic. Just fantastic. Look at these jails . . . It used to be so beautiful here those days . . ."

Chapter 12   PRISON: AN IDEA OR A PLACE?

It would be impossible for me to say imprisonment is *worse* for women than it is for men. Imprisonment is terrible for everybody. Imprisonment is *different* for women because women are different from men. But we are *each* different; we each experience life from our own perspective. We each have a separate reality and everything we see, touch, feel, hear is perceived slightly differently from the next person.

Men may cope with prison in different ways than women—but they too are treated as children. They too are forced into a state of dependency. They suffer the same powerlessness and mistreatment. There are plenty of men and, therefore, male prisoners who are gentle, tender or frightened people. Just because stereotypes label them as bruisers, as strong, tough individuals, doesn't mean they are. We are all fragile. We are all unique. We all have the potential to grow and change and contribute to life.

But prison is a concrete womb for everyone. It is a place we send people for *change*. We expect them to grow and become responsible on literally concrete ground. We force-feed dependency and regression to people and then hurl them back into society expecting them to be independent. It doesn't make sense.

In 1870 a Judge Carter from Ohio said he favored the abolition of prisons. At the National Congress on Penitentiary and Reformatory Discipline he said that *any* system of imprisonment or punishment was degradation and could not reform a person. He wanted to release all the people confined in prisons. The judge said he felt certain that prisons would be abolished once women had won the right to vote, hold office and sit as judges and legislators. He maintained women would correct the injustices men had mandated as law.

His view, not surprisingly, was unpopular at the time. Although people at the Congress condemned prisons as a failure, they wanted to reform, not close down prisons. The majority were not willing to give up their belief that somehow prisons would work. Nor were they willing to give up the assumption that intemperance and prostitution were the *causes* of crime. But Judge Carter and several other people at the Congress argued intemperance was not the cause of crime and never had been. Neither was prostitution. They said that

if these activities brought people into crime, they might be the ante-
cedents, but they were not the immediate cause. Many spoke fer-
vently in favor of establishing an equitable society that would prevent
crime by eliminating poverty, desperation and hopelessness.

As I write this last chapter, I feel some real despair. I feel somewhat bitter that people live in such oblivion to one another that
books like this one must be written. Why don't people already know?
Why is the public unwilling to seek the truth of how they are hurting *themselves?*

For two hundred years, knowledgeable people in America have
been saying prisons don't work. They don't stop crime. They don't
deter criminal behavior. Prisoners, who know better than anyone,
have demonstrated what a destructive, sadistic and bitter failure
prisons have been. They have risked their lives to draw attention to
the conditions they live in. Women and men in prisons across the
country have responded to their environments by refusing to work,
refusing to eat or refusing to co-operate until conditions improve. In
Kansas, inmates went so far as to cripple themselves by cutting their
Achilles tendons in protest to their living conditions. The effect of
experiences inside prison is perhaps most dramatically reflected in
the fact that 80 *per cent* of all new felonies are committed by people
previously confined in what I have called a state of infancy. Four
fifths of all our major crimes solved are attributed to people already
processed at least once through the criminal justice system.

We are nearing the twenty-first century. We really don't have time
to be so foolish. We have repeatedly heard prisoners and ex-prisoners,
judges, attorneys general and even the President of the United States
say that prisons are a blight on America: a reflection of our inhumanity and character. Former Associate Justice of the U. S. Supreme
Court Arthur J. Goldberg said, "During my service as a justice of
the United States Supreme Court, I had the unique opportunity to
observe how self-defeating and destructive simplistic approaches to
crime and punishment can be. Repressive measures and increased
penalties are *not* the answer. These solutions will be no more successful in our own era than they have in times past."

I am astounded when I hear people calling for preventive detention, longer sentences, more severe punishment. They denounce the
"coddling" of prisoners and cry for state-inflicted vengeance. These
same people maintain the theory that imprisonment will decrease
crime on the streets and rehabilitate the offender. Like their fore-

bears, they maintain that drugs, a replacement for alcohol, are the *cause* of crime, not the antecedent. These people don't understand what they're talking about. They are locked in prisons of their own making. They do not realize that ultimately society suffers, we all suffer from the continuation of an unworkable theory, founded only in blindness and maintained through rigid stubbornness. We are using precious resources and energy to hurt ourselves.

In his book *Crime in America*, former Attorney General Ramsey Clark points out that what we do in the field of penology has practically no relationship to what we say we do. He says that the effect of imprisonment—where the individual's integrity and personality have been almost totally abused—is to make prisoners come out of prison a threat to society.

"If we are to deal meaningfully with crime," Clark writes, "what must be seen is the dehumanizing effect on the individual of slums, racism, ignorance and violence, of corruption and impotence to fulfill rights, of poverty and unemployment and idleness, of generations of malnutrition, of congenital brain damage and prenatal neglect, of sickness and disease, of pollution, of decrepit, dirty, ugly, unsafe, overcrowded housing, of alcoholism and drug addiction, of avarice, anxiety, fear, hatred, hopelessness and injustice. These are the fountainheads of crime. They can be controlled. As imprecise, distorted and prejudiced as our learning is, these sources of crime and their controllability clearly emerge to any who would see."

Even the most conservative administrators of prisons for both men and women will admit that imprisonment doesn't work; it is self-defeating. Officials have told me frankly that there is nothing they can do. That "you need to start with pre-schoolers and get set programs where kids can have a healthy diet and a healthy environment." "These places just don't rehabilitate anybody." And so on.

The National Council on Crime and Delinquency has taken the position that no new detention or penal institutions should be built before alternatives to imprisonment are fully explored. They have called for a halt on construction of all new prisons, jails, juvenile training schools and detention homes until the funding, staffing and utilization of non-institutional corrections has been attained.

In formulating this policy statement, the Council pointed to the fact that a three-year project in Saginaw, Michigan, demonstrated that 80 per cent of felony offenders can be placed on probation without danger to the community. They documented other research leading to the conclusion that of some 400,000 men, women and children imprisoned in America on any given day, very few need to be locked up for the protection of society; that imprisonment is necessary only for the tiny minority of offenders so dangerous as to pose a serious threat to society if allowed at large. On that basis, NCCD pointed out we have vastly more institutional space than is possibly needed.

Thorough research and even a brief glimpse of history support this position. But in November 1968, President Richard Milhous Nixon gave the U. S. Attorney General a thirteen-point correction program that ignores all of these recommendations. He has also called for further pretrial detention, a plan contradictory to the Constitution of the United States. Under the President's program, the Bureau of Prisons has developed a ten-year plan calling for the construction of sixty-six new institutions at an estimated cost of $700 million. Estimates of annual operating costs would add more than $150 million—if we can trust the normal ratio of average construction costs to average operating costs.

In addition to the sixty-six new federal institutions, plans are being developed by state and local authorities for the construction of more jails for sentenced offenders *and* for people awaiting trial and sentencing—still a violation in effect of the principle that people charged with a crime are considered innocent until proven guilty.

In Connecticut, where jails are state-operated, new jail construction is already in progress and the planning of replacements for local jails is being financed by the Law Enforcement Assistance Administration—the same agency that financed the task force report on "The Challenge of Crime in a Free Society," which held that prisons don't deter crime or protect society.

The National Jail Census reported in 1970 the total planned jail construction expenditures for that year were over $170 million.

According to the U. S. Bureau of Prisons, eight federal correctional centers for guidance and detention are being planned in metropolitan areas. Construction funds have been appropriated for one center in New York City and funds are also being used to plan similar construction in Chicago, Philadelphia, San Diego and San Francisco.

The multimillion-dollar federal institution planned for construction in lower Manhattan is adjacent to the property where the city of New York proposed to construct the $60-million city jail. No joint planning has been done by state, federal or local authorities to determine whether both facilities are needed or the extent to which alternative measures in lieu of pretrial detention would reduce the estimated numbers of people imprisoned in either.[1]

It would seem clear that we allow government and the machinery of bureaucracies to roll on even when we know that machinery to be crushing us all. None of us seem to feel we have the power to stop an unworkable and devastating system. Are we so locked into the prisons of the past that we are afraid to look into the future? Afraid to accept the responsibility of our own power?

We continue to produce new prisons with illogical enthusiasm. But as we have produced prisons, we have also produced apologetic reforms. Since the establishment of penitentiaries, people have apologized for their errors with tokens of change, the tokens still based on the same theories—thus becoming part of the old cycle. None of the reforms have reduced the number of people being punished in prison. They haven't reduced crime. If anything, many good intentions and reforms have expanded an unjust system, and increased crime.

A lot of people have asked me if I was going to write about this program or that program, this organization or that organization working for prison reform. Some prisoner support groups have been quite effective. Some projects have meant new opportunities for people confined. Tremendous perseverance has been shown on the part of many community people and corrections personnel dedicated to change; enormous efforts have been made to maintain individual rights and as much freedom as possible within prison walls. Work release programs and post-imprisonment employment banks have provided new opportunities. These immediate steps are constructive, important, even vital.

But I have chosen not to write about the reforms and innovations in depth because in fact they affect only a *minority of prisoners*. Their success is minuscule in relation to the total picture. The basic conditions remain the same. The basic realities for people in prison are as true today as they were in 1840 and 1870 and 1940. The basic questions still exist despite changes. And if we don't deal with those questions people may be still writing about the same basic issues in 2070, and 2170, if we survive that long.

It also seems those of us who want change have been as blind to

1. National Council on Crime and Delinquency, *Policies and Background Information* (Hackensack, N.J., 1972).

history as we have been to the *expansion* of the system through sincere efforts to reform it piecemeal.

As I pointed out above, the concern of reformers with the neglect and mistreatment of women in prison at the turn of the century led to the establishment of separate prisons for women. Since that time *more* women have been funneled into the system. The concern about juveniles has led to the reform establishment of a juvenile system of justice—with family courts, juvenile probation officers and juvenile jails and prisons. Since most state institutions for women and children have been built without walls and with "nice" conditions, judges have been less hesitant about incarcerating them. Sending a mother or a child to a "reformatory" or a "center" isn't as distasteful as sending them to a "prison." The same semantic change is being used in correctional institutions for men. And yet it is plain to see that vocabulary or the lack of high walls and armed guards don't change the realities of imprisonment and degradation, of coercion and attempts to force change and create dependency. Through reform, imprisonment has expanded.

The establishment of the U. S. Bureau of Prisons was a reform measure of the 1930s—when there were seven federal prisons being funded by Congress and functioning autonomously. At that time, 12,000 offenders were confined in those institutions and an equal number of federal prisoners were held in state and local facilities. Today the Bureau operates thirty-eight institutions throughout the country, housing approximately 20,000 people. More than 36,000 people are under the supervision of the federal probation system—another reform.

It is apparent that changes created with the best of intentions have often led to an increase and expansion of custody—both within institutions and in the community. When prison sentences were deemed unconscionably long (and we have the longest prison sentences in the world), the parole system was established. Once parole was available, judges began to respond by giving offenders even longer sentences, on the theory that they would need more control over the person's behavior in the street. Parole has justified governing personal and private life—with an emphasis on middle-class morals. It has become an effective harness on behavior which has no relationship to crime.

We also can see from history that when one small part of the system is changed, other parts often seem to work so as to co-opt the effect of the reforms. For example, in Wisconsin, it's now possible for an offender to have an attorney of her own if she is in danger of having her probation or parole revoked. This was a sound attempt to protect the civil liberties of the offender. But authorities in Wisconsin report that since the ruling, judges are now less willing to grant probation and parole boards are less willing to grant parole. So what looks like a humanitarian change has in fact led to a more rigid system.

Today when I hear about community treatment centers being established that are chiefly residential, I know they are a step forward from custody-oriented prisons. Plans for many centers include diagnostic services for courts to give judges more information to determine appropriate sentencing; intensive short-term treatment; and units for counseling and guidance of inmates being prepared to return to the community. There is also vocational and family counseling in a few existing centers.

But I have the sense that the same historical error is being repeated in the move toward community treatment centers that has made reforms fail in the past. These centers are being planned *in addition to* existing and planned prisons. There have been few stated intentions to close down prisons; to replace prisons with community treatment centers. The centers threaten to become another appendage to a growing machine that is already out of whack; a system that could more correctly be termed a non-system for injustice.

Community treatment centers will, in effect, be trying to repair damage done by mass institutionalization, by infancy treatment in the prisons . . . for the minority of people allowed to enter them. They are on a continuum with theories of the past—that by treating or rehabilitating less than 2 per cent of the lawbreakers reported, we will reduce crime in America.

It doesn't make sense.

Sometimes it seems to me that the efforts of the state are unwittingly directed at further disrupting the family units of poor people— and that efforts at rehabilitation are merely an attempt to rehabilitate people from lower-class morality into middle-class morality. An attempt to force people into accepting the values of production and a sound economy; an effort to keep them distracted from the plight of the environment around them. It seems that little of what we call criminology and penology has much to do with crime. It has more to do with economics. Maybe the real questions we should be asking don't revolve around crime as much as they do around our fears, our values and the quality of life. Maybe they have more to do with how we all fail to take care of each other.

Obviously we should experiment with new ways of preventing crime and supporting one another in life-giving ways. The prison system has indeed been maintained on an historical continuum. A continuum of ideology and practice that has become so imprinted into our consciousness that we have never been willing to break away from it. It is apparent that this continuum is obsolete.

Fresh thinking is needed and it is badly needed. We need to break the continuum, break with the past. The only block is our own resistance—our own inner prisons—that stifle creative thinking and change. We have all the material, economic, technical and intellectual tools necessary to realize a society that would allow equal education, income, opportunity, support and self-realization for all citizens.

It is possible to abolish poverty and hunger. It is possible to have life-giving work available. It is possible to shut down prisons as we know them and share space and life with people now rejected, neglected and abused. It is possible for us to care about ourselves and accept our differences, to think in larger perspectives; to accept our different realities and learn from the richness of all the cultures in this country.

All of us—in the general society and in the prison society—need to assert a sense of responsibility and determination over our own futures. We all have a need to be at peace with ourselves. We have a need for privacy and the opportunity to experience without fear the natural and social environment.

We need to reorganize totally the systems that drain our energies and make us dependent on waste and ruin. A total structural change could allow human relationships to develop along with creative life-giving forces. But to have fresh thinking—to create new channels for our energy which would prevent crime and destruction—would mean that we would have to break the continuum. Willfully and determinedly, we would have to contradict and negate destructive theories and practices in a very pragmatic way. We would have to stop placing blame for the immense problems of our socitey on a "criminal class." We would have to establish new priorities. We have no model. Nor do we know what is feasible. What is not feasible shows itself only after the fact . . . The criminal justice system is one area that has showed itself not feasible. It is a microcosm of our society; it concerns human behavior. It is a good place to begin.

I know there is a large group of people who are imprisoned unjustly and punished unfairly. They are held in jail long periods of time awaiting trial. Or they are people who are being punished for punishing themselves.

There is a second group of people—the vast majority—who do not get punished because of an ability to manipulate the system or avoid detection. The discretion of the law protects the majority of middle-class people. They break laws—fornication, adultery, traffic, liquor, drug laws, business infractions, tax evasions—crimes other people are serving time for. Studies have told us that the average urban resident commits eighteen felonies a year, each punishable theoretically by a year or more imprisonment.

There is a third group of people—some who fall into the first category—to whom prison is an essentially normal part of culture. These are people unprotected by the discretionary power of the law. They serve as "examples" for the rest of us. Many of this group give lip service to such concepts as rehabilitation and getting out of the system—but essentially lack the tools or the motivation to do so. Some of this group resist all attempts to do what they say they want to do. They do not want to give up drugs or the minor moneymaking systems of survival that involve hustling and stealing and living fast and dangerously. They do not want to give up the life. They demonstrate this by not giving it up—no matter how much punishment they suffer as a result.

Their position is: why should *they* change when society doesn't change? A strong analogy could be made between them and the public that gives lip service to providing rehabilitation without ever effectively offering it. We say we are against punishment and punitive imprisonment, but we do not demonstrate this by giving it up.

We expect lawbreakers to change, but we are not willing to change. We expect them to want to give up their cultural and survival values, but we are not willing to give up ours. Why do we allow the mindlessness of middle-class self-destruction and not the mindlessness of lower-class self-destruction? Is one so much wore than the other? Is an embezzler any better than a numbers runner? Expecting that anyone or everyone who has broken a law should change or be willing to give up her culture is not very logical. We all hold on to what is familiar to us. We are being foolish Goodie Two-Shoes to try to change other people's behavior without fully understanding their culture or offering viable alternatives.

I know that there are a lot of people who put themselves in bondage, or keep themselves in bondage both inside and outside jails. There is a whole culture in America that depends on being controlled and imprisoned—either with drugs, with alcohol or in jail. The concrete womb is security. The bottle is security. Heroin is security. Of course they are artificial security—but they are a response to fear. Fear of an overwhelming society, fear of powerlessness, fear of the unknown and fear of the known. All these "places" contribute to escape, to abandonment of responsibility. For many, outside pressures and people are more frightening and more evil than dependency.

Some people in prison say openly they would prefer prison if they could just have their families with them and have more freedom to do what they want to do.

It is an ironic cycle: society has an exaggerated fear of crime because of the minority of truly violent experiences and they lock a minority of lawbreakers away to help them feel safer. As a result, their actions work against them to make them in fact less safe. The people they are afraid of—the people labeled "criminals"—are afraid of the people who are afraid of them, which ultimately makes them more of a threat.

The cycle must be broken if any of us are ever to go forward. Communication has to open up. The community must go into the prisons and prisoners must be accepted and welcomed back into society; integrated, not alienated.

I would submit that even the most dependent persons or the few people who have committed the most heinous crimes don't need the environment they are now subjected to in prison. And certainly the vast majority of prisoners shouldn't be incarcerated at all. Allyn Sielaff, Commissioner of the Bureau of Corrections, in Pennsylvania, estimated that *less than 1 per cent* of all imprisoned felons in the state need maximum-security confinement.

Even the most conservative view would indicate that some of these conditions must be immediately changed—that prisoners must be granted their full civil rights. People must be given fair, speedy trials. Prisoners must maintain the right to vote; furlough programs must be expanded; family ties must be maintained. As long as any kind of prisons exist, inmates should be given the opportunity to earn decent wages to support their families. They must be *allowed* to become contributing members of society *if they so choose*. They should be able to be doctors and nurses and architects and licensed technicians and recreation directors—people contributing to life, to growth, to change. In times of national crisis from natural disasters of floods and hurricanes, prisoners have come out of prisons to help clean up disaster areas and save lives. They have volunteered to contribute to the community—and during times of crisis the community appreciates their work and their spirit. But normally, all avenues of growth or possibility for human contribution are closed off to people labeled "criminal."

Sometimes the horror of what I have seen happening to human beings I've met in prisons closes in on me and gives me Kafkaesque nightmares. The Catch-22's and contradictions inside that erode people's spirit, the horrible powerlessness and agony of people both "guilty" and "innocent" in the eyes of the law, the calls I have gotten in the middle of the night from women afraid of sticking a needle in their arms again or wondering what to do about their sick children, the fear that is so overwhelming when they try to "adjust" again is all too much to hold inside or vomit up . . .

I retaliate by fantasizing what could be possible. I imagine taking my grandchildren by the hand and walking through the rubble of Holmesburg Prison and the House of Correction and Riker's Island. I imagine being an old white-haired woman feeling a sense of peace and quietness—telling them that these were terrible places where men and women were locked up in small concrete cells and made to labor for the mother state. I tell them the ruins are here as a reminder for generations to come; they're a monument of the death of our inhumanity to one another.

I imagine telling them that people of my day realized that they didn't know what they were doing when they imprisoned each other —that they had an idea that was wrong, that was brutal, so they gave up thinking they were right and risked new possibilities. "It's never too late to change," I tell them, "as long as you have the will to face the fear of being wrong and the will to face the unknown." I tell them about the days when hospitals and health centers were built in abundance and when clinics instead of criminal laws became available to people with problems they needed to solve. People who stole and threatened one another were remanded to groups of neighborhood people who helped them work out their problems and repay their victims; community judges and juries started ordering recreation for people who needed to learn how to play and laugh. I tell them that although it's beyond their comprehension, "In my day, no one would have ever thought of a judge ordering a man and woman who stole to play frisbee in the park with their neighbors. Can you imagine?! No one ever thought of getting to know someone who took something from them to find out what they needed. No one ever thought of replacing bad habits and self-destructive environments with music and theater in every neighborhood . . .

"It was all really very silly," I tell them, "but the silliness destroyed a lot of lives. People then actually locked people they didn't like *away* from society so they could adjust to society. It didn't make any sense at all."

Realistically, I doubt my fantasies will come true—or that prisons will in fact be abolished during my lifetime. But I feel an urgency about the situation—perhaps more so than many people who have not been imprisoned, because of the places I have been to, the people I have met and the people I have learned from. I remember the child's writing in the visitors' bathroom at California Institution for Women: "I LOVE MY MOM." Each letter was scratched in large penciled marks, etching forever in my mind the loneliness we all share. The alienation, the fear, the sense of powerlessness and longing . . . The grief of never realizing our own potential.

And as I sit here at my desk, I have a letter in front of me as a reminder, a letter from a woman in prison whose clarity and concerns have become a part of my world. She asked me not to use her name since her parents still don't know she is in prison. She has spent two years behind bars, but she writes to them from a friend's address. She says they have suffered enough, she doesn't want to worry them with additional burdens . . . I quote her letter since I believe her perspective should make us all acutely aware of the need for new and creative thinking—followed by new and untried paths of action:

July, sometime, 1972

DEAR KITSI,

I know you will write the book and I know some people will listen to you—but I just hope you can make them feel prison from the inside. I hope you can make them feel how the time ticks away on you here and how no matter how hard you try to maintain yourself and some degree of independence and self-respect, the daily process eats away your spirit. I have always thought of myself as a pretty strong and open woman, but this joint has taken some of my gentleness, some of my womanhood. Kitsi, I'm not the same warm person I remember myself to be. I find myself withdrawing from people in here—and even though I know it's a natural reaction, I know it will affect the way I relate to people, especially my own children, outside. I feel the walls around me all the time. And I'm afraid I'll carry them outside with me when I leave. Do you think I'll be able to be a good mother when I get my children back? I worry, I worry more than I should when I can't do anything about it.

I heard that state senator on the radio again yesterday and he was knocking the furlough program because of one man's escape. He was saying it's a crime that these "dangerous criminals" are let out of a "correctional institution" for a weekend, that nobody should be let out on a furlough until a few months before they get out. There's a lot of pressure around here. (They're going to put armed guards around the perimeters, too.)

As I was listening to that senator, I was thinking he's ignorant. He doesn't know what he's saying. He can't know what he's talking about. I'd like to get on the radio, too, and say that if you don't let people out, if you don't let them feel the world out there again slowly and let them be part of it, then you're *making* them dangerous. He's just asking for more trouble, more crime, because he's not recognizing us as human beings who have broken laws that don't even affect him. He doesn't know what a prison is. He doesn't know how it feels inside and what it does to a person. Isn't there some law about equal time? I'd like equal time to talk to people.

You know the truth, Kitsi, we are imprisoned in an idea, not just in a place. Prison doesn't work to change people except for the worse, so the idea must be wrong.

All people see is that they are safe from us because we are inside this concrete womb. This damn concrete womb. But I don't think there is any other place anywhere where people are expected to be so completely grown up and self sufficient and sensible when they have been made for such a long time to feel so little and helpless and dependent. And this womb isn't even nourishing!

Somethin's got to change. And I guess the idea has to change before anything else. For now all I can hope is that I will be able to grow again when I get out . . . and get rid of the walls around me. I know it's gonna be hard leaving this womb and staying away. I just hope I have the strength to make it. I know it's a matter of will. But damn it, I want so much to feel big again, to feel like a whole woman again. I want to feel like a real self-sufficient person again . . .

If you can, tell society to make some room for me and for the other men and women locked into their ideas, their prison camps. Tell people to keep their children out of these places, just to love and nourish them. Tell people we need them and they need us, even though they don't realize it yet. Tell them to claim us so we can claim them. It's overdue, but it's not too late.

Love, and power to you . . .

When Will We Learn?

We the living are now and throughout time responsible for what happens to the earth, to man, to life.

Shall we not learn from life its laws, dynamics, balances?

*Learn to base our needs not on death, destruction, waste, but on renewal?**

* Ansel Adams and Nancy Newhall, *This Is the American Earth* (San Francisco: Sierra Club, 1960).

Glossary:

Prison and
Prison-related Terms

Prison and Prison-related Terms These words and definitions are not used in the same manner throughout the country; they only express the way they are used in the various places I have found them.

Acting out Emotional or uncontrolled behavior on the part of a prisoner. The term (used by staff) covers a wide range of expression—from breaking a window to crying.

Adjustment center Area of solitary confinement cells where prisoners are kept in maximum security confinement.

Administrative segregation "Solitary confinement" that is administratively ordered instead of being "punitively" ordered through a disciplinary proceeding for violation of institutional rules. Emotionally disturbed women, for instance, are often kept in maximum security confinement throughout their incarceration—as are women sentenced under the death penalty.

Appeal A procedure whereby a person who has received an adverse decision in a lower court may have the decision reviewed by a higher court, usually known as an "appellate court." It is an "appeal" because the higher court may grant or deny the review.

Back time The amount of unserved time remaining from a previous sentence which has to be served as a result of violating parole. When parole is revoked because a person has been convicted of a new crime committed on parole, the new sentence being imposed is known as "front time" and that portion of the old sentence imposed upon the parole revocation is known as "back time." (For instance, if a woman has been on parole six years and during the seventh year is arrested and convicted of a new crime, the judge may give her a new sentence and additionally demand she serve all her back time for six years.)

Bad way (to be in) To be sick or feeling very depressed or upset.

Bags Slang for packets usually containing heroin or cocaine.

Beef (*n*) Sentence or time. (*v*) To have a complaint.

Behavior clinic Disciplinary "court" that determines punishment for infractions of institutional rules.

Benny An amphetamine pill.

Bing Solitary confinement.

Black lock Solitary confinement either in an isolation cell or in your own cell for a period of three days or more.

Blowing it Losing the opportunity to do something desired; i.e., "blowing parole" means not making it, failing.

"Blue room" Solitary confinement cell painted blue. (This euphemism used at Cook County Jail in Chicago.)

Boosting Shoplifting.

Bounce Writing a bad check. Can also mean to throw out, e.g., somebody being "bounced" from a program.

Brainwashing Indoctrination aimed at changing a person's basic convictions or attitudes and replacing them with a fixed or unquestioned set of beliefs.

Bull dyke Woman who plays a masculine role in a lesbian relationship. Also a derogatory term used to describe any woman who looks masculine or tough.

Bust A police raid or a raid from institutional staff.

(To get) Busted. To get arrested. In prison, to get written up for an infraction of rules.

Campus Prison grounds.

Cellblock A section of a prison or jail containing any number of cells, usually arranged perpendicular to a long, narrow walkway.

Clients Prisoners.

Coke Cocaine.

Con (*n*) Convict or prisoner. (*v*) To fool or swindle another person.

Con artist A person skillful at convincing someone else of their good intentions while defrauding them. A con artist can make almost anyone believe almost anything.

Con game A swindle or intelligence game in which a person is defrauded after his confidence has been won.

Continuance Legalese for a postponement. When a case is listed for a hearing in court on a particular date and the hearing is postponed for some reason, the case is said to have been "continued." The same term is used for a person who has been given another date for a parole hearing.

Contraband Goods prohibited by law or regulation from being brought into or kept in the prison. Contraband is anything so determined by the particular institution—from postage stamps to food products to personal items such as cosmetics or wedding rings.

Control center The central point for prison surveillance—either in a particular living area or in the whole institution. In modern institutions, guards press buttons to slide cell doors open and lock them, from the center.

Cop (to cop) To steal or acquire.

Cop a plea To plead guilty, on a previous arrangement with the defense attorney and the prosecution for a lesser sentence.

Cop out To quit. Or to fail to keep a promise.

Correctional counselor Prison employee whose job usually includes both counseling and surveillance.

Correctional institution Prison. Technically, an institution which aims to "correct faults."

Correctional officer Guard or matron.

Corrections Recent terminology for the field of penology which states it is treatment-oriented rather than custody-oriented. (Most state organizations previously called Bureaus of Prisons are now called Bureaus of Corrections.)

Cottages Residential houses containing cells or locked rooms for prisoners. The term is basically used in women's and juvenile institutions that have housing in smaller units than the mass penitentiary.

Count Population inventory usually held from three to nine times a day in any prison. A security precaution against escape attempts.

Detainer A writ authorizing further detention of a person in custody pending action.

Detention Keeping a person in custody or confinement usually awaiting trial.

Detention center A jail used primarily for persons held awaiting trial.

Determinate sentence See *Sentence.*

Dig it Understand what is being said. Know what I mean?

Discretionary power A term used to describe the power exercised by the courts in placing a person on probation, suspending a sentence or assigning a conviction. It is also commonly used to describe the power exercised by administrative bodies in making their decisions; e.g., parole boards usually have broad discretionary power to decide whether a prisoner should be placed on parole or kept in prison. Their decisions can only be overturned in a court proceeding if they can be shown to constitute an abuse of discretion. Since their discretionary power is so broad, however, they are rarely called to account for abusing their discretion.

Disciplinary board A group of two or more staff members that determines punishment for infraction of institutional rules.

Discipline Punishment.

Do time To serve a prison sentence. A common expression is, "Do your time, don't let your time do you." In other words, serve your sentence your own way, don't let it destroy you.

Dope (*v*) To administer a narcotic or medication to someone; to drug them or "dope them up." (*n*) An addictive drug or marijuana.

Dorm Living area or cellblock in a prison for multiple residence where beds are normally lined up in military fashion.

Drop her belt To switch from playing the masculine role back to the feminine role. When a woman *drops her belt* she is often said to have "curled up her hair" again. When a woman *drops her belt* it usually implies she has left the relationship in which she played the male role.

Dude Man.

Feeding time Official prison euphemism for prisoner meal time. Meals are often referred to by jail administrators as "feedings," such as "feedings" given babies or animals.

Fix An intravenous injection of heroin or another opiate.

Flat timer A person serving a set amount of time or a fixed prison sentence without eligibility for parole, e.g., "two years flat time." Flat timers are often envied because they have no uncertainty about when they will be getting out; they do not have to worry about how to meet conditions of parole.

Flip out To lose touch with reality; to go berserk or insane. In prison this can mean merely a loss of control over emotion.

Fog procedure Maximum security procedure followed in institution during fog, rain or heavy storm to guard against escape.

Free world The world outside prison; society at large.

Front time See *Back time.*

Grapevine Informal word-of-mouth communication used in prison or the "underworld" as a way of spreading news usually unknown to authorities or the general public.

Go off To get angry, scream or shout; to "blow your cool."

Guards Custodial personnel assigned to supervise and control prisoners. Guards are also referred to as *matrons, staff, correctional officers* and *police.*

"H" Heroin.

Habit Addiction to narcotics; to *have a habit.*

Heat The police; the authorities; prison guards or staff members.

High Intoxication or euphoria induced by a stimulant or a narcotic.

Hit the fence Escape.

Hole Solitary confinement.

Hooch Homemade wine or alcoholic beverage illegal in prison—often made from potato peelings or sugar and fruit.

Hooked (to be) To be addicted to heroin or other narcotics.

Hooked up To be attached to a person or involved in a relationship.

Horse Heroin.

Hot Stolen or illegal.

House Cell or room. Prisoners often refer to their individual cells as "my house."

Hustle To obtain money in legally questionable ways that involve quick wit or movement, e.g., to solicit customers for or as a prostitute.

Hustler A person who makes money in ways which often involve deception; a person who lives by wit. In some areas prostitutes are referred to as *hustlers.*

Hype Drug addict.

Incorrigible A term used by courts and prison officials to describe someone who will not be reformed, corrected or tamed. The term is often synonymous with uncontrollable; many juveniles are incarcerated for being "incorrigible" when they have broken no criminal law.

Indeterminate sentence This can be a sentence to prison which stipulates no maximum or minimum time. However, it usually means the sentence states the maximum term only and thus the prisoner can be released any time up to the maximum depending on her institutional record and parole approval. People traditionally serve longer terms in prison under this sentencing procedure, although it was not intended to achieve this effect.

Inmate code Unwritten rules of procedure and conduct for prisoners which define loyalties and unity. To "break the code" means to go against the standards of behavior accepted by peers.

Institutionalization Acceptance of institutional values and standards of behavior as one's own.

Isolation Solitary confinement.

Jacket Institutional file on each prisoner which includes data on her family history, education, past employment and arrest record. Medical, psychiatric and disciplinary reports as well as behavioral evaluations and records of visitors and correspondents are kept in the jacket. The prisoner is not allowed to see what is in her jacket but the information is accessible to police, federal agents, the institution and parole board.

Jag A drug habit.

John A prostitute's paying customer. The term is also used to refer to a toilet.

Joint Prison or jail.

Jones A strong desire for something or someone; also a habit.

Junk Heroin or other drugs.

Junkie A person addicted to narcotics.

Juvie Juvenile hall; reform school.

Kick the habit To break or cure the addiction to narcotics.

"Ladies" Women prisoners.

Life, The Way of living on the streets that involves illegal moneymaking activities; a culture separate from mainstream society.

Mainline To inject drugs directly into a major vein.

Mind blower A discovery; a surprise or realization that is shocking.

Minimum sentence A term of imprisonment which in most states cannot be more than one half of the maximum sentence imposed. An offender is not usually eligible for parole before the expiration date of her minimum sentence. (See *Sentence*.)

Movement (as in inmate movement) Refers to major inmate "traffic" or the actual physical motion of inmates walking or being transferred from one part of the institution to another for any purpose.

My heart A favorite child or someone dear and close to the person speaking.

Nickel bags Packets of heroin or another drug costing five dollars each. A *dime bag* costs ten dollars. (*Doing a nickel* means serving a five-year sentence.)

No shit Something that is the truth. This expression is also used sarcastically or as an exclamation.

"Off Limits" Areas in the prison where inmates are not allowed without express permission.

Old man A woman's husband or lover; is also used to refer to someone's father.

"Out of Bounds" Same as *Off Limits*.

P & Q "Peace and Quiet" unit for maximum security confinement; the same as the "Adjustment Unit," primarily for women with mental problems or chronic disciplinary infractions. Assignment is made administratively.

Paperhanger Person who writes bad checks.

Parole That period of time which a person serves "on the street" following release from imprisonment while she is still under jurisdiction of the court until the date her maximum sentence expires. Most people sentenced to imprisonment are released sometime before the maximum term of their sentence expires. They are usually under the jurisdiction of an administrative body most often known as a state "parole" board and must follow a certain code of behavior during the period on parole. Failure to obey the rules of parole may result in the parolee's return to imprisonment.

Parole Board Administrative agency of the federal, state or local criminal justice systems. The board sends one or more representatives to interview inmates at "parole hearings" and a majority of the board later determines whether the inmate will be released prior to expiration of sentence. The board sets its own rules and regulations immune from other governmental sanctions. The Federal Parole Board, for instance, has never announced the rules or principles guiding its determinations and gives no reasons for its decisions to approve, deny or continue. Its discretion is unchecked by legal standards or judicial review. Nine people make up the Federal Parole Board. They make about 17,000 decisions per year on individual prisoners—an average of seventy decisions a day.

Parole violation Failure to obey the rules set down by the parole board that results in return to prison. A parolee may also be returned to prison if she is arrested for the commission of a new crime while on parole. If she is convicted, she will be made to serve not only the new sentence, but also all the time remaining on the sentence for which she was paroled without any credit being given for that time she was on parole.

PBX training Telephone switchboard training.

Penitentiary thing Something that happens only in prison.

People A person's family in the outside world. "My little people" are "my children."

Players Heterosexual women involved in homosexual roles in prison; women "playing a role."

Playing To be involved in homosexual role playing.

Playing the dozens Playful and sometimes hostile exchange of rhymes in a certain pattern—usually aimed at being derogatory either to a person or the person's mother.

"Police" Guards, matrons or other prison staff members; also law enforcement officers.

Pop a door Open a door by pressing an electronic control that triggers release of lock.

Post-conviction remedy A procedure whereby a person who has been convicted of a criminal offense may have the proceedings reviewed in a supplemental proceeding. The best-known post-conviction remedy is that of *habeas corpus*, which is initiated by the filing of a petition.

Pre-sentence investigation A report usually prepared by the probation department to provide information to the judge concerning the background and personality of the person to be sentenced. It may also contain many suggestions as to the disposition of the case. Unfortunately only a small percentage of judges order these reports on people before sentencing them to prison.

Prisoners Persons held in custody, captivity or a condition of restraint. Women prisoners are also referred to as *clients, residents, inmates, convicts, patients, girls, ladies* and *students.*

Probation Wherever a judge has the power to impose a term of imprisonment for conviction of a criminal offense he is usually also given the power to suspend the imposition of such sentence and place the person under the jurisdiction of a state or county administrative body to which she must report at regular intervals. She must also follow certain rules or regulations set down by this administrative body.

Probation revocation Annulment of probation for failure to follow rules and regulations of probation. A person whose probation has been revoked may be sentenced by the judge as if she were being sentenced immediately following her trial—that is, to any period of time up to the maximum term for which the offense is punishable. She is not given credit for the time she served on probation.

Public defender An attorney under contract to the city or a privately funded agency to represent indigent defendants. Because the majority of people going to trial are indigent, PDs represent the majority of

people sentenced to prison. Prisoners who believe the defense to be inadequate often refer to PDs as "prison deliverers."

Pulled out To be taken out of the prison to go to court or to be transferred to another institution.

Pull my coat Help me out; call my attention to something that's going
on to keep me out of trouble.

Punitive segregation Solitary confinement ordered as punishment.

Rack Solitary confinement (as in getting sent to the rack).

Rap A conviction. A bad rap is a heavy sentence or a bad break. *To
take the rap* means to take the conviction. Women prisoners often say
that women "take the rap" for their men; men prisoners say that men
"take the rap" for their women.

Rat A person who is an informer or a snitch.

Red devils Seconal.

Reform (*v*) To correct an evil or an abuse; to improve by alteration;
to cause a person to abandon irresponsible or "immoral" behavior.
(*n*) An action that attempts to improve social or political institutions
or conditions without radical change.

Reformatory A prison usually designed for women or children; a place
designated for the *reformation* of prisoners.

Rehabilitate To restore a handicapped or delinquent person to useful
life through education or therapy; to restore original rank, privilege or
rights of a person; to indoctrinate a person into accepting a system of
values or morals different from her own.

Re-integration The readjustment and reorientation of a person back
into society. Current emphasis on re-integration of prisoners recognizes
the disabling effects of isolation and imprisonment and encourages
work release programs, home furloughs and halfway houses to cushion
the shock of re-entry.

Release on recognizance To be released prior to trial on the basis of
personal affirmation of the obligation to appear in court. The decision
to release a person on her own recognizance is based on her stability,
family background, history of employment and residence and prior arrest record. Personal recognizance is ordered as a substitute for the
posting of money bond.

Repentance Remorse or contrition for past conduct or "sins."

Reservation A tract of land set apart by the federal government for a
specific and limited purpose; i.e., a prison such as Alderson or an area
reserved for original Americans.

Residents Prisoners.

Restitution Compensation for loss, damage or injury. A reparation.

Run a check/Run a make This is a term used when officials or prospec-
tive employers make a background check on a person's police record.
Prosecutors usually "run a make" on a person coming before the court

to see if they have any open or pending cases. If an employer runs a check and finds the person has a prison or arrest record she has not listed, he can dismiss her for "falsifying records."

Sentence An order made by a judge directed at a person convicted of a criminal offense. It can consist of either a fine or a prison term. A judge may also suspend a sentence completely or suspend imposition of a sentence and place a person on probation or under the jurisdiction of a private program. The laws of various states differ in the manner in which they direct the judge to impose a sentence, and sometimes the laws of one state may have differing sentencing statutes relating to men and women. There are basically two types of sentences. In one the judge imposes only the maximum term to be served. In the second type the judge imposes a minimum and maximum term. The minimum term is that period of time which must be served before the person can be considered for parole. A sentence which states the maximum term only is referred to as an indeterminate sentence and a sentence which states both a minimum and a maximum may be called a definite sentence. However, the reader is cautioned that these terms are not used uniformly throughout the various jurisdictions and sometimes a sentence stating a minimum and a maximum is also called an "indefinite" sentence.

Shackle A metal fastening that encircles and confines the ankles or wrists to hobble a person and restrict movement.

Shakedown A thorough search of a prisoner's room or person and of the premises for drugs, weapons and other contraband. Extortion of money by blackmail or fraud is also known as a shakedown.

Shank To cut someone with a knife.

Show respect Stand at attention.

Shiv A knife or razor used as a weapon. In prison, some women carry shivs made from various objects for self-defense or for use in fights, etc.

Shrink Psychiatrist or psychologist.

Signifying Putting someone down; using derogatory language about a person.

Snitch An informer; a person who violates inmate code by telling police or prison staff about the activities or plans of other prisoners.

Solid An agreement, a confirmation meaning right or true. A "solid person" is a trustworthy person.

Solitary confinement The confinement of a prisoner in a maximum security cell where she is isolated from everyone else for the purpose of punishment or discipline. Solitary confinement usually means a loss of all prison privileges, such as mail, visitors, etc., in addition to the physical isolation. Solitary is also referred to as the *bing/rack/hole/*

reflection/the quiet room/isolation/lockup/segregation/punishment/adjustment.

Sprung (to get) To be released from jail on bail pending trial or appeal; to be released.

Square business Anything that is "real," true or factual.

Stable A group of whores or prostitutes who belong to one pimp who "protects" them and collects half their earnings or more.

Staff Prison employee(s) or guard(s).

Stash (*v*) To hide. (*n*) Anything saved or hidden. Usually any stash in prison is considered contraband.

"Stone cop" A prison staff member who strictly adheres to rules without exception; a guard who searches for anything illegal or out of the ordinary and reports it to authorities. (Can also be applied to an inmate who is a snitch.)

"Straight police" A guard who will not make exceptions—who follows rules as they are written. Often "straight police" are considered fair by prisoners because they are predictable and do not discriminate.

Street, The The world outside prison. Usually refers to low-income culture where people basically communicate from the front stoop or on the street.

Street time Slang used to describe the period a person spends on parole or on probation.

Stud broad A woman who appears to be masculine or who plays the male role in a homosexual relationship.

Stuff Narcotics, usually heroin.

Suspended sentence A judge sometimes suspends a sentence for a period of time, after which, if the defendant has not been re-arrested, she has her case closed. The complete suspension of sentence is rare, except in cases where a judge is sentencing a defendant on multiple bills of indictment—and imposes a sentence on some of the bills and suspends sentence completely on others.

Trick A male who pays a woman to have intercourse, or to give him some form of sexual gratification.

Trick baby Child born to a woman prostitute by a paying customer.

Tricked up (to be) To be confused, disoriented.

Turn a trick To have a male customer and get paid.

Walk To get out of prison. To walk free without restrictions of parole or probation.

Wire Information or a message.

Write-up A disciplinary report on the violation of a rule; an infraction that is reported by a staff member.

Bibliography:

Consulted Works and
Recommended Reading

Adams, Ansel; and Newhall, Nancy. *This Is the American Earth*. San Francisco: Sierra Club, 1960.

American Association of University Women, Pennsylvania Division. *Report on the Survey of 41 Pennsylvania County Court and Correctional Services for Women and Girl Offenders, Jan. 1, 1965–Dec. 31, 1966*. Reported by Margery L. Velimesis, Division Project Director. Philadelphia, Jan. 1969.

American Correctional Association. *Manual of Correctional Standards*. Washington, D.C.: ACA, 1969.

American Foundation Institute of Corrections. *The County Jail and Related Criminal Justice Services, Polk County, Florida*. Philadelphia: AFIC, 1966.

American Foundation Studies in Correction. *The County Prisons and Jails of Pennsylvania*. March 1965.

American Friends Service Committee. *Struggle for Justice—A Report on Crime and Punishment in America*. New York: Hill & Wang, 1971.

Annual Report of the Los Angeles County Jail Division. Los Angeles, Calif.: 1971.

Annual Report of the New York City Board of Correction. *Crisis in the Prisons: New York City Responds. A Commitment to Change*. New York: Department of Corrections, 1971.

Annual Report Ohio Reformatory for Women. July 1, 1970, to July 1, 1971. Marysville, Ohio: 1971.

Artis, William, Jr. ". . . And Justice for All?" An Interview with Haywood Burns, National Director of the National Conference of Black Lawyers. *CRJ Reporter*, Sept. 1972.

Balchen, Bess. "Prisons: The Changing Outside View of the Inside." *AIA Journal*, Sept. 1971.

Barros, Colleen; Slavin, Andrea; McArthur, Virginia; and Adams, Stuart. *Movement and Characteristics of Women's Detention Center Admissions, 1969*. Research Report No. 39. District of Columbia Department of Corrections, May 1971.

Bartlett, Donald L., and Steele, James B. "Crime and Injustice." The Philadelphia *Inquirer*. February 1973.

Beck, Robert. *The Naked Soul of Iceberg Slim*. Los Angeles: Holloway House, 1971.

Beckman, Lanny. "Psychology as a Social Problem: An Investigation into the Society for the Psychological Study of Social Issues." *Radical Therapist*, Vol. 2, No. 6, 1972.

Benjamin, Harry; and Masters, R. E. L. *Prostitution and Morality: A Definitive Report on the Prostitute in Contemporary Society and an Analysis of the Causes and Effects of the Suppression of Prostitution.* New York: Julian Press, 1964.

"The Black Prisoner: Featuring the Writings of Black Prisoners," *The Black Scholar*, April–May 1971.

Blake, James. *The Joint.* New York: Doubleday, 1971.

Booth, Maud Ballington. "The Shadow of Prison." *Proceedings of the 58th Congress of the American Prison Association*, 1928.

Brown, Barbara A.; Emerson, Thomas I.; Falk, Gail; and Freedman, Ann E. "The Equal Rights Amendment: A Constitutional Basis for Equal Rights for Women." *The Yale Law Journal*, Vol. 80: 871; 1971.

Bullough, Vern L. *The History of Prostitution.* New Hyde Park, N.Y.: Univ. Bks., 1964.

Byrnes, Inspector Thomas. *1866 Professional Criminals of America.* Introduction by Arthur M. Schlesinger, Jr., and S. J. Perelman. New York: Chelsea House Pubs., 1969.

Cameron, Mary Owen. *The Booster and the Snitch.* London: Macmillan, 1964.

Campbell, Joseph. *The Masks of God: Creative Mythology.* New York: Viking, 1968.

Carroll, Lewis. *Alice's Adventures in Wonderland.* New York: Harper & Brothers, 1901.

Case, John D., Warden, Bucks County Prison and Rehabilitation Center. Testimony at Philadelphia Hearing of Legislative-Executive Task Force on Reorganization of Government. Aug. 13, 1970. *Toward Reducing Crime in Pennsylvania*, Vol. II, Sept. 15, 1970.

Chevigny, Paul. *Police Power.* New York: Pantheon, 1969.

Citizens Task Force. *Report on State Correctional Institution at Muncy, Pennsylvania.* Distributed by Pennsylvania Program for Women and Girl Offenders, Inc. Philadelphia, 1970.

The Clarion. Inmate Publication at California Institution for Women, bi-monthly issues Oct. 1970 through Dec. 1972.

Clark, Ramsey. *Crime in America: Observations on Its Nature, Causes, Prevention and Control.* New York: Simon & Schuster, 1970.

Cleaver, Eldridge. *Post-Prison Writings and Speeches.* Ed. Robert Scheer. New York: Ramparts Press, 1969.

———. *Soul on Ice.* New York: Dell, 1968.

"Coeducational Prison Is a Test in Rehabilitation," *New York Times*, July 8, 1972, p. M 27.

Cole, Larry. *Street Kids*. With Ralph Romero, Pauli Vizzio, Eddie Burgos, and Charlie Galetti. New York: Grossman Pubs., 1970.

Committee on Classification and Case Work of the American Prison Association. *Handbook on Classification in Correctional Institutions*. Revised and reprinted by the American Foundation Studies in Corrections. Philadelphia, 1965.

Committee on the Model Act. "A Model Act for the Protection of the Rights of Prisoners." National Council on Crime and Delinquency, 1972.

"The Costs of Preventative Detention." *Yale Law Journal*, Vol. 79: 926; 1972.

Cray, Ed. *The Big Blue Line: Police Power versus Human Rights*. New York: Coward-McCann, 1967.

"Creation: The Arts In Prison." Supplement, *The Penal Digest International*, Vol. 1, No. II, July 1972.

Cunningham, Gloria. "Supervision of the Female Offender," *Federal Probation*, XXVII, Dec. 1963.

Cyert, Margaret, Chairman of the Citizen Task Force to Propose a Community Treatment Center for Women Offenders. Testimony at Pittsburgh Hearing of Legislative-Executive Task Force on Reorganization of Government. Aug. 21, 1970. *Toward Reducing Crime in Pennsylvania*, Vol. II, Sept. 15, 1970.

Davis, Angela Y.; Magee, Ruchell; the Soledad Brothers; and other Political Prisoners. *If They Come In the Morning*. New York: Signet, 1971.

Dawson, Robert O. "The Decision to Grant or Deny Parole: A Study of Parole Criteria in Law and Practice," *Washington University Law Quarterly*, Vol. 1966, No. 3, June 1966.

Day, Dorothy. "Thoughts After Prison," *Liberation*. Sept. 1957.

D.C. Citizens Council for Criminal Justice. *The Treatment of Women Offenders in the District of Columbia*. Washington, D.C., March 1972.

Deans, Ralph C. "Racial Tensions in Prisons," *Editorial Research Reports*, Oct. 20, 1971.

Deming, Barbara. *Prison Notes*. New York: Grossman Pubs., 1966.

Douglass, Frederick. *The Life and Times of Frederick Douglass*. Reprinted from the revised edition of 1892. London: Collier-Macmillan, 1962.

Duster, Troy. *The Legislation of Morality*. New York: Free Press, 1970.

Eastwood, Mary. "The Double Standard of Justice: Women's Rights Under the Constitution," *Valparaiso University Law Review*, Symposium: Women and the Law, Vol. 5, No. 2, 1971.

Edmundo, A. *Psychological Striptease*. Unpublished book of poetry by inmate in Huntingdon Prison, Huntingdon, Pa. 1971.

Eldridge, Stanley. *Return Me to My Mind*. New York: Fortune Society, 1970.

Erikson, Eric H. *Childhood and Society*. New York: Norton, 1964.

"Excerpts from Opinions on Death Penalty," New York *Times*, June 30, 1972, p. L 34.

Eyman, Joy S. *Prisons for Women. A Practical Guide to Administration Problems*. Springfield, Ill.: C. C. Thomas, 1971.

Faustini, Gino. "La delinquenza fra le adolescenti in Italia." *Esperienze di Rieducazione*. 16 (1): 71–112, 1969.

Fernald, Mabel Ruth; Hayes, May; and Dawley, Almena. *A Study of Women Delinquents in New York State*. Patterson, N.J.: Smith, 1920.

Flynn, Elizabeth Gurley. *The Alderson Story: My Life as a Political Prisoner*. New York: International, 1963.

Foote, Caleb. "The Bail System and Equal Justice," *Federal Probation*, Sept. 1955.

Forer, Lois G. *No One Will Lissen; How Our Legal System Brutalizes the Youthful Poor*. New York: Grosset, 1970.

———. "Youth and the Law," *The YWCA Magazine*, Feb. 1972.

Frankl, Viktor E. *From Death Camp to Existentialism*. Trans. Ilse Lasch. (First published in German, 1946, *Ein Psycholog Erlebt das Konzentrationslager*.) Boston: Beacon Press, 1959.

Geller, William. "The Problems of Prisons—A Way Out?" *The Humanist*, Ethical Forum, May–June 1972.

Giallombardo, Rose. *Society of Women. A Study of a Women's Prison*. New York: Wiley, 1966.

Gillan, John L. *Criminology and Penology*, New York, London: Appleton-Century Co., Inc., 1945.

Glaser, Daniel. "Societal Trends: From Revenge to Resocialization: Changing Perspectives in Combatting Crime," *The American Scholar*, Vol. 40, No. 4, Autumn 1971.

Goffman, Erving. *Asylums*. Garden City, N.Y.: Doubleday, 1961.

Gold, Sally. "Equal Protection for Juvenile Girls in Need of Supervision in New York State." Unpublished paper available in Yale Law Library, 1970.

Goldman, Emma. *Living My Life*. New York: Dover, 1971.

Goodell, Charles; and Von Hirsch, Andrew. Testimony before Subcommittee No. 3 of the House Judiciary Committee. "On H.R. 13118. The Parole Procedures and Improvement Act of 1972." *Corrections—Part VII-A*. Washington: U. S. Government Printing Office, April 1972.

Graham, Fred P. "Criminal Statistics," *Information Review, Crime and Delinquency*, Aug. 1969.

Grant, Joanne (ed.). *Black Protest. History, Documents, and Analysis 1619 to the Present*. Greenwich, Conn.: Fawcett, 1970.

Greenberg, David. *The Problem of Prisons*. Distributed by the American Friends Service Committee, 1970.

Halleck, Seymour, M.D. *The Politics of Therapy*. New York: Science House, 1971.

———. *Psychiatry and the Dilemmas of Crime*. New York: Harper, 1967.

Harmon, Sasha. "Attitudes Toward Women in the Criminal Process." Unpublished paper available in Yale Law Library, 1970.

Harris, Sara. *Hell Hole*. New York: Dutton, 1967.

Health Law Project Report. *Health Care and Conditions in Pennsylvania's Prisons*. Philadelphia: Univ. of Pa. Law School, 1972.

Hearings before Subcommittee No. 3 of the Committee on the Judiciary, House of Representatives. "Illinois: The Problems of the Ex-Offender." *Corrections: Part VI*. Washington, D.C.: U. S. Government Printing Office, Jan. 1972.

———. "Prisons, Prison Reform and Prisoners' Rights: California." *Corrections: Part II*. Washington, D.C.: U. S. Government Printing Office, Jan. 1972.

———. "Prisons, Prison Reform and Prisoners' Rights: Massachusetts." *Corrections: Part V*. Washington, D.C.: U. S. Government Printing Office, Oct. 1972.

———. "Prisons, Prison Reform and Prisoners' Rights: Michigan." *Corrections: Part VIII*. Washington, D.C.: U. S. Government Printing Office, March 1972.

———. "Prisons, Prison Reform and Prisoners' Rights: Wisconsin." *Corrections: Part IV*. Washington, D.C.: U. S. Government Printing Office, Nov. 1971.

Hecht, Judith A. *Effects of Halfway Houses on Neighborhood Crime Rates and Property Values: A Preliminary Survey*. Research Report No. 37. District of Columbia: Department of Corrections, 1970.

Helfer, Ray E.; and Kempe, Henry C. *The Battered Child*. Chicago: Univ. of Chicago Press, 1968.

Hendrix, Omar. *A Study in Neglect: A Report on Women Prisoners*. New York: The Women's Prison Association, Fall 1972.

Henry, Joan. *Women In Prison*. New York: Doubleday, 1952.

Herbert, Rachel Bluntzen. *Shadow on the Nueces, The Saga of Chepita Rodriguez*. Emory University, Ga.: Banner, 1942.

Hickey, William L. "Strategies for Decreasing Jail Populations," *Crime and Delinquency Literature*, Vol. 3, No. 1, March 1971.

Holder, Angela R., J.D. "Law and Medicine: The Prisoner's Right to Medical Treatment," *American Journal of Correction*, Vol. 33, No. 4, July–Aug. 1971.

Holiday, Billie. *Lady Sings the Blues*. With William Dufty. New York: Lancer, 1969.

Holt, Norman. "Temporary Prison Release—California's Prerelease Furlough Program," *Crime and Delinquency*, Vol. 17, No. 4, 1971.

Iowa Central Community College and Iowa Women's Reformatory. *Special Needs Proposal: Educational Program in Corrections for Clients at the Iowa Women's Reformatory.* Presented to the Iowa State Department of Public Instruction. March 1971.

Jackson, George. *Soledad Brother: The Prison Letters of George Jackson.* New York: Bantam, 1970.

Jackson, Lorraine A. *Impact of the Women's Detention Center on First Timers.* Research Report No. 41. District of Columbia: Department of Corrections, April 1971.

James, Howard. *Children in Trouble: A National Scandal.* Boston: Christian Science Pub., 1969.

Johnston, Norman; Savitz, Leonard; and Wolfgang, Marvin E. *The Sociology of Punishment and Correction.* New York: Wiley, 1970.

Joint Commission on Correctional Manpower and Training. *The Public Looks at Crime and Corrections.* The American Correctional Association, Feb. 1968.

————. *Volunteers Look at Corrections.* American Correctional Association, Feb. 1969.

Jones, Georgia. "Heritage: Three Women," *Off Our Backs. A Women's News Journal*, Vol. II, No. 8., Washington, D.C., April 1972.

Jones, Rochelle. "Females Without Freedom," seven-part series, Palm Beach *Post-Times*, Oct. 1970.

Kafka, Franz. *The Penal Colony.* Translated by Willa and Edwin Muir. New York: Schocken, 1970.

Kairys, David. "Juror Selection: The Law, A Mathematical Method of Analysis, and a Case Study," *The American Criminal Law Review*, Vol. 10. No. 4, 1972.

Kanowitz, Leo. *Women and the Law.* Albuquerque: Univ. of N. Mex. Press, 1969.

Keely, Sara F. *The Organization and Discipline of the Indiana Women's Prison.* Proceedings of the Annual Congress of the National Prison Association, 1898.

Kittrie, Nicholas N. *The Right to Be Different.* Baltimore and London: Johns Hopkins Press, 1971.

Klapmuts, Nora. "Children's Rights—The Legal Rights of Minors in Conflict with Law or Social Custom," *Crime and Delinquency Literature*, Vol. 4, No. 3, Sept. 1972.

Knight, Etheridge. *Poems from Prison.* Detroit, Mich.: Broadside, 1968.

Kopkind, Andrew. "White on Black: The Riot Commission and the Rhetoric of Reform," *Hard Times*, No. 44, Sept. 1969.

Kratz, Althea Hallowell. *Prosecutions and Treatment of Women Of-*

fenders and the Economic Crisis: Philadelphia, 1925–1934. Philadelphia: Univ. of Pa. Press, 1940.

Landis, Judson R. (ed.) *Current Perspectives on Social Problems.* Belmont, Calif.: Wadsworth Pub., 1969.

Lee, Henry. "The Ten Most Wanted Criminals of the Past 50 Years," *Liberty,* Fall 1972.

Lekkerkerker, Eugenia C. *Reformatories for Women in the United States.* Batavia: J. B. Wolters, 1931.

Lemmert, Edwin M. "The Juvenile Court: Quest and Realities." *Task Force Report: Juvenile Delinquency and Youth Crime.* President's Commission on Law Enforcement and the Administration of Justice. Washington, D.C.: U. S. Government Printing Office, 1967.

Lester, Julius. *Long Journey Home.* Stories from Black History. New York: Dial, 1972.

Levine, Stephen. *Death Row: An Affirmation of Life.* New York: Grove, 1971.

Levy, Howard; and Miller, David. *Going to Jail: The Political Prisoner.* New York: Grove, 1971.

Lindsey, Richard W. *Pennsylvania Board of Probation and Parole: Media Fact Sheet.* July 1971.

Loveland, Frank; Vander Weil, Ronald W.; Wellford, Charles F.; and Durborow, Doris W. *The Correctional Institutions and Services of Connecticut.* Philadelphia: The American Foundation Institute of Corrections, 1966.

Lucey, D. J., III, M.D.; and Keene, J. C. "Women in Prison: The Treatment Model; the Muncy Experience," *Social Welfare Law,* C.P. 735, 1972.

Lundberg, Emma O. *Unmarried Mothers in the Municipal Court of Philadelphia.* Philadelphia: Thomas Harrison, 1933.

Malcolm X. *The Autobiography of Malcolm X.* New York: Grove Press, 1965.

Mapes, Glynn. "Unequal Justice: A Growing Disparity in Criminal Sentences Troubles Legal Experts," *Wall Street Journal,* Sept. 9, 1970.

Mead, Margaret; and Baldwin, James. *A Rap on Race.* New York: Lippincott, 1971.

Menninger, Karl. *The Crime of Punishment.* New York: Viking, 1968.

Melville, Sam. *Letters from Attica.* New York: Morrow, 1972.

Merriam, Eve. *Growing up Female in America: Ten Lives.* New York: Doubleday, 1971.

Millett, Kate. *Sexual Politics.* New York: Doubleday, 1970.

Minton, Robert. *Inside: Prison American Style.* New York: Random House, 1971.

Mitford, Jessica. "Experiments Behind Bars." *Atlantic Monthly*, Jan., 1973.

————. "Kind and Usual Punishment in California," *Atlantic Monthly*, March 1971.

Monahan, Florence. *Women In Crime*. New York: Washburn, 1941.

Morris and Breithaupt. "Compulsory Sterilization of Criminals—Perversion in the Law," 15 *Syracuse Law Review* 738, 1964.

Murton, Tom. "Drugs Used to Control Inmates." *The Freeworld Times*, Vol. 1, No. 2, Feb. 1972.

Nagel, William G. *The New Red Barn: A Critical Look at the Modern American Prison*. New York: Walker, 1973.

"The National Committee for Prisoners Rights," *Prisoners Rights Newsletter*, Vol. 1, No. 1, State University of New York at Buffalo, School of Law, Sept. 1971.

Nussbaum, Albert F. "The Rehabilitation Myth," *The American Scholar*, Vol. 40, No. 4, 1971.

Ohio Department of Mental Hygiene and Correction. Annual Financial and Statistical Report 1970–1971. Bureau of Statistics, 1971.

Parker, Tony. *Women In Crime: Five Revealing Cases*. (First published in Great Britain under the title *Five Women* by Hutchinson & Co., 1965) New York: Delta Books, 1968.

Pell, Eve. "The Soledad Brothers: How a Prison Picks Its Victims," *Ramparts*, Aug. 1970.

Pollock, Otto. *The Criminality of Women*. Philadelphia: Univ. of Pa. Press, 1950.

President's Commission on Law Enforcement and the Administration of Justice. *The Challenge of Crime in a Free Society*. Washington, D.C.: U. S. Government Printing Office, 1967.

"Reading of Lawyer-Inmate Mail Barred," *The Prison Law Reporter*. Vol. 1, No. 12, Sept. 1972.

Reckless, Walter C.; and Kay, Barbara Ann. *The Female Offender*. Unpublished paper submitted to the President's Commission on Law Enforcement and the Administration of Justice, 1967.

Reiss, Albert. "Police Brutality—Answers to Key Questions," *Transaction*, July–Aug. 1968.

Report of the Legislative-Executive Task Force on Reorganization of Government. (Dept. of Corrections). *Toward Reducing Crime in Pennsylvania*. Vol. II, Sept. 15, 1970.

Richette, Lisa Aversa. *The Throwaway Children*. Philadelphia and New York: Lippincott, 1969.

Richmond, Al. *Native Daughter, The Story of Anita Whitney*. San Francisco: Anita Whitney 75th Anniversary Committee, 1942.

Rogers, Helen W. "A Digest of Laws Establishing Reformatories for Women," *Journal of Criminal Law and Criminology*, XIII, Nov. 1922.

————. "A History of the Movement to Establish a State Reformatory for Women in Connecticut," *Journal of Criminal Law and Criminology*, XIX, 1929.

Rosenberg, Ethel. *Death House Letters*. New York: Jero Publishing Co., 1953.

Rothman, David J. "Of Prisons, Asylums, and Other Decaying Institutions," *Public Interest*, No. 26, 1972.

————. *The Discovery of the Asylum*. Boston: Little, 1971.

Rudovsky, David. *The Rights of Prisoners*. New York: Avon, 1973.

Rundle, Frank, M.D. "Institution vs. Ethics: The Dilemma of a Prison Doctor," *The Humanist*, May–June 1972.

Sarrazin, Albertine. *The Runaway*. New York: Grove, 1967.

Schulder, Diane B. "Does the Law Oppress Women?" *Sisterhood Is Powerful*. An Anthology of Writings from the Women's Liberation Movement. (Ed.) Robin Morgan. New York: Vintage, 1970.

Schur, Edwin. *Crimes Without Victims*. Englewood Cliffs, N.J.: Prentice Hall, 1965.

Serge, Victor. *Men In Prison*. Garden City: Doubleday, 1969.

Slim, Iceberg. *Pimp: The Story of My Life*. Los Angeles: Holloway House, 1969.

Shaw, George Bernard. *The Crime of Imprisonment*. New York: Citadel, 1961.

Smith, Ann D. *Women In Prison*. London: Stevens, 1962.

Spaeth, Edmund B., Jr. "The Court's Responsibility for Prison Reform," *Villanova Law Review*, Vol. 16, No. 6, Aug. 1971.

"Toward Social Justice—Bridging Idealism and Realism," Proceedings of the 18th National Institute on Crime and Delinquency, *The Quarterly*, Vol. XXVIII, Nos. 2 & 3, Pennsylvania Assn. on Probation, Parole and Correction, Autumn 1971.

Spencer, Carol; and Berechocea, John E. *Vocational Training at the California Institution for Women: An Evaluation*. Sacramento: S.8139 California Corrections Department, 1971.

Starobin, Robert S. *Industrial Slavery in the Old South*. New York: Oxford, 1970.

State Law Enforcement Planning Agency. *1971 New Jersey Plan for Criminal Justice*. Dissemination Document No. 9, Jan. 1971.

Sterling, Dorothy. *Tear Down the Walls! A History of the Black Revolution in the United States*. New York: Signet Books, 1970.

Strouse, Jean. "To Be Minor & Female: The Legal Rights of Women Under 21," *Ms.*, Oct. 1972.

Summary of Completed Research: 1967–1971. Summary Report No. 1. District of Columbia Department of Corrections. Jan. 1971.

Sutherland, Sidney. "The Mystery of the Puritan Girl: Did Lizzie Borden Kill Her Parents?" originally published in *Liberty*, March 1929; reprinted in *Liberty*, Fall 1972.

Sykes, Gresham M. *Crime and Society*. New York: Random House, 1967.

Szasz, Thomas Stephen. *Law, Liberty and Psychiatry: An Inquiry into the Social Uses of Mental Health Practices*. New York: Macmillan, 1963.

————. *Psychiatric Justice*. New York: Macmillan, 1965.

Tassin, Ida Mae. *Proud Mary, Poems from a Black Sister in Prison*. Printed by Buffalo Women's Prison Project, 1971.

Taylor, Victor E. "Drug Abuse Control: Heroin and the Black Community," *The American Scholar*, Vol. 40, No. 4, 1971.

————. "The Correctional Institution as a Rehabilitation Center—A Former Inmate's View," *Villanova Law Review*, Vol. 16, No. 6, Aug. 1971.

Temin, Carolyn E. "Criminal Sentencing Procedures—A Judicial Straitjacket," *The Shingle*, The Philadelphia Bar Association, Vol. XXXII, No. 7, Oct. 1969.

————. "Discriminatory Sentencing of Women Offenders: The Argument for ERA in a Nutshell," *The American Criminal Law Journal*, Spring 1973.

Transactions of the National Congress on Penitentiary and Reformatory Discipline held at Cincinnati, Ohio, 1870. Edited by E. C. Wines, D.D., LL.D. Albany: Weed, Parsons and Co., 1871.

Tyler, Gus (ed.). *Organized Crime in America, A Book of Readings*. Ann Arbor: Univ. of Mich. Press, 1962.

"Use of Group Dynamics and Bibliotherapy in Total Institution Training for Human Development." Workshop on self-worth and self-development at Iowa Women's Reformatory. (Available from Morris A. Lotte, Library Consultant. Iowa Department of Social Services.) 1972.

Velimesis, Margery L. "Criminal Justice for the Female Offender." *Journal of the American Association of University Women*, Oct. 1969.

Walker, Nigel. *Sentencing In a Rational Society*. London: Allen Lane, 1969.

Ward, David A.; Jackson, Maurice; and Ward, Renee E. "Crimes of Violence by Women." Task Force on Individual Acts of Violence. U. S. National Commission on the Causes and Prevention of Violence. *Crimes of Violence*, Vol. 13. Washington, D.C.: U. S. Government Printing Office, 1969.

Ward, David A.; and Kassebaum, Gene. "Homosexuality: A Mode of Adaption in a Prison for Women," *Social Problems*, Fall 1964.

Ward, David A.; and Kassebaum, Gene. *Women's Prison: Sex and Social Structure*. Chicago: Aldine Pub., 1965.

Weatherman. Ed. Harold Jacobs. San Francisco: Ramparts Press, 1970.

West, Celeste. "Kept Women," *Synergy*, Jan.–Feb. 1971.

Wolfgang, Marvin E.; and Cohen, Bernard. *Crime and Race: Conceptions and Misconceptions.* New York: Institute of Human Relations Press, 1970.

Wolfgang, Marvin, E.; and Ferracuti, Franco. *The Subculture of Violence: Towards An Integrated Theory in Criminology.* Great Britain: Tavistock Publications, 1967.

Wolfgang, Marvin E. "Making the Criminal Justice System Accountable," *Crime and Delinquency,* Vol. 18, No. 1, Jan. 1972.

————. (ed.) *Studies In Homicide.* New York: Harper, 1967.

Woods, Paul, J., Ph.D. *A Study of Anger in the Federal Reformatory for Women.* Federal Reformatory for Women, Alderson, West Virginia, July 1970.

Yablonsky, Lewis. *The Violent Gang.* New York: Macmillan, 1962.

Young, Clifford M. *Women's Prisons Past and Present.* Printed at Elmira Reformatory, New York: 1932.